JUDAS

JUDAS

A Biography

SUSAN GUBAR

W. W. NORTON & COMPANY

NEW YORK   LONDON

For information about permission to reproduce selections from this book,
write to Permissions, W. W. Norton & Company, Inc.,
500 Fifth Avenue, New York, NY 10110

For information about special discounts for bulk purchases, please contact
W. W. Norton Special Sales at specialsales@wwnorton.com or 800-233-4830

Manufacturing by R R Donnelley Harrisonburg
Book design by Lovedog Studio
Production manager: Julia Druskin

Library of Congress Cataloging-in-Publication Data

Gubar, Susan, 1944–
    Judas : a biography / Susan Gubar.—1st ed.
        p. cm.
    Includes bibliographical references and index.
    ISBN 978-0-393-06483-4 (hardcover)
    1. Judas Iscariot. I. Title.
    BS2460.J8G83 2009
    226'.092—dc22
    [B]
                            2008042967

W. W. Norton & Company, Inc.
500 Fifth Avenue, New York, N.Y. 10110
www.wwnorton.com

W. W. Norton & Company Ltd.
Castle House, 75/76 Wells Street, London W1T 3QT

1 2 3 4 5 6 7 8 9 0

FOR MARY JO WEAVER,
BELOVED FRIEND

Delivering up was done by the Father, delivering up was done by the Son, delivering up was done by Judas; one thing was done.

—Augustine,
Tractates on the First Epistle of John

God does not forgive the sins He makes us commit.

—José Saramago,
The Gospel according to Jesus Christ

Love is the weather. Betrayal is the lightning that cleaves and reveals it.

—Toni Morrison,
foreword to *Love*

CONTENTS

ILLUSTRATIONS

COLOR PLATES

PREFACE

Every great man has disciples, Oscar Wilde often quipped, but Judas usually writes the biography.[1] According to this sly proposition, malice motivates biographers, who divulge incriminating evidence that most people would prefer to incinerate before their demise or at least lock in a vault for a good long time. But with respect to Judas, what dirty secrets haven't already been aired? For more than twenty centuries, poets and painters, novelists and dramatists, theologians and moviemakers have berated him every which way for . . . "whatever," as my younger daughter might have once phrased it. That Christ's betrayer is a fascinating figure whose life has mattered finds immediate confirmation in the first-name basis Wilde assumes with a personage holding sway over his imagination. But before the publication of *Judas: A Biography,* no book had examined the chronological evolution of the twelfth apostle over the extensive span of his multimedia existence. There are a number of reasons for this curious paucity of scholarly and critical studies.

How can one possibly set out to write the life story of someone about whom so very little is known? Most biographical studies begin or end with sentences like "Born in the town of B during the year of C, our subject eventually died at H from Q in the time of W." They include family genealogies, interviews with descendants and friends, descriptions of homes and haunts, quotations of public speeches, snippets of private letters and journals, accounts of formative child-hood experiences, evidence of flings or significant relationships in youth and later adulthood. None of these facts is available in the case of Judas. This may be why—despite the plethora of creative material produced over the centuries—there is so little scholarly or critical analysis of the twelfth apostle in contemporary times. Judas's life cannot be reconstructed as a factual record. It can be approached only through pictures and stories and sermons that represent his varied development from its biblical beginnings to the present, though Wilde's adage reminds us how firmly that development remains attached to treachery.

A second reason why the open secrets of Judas's nefarious past have never received adequate scrutiny may relate to another facet of the genre of biography. Despite its fine edge, Wilde's surmise—which would make me the betrayer of the betrayer—is less personally unnerving than the more common assumption that biographers aid and abet their subjects. Scholars of biography claim that though its authors may become bitter enemies, they more frequently become close allies of the individuals they study.[2] The prominence of biographies about ennobling moral exemplars, as well as the assumed affinity of biographers with their subjects, probably clarifies why so few people have focused on the long iconographic career of Judas Iscariot. Put otherwise, if biographers find themselves drawn to figures who serve as reflections or projections of themselves, as is generally acknowledged, then the biographer of the twelfth apostle faces a huge impediment. A money-grubbing snitch and scheming turncoat, at least by popular consensus, Judas surely cannot and should not be anyone's role model. So repellent is he that he provokes the only instance (to my knowledge) of a biblical text conceivably justifying abortion: it might have been better, the New Testament tells us, if he had not been born.

No wonder, then, that except for a flood of publicity occasioned by the recent recovery of an ancient Gospel of Judas (media exposure that concentrated on Gnosticism in antiquity), the twelfth apostle has attracted very little attention. Yet, at least to my sensibilities, the creative Judas characters inspired by the canonical Gospels are much more resonant and multifaceted than is the Gnostic Judas. Actually, the words *resonant* and *multifaceted* hardly convey the mystic incongruities of a character captivating precisely because he could be imagined not just as a better-unborn demon working Satan's evil will but also, and antithetically, as a divine agent facilitating the resurrection of God's Son and the salvation of humanity. Without setting out to do so, I found myself eventually contending that the condition of Judas—an unexpectedly relevant character in the Bible—profoundly reflects some of the most stubborn psychological and ethical issues human beings face now, as always.

Like Wilde, most people are on a first-name basis with Judas, as they are today with, say, Elvis or Madonna, for the betrayer often served to typify Jewish people; however, he rarely gets mentioned in the voluminous scholarship that studies the dynamics and history of anti-Semitism. Since many Jews have never opened the New Testament, he is much better known by Christians than by Jews. But Christians, too, often remain vague about Judas, and not only because of the understandable embarrassment about racist agendas that he at times has fueled or fanned. Even scrupulous readers of the New Testament have to be mystified by Judas, because there are so few verses devoted to him and because these accounts frequently contradict each other. The four Gospels disagree on when Judas decided to hand Jesus over, how he did it, and why. The Gospels also disagree about the timing of the event, about who Judas brought with him, and about what happened to him afterward. With respect to a minor character who performs a major role, only two facts emerge uncontested and unanimously from all of the Gospel accounts: that he was one of Jesus' apostles and that he gave Jesus over to the hostile Temple authorities, thereby precipitating a chain of events leading to the crucifixion.

Jews and Christians know little about Judas because there is little to know. Yet although the little that postbiblical artists and thinkers knew about Judas continually drove them to elaborate on his story through a succession of incongruous reinventions, I could not find a readable or comprehensive book about Judas's long representational life from the Gospels to the twenty-first century. I would like to think, then, that neither tell-all treachery nor projected affinity brought me to the subject of Judas, but instead the need to comprehend what contrary uses various historical ages have made of him. Intellectual curiosity, pure and simple and at times relentless, propelled me to learn more about a character I knew to be important, but about whom I knew little else.

This biography traces how Judas was seen from his inception in the New Testament to contemporary film and fiction. Since I recount a narrative about a betrayer who has always attracted theologians and artists to reassess his character, *Judas* is in some sense a metabiography: a biography of multiple pseudo-biographies of a twelfth apostle with a multiple personality disorder (which is only one—if the most chronic—of many afflictions he suffers). At times, I turn to painters and novelists whose main interest lies in Jesus and, perhaps, Peter or John, but whose inclusion of a marginalized Judas nevertheless illuminates his condition. In subsequent chapters, I try to make visible Judas's iconic centrality throughout Western history, especially in European and in South as well as North American contexts. Studying Judas, I will argue, provides a way of mapping Christianity's growth out of and then its differentiation from Judaism, and what such a collective or interfaith legacy means for Christians of all denominations and Jews from various backgrounds.

Poems and paintings, novels and dramas, tracts and movies inspired by Judas have made it possible to provide what readers of biographies expect: first, candid pictures of Judas, alone in youth and in old age as well as with his most important dining companions and mentors, or actively engaged in the activities for which he is most famed; then genealogical speculations about his ancestry as well as unsubstantiated but recurrent innuendos about his anatomy and destiny, and intimate close-ups of his successive lifestyles, some of which eventuate in salacious intrigues and perverse crimes; and finally, a heartwarming sinner-to-saint story of recovery and redemption, albeit frequently accompanied by recidivism and backsliding. I depend on foundational stories about my subject's origins, in Judas's case the Gospels of the New Testament, fully aware that no fact-checker could certify any of their assertions, and I do so in the manner of many biographers who seek to tell the truth by compressing events, embroidering on details, and inventing forms of narration. Hence, *Judas* cannot pretend to be a definitive biography, even with respect to available archives. I have made no effort to track down each and every painting, poem, play, or novel about the betrayer; nor could I have done so, given space and time constraints. Moreover, though the twelfth apostle has been repeatedly killed, he refuses to be laid to rest and so his life and biography necessarily remain incomplete.

This book could not have been undertaken without the help of a number of specialists in fields with which I have had to become conversant. At Indiana University, my greatest debt is to J. Albert Harrill, whose religious studies course "Jesus and the Gospels" gave me an excellent foundation for understanding Judas's various roles in the New Testament. I am also greatly indebted to David Brakke, whose class "Jesus in the Movies" helped me consider Judas's celluloid morphing and whose profound knowledge of antiquity led to numerous insights into ancient texts. Important, too, was the scholarly and technological expertise of my assistant, Jamie Horrocks, who digitalized innumerable articles and images so that I could study them, and who also offered creative suggestions that led me down rewarding paths. As readers of portions of this manuscript in draft form, Bert, David, and Jamie were invaluable, though of course they are in no way responsible for any faults in the presentation here.

Three dear friends brought their good eyes to the visual images discussed throughout this book. On one glorious afternoon in the fall of 2006, Shehira Davezac, Jan Sorby, and Jayne Spencer enriched my interpretations of the artwork reprinted on subsequent pages. Other assistance was provided for research in particular areas of expertise. I am grateful to Bonnie Erwin for translations of Old English works, to Julie Wise for assistance in nineteenth-century cultural history and general bibliographic accuracy, and to James Rasmussen for knowledge of German texts and contexts. My collaborator, Sandra M. Gilbert, who always provides an inspiring pattern of imaginative honesty, fortified my efforts at various crucial junctures.

Numerous colleagues, friends, correspondents, and students furnished suggestions or read and critiqued drafted chapters, in particular Matt Brim, Judith Brown, Sarah Burns, Fred Cate, Linda Charnes, Amanda Ciccarelli, Pauline David, Lee Edelman, Dyan Elliott, Yakir Englander, Mary Favret, Jennifer L. Fleissner, Eileen Fry, Sander Gilman, Paul Gutjahr, Susannah Heschel, Marianne Hirsch, Amy Hungerford, Patricia Ingham, Ken Johnston, Georgette Kagan, Jon Lawrence, Deidre Lynch, Ellen MacKay, Sandra Macpherson, Shaul Magid, Maurice Manning, Michael McGerr, the late Diane Middlebrook, Andrew H. Miller, Richard Miller, Michael Morgan, Laura Nash, William Rasch, Alvin Rosenfeld, Adam Rovner, John Schilb, Miryam Segal, Kathy Smith, Helen Sword, Ovir Tzur, Alison Umminger, Shane Vogel, Stephen Watt, Steven Weitzman, Rob White, Nicholas Williams, and Judith Wilt. The director of *Sorry Judas,* Celia Lowenstein, generously sent me a DVD of the film. Curators and archivists at various museums and film still archives as well as artists helped make possible the illustrations reprinted here: particularly helpful were Nanette Brewer and Adelheid Gealt at the Indiana University Art Museum, Betsy J. Rosasco and Laura M. Giles at the Princeton University Art Museum, Ron Mandelbaum at Photofest, Dave McCall at BFI, Christoph Eggenberger at Zentralbibliothek Zürich, and Geoff Todd.

Two grants, funded by Indiana University, freed me from teaching duties so that I could complete the manuscript with dispatch: a fellowship from the College Arts and Humanities Institute and another from the New Frontiers grants. My thanks go to Andrea Ciccarelli and Michael McRobbie for these awards, to Ellen Levine for representing the project as an agent, to Jill Bialosky at W. W. Norton for overseeing it as an editor, and to Jill's capable assistant Paul Whitlatch for infinite patience with my innumerable questions about production issues. Ever supportive, Adrienne Davich moved the manuscript through its final stages with alacrity. My copyeditor, the indispensable and wise Alice Falk, has become a dear friend through many thick and thin projects, and one from whom I always learn.

As always, the companions who keep me company daily in physical and electronic venues provided encouragement in too many ways to enumerate. Donald Gray, who read every draft and whose editorial skills honed each chapter, traveled with me to museums, watched movies, and deeply enriched my understanding of what we have discussed together. The astonishing independence of my mother, Luise David, freed me to wander creatively in whatever intellectual realm beckoned. My son-in-law Kieran Setiya guided my efforts to learn from his insights into philosophical approaches to ethics, and my stepdaughter Julie Gray facilitated my understanding of French texts and contexts. The loving kindness of Kieran and Julie and of my treasured daughters, Marah and Simone Gubar, buoys up my sometimes faltering faith in the future. My dear cousins Bernard David and Colin David provide ballast to and adventure in my life. Along with Susannah Gray and John Lyons, all the members of my family invariably enrich my thinking. For the inspiring and joyous exuberance of Jack Lyons and Elliot Gubar Setiya, I can only give heartfelt thanks.

This book is dedicated to my lifelong friend, Mary Jo Weaver, whose deep knowledge of Christianity and whose staunch commitment to linguistic lucidity shaped not only each chapter but also the sort of conceptualization that occurs much earlier in the writing process. As her many friends and students know, Mary Jo's loyalty, integrity, plain-speaking, and liberality of mind stand in stark contrast to Judas's conventional reputation. Yet no one understands better than Mary Jo the vagaries of the human spirit, which Judas's obscured progress so intensely registers, as well as the profound importance of dialogues among people from divergent faith communities, which Judas's evolution most definitively proves.

JUDAS

INTRODUCTION

WHO DOES NOT KNOW that Satan damns, Eve tempts, Cain murders, and Judas betrays? One of the earliest documents that has come down to us from biblical times (from the 50s C.E.) suggests that Paul may not have known about Judas. An absent presence surrounds the first account of Jesus' betrayal, because Paul uses the passive voice when he writes about Jesus being handed over—without mentioning the agent of the act: "the Lord Jesus on the night when *he was betrayed* took a loaf of bread, and when he had given thanks, he broke it and said, 'This is my body that is for you' " (1 Corinthians 11:23–24; emphasis mine). Someone informed on Jesus or handed Jesus over, according to the preeminent missionary of the first century, though the identity of the defector remains shrouded in mystery. Yet elsewhere the New Testament fastens the name of Judas Iscariot to treachery: Mark, Matthew, Luke, and John all associate Judas with betrayal. All four also describe a scene in which the twelfth apostle surrenders Jesus to his enemies. Exactly who was Judas Iscariot, and why over the past two thousand years have so many thinkers and artists tried to answer this question? Was he an actual person? Where did he come from, what were his motives, how and why did he enact his role, with what personal consequences?

The obvious place to begin resolving all these puzzling matters is the New Testament. Foundational as the Gospels are to an understanding of Jesus' antagonist, their authors leave many blanks in Judas's life story, even as they provide contradictory sketches of his personality, motivation, and fate. Very few verses are devoted to Judas in the Bible, and they agree only on his being the disciple who gave Jesus over to the Jerusalem authorities. All other biblical claims about the twelfth apostle—about, for instance, how he betrayed or when he began thinking about betrayal—are negated or qualified by opposing or incongruent contentions. The recent recovery of an ancient Gospel of Judas has fanned interest in him but has not filled in the blanks; it has, instead, accentuated the contradictions. Because of these gaps and inconsistencies, painters and theologians, poets and dramatists, novelists and filmmakers have returned to a crucial figure at the heart of the Passion narrative, one whose baffling act of betrayal initiates the crucifixion but also and just as enigmatically the resurrection.

"Judas is the most important figure in the New Testament apart from Jesus," the highly regarded Protestant theologian Karl Barth explained: "For he, and he alone of the apostles, was actively at work . . . in the accomplishment of what was God's will and what became the content of the Gospel. Yet he is the very one who is most explicitly condemned by the Law of God" (*Doctrine* 502). Centuries earlier, Augustine had laid the groundwork for Barth's claim by imagining a trinity of God, Jesus, and his twelfth apostle: "Delivering up was done by the Father, delivering up was done by the Son, delivering up was done by Judas; one thing was done" (*Tractates* 222–23). Only some 1,200 words are composed about Judas in the New Testament; they furnish the bare bones of a significant life later elaborated on repeatedly.

Also because of these blanks and contradictions, the factual Judas is dwarfed—in the history of Western civilization and in the pages to come—by his dazzlingly various and invented forms in postbiblical times. Scarcity of information about a historical Judas Iscariot, along with obscurities in the written records from the first century C.E., has stimulated all sorts of people to produce a plethora of stories about an individual who turns into one of the most multifaceted characters in Western culture. Especially in medieval legends and in Renaissance painting, Judas takes on flesh and personality through a succession of distinct and often incongruous portraits, as he does in subsequent literary works: first, the biblical anomaly becomes Satan's greedy agent and thus the most detestable villain in Western societies; but then, also and oddly, he appears to play the part of the passionate lover of Jesus, his heroic counterpart, and even his savior. Before and after the 2006 recovery of a Gnostic Gospel of Judas, the centrality of the twelfth apostle in the history of Christianity has gone largely ignored. How and why did a figure of disgrace eventually turn into a dignitary: Judas the saint, the martyr, the divine, even (in one Islamic-influenced gospel) Judas the Jesus look-alike, dying (instead of Jesus) on the cross? This is the question I answer through a biography of Judas's long cultural life.

Somewhat of a conceit or metaphor, the biographical framework nevertheless helps me narrate the patterns of development at work in changing conceptualizations of a figure with multiple personalities during the trajectory of a convoluted career.[1] In brief, *Judas: A Biography* maps the origins of the atypical twelfth apostle in biblical times, his fiendish adolescence during antiquity and the premodern period, his erotic coming of age during the Renaissance, his heroic maturation in modernity, his death as well as his astonishing resurrection during the course of the twentieth century, and his venerable afterlife into the twenty-first. It uses the periods of Judas's represented evolution as phases in an unfolding figurative life. The biographical scaffolding serves to emphasize the fact that the book in your hands is not about theology or history, but instead about character and representation. The next chapter will explain and (I hope) justify why I have chosen such a quirky approach to an infamous personage whose dates, ancestry, place of origin, aspirations, acts, and values remain unknown. To begin with, though, Judas in his most notorious persona has to be approached as the principal figure through whom Christians have understood Jews and Jewry.

Anomaly, pariah, lover, hero, savior: Judas has undergone as many imaginative transformations as Satan, Eve, and Cain, to whom he is regularly compared. Unlike Satan, Eve, and Cain, however, Judas Iscariot does not appear in the Hebrew Bible, and he has not been relegated to a purely mythic realm. And unlike Satan and Eve, if not Cain, the twelfth apostle has often been made to represent what is thought to be a religious or ethnic or racial group.[2] Originally neither more nor less Jewish than Jesus or, for that matter, Matthew, Peter, and John, Judas was frequently conflated with the Jewish people. How, when, and why did Judas come to stand for the Jews, and with what shifting repercussions? What does it mean that at certain representational moments Judas is *not* Jewish? Answers to these questions can be briefly sketched within the next few pages, though their long-term implications will become fully apparent only at the book's conclusion.

That Judas's name was used against Jews by Christians in postbiblical times confers on him an especially important part in the history of the relations between Jews and Christians. As early as the fourth century Saint Jerome asked, "Whom do you suppose are the sons of Judas?" Without skipping a beat, he went on to answer, "The Jews. The Jews take their name, not from that Juda who was a holy man, but from the betrayer" (259). Indeed, "no matter how you interpret it," Jerome argued, "Iscariot means money and price" (260). Nor did his view expire in antiquity. In the sixteenth century, Martin Luther attributed Jewish biblical responses and commentaries to the foul influence of Judas. After Judas exploded, with his intestines as well as his bladder bursting, Luther explained, the Jews "caught the Judas-piss" and "mixed it into the excrement and ate it among each other and drank it so that they developed such sharp eyes" (Luther, *Vom Schem Hamphoras* 214). According to Luther, it seems, Jews ingested concoctions of Judas's urinary and fecal waste, presumably to offset inborn astigmatism or to cultivate some kind of threatening X-ray vision. Luther's approach signals the disgust that Judas (and his presumed influence) could and often did arouse in Gospel readers and audiences.

With decidedly less mind-boggling (not to say unappetizing) rhetoric, in 1911 the American scholar W. B. Smith published a perfectly conventional essay in which he stated that the twelfth apostle "*stands for Jewry, for the Jewish people*" (539). And in 1942, the highly regarded Protestant theologian Karl Barth elaborated on a personification that also functions as a synecdoche: bread often stands for food, head for cattle, Judas for the Jewish people. Barth had published a second volume of his *Church Dogmatics* in Switzerland because his active resistance against Hitler made his stay in Germany impossible, and still he buttressed Jerome's view. "Judas and all Israel, Judas and in and with him the Jews as such," Barth exclaimed, adding that "Like Esau, the rejected of God, they sold their birthright for a mess of pottage. They did not do so with closed but with open eyes. Yet these were obviously the eyes of the blind" (465).[3] In contrast to his brilliant insights into other textual matters related to the twelfth apostle, Barth's judgment that "Israel always tried to buy off Yahweh with thirty pieces of silver" (464) teeters toward Luther's in its nauseated (and, in turn, repellant) disgust. This idea that Jews dishonorably and habitually attempt to suborn or bribe God issues from a principled opponent of the Nazis just at the time the "final solution" gets under way.

After conducting a survey in 1966, the Anti-Defamation League of B'nai B'rith published an inquiry into American anti-Semitism. The assessment, which addressed popular ideas about Jesus' Passion, garnered disturbing responses to the question "When you think of Judas, who betrayed Christ, do you think of him as . . . ?" The authors' findings flatly stated that "Seeing Judas as a Jew is not meaningfully related to denomination": "44 per cent of the Protestants and 47 per cent of the Roman Catholics thought Judas was a Jew (only 13 and 19 per cent of these groups thought the apostles were Jews)" (Glock and Stark 49). Since one would expect this last sentence to explain that such-and-such a percentage of people "thought the *other* apostles were Jews," even the investigators seem unable to grasp the discipleship of Judas. In 2005, looking back at his "church's Sunday school curriculum," John Shelby Spong, the retired Episcopal bishop of Newark, explained that "it was easy to identify the Jews. They had names like Pharisees, Sadducees, scribes, Caiaphas, Annas and Judas Iscariot. Those names dripped with hostility as these stories were told"; however, "no one told me that Jesus was a Jew" (194).

Up until today, and despite overwhelming academic and theological agreement to the contrary, some people have remained convinced that Judas was Jewish, Jesus and his other eleven disciples Christian. The words of a contemporary cultural historian can summarize the quintessential Jewishness of Judas: according to Jeremy Cohen, "the very name of Judas or Judah (*Yehudah* in Hebrew) signifies the entire Jewish people, in the language of Scripture and in subsequent writings, too. As the ultimate expression of evil and betrayal, the character of Judas resides within each and every Jew" (259). With Judas's departure from the Last Supper, George Steiner argued in characteristically striking language, "not merely those thirty pieces of silver but the daemonic ambiguities of money itself . . . will cling to the Jew like leprosy" (*No Passion Spent* 417).[4] The "daemonic ambiguities of money" stick "like leprosy" to Judas (and the Jews he personifies) by means of clinking (silver or gold) precious coins, rather than the flimsy paper currency issued by civic states.

The query "what does Judas look like?" may call to mind a constellation of stereotypically anti-Semitic traits. Early writings tell us nothing about Judas's physiognomy, just as they furnish no description of Jesus' physical features, but the twelfth apostle often appears with a hook nose, blind eyes or (in profile) one suspicious eye, red hair, wrinkled or warty skin, and a malevolent mouth.[5] Judas as he was used against Jews by Christians is perhaps most graphically protested by the Australian expressionist Albert Tucker, whose satiric portrait *Judas* (1955; plate 1) captures a totally degraded depravity: squatting and straining in brown with his bottom low to the ground, his buttocks just inches from the earth, he cannot but recall the feces often associated not only with filthy lucre but also with early biblical descriptions of and later elaborations on Judas's foul end, the explosion of his bowels. Throughout his pictorial history, reddish hair links Judas to Satanic sins, bloody passions or designs.

As if bowed down by the weight of his past, Tucker's spiritually blind Judas has no eyes, no vision at all, but exhibits the shadowed lids, sallow complexion, and large nose stereotypically ascribed to Jews. He also displays a scowling or frowning intensity that, in this case, marks Judas's brow with an imprint or brand reminiscent of Cain's. With his thick and rooted feet, his crouch captures the gravity of an earth-bound but hardly human creature. No matter what it is that slithers over the tunic taut between his spread knees—braids of the broken hanging rope? a flaccid penis, a telltale trunk, or tails? turds? bowels? intestines?—the two excrescences look as monstrous as Eve's snaky familiar. Part animal and part human, a transgenic Judas seems quite old here.

Out of his bulimic mouth Tucker's Judas spits his innards, only five of the thirty silver coins he earned through deceit and treachery so sickening that they must be vomited or spewed or defecated from the filthy hoard or slot machine his body has become. Hands firmly grasping his ankles, he regurgitates the coins while one of the more penile of the two excreta looks to be making its way toward his extended lips, an organ he might himself suck or swallow (as the satanic snake does its tail) if it does not gag or choke him first. Having gorged on money but now having to regurgitate the indigestible, Judas—expectorating from his funnel-like aperture—has a rigid block-shaped pose that calls to mind a figure tortured in the stocks against a tellingly yellowed sky. Often the color of Judas's robe in Renaissance oil paintings, yellow (required on badges assigned to Jews in the medieval period and in Nazi Germany) was thought to symbolize Judas's greed (for gold) as well as his envy, cowardice, and dishonesty. (The American phrase "green with envy" corresponds to the German "gelb vor Neid," or yellow with envy.) All head, bottom, limbs, appendages, and members, Judas appears heartless and soulless, like an open dirty book. There is no grace abounding to this chief of sinners.[6]

Does Tucker's portrait subvert or reaffirm an anti-Semitic stereotype? By treating this painting as satire (in part because of its use of exaggeration), I have been assuming that its painter criticizes the caricature he recycles; however, the volatility of visual representation leaves the interpretive consequences of each recycling up for grabs, dependent on how individual viewers perceive it. No wonder that the nefarious propaganda exploiting Judas has made both Christians and Jews leery about confronting his cultural history. Repellant as he is, Tucker's Judas reflects either the vilification of Jews or fully justified anger at the vilification of Jews, both of which have been fueled by some approaches to the Passion narrative. Yet Tucker's spitting, squatting, squinting Fagin embodies only one facet—if the most gruesome—of Judas's multifaceted character.

Before but especially after the Holocaust demonstrated the catastrophic consequences of anti-Semitism to many Americans, Judas began to be depicted more sympathetically in popular culture. Consider the contrast between an alienated Judas in Cecil B. DeMille's silent film *The King of Kings* (1927) and the heroic Judas in Nicholas Ray's blockbuster remake, *King of Kings* (1961). Cecil B. DeMille, himself partly Jewish-identified, presented a misguided and self-serving but good-looking Judas who broods over the heap of coins offered by a much guiltier Caiaphas.[7] More attuned to the political perplexities of the twelfth apostle, Ray's adaptation depicts Jews massacred by sadistic Romans and a rebellious Judas so outraged by the carnage that he seeks any and all means to liberate Jerusalem: he betrays Jesus only in order to force his messiah's hand.[8] An anguished but handsome and courageous Rip Torn stars as Judas in the remake (illustration i.1). Decades after World War II and while Adolf Eichmann was being tried in Israel (raising consciousness about the horror of the Shoah), Ray's idealistic Judas convinces himself that an arrested Jesus will strike back against the genocidal Romans and thereby free the Jews from what is shown to be horrific slavery.

Actively militant on Judas's behalf, Martin Scorsese used the cli-

i.1. Judas, played by Rip Torn, in Nicholas Ray's *King of Kings* (1961). Source: British Film Institute.

max of his movie *The Last Temptation of Christ* (1988) to feature a righteous, self-sacrificing, and eminently noble Judas (played by Harvey Keitel) who ascertains that "God gave [Jesus] the easier job" in Jerusalem, and then rescues Jesus from Satanic thrall so that he is empowered to deliver redemption to humankind.[9] Scorsese's Judas—adamant, loyal, and looking in publicity stills like a snazzy model in a Nazareth fashion catalogue—saves a hesitant Jesus as well as Jesus' saving mission.[10] One critic, noting the sustained dramatic interaction between Jesus and Judas, sees the film taking on "aspects of the Hollywood 'buddy' movie with two friends aiding each other in a joint quest" (Humphries-Brooks 86); another traces how the "homo-erotic undertones" in the relationship between Jesus and Judas propel the plot (Reinhartz 176). With a confused Jesus, the plot of *The Last Temptation of Christ* features a trusty Judas-comrade who, against great odds, comprehends and carries out God's divine will.

And we now know that Scorsese's approach, like that of the Greek novelist who furnished his source, can find confirmation in the recently recovered Gospel of Judas, which appears to provide a humane take on this apostle's nature, as do (albeit to a lesser degree) the first two Gospels in the New Testament. In none of these instances do we find Judas marked as more or less Jewish than the other figures in the Passion narrative. The earliest canonical and noncanonical texts rarely isolate Judas from the other eleven apostles, rarely conflate him with the Temple authorities, rarely classify his distinctive religious or ethnic affiliation. Neither do Ray and Scorsese. These and other examples explain why the author of a wide-ranging German-language treatment of Judas traditions considers it eminently reasonable to declare, "One cannot say that Judas was generally seen as the exponent of Judaism in contrast with the other apostles, nor that the hatred for that ethnic minority was generally carried over onto him" (Dinzelbacher 80).[11]

Such varied depictions of Judas's loyalties and nature—sometimes a stereotyped Jewish foe, sometimes Jesus' most intimate friend—help clarify why numerous scholarly analyses of anti-Semitism refrain from mentioning the influence of the twelfth apostle. Even the most responsible theologians and religious historians engaged in Christian-Jewish dialogues today ignore the role of Judas.[12] They disregard him in part because anti-Semitism does not necessarily depend on Judas; Judas was not always viewed as Jewish or as a prototype of Israel, and therefore any kinship between Judas and the Jews is patchy or wavering. At various stages in his development, Judas intermittently speaks as a Jew, as a Christian, and as a person with no religious affiliation at all. How can this be, and what does it mean? The chapters that follow propose that Judas's shifting affiliations date back to (and reflect the repercussions of) the inseparability of Judaism and Christianity from biblical times until late antiquity. To trace the genesis of

Judas is to delineate the origins of those species of religion we call Judaism and Christianity. Indeed, Judas was vigorously deployed to differentiate Judaism from emergent Christianity. Precisely because of his instrumentality and because his beginnings are so rife with blanks and contradictions, gaps and incongruities, a multitude of thinkers and artists have been moved to delineate his astonishingly various incarnations over twenty centuries.

Juxtaposing contemporary neglect of (or embarrassment about) Judas against his spectacularly influential past, *Judas* was written neither to repress nor to excuse anti-Semitic ideologies hinged on the figure of Judas, but rather to explore what his morphing signifies in terms of Jewish-Christian traditions and interactions. As I hope to show, mutating avatars of Judas Iscariot illuminate the relationship between Judaism and Christianity as well as changing Western attitudes toward the body, blood, and money; greed, hypocrisy, and betrayal; suicide and repentance; friendship, homosexuality, and divinity. At its most basic level, and whether or not Judas appears to be Jewish, his story of betrayal invariably raises the question of evil. Why do human beings commit acts of iniquity? Why does an omniscient and omnipotent God allow immoral crimes to occur? And if God sanctions or requires bad actions, should individual human actors be held accountable? Can they or should they place their faith in such a God? These are the important issues—central to the problem of free will and determinism, trust and faith—to which thinkers and artists absorbed by Judas recurrently returned, not just in past times and in high art, but also in postmodern times and in popular forms.

By making use of the periods in cultural history as if they were developmental stages in a continuous but continually changing (though unusually long) life, the plot of *Judas: A Biography* follows an enigmatic loner in ancient times who was mercilessly bullied during a fiendish adolescence in premodern societies until he unexpectedly attained a seductive and ethical maturity at moments in the medieval period and with frequency after the Renaissance. As Brendan Kennelly has observed in the preface to his remarkable book of poems *The Book of Judas* (1991), "A learned hate is hard to unlearn" (9). Yet throughout the eighteenth and nineteenth centuries, Judas grew in erotic, political, and moral power, taking on the stature of a hero, albeit a brooding and conflicted one. In short, over the long haul the twelfth apostle progresses from disgrace to dignity. The questions such a trajectory raises are multiple. Why did a character treated as one of Jesus' intimate apostles by Mark and Matthew turn into a demonic Antichrist in antiquity? How could such a pariah then be pictured as Jesus' lover in the Renaissance or as his champion in the nineteenth century? Was Judas in fact doomed by a return of his repressive tormentors, by a regression to his satanic past, during the reign of the Third Reich? For what reasons did Judas's vindication fail—and how did Nazi villifications finally miscarry? Can it persuasively be argued that Judas moves from disgrace to dignity, if he has recurrently stood for a stereotyped people? These are the mysteries *Judas: A Biography* seeks to solve.

In the first chapter, the contrast between how little we know about the historical Judas and the proliferation of Judas allusions and fictive Judas spin-offs serves to make a case for the biographical format of the rest of the book. Here I also explain how it is possible for Judas to progress from early damnation toward a weird sort of beatification, even though he recurrently regresses to the role of Jewish pariah. My second chapter, "Alone of All His Sex," focuses on the singularity of this apostle's initial development in the Gospels, a point later made by numerous visual depictions of his vexed relationship to his community—Judas as the only apostle without a halo, on the wrong side of the table, with red hair, a money bag, or a yellow robe—as well as conflicting accounts of his motives, means, and ends. In the New Testament, Judas evolves from a wayward apostle to a demonically possessed thief. Taken together, the emergent figures of Judas in the Gospels illuminate the permeability of Judaism and Christianity in ancient times. He therefore reveals when, how, and why two characters born into and committed to the same faith seem to undergo antithetical conversions as Judas becomes Jewish, Jesus Christian.

The biblical paradoxes posed by the four canonical Gospels, as they coalesced together in the Christian imagination, generated Judas's subsequent incarnations, which solve or dissolve, contest or confirm multiple knots or cruxes in the New Testament. Part II of this book rests on the assumption that Judas was vigorously reinvented from antiquity to the present precisely because of the blanks as well as the contradictions in the earliest Gospel accounts of his instrumental role in the Passion. Many thinkers and artists—persuaded that Judas's part had not been accorded a logical narrative—re-create the twelfth apostle with a host of dissimilar faces and postures: the succession of incarnations described in Part II. Regardless of which prototype he manifests in a long series of plausible and implausible reconstructions, each is partial and incongruent with the others. In all of Judas's postbiblical personae, inconsistencies are resolved by denying or eliding some aspects of the New Testament accounts. Inevitably, then, multiple Judas figures emerge, with markedly different demeanors and temperaments. Though for the purposes of clarity I will attempt to keep the anomaly distinct from the pariah, the lover from the hero and the savior, Judas occasionally confounds such compartmentalization.

Part II opens with the third chapter, "Damned Miscegenation," which examines Judas as a scapegoat or pariah. During antiquity and the premodern period, when most people could not read the Bible and legends proliferated, a vilified Judas warned against commercial enterprises as well as religious heresies that accompanied the establishment of medieval and Renaissance societies. From the theological meditations of the church fathers to the earliest recorded ballads, legends, and mystery plays, Judas emerges as a figure of miscegenation, blurring the boundaries between person and animal, human and satanic, the living and the dead. An absorption with the anal and oral crimes attributed to Judas influenced innumerable European illustrations of the bloody or fecal entrails and bowels, toothy mouth, black demons, and parasites often associated with Judas, along with folk-lore about the so-called Jewish stench, host desecration, ritual human sacrifice, vampirism, and cannibalism. But why did Judas recurrently star inside the Oedipus story, and what did that melding signify about his progressing out of the anal and oral phases, his arrival at the phallic stage?

The fourth chapter, "Arresting Kisses," explores representative stained-glass windows, Psalters, woodcuts, and oil paintings from the twelfth century to the Renaissance depicting the antagonists Jesus and Judas in a close embrace. One scene in particular engages the painters: the betrayal kiss. Judas, emerging as a prototype of general human depravity, predictably raises the problem of the proximity of evil to good. Many painters use the story of Judas's captivating embrace and kiss to linger on sadism, love spilling over into a cruel eroticism labeled deviant, but others less predictably depict adver-saries enacting an amorous or spiritual union. Chapter 4 poses the question, what does it mean that the most widespread cultural image we have of two men embracing derives from Judas's act of betrayal? At least visually, the twinning of Jesus and a loving Judas could and did modulate into a homoerotic or homosexual clasp.

Counterintuitive though it may seem, pictures of the betrayal kiss set in motion the humanization of Judas first as a remorseful peni-tent, then as a passionate crusader for Jesus. The fifth chapter, titled "In a Modern Glass Darkly," traces a secular tradition that translates erotic and spiritual brotherhood into psychological and ethical dou-bling: authors depicting this parallelism have presented, at the least, a sincere Judas and, at the most, a heroic Judas "ordained of heaven / To urge the great work of redemption on / Commencing with Christ's Kingdom upon earth," as Richard Hengist Horne put it (154). In this guise, a glamorous twelfth apostle—somewhat like Prometheus—typifies rebellion (against the unjust authority of Rome) and idealism (in helping his comrade Jesus quicken the coming of a new age of justice). Even when Judas's moral rehabilitation fails, he takes on pathos either as an isolated figure trapped within the brutal role he had to play in a story that brings redemption to everyone else or as a miserable soul inexplicably estranged from grace. A number of artists identify Judas with the desperate cases and lost causes sponsored by the saint whom he often eclipsed, Saint Jude, or with the isolating agony lamented by an inexplicably afflicted Job. Whether Judas was motivated by good or by obscurely compulsive instincts, modern narratives that issue in his destruction tend to approach him sympathetically and at times use his dismal fate to question the justice of God or God's Son.

Despite such concerted efforts at exonerating Judas, the sixth chapter of this book—"Twentieth-Century Deaths and Resurrections"— asks the question, was the return of the medieval pariah-Judas responsible for the Holocaust? Even though I will answer this question with a decided no, Nazi-sponsored propaganda indisputably did recycle the pariah-Judas. A number of historians have shown, too, that Nazi clerics went beyond linking Judas with the Jews when they preached sermons about a non-Jewish, Aryan Christ. Prominent religious thinkers continued to blame Judas with the Jews for nailing Christ to the cross, necessitating the repudiation by postwar Christian authorities of any and all efforts to misuse the Passion so as to collude in anti-Semitism. All these phenomena seem all too predictable. But then Judas's life story took quite an unexpected turn, one that allows me to discuss two widely ignored climaxes in his iconographic later existence. Born in the Gospels, the Jewish pariah-Judas was consigned to death at Auschwitz (by the Nazis) and after Auschwitz (by their Christian postwar adversaries), but news of his demise has been greatly exaggerated.

Rigorous attempts to murder the Jewish pariah-Judas were accompanied by the apotheosis of the twelfth apostle in semblances more resplendent and contradictory than any of his earlier guises. Chapter 6 will account for a surprising phenomenon at the end of the twentieth century: Judas's manifestation, first, as a savior of humanity's savior and then as an omnipotent deity, an all-consuming figure of humanity's damned and doomed condition within a world in which the Holocaust happened. Toward the end of the twentieth century, Judas the divine emerges to stand for the precarious efficacy of Jesus' atonement and its consequences: sorrowful disappointment, painful alienation, and the corrupt exploitation of an unredeemed world. Contemporary writers brood on the repercussions of a conviction Mircea Eliade traced back to Nietzsche, the proposition that "As a historical being, man killed God, and after this assassination—this 'deicide'—he is forced to live exclusively in history" (48). An ecumenical Judas—neither more nor less Jewish than Jesus—remains alive and well: a powerful iconic presence.

The partial eclipse of Jesus from my history of Judas's long cultural life and the predominance of Christian artists drawn to interpret the Passion spurred me to consider in the final chapter what the twelfth apostle signifies from an often-disregarded Jewish perspective and how the nature of Jesus changes over two thousand years, depending on the Judas with whom he is conjoined. Despite the disjointed personalities exhibited throughout the twenty centuries of Judas's representational life, this book concludes with a meditation on the enduring import of the betrayer for people from all faith communities. Much to my own surprise (since my project here was motivated less by any thesis than by curiosity), I end up contending that the complex psychological and ethical quandaries Judas invariably addresses make him one of the most relevant biblical characters today.

Judas remains meaningful because of a negativity that reflects the contradictions in which he is rooted. The core of my argument pertains to the incongruities and inconsistencies that continually propelled his reincarnations. In other words, the genesis of Judas in the knots and cruxes of the Gospels illuminates not only the origins of those religious species we call Judaism and Christianity but also the specious or virtual species of Judases who have populated the imaginations of countless people throughout the postbiblical history of Western culture. And what that specious species in turn clarifies—

perhaps more starkly than any other public or private iconography in Western culture—is the conundrum of betrayal (treachery), itself a notoriously ambiguous moral category . . . one so slippery that sometimes it can mean, antithetically, that a slip (of the tongue or a gesture) betrays us into revealing exactly who we are. Considered "fascinating . . . because it is often enormously puzzling," betrayal constitutes a violation of trust, of course, but a violation of trust that has to be judged in terms of a complex of extenuating factors, or so philosophers of ethics remind us (Shklar 141).

The artists discussed in *Judas* address a host of factors clustered around the betrayal of trust: the discrepancy between or conjunction of feeling betrayed, being betrayed, and becoming a betrayer; whether or not deception accompanies betrayal to conceal it; the difference between betrayers deliberately exercising power over someone so as to be hurtful or being themselves betrayed by uncontrollable emotions; the curious and disturbing paradox that misplaced or misconstrued loyalty can itself constitute a betrayal; the equally odd phenomenon that collaborative betrayal can occur when someone is driven to betray by or for another; the irony that betrayal of evil forces may constitute a supreme good or that betrayal of one cause can mean loyalty to another. By dwelling on a mystic messiah— who is generally considered eminently trustworthy and whose trust is betrayed—the Passion crystallizes such issues. Interpreters of Judas and the New Testament play variations on this theme in order to multiply the meanings of trust's betrayal.

Whereas Jesus proffers *euangelion,* the "good news" of the Gospels, the apostle who betrays heralds "dusangelion," the bad news related to the Greek verb *dusangelein* (to announce bad news) and the Greek adjective *dusangelos* (announcing evil).[13] Judas's bad news proclaims that some human beings, experiencing their evildoing or suffering as neither intentional nor deserved nor ennobling, mourn the limits of redemption or God's broken covenant. Caught in a narrative antagonistic to his own well-being, Judas testifies for all those who chaff against forces conspiring to doom them to mortification or damnation. He represents casualties about whom luckier people murmur, there but for the grace of God. . . . This phrase itself suggests the scandalous caprice of grace and disgrace. When, in one of my epigraphs, Toni Morrison calls love "the weather," betrayal "the lightning that cleaves and reveals it," she suggests the fungible exchanges of love and betrayal. Just as our belief in the possibility of a progressive history of Western civilization must always be adjudicated against a realization of its recurrent subversion, so the Passion story weighs Jesus' rise against Judas's fall, even as it asks whether one would be possible without the other.

Yet that Judas alone has been stuck in the role of scapegoat seems indisputably unfair, given the number of human and divine agents who participate in the handing over of Jesus in the New Testament.[14] Even though it was Judas who delivered Jesus to the chief priests in the Gospels, the chief priests handed Jesus over to Pilate, and then Pilate gave him over first to the Jewish mob and then to the Roman soldiers, and of course it was the Roman soldiers, operating under imperial rule, who crucified him. According to John, Jesus insisted on his followers understanding that he exerted control over his own fate: "I lay down my life in order to take it up again," John's Jesus proclaims; "No one takes it from me, but I lay it down of my own accord. I have power to lay it down, and I have power to take it up again" (10:17–18). In Romans, it is God himself "who did not withhold his own Son, but gave him up for all of us" (8:32). Precisely the uncanny parallelism or collaboration between Judas, the chief priests, Pilate, the Jerusalem crowds, Roman soldiers, Jesus, and God destabilizes guilt and responsibility for a morally culpable act that brought about what many hold dear as the redemptive promise of resurrection. Judas—frequently excluded from the salvation he helps facilitate—delivers bad news that stays news, for his dogma of damage and despair testifies to the most profoundly distressing nature of the human condition.

PART I

MYSTERIOUS ORIGINS

JUDAS, FACT OR FICTION?

Is Judas's mythic stature derived from any historical basis? If Judas was a real person, why did he betray Jesus and what was his fate? The answers to these questions, coupled with Judas's magnificent morphing over such a long period of time and in so many various venues, make biography a feasible approach.

SOME OF THE FINAL WORDS JESUS speaks to his disciples before his death pertain to the twelfth apostle: "Get up, let us be going. See, my betrayer is at hand" (Mark 14:42; Matthew 26:46). Although Judas may be a minor character in the Passion, his is hardly a bit part. "For the world to be saved," a character in Nikos Kazantzakis's novel *Christ Recrucified* (1948) explains, "Judas is indispensable, more indispensable than any other Apostle" (25). Karl Barth made a similar point when he argued that "Judas does what God wills to be done. He and not Pilate is the *executor Novi Testamenti*" (*Doctrine* 502). Without Judas, the contemporary author Mario Brelich reminds us, neither the Gospels nor Christianity would exist. Given "the tremendous benefits accruing" from his acts, "We are all accomplices to the Crime of crimes," Brelich asserts, claiming paradoxically: "the one person in the world and in History who had nothing to gain from committing it, or to put it more exactly, the only one who had everything to gain from not committing it, was, precisely, Judas Iscariot himself!" (218).

Yet remarkably few scholarly studies center on this apostle. Both Jewish strictures and Christian apologies about the anti-Semitic uses to which Judas has been put have obscured the significance of his evolution as well as the complexity of his protean character, an evolution that does not hinge simply on whether he becomes typecast as the sole Jewish disciple. For at times, the twelfth apostle becomes the only homosexual disciple, at other times the only African one, at still other times the only mentally unstable or disabled or agnostic one. A handful of books have dealt with Judas, all meant for specialists in the history of Christianity and all neglectful of the central role he has played in the visual arts and in contemporary literature. The most useful of these is Kim Paffenroth's *Judas: Images of the Lost Disciple* (2001). To the extent that I deal with Judas's temporal development from ancient times to the present, my chronological approach differs from his typological one, for I start with the Gospels in the order of their composition, and then proceed by visiting early Christian thinking, medieval ballads and mystery plays, Renaissance painting, eighteenth- and nineteenth-century poetry, and twentieth-century theology, fiction, and film. Groundbreaking as his study was, Paffenroth's decision to ignore chronology and to provide so many meticulous summaries of so many (often banal) texts left me confused about the historical trajectory of Judas from biblical times to the present.

Besides gauging Judas's progress as an index of modifications in Western civilization's ideas about betrayal and trust, free will and determinacy, I try to avoid the tendency of other thinkers to decry Judas's vilification or to vindicate his actions. In *Judas Iscariot and the Myth of Jewish Evil* (1992), Hyam Maccoby emphasizes the conflation of the name of the Jewish people with the name of Jesus' betrayer, and then attributes Christian anti-Semitism to the degrading mythologizing of Judas. William Klassen in *Judas: Betrayer or Friend of Jesus?* (1996) seeks to invent a less murderous script from the Gospels: Klassen translates the Greek term for Judas's betrayal as an act of handing Jesus over to the high priests, thereby exonerating it as a divinely countenanced task. Whereas Maccoby castigates an evil-through-and-through Judas, Klassen pities a well-intentioned if unappreciated Judas. Unlike these two authors, I come neither to bury Judas nor to praise him.

Reviewing the extensive trajectory of Judas's diverse incarnations, I draw on recent theological attempts to grapple with the shocking moral challenge that fuels the drawing power of Judas. The theologian Anthony Cane put it this way: "if the salvation of humankind has in any measure a dependence on the damnation of one man, this is an injustice that radically undermines it" (156).[1] Since Judas was the only apostle to facilitate God's will—by helping to bring about the crucifixion and resurrection—does the doom or damnation he (alone among the disciples) suffers in the Passion qualify or call into question the mercy or efficacy of God or of God's Son? By thinkers in every conceivable historical period, Judas was reimagined, as he still is today, so as to clarify, resolve, or decry this enigma. In the popular imagination, for quite some time, Judas the turncoat, snitch, and thief often predominates, but that is not the case in his transnational, centuries-long legendary life in art and letters. For more than twenty centuries, Judas matures in poems and plays, novels and movies from a disgraceful pariah to a dignified lover, hero, and savior.

Given his long-standing cosmopolitanism, Judas's biography inevitably takes a different form from that of, say, Jane Austen or Albert Einstein. This life study of Judas follows the conventions of other biographies but with some salient changes. Many biographers open with a chapter on "Beginnings," though in Judas's case his origins remain textual: they can be traced only through the accounts of the four Gospels. "First Achievements" or "The Political Activist" or "Midlife Perplexities" might be chapters in a standard biography, in which every stage is pigeonholed into clearly demarcated sections of an existence. For Judas, however, incompatible personae recycle perpetually, for each of his roles is rooted (or finds confirmation) in some aspect of his contradictory textual origins. Yet throughout the consecutive phases of his temporal development, one character type predominates over the others as he moves from a premodern fiend to a Renaissance acolyte to an Enlightenment insurrectionist to a twentieth-century collaborator with Jesus.

The jolting phases of Judas's successive evolution over time contrast with the curious fact that he manages to stay the same horrid miscreant as the centuries roll by. Since a focus on what stays the same would inevitably be enervating and since the twelfth apostle does grow better and wiser, does gain ethical insight and a profound sense of responsibility regarding his teacher's mission, the chapters that follow trace Judas's progress and maturation, though this first chapter will conclude with a reminder that today Judas continues to display all his discordant guises. Here, too, I will attribute Judas's ability to stay the same even as he grows wiser to gaps and contradictions in a biblical genesis that also explain why he embodies the hyphen in Judeo-Christianity.

Whether marked as a demon or a martyr, the go-between Judas has provoked profound reflections on the problem of betrayal in virtually every medium and genre. By making it difficult to explain that problem away, Jesus' most notorious disciple emerges as a resonant contemporary. He does so despite—and paradoxically because of—his nebulous historical status. Uncertainties about Judas's historical reality, coupled with his incongruous roles, prompted my biographical approach to Judas's long cultural existence. For the absence of facts about a real Judas Iscariot propelled the fictional Judas's long succession of reinventions, all of which shed light on the dark night of a soul alienated from the rest of humanity and from the powers ruling humanity's destiny.

THE HISTORICAL JUDAS

Over and against the handful of publications about Judas that constitute the scholarly corpus of recent work done on him in English, hundreds of books about Jesus could be listed, all composed within the past several decades.[2] The story of Judas's life and death in the

Gospels has been eclipsed by the astonishing proliferation of books, films, and television series about the birth and crucifixion of Jesus, works that often contain hardly a mention of Judas at all. Since there are so few verses about Judas in the New Testament, this inattention is perfectly comprehensible.

In addition, it can be partly attributed to the emphasis that recent biblical scholarship has placed on historical investigation. When scholars remain relentlessly historical in their approach, in other words, they ignore (and have to ignore) Judas. In 1998, *Frontline* produced four sixty-minute television shows titled *From Jesus to Christ*, featuring interviews with eminent New Testament scholars and footage of archaeological evidence, found throughout Israel, about the origins of Christianity. Not once in these excellent programs is Judas's name mentioned. The reason for this omission has everything to do with the historical bent of the producers, for a number of investigators argue that the earliest accounts of Jesus' life and death in fact contain no real-life Judas-betrayer. Biblical scholars call the source (besides Mark) on which the Gospel authors Matthew and Luke relied "Q"-for *Quelle*, which means "source" in German—and hypothesize that in it there is no Judas-betrayer at all.[3] In the Talmud, the compilation of rabbinic literature produced from the first to the sixth century, the scarcity of Jesus references "can be compared to the proverbial drop in the *yam ha-talmud* ('the ocean of the Talmud')" (Schäfer 2); and there is no allusion to an apostle named Judas Iscariot.[4]

On the one hand, does the fact that Judas "bears the name of the Jewish people" mean that the tale was invented as an anti-Semitic myth, as Hyam Maccoby has proposed (ix)? Maccoby believes that a story about the struggle between Jesus and "the Jews as a Judas-nation" was what enabled Christians to divorce Christianity from Judaism (80).[5] Similarly, but more recently, John Shelby Spong has speculated that the idea of Judas arose decades after Jesus' death, when early Christians tried to curry favor with Romans by blaming the crucifixion on Jewish authorities. Or, on the other hand, did the narrative necessities of a betrayal plot generate a betrayer after the fact so that, according to Frank Kermode, "It is not unreasonable to conjecture that there was originally no Judas at all" (*Genesis* 94)?[6] Provocative as such conjectures are, one should not simply assume that Judas was merely a stereotyped Jew, the offshoot of a survivalist strategy to gain Gentile support for the church, or the fictive by-product of a narrative necessity. Judas's absence from or marginalization in the earliest sources cannot definitively prove his fictitious nature.

Those thinkers who study the tasks Judas performs remain even more divided about the imaginary or historical status of Judas's deeds and sayings than they are about those of Jesus. Recently, scholars have elaborated several criteria for using faith documents as historical sources, and a number of these principles can help in a search for the real-life Judas. Such a quest may be doomed to falter, but it nevertheless does propose a historical basis for his character and acts, even as it shapes the more rewarding pursuit of a mythic Judas who, within the Gospels and afterward, metamorphoses in a spectacularly protean manner. Here, in capsule form, are the historians' criteria that best help ascertain the legitimacy of ancient testimonies about Judas.

First, earlier sources are given more credence than later ones. Second, multiple witnesses from independent informants authenticate material as likely. Third, contextual credibility counts (so that, for instance, anachronisms can be ruled out). Fourth, the less theologically motivated the testimony, the more valuable: controversial or quirky statements (that do not support a decidedly Jewish or Christian agenda) may contain facts precisely because of their unpredictability or incongruity.[7] Biblical scholars rely on these suppositions to evaluate the Gospels, all written in Greek by anonymous authors who were not eyewitnesses and who composed approximately thirty-five to sixty-five years after the events narrated. With such standards in mind, most thinkers deduce from the chronology of the four Gospels now established that Mark must be accorded a place of primacy. If the Gospel of Mark was written in the mid-60s or early 70s C.E., as most scholars agree, then it predates Matthew and Luke (80s) and John (90s).[8] The additions of each subsequent author illuminate areas of consensus and discord.

Before we turn in the next chapter to Mark and his successors to gain an appreciation of how radically the character of Judas was altered by four of the authors in the New Testament, the earliest source quoted at the start needs to be briefly revisited. Because in 1 Corinthians Paul writes in the passive voice, without mentioning Judas at all, a reader may wonder if Paul even knew of a disciple by that name: "the Lord Jesus on the night when *he was betrayed* took a loaf of bread . . ." (11:23–24; emphasis mine). To make matters murkier, scholars have also questioned whether Paul actually described a betrayal. Since in the New Testament "there are *no examples* of *paradidōmi* [hand over] being translated as 'betray' outside the Judas tradition," quite a few biblical thinkers argue, Paul should be understood as explaining what happened "on the night when [Jesus] was handed over" (Saari 22; emphasis mine).[9] Perhaps, in other words, Paul is describing the night when Jesus was handed over by God who, elsewhere we are told, "did not spare his own son, but handed him over for all of us" (Romans 8:32). Throughout the New Testament, the apostles *hand over* the good news and God *hands over* sinners to perdition. Therefore, they claim, the handing over described by Paul need not constitute a betrayal. Nor need the handing over of Jesus by Judas in later Gospels.

Yet, given the criteria of contemporary historians, Paul's testimony can help establish Judas as a historical being, for Paul supplies a counterintuitive, unpredictable claim, one that creates persistent problems for the theologically minded. It is, moreover, an assertion made by multiple independent witnesses whose motives could not possibly be theological.

In the earliest documents in the New Testament, Paul states that the resurrected Jesus was seen by all twelve apostles: Paul testifies about Jesus "that he was raised on the third day in accordance with the scriptures, and that he appeared to Cephas, then *to the twelve*"

(1 Corinthians 15:4–5; emphasis mine). The Gospel authors refer to eleven viewing the resurrected Jesus or mention no number at all. Yet Matthew and Luke contain statements by Jesus himself, saying to the twelve disciples that "in the new world, when the Son of Man shall sit on his glorious throne, you will also sit on twelve thrones, judging the twelve tribes of Israel" (Matthew 19:28; cf. Luke 22:30). According to the biblical historian Bart D. Ehrman, "This is not a tradition that was likely to have been made up by a Christian later, after Jesus's death—since one of these twelve had abandoned his cause and betrayed him. No one thought that *Judas Iscariot* would be seated on a glorious throne as a ruler in the Kingdom of God. That saying, therefore, appears to go back to Jesus, and indicates, then, that he had twelve close disciples whom he predicted would reign in the coming Kingdom" (*Jesus* 186).[10] It is worth stressing, too, that some Gospel authors list one or another apostle unmentioned by others; Judas, in contrast, is named by all four.

Moreover, witnesses in accord with Paul and with Matthew's Jesus as well as Luke's multiply after the period in which John wrote. While gospels were proliferating in the ancient world, and before some (and not others) were designated canonical in the fourth century, the leaders of various communities continued to record the parables that Jesus had framed to instruct his followers. For example, at the conclusion of the fragmentary, noncanonical Gospel of Peter, discovered in 1886 and known to have been in circulation around 175 C.E., the author explains that after the crucifixion and on the last day of the feast of unleavened bread, "We, *the twelve* disciples of the Lord, cried and mourned" (Cartlidge and Dungan 79; emphasis mine). Similarly, at the beginning of a late second-century Coptic "secret book" titled the Apocryphon of James, Jesus returns many days after he rose from the dead to instruct those banded together to mourn him: "*the twelve* disciples [used to] sit all together at the [same time], remembering what the Savior had said to each one of them, whether secretly or openly, and setting it down in books" (Cartlidge and Dungan 111; emphasis mine). Like the other eleven, Judas, we will see in the third chapter, appears in a number of narratives that were not incorporated into the Christian Bible but that proliferated during antiquity.

By virtue of the overlapping criteria of historical credibility, in other words, it seems clear that Jesus chose twelve disciples, presumably to represent the twelve tribes of Israel. Of course twelve may bring to mind the number of months in a year, the total signs of the zodiac, or half the number of hours in a day, and thus may seem predetermined. But all three synoptic authors (Mark, Matthew, Luke) and John include Judas in their number. Even his name has been taken as a signature of his contextual credibility. A Greek form of the biblical *Yehudah* or *Judah,* Judas was a very common Jewish name: think of the heroic Judas Maccabee (of Hanukkah fame), as well as several minor Judah and Judas characters in the Hebrew and Christian Bibles.[11] Saint Jerome's interpretation notwithstanding, "Iscariot" might derive from *sicarii* (assassins), the name given a group of violent Jewish patriots famed for concealing their daggers beneath their garments, stabbing their victims in crowds, and then defying detection by melting away. The *Catholic Encyclopedia* takes Iscariot to mean "a man of Kerioth," a city of Judea, and states that all the other apostles were Galileans (s.v. "Judas Iscariot"), but this claim has not been fully accepted by all scholars.[12]

Still, it appears that Judas Iscariot, the disciple, should gain credence historically. And even though his act of betrayal may generate doubts, these same criteria of historical authenticity tend to ground it historically as well.[13] For all three of the synoptic authors and John testify that the betrayal was engineered by Judas.

To be sure, when the Gospel of Peter asserts that "We, the twelve disciples of the Lord, cried and mourned," it appears to detach the twelfth apostle from betrayal, as does the Apocryphon of James with its claim that the twelve were engaged after Jesus' death in writing their accounts of his ministry. Yet Ehrman persuasively speculates that Judas's treachery "is about as historically certain as anything else in the tradition" (*Jesus* 216), because the betrayal is multiply witnessed (in the accounts of Mark, John, and Acts), and because it furnishes a problem the theologically inclined would hardly welcome: it raises the crucial conundrum, why would Jesus have chosen as an apostle a man capable of doing such a deed? Proposed answers to this age-old query only add to the perplexity. If Jesus did not comprehend Judas's character, how wise was Jesus in selecting his inner circle? If he did, could it be possible that Jesus would doom one of his beloved disciples to enact his personal damnation, and would Jesus do this in order to secure his own glorification (through suffering)? Inexplicable or unpredictable stories make good history, or so scholars of antiquity suppose, and therefore we can assume that Judas's betrayal probably occurred.

The operative word is "probably." What Harold Bloom claims about Jesus—that "'Jesus: A Biography' is always an oxymoron" and that we must "admit how hopelessly little we actually can know about Jesus" (*Jesus* 11, 22)—holds true for Judas as well.[14] Maybe my "probably" should be chalked up to a biographer's wish to establish the legitimate lineage of her subject. A better word might be "possibly." Many contemporary thinkers agree that the Passion story of Jesus' arrest, trial, and crucifixion derives from the earliest period of Christianity. Some, pointing to two independent sources (etiological legends discussed in the next chapter), connect Judas to a potter's field of red clay in Jerusalem called the Field of Blood.[15] This much— the historical probability or possibility of Judas's existence in ancient Judea and of his deed—but only this much can be claimed about the contradictory narratives told by Mark, Matthew, Luke, and John about the traitor in the Passion. As the biblical historian E. P. Sanders cautions, "There is nothing in the gospels about Judas' ambitions at all" (74).

Why did Judas betray—but also, what information exactly did Judas betray? Readers of the New Testament can only guess. The Greek verb associated with Judas's action, *paradidōnai*—Raymond E. Brown provides the translation "to give over" (2:1399)—suggests what may have happened: that Judas arrived on the Mount of Olives with those determined to arrest Jesus, showed them where to find

Jesus, and distinguished Jesus from among others.[16] To sum up in the words of another scholarly authority, John P. Meier, "we know only two basic facts about [Judas]: (1) Jesus chose him as one of the Twelve, and (2) he handed over Jesus to the Jerusalem authorities, thus precipitating Jesus' execution" (208).

These "two starkly contrasting facts" constitute "the colliding flints" that have "set ablaze Christian fantasy ever since" (Meier 208). Where Judas came from, when exactly he met up with the other disciples, why he was motivated first to follow and then to betray Jesus, what exactly he betrayed and precisely to whom, how and where he met his end: these matters remain shrouded in mystery because historians of the ancient world have found scant sources of information about Judas outside the New Testament.[17] Indeed, no one has succeeded in locating any sources about Judas independent of retellings of the New Testament narratives, which is why reputable thinkers can continue disbelieving in his historical reality. And of course the inconsistent Gospel portraits were composed not to furnish an objective record but to shape events in such a manner as to teach doctrine and inspire faith. Precisely these gaps in our knowledge about the real-life Judas and the "colliding flints" in his story have teased and inspired creative artists to fill in his lineaments.

Given the tension between the Jerusalem authorities and the apostles that historians trace through the Gospels, it is possible to speculate that their collision may well have sparked Judas's propensity to be castigated as a stereotyped Jewish foe at some times and to be celebrated as Jesus' most intimate friend at others. For Judas, unlike the other eleven, worked not only with and for Jesus and his followers but also with and for the Temple and its priests. A Jew, like Jesus, Judas emulated his teacher, but he also collaborated with the Temple priests whom Jesus challenged. He stands ambivalently in between Jews who accepted Jesus as the messiah and Jews who did not. Put more precisely—taking into consideration that the Gospels reflect less the time in which Jesus lived and more the later period in which they were composed—one can see that Judas stands for a spectrum of beliefs within a complex Jewish society characterized by widespread messianic expectations.

Before the Jewish Jesus sect turned into a Gentile religion, Judas must have resembled many Jewish Christians who believed in Jesus as messiah but on different terms from those prescribed by the Jewish authors of the New Testament.[18] During a period when Jewish Christians and non-Christian Jews shared the Hebrew scriptures and when numerous sects multiplied within each group to dispute all sorts of religious issues, gradations between belief communities did not divide populations as easily as they do today between a distinctly separate Judaism and a distinctly separate Christianity.[19] Scholars of antiquity have explained that from biblical times until the fourth century, Jewish Christians and non-Christian Jews proliferated, along with Gentile Christians; within all these groupings, some people passionately subscribed to the discipleship of Jesus, some passionately denied it, and many debated its nature (though undoubtedly quite a few gave not a hoot).

As Daniel Boyarin puts it about the impossibility in antiquity of distinguishing between a detached entity termed *Judaism* and a separate faith called *Christianity,* "Judaism is not the 'mother' of Christianity; they are twins, joined at the hip" (5).[20] One way of viewing that join or joint is through the figure of Judas. At times a celebrant with the apostles, at times an instrument of the Temple authorities, Judas incarnates the inseparability of Judaism and Christianity, their scandalous melding or permeability, which would be recurrently disowned, acknowledged, and championed by a host of later thinkers and artists. Judas, I will contend, exemplifies shifting attitudes toward Judeo-Christianity before and after various authorities constructed walls of orthodoxy that ensured its partition into a Christianity opposed to Judaism.[21] The twelfth apostle's ambivalent identifications and ambiguous attachments have mystified and thereby attracted writers and painters up till the present day.

WHY BIOGRAPHY?

Since a historical approach casts so little light on Judas, his representational transformations as an imagined personage take center stage in this study. A folkloric villain, Judas in his progress personifies Western culture's changing ideas about an evil that must and should and will be punished or about a degraded existence eminently dispensable. Throughout the Mediterranean, in Central Europe, and in Spain, Mexico, and South America, up to and into the twentieth century, wooden or papier-mâché effigies of Judas were paraded, cursed, pierced, flogged, hung, or burned at Easter in popular folk rituals thought to ensure prosperity (see Taylor, "Burning" and "Gallows"). The sheep, goat, and cow used to lead other sheep, goats, and cows to slaughter, the quail employed to trap other quail, are called Judas animals. Blinded and caged, the Judas quail whimpers its distress, thereby attracting other birds, which can then be caught.

Whether huge or minuscule, Judas life-forms destroy their own species. When 200-pound, 20-foot pythons threatened native wildlife in the Everglades recently, scientists inserted radio transmitters into the body cavities of females, who served as Judas snakes by luring mate-seeking males to the kill. Considerably smaller, the silkworm that dies, ensnared and hanging from a tree, without spinning its cocoon is a Judas (Gillet 326). A novel called *The Judas Strain* (2007), by James Rollins, hypothesizes a microscopic Judas virus that "turns friend into foe," betraying and threatening to exterminate existence: "This organism has the capability to travel through the planet's biosphere, transforming all bacteria into lethal, life-destroying organisms" (123). Within less fantastic, more historical human environments, Judas similarly stands for self-betrayal or treachery. "Opium is the Judas of drugs; it kisses and then betrays" addicts into physical and mental agonies, including "overwhelming suicidal impulses": so one William Rosser Cobbe argued on the title page of his 1895 book, *Doctor Judas: A Portrayal of the Opium*

Habit. The peephole in a prison door, through which guards spy, is a Judas hole. For centuries, devious statesmen accused of informing on or conspiring against their own people were tarred with the Judas libel. Such politicians may promote Judas compromises that render a homeland vulnerable to enemies thereby licensed to destroy it.

As Judas became an icon of alleged Jewish iniquity, he reflected or even may be thought to have embodied the history of anti-Semitism: the toxic belief that Jews constitute a degraded and thus dispensable life-form that must or should or will be destroyed, for they threaten the health and welfare of the human species. Indeed, his trajectory, we will find, serves as a sort of barometer by which shifting attitudes toward the Jews and Judaism can be measured, although at certain representational moments Judas Iscariot is not Jewish and is instead contrasted with the Jews (usually to the detriment of the latter). Still, Judas could be said to be the most obvious candidate for the role of muse of the Holocaust, mainly because his collaboration in deicide was invoked to justify the genocide.[22]

During a scene before a Catholic church in Claude Lanzmann's documentary film *Shoah* (1986), a Polish crowd explains their past acquiescence in murderous acts against the Jews of their own community. The bystanders justify the Nazis' roundup and killing of Jewish neighbors by recycling the blood curse in Matthew. They thereby attribute the annihilation of the six million in the "final solution" to God's rightful retribution against the Jews, who condemned an innocent Christ to death fully realizing that "His blood [would and should] be on us and on our children!" (27:25).[23] In Matthew's Gospel, Judas effectively collaborates with wicked Jews, for their evil willfulness takes precedence over Pilate's qualms of conscience about sentencing Jesus to crucifixion. From 1860 until 1990, Bavarian actors performed a version of the annual Oberammergau Passion play in which Judas admits his evil—"where can I go to hide my shame, to escape the torments of conscience?"—and then asks for extermination: "O earth, open and swallow me up! I can no longer exist" (W. Stead 196).[24] Thus, Auschwitz might be understood as the consummation so devoutly wished by the repugnant wrongdoer, so clearly earned by his nefarious partners in crime as well as by their descendants.

Given the guilt heaped on Judas and the Jews as co-conspirators in the murder of Jesus, was Judas a necessary, a sufficient, or only a contributory cause of the Shoah? Important as Judas was in anti-Semitic ideologies, his erratic trajectory makes his utility for understanding Nazi genocide as perplexing as the "final solution" itself. In the nineteenth century, Judas was approached by Thomas De Quincey through German thinkers who viewed him as a patriotic Hebrew revolting against Roman rule, one who gleaned Christ's need for a betrayer: Judas "supposed himself executing the very innermost purposes of Christ," according to De Quincey; and "As regards the worldly prospects of this scheme, it is by no means improbable that Iscariot was right" (181).

The chapters that follow contend that Judas can be considered a contributory cause of the Holocaust, but neither a necessary nor a sufficient one: first because virulently anti-Semitic images of the Jewish Christ-killer Judas occur in virtually every European and American context, not just in Germany; second because virulently anti-Semitic rhetoric about Jews as Christ-killers has surfaced, even in antiquity, without any need whatsoever to invoke the figure of Judas;[25] and third because after the Enlightenment Judas was often reinvented as a Romantic rebel, sometimes with and sometimes without a cause. Many nineteenth-, twentieth-, and twenty-first-century portraits of Judas explore his predicament so as to plumb the depth of human perplexity or despondency at insurmountable political, psychological, and ethical dilemmas faced by people of any and all faiths. To this extent, he becomes a sympathetic character and a sort of everyman.

How can one account for Judas's progress before, during, and after the Shoah? Along with the gaps and incongruities in the New Testament, the impossibility of establishing Judas's real dates, ancestry, place of origin, aspirations, acts, and values spurred numerous theologians and artists to produce a succession of discordant portraits of the twelfth apostle that can be traced in an evolving trajectory through successive phases.

A biographical approach to the legendary life of Judas over twenty centuries adds verisimilitude to an otherwise bald and unconvincing narrative—bald and unconvincing because of the incongruity of his manifold guises. Whereas a biting and excreting Judas horrified premodern thinkers, Renaissance painters presented a tender Judas engaged in a brotherly embrace with his beloved mate; whereas a politically ambitious Judas heroically struggles to advance his teacher's mission during the Enlightenment, a contemporary Judas doubts the efficacy of that mission. Yet all the painters and novelists, dramatists and preachers, poets and filmmakers claim to be describing the same disciple. All elaborate on some portions of the conflicting accounts of Mark, Matthew, Luke, and John in the New Testament. To cope with the jarring stages in Judas's chronological evolution as well as the trajectory of those stages, this book tracks the fiendish premodern Judas, the loving Renaissance Judas, the heroic Enlightenment Judas, and the contemporary skeptical Judas, paying particular attention to the twelfth apostle's exceptionally complex development during the cataclysms of the twentieth century.

The course of Judas's extended existence never does run smooth, because at each and every postbiblical moment competing figurations of Judas—as anomaly, pariah, lover, hero, and savior—circulate. Indeed, as the introduction proved, the stereotyped Jewish miscreant in particular resurfaced from the time of Jerome to the periods of Luther, Barth, and Tucker. Yet during certain historical intervals, different avatars prevail. The anomaly and pariah predominate before the Renaissance, the lover and hero and savior in later ages: this arc moves the twelfth apostle from demonization to a curious sort of beatification. Like all human beings, legendary Judas changes his bodily shape as he sloughs off certain behaviors during the passage of years, taking on new beliefs and ambitions. More frequently than those human beings who regress to habits they thought they had outgrown or discarded, though, legendary Judas adopts and flaunts new lifestyles while retaining old ones.

Biography allows me to attend to the prominence of different facets of Judas as he advances from antiquity to contemporary times, even as it enables me to assume that he retains his biblical origins and therefore a capacity to embody all of his initial clashing identities at every stage of his development. With grievous consequences, the propaganda industry of the Third Reich did retrofit a demonic Judas to facilitate the Shoah; however, we will see that growing apprehension about the scale of the genocide led to widespread efforts to expunge the Jewish Judas-pariah, catapulting this apostle to unpredictable heights during the postwar decades. Only after the toxic consequences of the Jewish Judas-pariah had been made evident did he become illegitimate (at least in high culture). His demise triggered an apotheosis of Judas avatars accorded saintly or godlike powers. After maturing over many centuries and then shockingly regressing at the middle of the twentieth century, Judas ultimately undergoes first a deification and then a change of life that returns him to his anomalous origins.

Life history, then, furnishes the framework of the pages to come, as I attempt to recount a mythic career over the passage of many historical periods and in most Western societies. My somewhat eccentric approach to the genre of biography derives from two quite distinct models, both of which tackle subjects far removed from mine, but both of which nonetheless provide a suitable conceptual structure for a figure who transmutes in so many different media and contexts. In Jack Miles's *God: A Biography* (1996), a divine protagonist is characterized by passions and concerns that develop in God's character as he interacts first with Adam and Eve and later with Noah, Job, and Daniel in the Hebrew Bible. In Virginia Woolf's earlier and inventive *Orlando* (1928), a fictive male artist born in the Renaissance grows up to become a celebrated female artist in modern times. Both authors implicitly subscribe to the idea, expressed by Woolf and informing these pages about Judas, that "a biography is considered complete if it merely accounts for six or seven selves, whereas a person may well have as many thousands" (309).

Different as Miles's and Woolf's texts are, their frameworks posit a quasi-real, quasi-mythical personage in progress over an unusually long duration of time. Such an assumption is particularly useful for the possibly historical but quickly legendary creature known as Judas, whose mythological life spans twenty centuries. Given this longevity, only touchstone moments of Judas's career, only "six or seven selves," can be fully delineated in the pages to come. In my recounting, those six or seven selves frequently crowd out, flatten, or diminish the other characters with whom Judas interacts because, as Janet Malcolm has explained, biographers "must cultivate a kind of narcissism on behalf of [their] subject that blinds [them] to the full humanity of anyone else" (58). What makes Miles's and Woolf's stretching of biography apt for Judas Iscariot is not just the continuity (from ancient times to the present) of his name with betrayal but also his somewhat historical, somewhat fictive stature. Judas is firmly attached to an act of treachery that results in a horrific death, but no one knows his actual origins, intentions, personality, or ultimate fate.

Such an investigation into murder—whether deicide or homicide—requires an engagement with religious studies scholarship, in which I have immersed myself, and aspires to a daunting chronological, geographic, and generic scope. To cover the extensive path of Judas's life, I have had to bounce from antiquity to the late medieval period, conflating this long passage of time under the rubric of premodern cultures, and to generalize about the seventeenth and eighteenth centuries, as if there were such a phenomenon as a monolithic Enlightenment. Flagrantly inaccurate period designations, accompanied by equally specious groupings of artists from quite distinct linguistic, geopolitical, and religious backgrounds, were adopted in order to track the entirety of Judas's convoluted evolution. While dealing with a particular textual or pictorial manifestation of Judas, I have parenthetically included specific dates of its composition as well as its place of origin in, for example, Ireland or Guatemala. But extended considerations of national conceits and customs have often been shelved here, as have the differences between, say, Anglican, Lutheran, and Eastern Orthodox approaches to the Passion story, although future investigations into Judas will assuredly furnish fascinating insights into the unique roles he has played in distinct locales and belief communities.

At times, to pursue the narrative thread of Judas's evolution, I have had to push into the background the formal complexity of a particular poem or novel, or to occlude the difference that genre or medium makes in representations with remarkably divergent forms. Partly because of my reliance throughout on works in translation, there are only a smattering of passages here that constitute original scholarship, if we take that term to mean the discovery of new artifacts and facts: in taking up ancient Greek, Coptic, old German, French, and Italian works, I depend on scholars in these fields. Besides doing my homework, however, I have provided ample footnotes to experts in particular areas of specialization for those readers wishing to delve into more academic sources or matters.

Yet this work is original in that it presents the first and only life history of one of the most resilient personages in Western civilization; in particular, it delineates a character who matured throughout many centuries but whose maturation was stymied or arrested in the middle of the twentieth century. Thus, the central questions: To what extent was a heroic Judas miserably typecast so as to produce or abet the "final solution"? If he did suffer such typecasting, how—why is too difficult to answer—was he doomed to replay his most demonic embodiment? And in what ways did the Holocaust in turn change conceptualizations of a contemporary Judas to reflect widespread anxiety (among people in quite varied faith communities) about what it means to live in an unredeemed and possibly unredeemable world? If throughout his progress Judas constitutes the hyphen joining Judaism to Christianity, what does his development tell us about the evolution of relationships between Jews and Christians?

In capsule, my answer will propose that at every historical stage of Judas's development, his multiple personae—anomaly, pariah, lover, hero, savior—persist, though inflected differently. While one period (say, the premodern) may emphasize one persona (the pariah), the other facets of Judas (anomaly, lover, hero, savior) never fully disappear, though they may be shadowed or partly eclipsed. Conversely, even during a period like the premodern, when Judas was predominantly represented as a demon, one can find resonant images of him as Jesus' champion. Christianity's problem child, Judas does not progress and grow on a straightforward path. Especially in the twentieth century, the views conveyed through Judas may strike some readers as blasphemous, for quite a few authors invoke him to criticize the uses to which the Son of God and God were put by secular societies unabashed about exploiting Christianity for decidedly non- and anti-Christian aims. Yet, as Søren Kierkegaard knew, "One will get a deep insight into the state of Christianity in every age by seeing how it interprets Judas" (*Journals* 512).

UBIQUITOUS RECYCLINGS

Because Judas's visage is multifaceted in every age, the visual illustrations I present throughout—mosaics, paintings, and movie stills—will sometimes cross conventional historical markers, undermining any simple trajectory in Judas's development through history. Daniele Crespi's *Last Supper* (1624–25; illustration 1.1) can exemplify this point, for—in stark contrast to the pariah-Judas satirized by Albert Tucker in 1955—it features an introspective, thoughtful Judas whose interiority mirrors that of Christ, whereas all the other boisterous apostles seem to be disputing among themselves, quarreling, cavorting, or maybe just being tipsy. Oblivious, the eleven tell tales or exchange confidences, but Jesus (holding the beloved disciple so often represented as sleeping at table) appears isolated, pensive, and passive, while Judas also gazes away from the present feasting as if to

1.1. Daniele Crespi, *Last Supper* (1624–25). Source: Bridgeman Art Library. © Pinacoteca di Brera, Milan, Italy.

interrogate the subsequent narrative into which (he realizes) he will be enfolded. He seems younger than Tucker had imagined him, closer to the thirty-something age of his teacher.

Crespi's Judas sits so as to be positioned closest to the viewer. He does not brandish a knife, as does an apostle on his right; nor does he steal the fish from the table or threaten to bite the host, as he will in depictions reprinted in subsequent chapters. He is not profiled as a two-faced cheater; nor is he accompanied by a dragon or bird, as he can be. Jesus and Judas, both wearing red and gray robes, are linked by means of a diagonal line that draws the eye from Judas to Jesus to the window above and to the putti or cupids holding a banner. Implicitly attached to each other, both men are detached from the others, partly because of their common tranquillity and silence, partly because they sit at the far ends of the oval table. Not demonic or hideous, Crespi's anomalous Judas looks anxious about the situation in which he finds himself.

An abstracted Jesus stares off into space, whereas Judas turns to look out—if not exactly at us, then somewhere toward or beyond us: this juxtaposition lends Judas an aura of conscience as well as an uncanny complicity with spectators who realize that upon rising, he will inevitably make his way to the chief priests in the Temple. In contrast with the other apostles, a frontal Judas peering at his viewers makes us his accomplice. Judas's perplexity is heightened by the contrary activities of his two hands: his right hand holds a piece of bread, as do the hands of other apostles around the table, but his left hand dangles down furtively, though with an open palm, as if he would— if he could—drop the partly concealed money pouch. Above all the diners, the horizontal banner declares "A man [or human being] has eaten the bread of the angels." The Latin phrase—"panem angelorum manducavit homo"—was recited daily by monks and priests as part of the Roman Breviary. As in Psalm 78, where "Mortals ate of the bread of angels" before "the anger of God rose against them" (25, 31), Crespi's Judas consumes what he craves before being laid low. The script makes it seem that Judas may be partaking of the gift of bread and wine, body and blood, offered by Jesus at the Last Supper in the accounts of Mark, Matthew, and Luke; however, the sliced loaf beside the place of the twelfth apostle recalls the contradictory report of John, with its description of Judas alone eating a sop that activated his demonic possession. Crespi's painting therefore ruminates not only on Judas's perplexity but also on the baffling indeterminacy of his story.

The history of art contains many such instances of approaches to Judas that do not conform to the prevailing ideology promulgated by theologians and literary writers in a particular period. Because of this and because Judas's maturation from disgrace to dignity was arrested during the Shoah, *Judas: A Biography* ultimately raises questions about human progress, about whether we can think of Western culture as homogeneous or coherent in each of its historical ages or as progressive over its successive ages—particularly in its capacity for toleration of ethnic or religious difference. The importance of that question goes without saying, given the rise of religiously motivated violence around the globe during the past fifty or so years. Ironically, in view of recurrent warfare between Islamic and Jewish people in the Middle East, the foundational Christian story has historically posed a greater menace to Jews than has any aspect of Muslim teachings.[26] Yet it is precisely the tense centrality of Jews in the Christian Passion that proves how intertwined the two religions have always been. And while the evolution of Judas demonstrates how powerfully Christian stories have been deployed to discipline and punish non-Christians, it also establishes that such divisive practices could be and have been reconfigured in almost every period of history through implicitly liberating iconographies and theologies promoting social justice and compassion among all people.

Judas: A Biography is a book written for readers interested in interreligious contacts and exchanges, especially Jewish-Christian relations. Throughout I use terms (such as the Passion or the Holy Spirit) in keeping with the language of the texts I am interpreting. Too often in the past, Judas has been approached by thinkers whose pro-Christian or pro-Jewish agendas replicated those of the poets, painters, and preachers who have portrayed him throughout his history. Key aspects of his changing character got lost because of polemics. On the pages to follow, I relinquish any attempt to solve historical uncertainties and theological conundrums as I seek instead to trace the literary and visual implications of works that held sway over many people's imaginations over many periods of time. In this effort, I rely on the supposition that cultural critics are trained to interpret such creative texts as incarnations of stages in intellectual history, an assumption that has animated numerous investigations into the dynamics of stereotyping in representations about subordinated or stigmatized people.

Because Judas acquires a wife as well as a sister, a mother, and various lovers in the long duration of his mythological career and because he is often depicted as a black man or in league with dark forces, his biographer has to factor gender as well as sex, sexuality, and race into an understanding of his life story. From Saint Jerome's time until the present, the Jews or "sons of Judas" were imagined as male, but, we will see, as rather peculiar in their particular manifestations of masculinity. In addition, from Daniele Crespi to Albert Tucker, portrait painters of Judas have for the most part been male, as have been the majority of his literary delineators. Indeed, Judas functions as a pivot in conceptualizations of masculinity, much as Eve does in cultural analyses of femininity. Just as Eve's appetite was said to have caused the fall of Adam, Judas's greed was believed to have initiated the crucifixion of Jesus. Often accompanied by animal familiars—though the snaky tails on Tucker's canvas seem to grow directly out of the human figure—both Eve and Judas enable the authors of spiritual as well as aesthetic works to grapple with a tempted and fallen figure made to shoulder responsibility for the mortality, suffering, and injustice so burdensome to humanity.

That Judas has been stuck in the role of scapegoat—the pariah whom Tucker so brilliantly delineates—seems indisputable. Perhaps, as Crespi's troubled figure hints, this task falls to him because of his refusal to believe in a redemptive future, which emanates a stubborn resistance to precisely the fulfillment, realization, hope, and good tidings of faith in general, and of Christian faith in particular. We will see that since ancient times Judas might therefore be said to embody what Edgar Allan Poe called "the imp of the perverse," what Kierkegaard called "the sickness unto death," or what Freud called "the death drive." Whether out of spiritual ignorance or ontological difference or a queer sort of depravity, Judas counters Jesus' pledge of life after death with the inescapable fact of death within life, for he is the linchpin in a plot that inexorably culminates in suffering and sacrifice. To the promise of salvation, futurity, peace on earth, and goodwill to men that Jesus holds out, Judas obstinately and intractably stands for what cannot be assimilated into such optimism: a gloomy but not therefore less profound acknowledgment of humankind's capacity for despair, damnation, destruction, rivalry, and self-hatred. How each of the canonical Gospel authors approached this disquieting apprehension, the subject of the next chapter, shaped subsequent reinventions and applications of Judas's name that continue up to the present day in popular as well as high culture.

Although I will stress the prominence of Judas as a pariah in antiquity, a lover in the Renaissance, a hero during the Enlightenment, and a savior in the twentieth century, his roles today riff on all these incarnations, as they did in previous eras. In rock music, on theatrical stages and movie screens, and in excavations, Judas kept on popping up during the last decades of the twentieth century, and he persists in doing so in the first years of the twenty-first century. Always chameleon, Judas continues to recycle his various personae to ring changes on the meaning of trust's betrayal. At a 1966 Bob Dylan concert in Manchester, England, for instance, one member of the audience was so offended by the folk singer's turn to electronic rock music that he famously denounced Dylan as "Judas." The epithet may or may not have been provoked by Dylan's Jewish origins, or by a pithy triplet he had produced three years earlier, which encapsulates an injunction that all the various artists considered in this book have taken to heart: "You have to decide / Whether Judas Iscariot / Had God on his side."[27]

"With God on Our Side" remains equivocal, if skeptical, about whether the twelfth apostle had been divinely authorized, but the counterculture in which Dylan participated produced singularly sympathetic renditions of a misunderstood Judas: Judas the anomaly. "I have no thought at all about my own reward," Judas repeatedly exclaims in *Jesus Christ Superstar* (1970), adding (also repeatedly) "I really didn't come here of my own accord." After Judas realizes he will be dragged through the slime for what he has done, he sings a reprise of the haunting song Andrew Lloyd Webber first has Mary Magdalene croon, "I Don't Know How to Love Him"; then

1.2. Judas, played by Carl Anderson, in Norman Jewison's *Jesus Christ Superstar* (1973). Source: Photofest.

an anguished Judas exclaims, "God! I'll never ever know why you chose me for your crime / For your bloody crime / You have murdered me!" One evocative still from the 1973 film version of *Jesus Christ Superstar*, in which the African American actor Carl Anderson was cast as the betrayer, frames a lynched Judas strung up alone in a desolate landscape (illustration 1.2). Drawing attention to a long linkage in the scapegoating of blacks and Jews, Anderson's Judas does not ascend into heaven but hangs on a barren earth ruled by the downward pull of gravity that tugs at one of his sandals (though he is resurrected in time to sing the title song at the end with a Motown backup group). "In American film tradition," one critic reminds us, "the lynched man is always innocent," and thus Judas's death turns into a "murder" inflicted by an Establishment "White God": "The target of the savage critique is the contemporary American religious establishment, not the unknowable, true God of Jesus" (Humphries-Brooks 65).

Approving in a different way, *Godspell,* staged in 1970 and then filmed in 1973, assumes that "Judas Iscariot / Had God on his side." For Judas refuses to kiss Jesus and is instead kissed by him. Just as forbearing, Monty Python's 1979 *Life of Brian* burlesques a young man mistakenly taken to be the messiah, along with a transsexual Judas called Judith, a leader in the parodic revolutionary faction Peoples' Front of Judea (PFJ), who unwittingly fails to intercede in the erroneous arrest. In 1989, when Denys Arcand's *Jesus of Montreal* was released in Canada, Judas's act of hanging himself became emblematic of the suicidal yearning Hamlet feels when he considers whether to be or not to be in a rotten world, which may explain why the acting troupe that goes on to stage the crucifixion relinquishes any allusion to the betrayer in the Passion.

More recently and more motivated by a decidedly Jewish perspective, an independent film titled *Sorry, Judas* (1993)—with a hip sound track featuring "You Always Hurt the One You Love"—tackled the anti-Semitism Judas had been used to trigger: Judas the pariah. Its wry director, Celia Lowenstein, and witty writer, Howard Jacobson, address the issue that Laurence Sterne raised in his novel *Tristram Shandy* (1759–67): that is, what parents would ever consider desecrating or dooming their offspring by naming the baby Judas. One of Sterne's characters puts the case against adopting Judas's name this way:

> "Your son!—your dear son,—from whose sweet and open temper you have so much to expect,—Your BILLY, Sir—would you, for the world, have called him JUDAS? . . . Would you, Sir, if a Jew of a godfather had proposed the name for your child, and offered you his purse along with it, would you have consented to such a desecration of him? . . . you would have trampled upon the offer;—you would have thrown the temptation at the

tempter's head with abhorrence . . . the sordid and treacherous idea, so inseparable from the name, would have accompanied him through life like his shadow, and, in the end, made a miser and a rascal of him, in spite, Sir, of your example."

Regardless of his surname, Judas will never smell sweet, or so one Shakespearean character tells another: "Judas Maccabaeus clipped is plain Judas" and thus "A kissing traitor" (*Love's Labor's Lost* 5.2.595–96). After tracing the grotesque stereotypes sponsored by Judas, Lowenstein and Jacobson nevertheless go on to fantasize about an obviously quixotic effort to canonize Judas for his martyrdom—his "only sin was that he facilitated Christianity"—and then imagine bottled beers, tube stations, credit cards, hospitals, and boulevards named in his honor! (Max Beerbohm had anticipated this spoof in his comic novel *Zuleika Dobson* [1911], whose heroine arrives at Oxford to wreak havoc on the men of Judas College.)

Two dramatic productions in 1998 approached the bond between Jesus and Judas from the perspective of the history of homosexuality: Judas the lover. David Hare's disturbing play *The Judas Kiss* features Oscar Wilde's risky love for a man who repeatedly betrayed him, Lord Alfred Douglas. About the "one flaw" in "the Christ story," Hare's Wilde comes to believe that "It would be artistically truer if [Jesus] were betrayed by John. Because John is the man he loves most" (117). A more ritualized reenactment of the Passion story, Terrence McNally's play *Corpus Christi* depicts Jesus getting into trouble with the High Priest after he has officiated at a gay marriage—and not because he then insists he is the son of God but rather because he vows that the openly gay Judas is, too: "The son of God is a cocksucker?" the High Priest scoffs, "I don't think so. We need sinners" (65). As witnessed by a grief-stricken Judas, Jesus—"the King of the Queers"—is crucified by homophobic church and state authorities (75). McNally's Passion play sought to heighten comprehension of and compassion for the divinity residing within all human beings, but ticket holders at the Manhattan Theatre Club had to pass through metal detectors because of anonymous phone calls threatening to burn down the hall.

In a theatrical work related to McNally's criticism of phobic approaches to a reviled disciple, Stephen Adly Guirgis's play *The Last Days of Judas Iscariot,* which opened in the spring of 2005 at New York's Public Theater, staged a retrial of Judas whose condemnation to eternal hell seems (to his defender) a flagrant denial of an all-forgiving God. Throughout this period, popular songs about Judas proliferated, and the band Judas Priest sold more than thirty million records with such albums as *Sin After Sin* (1977) and *Angel of Retribution* (2005).[28] But the aberrant and desirous Judas never eclipsed Judas the pariah. When Mel Gibson's *The Passion of the Christ* opened in 2004, theater audiences could take a breather from Jesus' bloody martyrdom by watching slow-motion frames of Caiaphas's money bag floating through the air, spewing coins then furtively collected by Judas. Later footage of Satan carrying the Antichrist links the devil to Judas, hounded by young boys—they wear *kepot,* or skullcaps—who turn into the pursuing devils he clearly deserves to encounter before and after he commits suicide.[29]

Nor would Judas the pariah block the luminous reappearance of Judas the savior. Around Easter time in 2006 and with vast media hoopla, plans got under way to publish a newly recovered fragment of the Gnostic Gospel of Judas that had surfaced after 1,700 years and that portrayed a visionary Judas who "will exceed" all the other disciples in Jesus' eyes, "For you will sacrifice the man that clothes me" (*Gospel of Judas* 43). The recovered text, though called the Gospel of Judas, did not claim to be composed by Judas; instead it focused on him as a celestial spirit imbued with precisely the wisdom and strength that Jesus needs and the other apostles lack. According to the Gnostics, it seems, Judas was utilized by Jesus in his advance from a fleshly being into an exalted divine power. Jesus is handed over by a Judas who fully understands that he will be stoned to death by the other disciples but who also knows that his own soul will join Jesus' spirit in eternity.[30]

This fourth-century Coptic Gospel of Judas—found in a cave at Muhazafat Al Minya in Middle Egypt, bought by a Swiss foundation, and published by the National Geographic—is probably based on a Greek version composed during the second century, and it confirms that even in the ancient world there were as many divergent attitudes toward Judas as there have been toward Jesus' other disciples.[31] On the Web page of the *Guardian,* an article declaring "we now know what [Judas's] excuse was" went on to supply the sound bite: "Jesus made me do it" (Borger and Bates). Yet according to Adam Gopnik in the *New Yorker,* a more humanized Judas "makes Jesus oddly less so, less a man with a divine and horrible burden than one more know-it-all with a nimbus" (81). Whether or not the rehabilitation of Judas diminishes Jesus, it will become evident in subsequent pages that the Gospel of Judas's central idea—that the twelfth disciple enacted what Jesus asked him to do—has a long and lively history.

The recovery of the ancient Coptic text certainly amounted to a momentous historical prize for scholars of antiquity, but creative writers and visual artists anticipated its perspective on the Passion long before it resurfaced and found its way into print in English. Some interpreters of the Gnostic fragment argue that its discovery "marks a turning point in the history of the Christian understanding of Judas" (Erhman, *Lost Gospel* 52). Yet numerous twentieth-century writers have produced pseudo-gospels purportedly recounted by a Judas presumed to be falsely characterized by the authors of the canonical Gospels in the New Testament.[32] Even earlier, Christian artists did *not* consistently portray Judas in a derogatory manner; they have at times envisioned a loving and powerful Judas who facilitates Jesus' divine mission.[33] Oddly, the host of scholars who produced a flurry of books quickly following the remarkable publication tended to choose the identical image by Giotto for their covers, as if countless other paintings of the twelfth apostle had not been produced, some much more attuned to the camaraderie of Judas and Jesus.[34] Even more oddly, this Coptic savior-Judas may have been the invention or wish-fulfillment of his hasty translators, for one professor from Rice

University has claimed that the Gospel of Judas actually features a demonic Judas who is informed about his betrayal so he will comprehend the suffering he deserves.[35] Whether true or not, the charge nicely suits a creature who resists stasis through his perpetual and perpetually incongruent reincarnations.

As in the ancient Gospel of Judas, each and every reinvention of Judas recorded within the rest of this book spawns a refiguring of Jesus because the two are so closely linked. With my attention fixed on Judas, I wait until my conclusion to ascertain what happens to the character of Jesus when the Gospel anomaly-Judas and the early pariah-Judas turn into the Renaissance lover-Judas, when the modern heroic-Judas emerges as the twentieth-century savior-Judas. *Judas: A Biography* proves that many artists and thinkers, in every conceivable venue, have retried Judas, sometimes finding him a habitual offender, sometimes letting him off scot-free, but always returning to his origins in the New Testament, where his ambiguous character first and most formatively appears. Postbiblical avatars of Judas—no matter how eccentric—demonstrate the rich and abiding significance of the various roles accorded to him by Mark, Matthew, Luke, and John. All of the Gospel authors describe Judas as the disciple who betrayed Jesus; however, they agree on little else about his character and fate.

2

ALONE OF ALL HIS SEX: GENESIS IN THE GOSPELS

How and why do Mark, Matthew, Luke, and John provide divergent, even contradictory portraits of the twelfth apostle? In the New Testament, multiple perspectives produce different betrayers. Although the accounts taken together generate a host of knots and paradoxes, the evolving figure of Judas illuminates the permeability of Judaism and Christianity in ancient times as well as the increasing anxiety or hostility this permeability began to generate.

A MAN ORIGINALLY WITHOUT a mother or a childhood, Judas springs up fully grown in the New Testament, where there are only twenty-two references to him. Oddly enough, as more time separates the Gospel authors from Jesus' death around 30 C.E., the number of words about Judas increases. Whereas Mark, writing in the mid-60s or early 70s, devotes just three verses to Judas, Matthew in the 80s mentions him five times; Luke in the 80s and later includes six verses; and John in the 90s inserts eight references. Though modest in scale, this progression anticipates an acceleration of interest in Judas among sacred and secular writers throughout the Middle Ages and the Renaissance. In many of these later spin-offs of the Gospel narratives, creative artists envisioned Judas as the arch-enemy of their Jesus, his other apostles, and thus of themselves. Curiously, however, the same claim cannot be made about the early Gospel writers, who establish the commonality of Judas's character with that of the other eleven disciples, and (albeit obliquely) even with Jesus himself.

How did Judas metamorphose from one of several complicit bystanders at the sacrifice of the Son of God to a pivotal perpetrator of the crucifixion? And why did Judas degenerate into the epitome of villainy, a singularly malevolent anomaly, in the later Gospels? My analysis of the New Testament, assisted by its early artistic illustrators as well as its later scholarly interpreters, provides some answers to these questions.[1] At first, Judas unnervingly exemplifies his companions; however, as the chronological gap between the Passion narrative and its narrators widens, his fate begins to isolate him in a culpability that makes him stand alone of all his sex, a traitor of humankind. To begin with, then, the handing over executed by Judas abets an overriding providential necessity, but eventually his treachery exemplifies shameful personal guilt.

Put simply, Judas is "one of us" in Mark and Matthew, where the *us* stands for Jesus' intimates and contemporaries, those who witness his miracles and hear his parables; however, Judas devolves into "one of them" in Luke and John, where the *them* stands for those who reject Jesus' miracles and scorn his parables. In the earlier Gospels, a self-condemned sinner can be forgiven, but in the later Gospels a wicked reprobate remains unforgivable. Judas develops in the New Testament from a typically obtuse apostle in Mark to a repentant sinner who atones through self-sacrifice in Matthew, from a self-destructing creature possessed by Satan in Luke to a devilish treasurer who collaborates in deicide with similarly devilish Jews in John. Probably this progressive vilification of Judas reflects the Gospel authors' (and their communities') intensifying need to distinguish the marginalized, persecuted followers of Jesus from the Jewish communities out of which they originated and with which they had to contend. In the aftermath of the Jewish-Roman War and the destruction of Jerusalem's Second Temple in 70 C.E., a number of scholars have argued, Jewish-Christian hostilities intensified.[2]

But my emphasis in these pages is less historical, more interpretive. In an effort to understand how Judas becomes increasingly Jewish-identified, I push to the background debates on the historical significance or prophetic status of the Gospels.[3] For as Judas is contaminated by his growing proximity to the Jews, his transmuting character provides an etiology of the split between "Christian" and "Jew," two terms that were originally intertwined: indeed, all the central players in the Gospels, with the exception of the Romans, were born Jewish and were responsive to what would later be called the Christian lessons preached by a Jewish Jesus to the Jews of Galilee and Judea. The emergent figure of Judas—who travels back and forth between the apostles and the Pharisees, or chief scribes of the Temple—illuminates the melding or permeability of Judaism and Christianity in ancient times. He therefore reveals when, how, and why two characters born into and committed to the same faith seem to undergo opposite conversions as Judas comes to be viewed as Jewish, Jesus as Christian.

Instead of combining or harmonizing the various Gospel accounts, I will begin by juxtaposing Mark's and Matthew's compassionate visions of Judas as "one of us" over and against Luke's and John's reproving depictions of Judas as "one of them." This tension sets the stage for Judas's much later cultural development, since his evolution from the Middle Ages into contemporary times functions as *midrash* (commentary) on or redaction (expanding or doctoring) of the New Testament. Like medieval scribes, secular artists who return to the Gospels might be considered pious correctors or impious corruptors of the original, ancient texts. Inevitably, they conflate four accounts that disagree about virtually every aspect of Judas and the role he performs. When the Passion narratives are amalgamated or fused—as they were during postbiblical times—incongruous or contradictory descriptions have to be explained, combined, expurgated, or forgotten. Judas the character would be launched into life by storytellers fitting the puzzling pieces together into a host of different personages. What makes the canonical Gospels, especially in their evocation of the

Hebrew Bible, so resonant is the coexistence in them of Judas's multiple personae—wayward apostle, doomed victim, loathed enemy—in a manner reminiscent of a Picasso face featuring several noses or mouths, a composite of multiple perspectives that also forecasts a Judas who would become in medieval and Renaissance paintings Jesus' lover and in nineteenth- and twentieth-century imaginative literature Jesus' militant comrade and rescuer. To understand how this fractured collage of divergent but related portraits of Judas originated, I now turn—not as a specialist in ancient history, religion, or language, but as a student of narrative—to a comparative analysis of the Gospels in the chronological order of their composition.

MARK'S ERRANT APOSTLE

The most striking and ironic characteristic of Mark's Judas is his resemblance to the other apostles in his appointment, his mission, his companionship with Jesus, his unbelief, and his infidelity. This commonality heightens the pathos of Jesus' isolation, vulnerability, and suffering in Mark's Gospel. Before Judas is named in this earliest of the Gospels, Jesus has been baptized by John and has heard the voice of God declare him "my beloved Son" (1:11); he has resisted the temptation of Satan and attracted large crowds by casting out unclean spirits, curing fevers, healing a leper and a paralytic, and restoring a withered hand. However, this last miracle, undertaken on the Sabbath, causes the Pharisees to begin conspiring against him (3:6). Still, people throng to listen to his parables, though neither the crowds nor his family or disciples fully comprehend him or his pronouncements (4:10–13, 3:21). Mark's Jesus speaks obliquely, contemporary scholars argue, because he believes that he must keep secret his efforts to become a messiah in order to redefine the messianic role.

First mentioned in Mark's listing of the twelve appointed "to proclaim the message, and to have authority to cast out demons" (3:14, 15), Judas is placed last and differentiated from the others as "Judas

Iscariot, who betrayed him" (3:19). But William Klassen's translation, "Judas Iscariot, who handed him over" (the Greek *paradidōni*
could also mean "delivered over"), would soften the epithet and thus
blur a condemnation that places a hard-and-fast distinction between
Judas and the other eleven (47–58). "The reader/listener does not
know if Judas' 'handing over' of Jesus is a negative act, nor to whom
Jesus will be handed over" (Saari 45). Since, as I mentioned in the
previous chapter, the apostles *hand over* the good news and God
hands over sinners to perdition, the handing over by Judas need not
involve treachery. Also, given Jesus' insistence in Mark that "the last
will be first" (10:31), Judas's position at the end of the listed disciples
remains ambiguous.

In any case, Judas indubitably is part of their company when Jesus
sends the apostles out with "authority over the unclean spirits" (6:7).
Judas presumably followed Jesus' instructions, taking nothing except
a staff on his missionary journeys—no bread or money—and in all
probability he, too, "cast out many demons, and anointed with oil
many who were sick and cured them" (6:13). Probably, like James
or Simon (Peter), he stayed at various houses and shook the dust off
his feet as testimony against those who refused to hear him (6:11).
Almost certainly, Judas resembled the other eleven in their bewilder-
ment at Jesus' words and deeds (6:51–52, 8:21).

Before their arrival in Jerusalem, the apostle treated most harshly
by Jesus is not Judas but Peter. At Caesarea Philippi, after Jesus cures
a blind man and Peter begins believing in him as "the Messiah," Jesus
"sternly ordered [the apostles] not to tell anyone about him," but
explains the future death and resurrection he would undergo. Peter's
shocked "rebuke" provokes Jesus' rebuke in turn, when he links
Peter with evil incarnate: "Get behind me, Satan! For you are setting
your mind not on divine things but on human things" (8:29, 32–33).
Like Jesus' attempts to keep his messianic fate secret, the admonition
reflects his effort to transform the concept of the messiah from the
figure of a miracle worker, an exorcist of demons, a powerful warrior,
or Davidic king to that of the suffering Son of God. But the disciples

in Mark remain clueless. "Their initial imperceptiveness about who he really is, and what his work is really about," Keith Nickle explains, "deteriorates later in Mark's narrative into purposeful, intentional misunderstanding that culminates in abandonment" (73).[4]

Even toward the beginning of Mark's story—for instance, when the twelve disciples witness Jesus walking on the sea—their astonishment as well as their fearful recalcitrance are related to their obdurate incomprehension, "for they did not understand" Jesus' miracles, "but their *hearts were hardened*" (6:52; emphasis mine), as Pharaoh's had been against the Jewish people. Frequently the apostles quarrel among themselves (for example, over who is the greatest [9:34]), or they are chastised on other grounds (in one instance, for not letting the little children come to Jesus [10:13–14]). Upon their arrival at the Temple, the provincial Galileans sound as dazed as Little Red Riding Hood viewing the big, bad wolf: "Look, Teacher, what large stones and what large buildings!" (13:1).[5] Yet two days before Passover, when the chief priests were searching out "a way to arrest Jesus by stealth and kill him" (14:1), it is only Mark's Judas who is said to have gone to them "in order to betray him," and they "promised to give him money. So he began to look for an opportunity to betray him" (14:10).

Horrific as it might be, the decision is given a possible motivation by an episode that directly precedes it: the story, set at the house of Simon the leper, describes Jesus being anointed by a woman with "very costly ointment" in an alabaster jar; though some scold her, Jesus defends the propriety of the service done for him.[6] Coming immediately after this tale, Mark's phrase "*Then*, Judas Iscariot, who was one of the twelve, went to the chief priests" (14:10; emphasis mine) hints that Judas might have been goaded by righteous indignation against the profligate wasting of a balm that others, too, felt could have been put to better use, "sold for more than three hundred denarii, and the money given to the poor" (13:5). Three hundred denarii, footnotes reveal, was roughly equivalent to a year of wages for a laborer. It is more than the large sum mentioned as the apostles' worried guess at the cost of food required—"two hundred denarii worth of bread"—to feed the five thousand whom Jesus miraculously nourishes with five loaves (6:37).

Whether or not all the other apostles were among the "some [who] were in anger" at Jesus' validation of the anonymous woman's wasteful use of the expensive salve, Judas could be said to be of that party when he "began to look for an opportunity" to betray Jesus (13:4, 14:10). Since the word "Messiah" literally means "Anointed [One]," such a sequence of events takes on social or theological significance: in a Gospel that depicts Jesus keeping the messianic secret (forbidding the cured and even demons to divulge the work of his healing, swearing the apostles to secrecy), does Judas object to some aspect of this evolving new role? The conflict he perceived between the legitimate messiah's duty to redeem Israel by serving as its king, on the one hand, and Jesus' willingness to be anointed for burial, on the other, might mean that "Judas's messianic hopes finally died at this moment and that he could see no other way out than to deliver Jesus over to the chief priests," as one commentator surmises: "Jesus had to be unmasked, for now he had broken definitely with all 'normal' messianic expectations" (Gärtner 21). Angered by squandered money that should have been donated to the needy or perplexed by the dissonance between traditional messianic expectations and Jesus' forecasts of his impending death, Judas may be acting out of high-minded principles. Just as important, and as Kim Paffenroth points out about Mark's version, "the offer of money by the high priests is an afterthought first mentioned by them, not Judas" (*Judas* 7). Judas might be distressed by the misspending on pricey spikenard, but avarice or greed does not appear to be his motive.

Even at the Passover meal, in which he fully partakes, Judas blends in with the other apostles, for he presumably helps them make preparations in the upstairs room and eats alongside them. When in Mark's version Jesus foretells that "one of you will betray me, one who is eating with me" (14:17), all of the distressed disciples protest, "Surely, not I?" and Jesus singles out "the one who is dipping bread into the bowl with me" (14:20): "woe to that one by whom the Son of Man is betrayed! It would have been better for that one not to have been born" (14:21).[7] Directly after this dire warning (which could refer to any one of the twelve), Jesus institutes the Lord's Supper, giving all twelve the loaf of bread and the cup of wine proclaimed to be his body and blood. And of course Jesus predicts "You will *all* become deserters" (24:26; emphasis mine) right before he goes to pray in Gethsemane, where those in attendance do desert him in his hour of need: although three times asked to keep awake, three times during this scene his disciples fall asleep. The commonality between Judas and the unconscious (but also unconsciously hostile because inattentive and disobedient) Peter, James, and John in Gethsemane is heightened when Jesus' prediction about Peter is fulfilled after the arrest; Peter repeatedly denies him before the cock crows twice (14:30, 68–72).

Never mentioned by name at the Last Supper, Judas decides to depart at a moment unspecified. At his reappearance with a crowd holding swords and clubs, Mark again characterizes him as "one of the twelve" (14:43). Mark's Judas has had sufficient time between visiting the chief priests and deciding to work as their agent to set the dialogue and designate a particularly sardonic signal:

Now the betrayer had given them a sign, saying, "The one I will kiss is the man; arrest him and lead him away under guard." So when he came, he went up to him at once and said, "Rabbi!" and kissed him. Then they laid hands on him and arrested him. (14:44–46)[8]

Jesus is thus delivered to his persecutors with what would look to be terms of endearment: the reverential epithet "Rabbi" and the kiss could only have come from an intimate.[9]

Often singled out in early visual representations, this scene—the arrest of Jesus—offers historians one of the best glimpses of Judas as he was imagined by artists over the centuries. One such depiction, an early sixth-century Byzantine mosaic in Ravenna, features Christ in a purple robe standing and facing frontally amid a group divided between apostles on one side, pursuers on the other (the S. Apollinare Nuovo cycle, illustration 2.1; see Schiller 2:52–53). Judas's sandals and his light robe mark him definitively as one of the apostles, though he has clearly moved from their side to that of the arresting party, and his hand uplifted in its caress parallels the arm of the sword-bearer about to take Jesus hostage. But Peter's sword also repeats this gesture, balancing the sword wielded by the captor. And the halo around Jesus' head encompasses Judas's as well, just as the arresting hand touches both men as a unit, emphasizing their union. Unlike later visual renditions, in which the disciples also have halos, here only Jesus sports this symbol of beatification. If one views the halo as uniting Judas and Jesus, then Judas's hand over Jesus' heart appears to be a pledge of allegiance. No one is stepping on anyone else's toes here, as they will in later depictions, and it almost looks as if the soldiers are trying to pull Judas away from Jesus for the capture. The Byzantine mosaic underscores Judas's commonality with the other disciples as well as his intimacy with Jesus.

After one person near Jesus cuts off the ear of a high priest's slave in the Gospel of Mark, Jesus proclaims, "let the scriptures be fulfilled"; and then "*All of them* deserted him and fled," including an anonymous follower in a linen cloth: "They caught hold of him, but he left the linen cloth and ran off naked" (14:51–52; emphasis mine). With this minor detail, David Friedrich Strauss explained long ago, Mark captures "the panic and rapid flight of the adherents of Jesus" (653), not one of whom accompanied him through his subsequent trials, beatings, mockery, and torment. Indeed, the eleven seem to have vanished from the text along with Judas: a Roman centurion facing the cross testifies to Jesus being "God's Son" (15:39); two women see the body in the tomb; and three women—informed that "He has been raised; he is not here" (15:6–7)—flee the empty tomb in fear, keeping secret the emptiness they saw as well as the message they received.

2.1. *The Kiss of Judas,* Scenes from the Life of Christ, Ravenna, the San Apollinare Nuovo cycle (520–526 C.E.). Mosaic. Source: Bridgeman Art Library. © Sant'Apollinare Nuovo, Ravenna, Italy / Giraudon.

Readers of Mark's Jesus, who is ultimately left bereft of all his male disciples, may find in Judas their representative: that is, a reflection of the other apostles and also of their own human frailty. For what exactly was the betrayal of Judas in Mark, and how pivotal to the plot is it?—these issues the narrative keeps indeterminate.[10] Presumably Judas revealed Jesus' whereabouts, but many have questioned whether this would have been necessary, noting that the Jewish authorities might have found Jesus quite easily on their own and therefore wondering whether it might be more important to consider what else Judas revealed. In front of the Council, the Sanhedrin, Mark's Jesus confronts many people giving "false testimony" (14:56, 57)—"We heard him say, 'I will destroy this temple that is made with hands, and in three days I will build another, not made with hands'"

(Mark 14:58); the frustrated high priest is therefore driven to ask if the testimonies are true. Jesus refuses to answer this question, but he does answer in the affirmative the next: "Are you the Messiah, the Son of the Blessed one?" The priest, tearing his clothes, then wonders, "Why do we still need witnesses? You have heard his blasphemy!" He thus makes it possible for readers to ask, why do we still need a betrayer? Jesus is condemned for blasphemy on the basis of his own admission, "I am [the Messiah]," and his own claim, "'you will see the Son of Man / seated at the right hand of Power,' and 'coming with the clouds / of heaven'" (14:62).[11]

As the narrative reads (not necessarily as history happened), Jesus is sentenced to death for what he knows and says himself to be, the "Son of the Blessed one." Has Mark's Judas simply revealed the truth to the chief priests about his teacher's professed identity?[12] Yes, Mark's Jesus repeatedly instructs all the apostles to keep his role secret (3:12, 5:43, 8:30), but Jesus himself provoked the plot against his life when he publicly, dramatically entered the Temple, overturned the money changers' tables, and proclaimed the sacred space "a den of robbers" (11:17); as he subsequently did again when he foretold the destruction of the Temple (13:2); and again when he announced himself the Messiah before the Sanhedrin. Judas may be the one who "handed over" Jesus, but he seems to be superfluous in terms of the climax of Mark's plot. And when Mark's Judas tells the arresting authorities to "lead [Jesus] away under guard," does he fear that Jesus will escape, or does he wish to keep him safe?[13]

In Gethsemane, Jesus had pleaded with "Abba, Father" to "remove this cup from me" (14:36); on the cross, he voices his anguish at being forsaken by God. Much more disturbing than Judas's betrayal, at least to Jesus on the cross, is God's abandonment. Because Mark's Jesus wants but is not allowed by God to let the cup of suffering pass, the first Gospel underscores Paul's view that it was God who "did not withhold his own Son, but gave him up for all of us" (Romans 8:32). To the extent that Paul did not limit the term "apostle" to the

twelve and made no distinction among the apostles (when he claimed
that the raised Christ "appeared to James, then to all the apostles"
[1 Corinthians 15:7]), Mark seems to be in accord with Paul, for
he views Judas as typical of the disciples, though in Mark's Gospel
they are fickle, vacuous, and never witness the resurrection. Judas,
introduced three times as "one of the twelve," contributes to Mark's
effort to "undercut the authority of 'the twelve' " (Saari 49). With its
emphasis on the guilt all must share for the crucifixion, the Gospel
of Mark could serve as the basis for the Catechism of the Council
of Trent (1566), which castigated the actions of all people against
the Lord: "Judas betrayed him, Peter denied him, and all abandoned
him" (quoted in J. Cohen 169).

In the earliest manuscripts of Mark's Gospel, Jesus' resurrection
does not occur and in no manuscript does Judas die. We are left with
Mark's priests stirring up the crowds whom Pilate soon seeks to pla-
cate by handing Jesus over to be crucified, and eventually with the
image of the empty tomb. According to Mark, Judas represents not
only the wayward disciples but also the pernicious high priests and
the cruel rabble, most of whom fled in fear from what they failed to
witness. More proactive than these others, Judas nevertheless functions like them as a bystander at the disaster, a repository or emblem
of human guilt and imperfection, the preeminent reason why Jesus
came to suffer and thereby ransom humankind.

MATTHEW'S REPENTANT SUICIDE

To readers familiar with the long history of Jewish anti-Semitism,
it may come as no surprise that the Gospel author most regularly
identified as Jewish, Matthew, creates one of the most anti-Semitic
narratives.[14] Matthew denounces the scribes and Pharisees as
"whitewashed tombs," "snakes," and "a brood of vipers" who cannot "escape being sentenced to hell" (23:27, 29).[15] What might be

surprising, however, is the suggestion that Matthew's Judas can be interpreted as a profoundly sympathetic sinner whose self-sacrificial repentance highlights and even reflects Jesus' innocence as well as his voluntary sacrifice. Matthew's more reverential approach to Jesus, who seems moody and isolated in Mark, enhances Judas's humanization by emphasizing two issues: Jesus' foreknowledge of his fate and Judas's suicide. To the extent that Judas, hanging on a tree, repents the grievous and possibly unintentional wrong he did to Jesus, who will be hung on a cross, an uncanny doubling links Matthew's betrayer to the Son of God. Yet Matthew's complex Judas also provided grist for later anti-Semitic mills.

The first revision Matthew makes of Mark—often noted but least understood in its consequences on Judas's character—is Jesus' growing ethical wisdom, the proliferation of his moral pronouncements: discourses, parables, sermons, sayings, rules, and prayers abound in the appreciably longer Gospel of Matthew. Much as Matthew's Jesus is genealogically related to David and Abraham, so Matthew is famed for his repeated citations of Jewish scriptures that hold out promises fulfilled by Jesus' life.[16] Since Matthew's Jesus views himself as a realization of Isaiah's prophecies, he comprehends what must happen and thus exhibits wise acquiescence about his life as a fulfillment of the Jewish Bible and about his betrayal as inexorably foreordained.

Among those with the power to cure diseases and cast out unclean spirits, "Judas Iscariot, the one who betrayed him" (10:4), is listed last by Matthew, following his source in Mark. Along with the other eleven apostles, Judas will proclaim the good news by becoming as wise as a serpent, as innocent as a dove. Also along with the other eleven, who seem more astute here than in Mark, Judas does comprehend the meaning of Jesus' walking on the water and falls down in worship of "the Son of God" (14:33). According to Matthew's Jesus, who cleaves to a militant ministry, the apostles are his mother and his brothers (12:49), all of whom must divorce themselves from earlier attachments and face ordeals during a period when, Jesus warns, "Brother will betray brother to death, and a father his child, and children will rise against parents and have them put to death" (10:21). Within the apocalyptic and conflicted world that Jesus is bringing into being, the apostles—less quarrelsome, more reliable than in Mark—are explicitly told by Jesus that they should aspire to act "*like the teacher*": although "not above the teacher," the disciple must "be *like the teacher*" during a time of discord and persecution (10:24–25; emphases mine).

Having arrived on earth not to bring peace but instead "a sword," Matthew's church-building Jesus has "come to set a man against his father, / and a daughter against her mother" (10:34). He frequently expresses to his followers his understanding of the suffering he will undergo at the hands of the chief priests because of his radical preaching (16:21).[17] Since the messianic message of Matthew's Jesus, replete with fulfillment citations, is never a secret as it is in Mark, those Jews who do not heed his words are more blameworthy for clinging to what is presented as an obsolete faith. From the beginning of this Gospel and throughout it, Jesus lambastes the scribes and Pharisees as blind hypocrites who view his exorcisms as demonically inspired, who condemn his work on the Sabbath as impious, and who fail to understand or follow their own Torah.

In Matthew's Gospel, Jesus' lament over Jerusalem mourns "the city that kills the prophets and stones those who are sent to it" (23:37). On the third occasion of foretelling his death and resurrection, Matthew's Jesus explicitly informs "the twelve disciples" that "the Son of Man will be handed over to the chief priests and scribes, and they will condemn him to death" (20:18). The long and furious diatribes against the corrupt chief priests and Pharisees in chapters 21–23 heighten the doom hanging over Jesus, for the Jewish authorities fully realize that the parables are attacks on their moral failings and seek to retaliate (21:45–46). As Jesus prepares for the holiday, he tells his disciples, "You know that after two days the Passover is coming, and the Son of Man will be handed over to be crucified"

(26:2). All of these forecasts combine to escalate the fatalism of a plot in which someone will have to do the handing over to Jewish scribes and Pharisees implacably set on revenge. To the extent that the events appear to be fated or overdetermined by a providential divine plan, Judas begins to look like a pawn and thus provokes compassion.

The second change made by Matthew, and much discussed by biblical scholars, involves the depiction of Judas's atonement through his own self-sacrifice, one that mirrors the sacrifice of Jesus himself. But first various smaller modifications pave the way for a more hypocritical Judas to be granted a decidedly penitential resolution of his story. In stark contrast to Mark's account about the scene at Simon the leper's house, Matthew's explicitly relates that "the disciples" were present and "angry" at the waste of ointment that "could have been sold for a large sum, and the money given to the poor" (26:6). When Judas's trip to the chief priests immediately follows—"*Then* one of the twelve" (26:14; emphasis mine)—the motive of irate alienation is strengthened: like the others and for reasons that are perfectly comprehensible, Judas objects to money being spent on an anointing ritual rather than the indigent.

Yet in Matthew's Gospel, it is Judas, not the priests, who brings up the issue of material gain by asking "What will you give me if I betray him to you?" Judas has profit on his mind, we assume now for the first time, but what does this money mean, given the sum mentioned by Matthew (and only by Matthew)? "They paid him thirty pieces of silver" (26:15): annotated editions of the Bible generally include a footnote here, explaining that this paltry amount comes from two references in the Hebrew Bible. In Zechariah 11:12–13, a pious shepherd of a flock (of sheep, of people) doomed to slaughter (by the Lord, who has lost patience with the recalcitrance of the sheep, the people) quits his job. Saying that the flock may pay him or not, as they see fit, the shepherd receives his wages of thirty shekels of silver: "Then the Lord said to me, 'Throw it into the treasury'—this lordly price at which I was valued by them." And in Exodus 21:32, one law, pertaining to a slave gored by an ox, states that "the owner shall pay to the slaveowner thirty shekels of silver, and the ox shall be stoned."

What to make of these bizarre allusions to Judas as a cheated shepherd or slaveowner, and to inadequate reparations for unvalued labors or irreversible wrongs? Both involve obviously measly sums of money that cannot compensate (for a flock not worthy of tending, for the dead slave). This is why in Zechariah the shepherd is told to throw it away and why in Exodus the ox must be stoned: that is, the money cannot meaningfully repay the labor done, the slave gone. Like the flock and the slave, Jesus is doomed to slaughter; however, unlike the recalcitrant flock, he has not abjured his God and, unlike the slave, he acts as a free man. Shockingly, then, the minimal sum paid by the chief priests belies the cost of Jesus' precious sacrifice. Elaine Pagels and Karen L. King put it this way: "'Thirty pieces of silver' was the contemptible price at which rulers of Israel valued Zechariah (Zechariah 11:12–13), exactly the same amount . . . that the Jerusalem leaders paid for Jesus, and with the same feelings of contempt" (18). "It is possible," A. M. H. Saari speculates, "that the payment of thirty silver pieces to Judas was meant to be symbolic: Jesus was purchased for the price of a slave, and through his redemptive death saved all humanity from being enslaved by sin and death" (120). Weirdly, though, the thirty pieces seem to identify Judas with righteous men defrauded of their goods and services, not with avarice.

That Judas takes such a pittance might suggest his awareness of its irrelevance in the drama into which he has been conscripted, for the priests (not Judas) set the exact amount. If Judas was outraged at the three hundred denarii squandered on anointing ointment instead of given to the poor, perhaps the thirty pieces of silver indicate that he may not have been motivated by material profit or avarice at all; he may instead have begun to resent the idea that Jesus, anointed as an object of worship, might subvert his preaching about the poor inheriting the earth. To protest the wasted three hundred denarii, Judas accepts a mere thirty pieces of silver: the money is only a bonus for an act he might have done for nothing. Curiously, however, a sum biblically marked as insufficient later surfaces to emblematize the greed or avarice of a mercenary apostle.[18]

In any case, Judas recalls the Hebrew Bible's Judah, who decides (while eating a meal with his siblings) that there is nothing to be gained by killing their brother Joseph and so sells him into Egyptian slavery for twenty pieces of silver (Genesis 37:25–28).[19] Matthew dates Judas's scheming from the moment he is paid the thirty pieces of silver; the payment causes him to begin "to look for an opportunity to betray [Jesus]" (26:16). A more subjective, deceitful Judas emerges from these calculations and also from an alteration in the ritual supper at Passover. After all the apostles worry aloud about betraying Jesus ("Surely not I, Lord?"), as they had in Mark, Matthew adds a new interjection by "Judas, who betrayed him," whose "Surely not I, Rabbi?" is answered with the equivocal, "You have said so" (26:22, 25). Jesus' motivation remains unclear here; but Judas's acceptance of the money, his search for an opportunity to betray, and his eating of the Passover meal have resulted in duplicity, even perversity: characterized by a fractured consciousness, with a lie or prevarication or self-delusion ("Surely not I, Rabbi?") Judas splits off his public persona from the private self Jesus may or may not perceive ("You have said so"). Judas distinguishes himself here from the other disciples, who follow Jesus' teaching to avoid titles (23:8–10), even as the term "Rabbi" begins to link him to the Jewish leaders (whose money he surreptitiously holds). The dissembling of Matthew's Judas at the Last Supper laid the ground for subsequent attacks on the deceitful impersonations in which Jews were said to engage.

As in Mark, in Matthew Judas participates in the Lord's Supper, hears Peter's denial foretold, and presumably slips away during subsequent events to reappear in Gethsemane with the crowd and chief priests and to give the sign of the kiss. Both Mark and Matthew preface the arrest through Jesus' announcement, "See, my betrayer is at hand" (Mark 14:42; Matthew 26:46). But in Matthew, Jesus responds to Judas's greeting and kiss by saying, "Friend, do what you are here to do" (26:50). To no other disciple does Jesus use the appellation "Friend."[20] Like "You have said so," this comment pointedly places responsibility onto Judas; at the same time, the word "Friend"—even if read as an instance of sarcasm—exemplifies Jesus' acquiescence to his fate as well as his intimacy with Judas. After the slave's ear is cut off, Matthew's Jesus again distinguishes himself by stressing the inevitability of the preordained script. Mark's earlier Jesus asks, "Have you come out with swords and clubs to arrest me as though I were a bandit?" Then he concedes, "But let the scriptures be fulfilled" (14:48, 50). Matthew's more pedagogic Jesus protests against the deed, because those who "take the sword will perish by the sword" and also because he could call on legions of angels: "But how then would the scriptures be fulfilled, which say it must happen in this way?" Finally Matthew's Jesus uses repetition to emphasize that "all this has taken place, so that the scriptures of the prophets may be fulfilled" (26:52, 54, 56).

Matthew's Judas and Jesus might thus to some extent be thought to act in concert, as if each realizes the necessity of the other in bringing about the narrative ending. Perhaps that is why Matthew provides a penitential denouement for Judas's life story. After Jesus is struck, slapped, and said to deserve death, Matthew describes the suicide of Judas:

> When Judas, his betrayer, saw that Jesus was condemned, he repented and brought back the thirty pieces of silver to the chief priests and the elders. He said, "I have sinned by betraying innocent blood." But they said, "What is that to us? See to it yourself." Throwing down the pieces of silver in the temple, he departed; and he went and hanged himself. But the chief priests, taking the pieces of silver, said, "It is not lawful to put them into the treasury, since they are blood money." After conferring together, they used them to buy the potter's field as a place to bury foreigners. For this reason that field has been called the Field of Blood to this day. (27:3–8).[21]

Like the shepherd in Zechariah, Judas wants to throw the money into the treasury; his labors have been worthless, or worse, he now concedes. Like Ahithophel, whose disloyalty to King David leads to his suicide (2 Samuel 17:23), Judas hangs himself, opening up the possibility that he had informed on Jesus without realizing the act would eventuate in the spilling of "innocent blood."[22] The phrase "When Judas, his betrayer, saw that Jesus was condemned" suggests that Judas may have had no intention whatsoever of bringing about Jesus' death. But his penance is spurned by the very people who scorn Jesus.[23]

Through Judas's suicide, Matthew drives a wedge between Judas and the Jewish authorities, even as he links Judas to Jesus. A conscience-stricken Judas flings the money into the Temple, whereas the Temple authorities hand Jesus over to death. That the chief priests take and use Judas's "blood money" implies that they are responsible for Jesus' death, for Judas is destitute and dead when the crucifixion occurs. Similarly, the chief priests remain supremely indifferent to Judas's sin of "betraying innocent blood," just as the Jews (now speaking "as a whole") remain indifferent to Pilate's qualms about betraying the innocent. In Matthew, Pilate has been warned by his wife's dream of Jesus' innocence, and therefore he "washed his hands before the crowd, saying, 'I am innocent of this man's blood,'" but the Jews accept full responsibility for Jesus' crucifixion in what has become an infamous malediction: "His blood be on us and on our children!" (27:24–25). Jesus' cup of wine is "blood of the covenant" for the forgiveness of sins (26:28); Judas attests to Jesus' "innocent blood"; his cast-off money subsidizes the Field of Blood, a cemetery for foreigners. Here, and frequently thereafter, Judas gains moral stature when severed from "the Jews."

To be sure, suicide as an act of remorse cannot be conflated with the crucifixion of an innocent man: referring to a person executed for a crime and hung on a tree, Deuteronomy explains that "anyone hung on a tree is under God's curse" (21:23). But in Galatians 3:10–14, Paul cites this axiom from the Hebrew Bible in order to annul it, because "Christ redeemed" his followers from "the curse

2.2. Ivory Crucifixion, plaque from a northern Italian casket (400–420 C.E.). Source: Bridgeman Art Library. © British Museum, London.

of the law."[24] Especially given the shame attached to crucifixion, an uncanny parallelism occurs when Judas (associated with the Field of Blood) and Jesus (dying in the place of a skull) voluntarily relinquish life on the wood of a trunk or a plank. The ideal of sacred suicide, of a Christ who committed suicide, dates back to ancient times: "Strange as the idea of the suicide of Christ may seem to some," Jack Miles explains about a Jesus who freely surrenders his life, "it is an idea that a Christian, even a devout Christian can entertain" (*Christ* 169).[25] Before Jesus acquiesces to crucifixion on a cross, then, Judas hangs himself on a tree. "Utterly alone, engulfed by self-reproach," Judas killed himself "without even waiting for Pilate's decision," and it is important to recall that "neither Testament contains a word against suicide" (Daube 312, 314).[26]

An ivory plaque from a Northern Italian casket (from 400–420 C.E.; illustration 2.2) captures the uncanny parallelism of Judas, limp as his robed body hangs down while his face turns upward, and Jesus erect and splayed on the cross. The contrast between Judas's dangling limbs and his upturned face lends pathos to his fate. Mary, another apostle, and a Roman soldier attending to the figure on the right hint that Judas's private tragedy has been eclipsed by the shocking public theatricality of the crucifixion. Not explicit in Matthew's text but resonant, nonetheless, is the realization bespoken by Judas's suicide—that he had mistaken the consequences of his act of informing on Jesus, and also that he had violated Jesus' golden rule: "do to others as you would have them do to you" (7:12). The discarded money bag lies below his feet. A remorseful Judas ultimately rejects, as Jesus does, what is shown to be the immorality of the Jewish authorities. In Matthew's Gospel, then, those authorities, not Judas, embody the vain hypocrisy of people who do not practice what they preach.

In stark contrast to Judas's repentance before Jesus' death, after the crucifixion Matthew's Jews successfully petition Pilate to place a guard at Jesus' tomb so his disciples cannot first steal the body and then broadcast the lie of his resurrection. When the tomb is found empty, the priests and elders bribe Roman soldiers to testify that while they slept the corpse was stolen by the disciples. The manipulations, bribery, and deceit of the powerful Jewish authorities stand in stark contrast to the silent suffering of the hanging men. Does Matthew's new inclusion of Judas's instantaneous repentance and death allow him to make his other substantial revision of Mark, namely the depiction of Jesus' resurrection and reunion with his disciples? The question arises because Judas can be viewed here as the first to realize—at the cost of his life—Jesus' divinity. The conversion of Judas forecasts what the resurrection proves, Jesus' incarnation. Whereas Mark's Gospel intimates what he seems to believe—that it was not Judas but God who "gave [his Son] up for all of us" (Romans 8:32)—Matthew hints about the crucifixion that it was "the Son of God, who loved me and gave himself for me" (Galatians 2:20).

Of course such an interpretation of the doubling between Jesus and Judas, which merely hovers like an aura around the details Matthew provides, cannot be propounded as schematic or definitive in any way. Yet the forsaken potter's Field of Blood links Judas with those who die on alien soil, without families, histories, their own rites and rituals. That Judas has grievously paid for his sins with his life is underscored when Matthew concludes by describing "the eleven disciples" going to Galilee to see the resurrected Christ (28:16). Regardless of Matthew's insistence on judgments against and punishments of those who sin, he makes it possible to perceive Judas as the patron saint of despair and diaspora, and as an uncanny precursor to Jesus, also a foreigner to the Romans in civic control and to the hypocritical Jewish leaders in social control of Judea. The fine line between suicide and martyrdom is addressed in the juxtaposition of Judas's self-inflicted death and Jesus' submission to his. Finally, in death Judas could be said to have successfully heeded what Jesus preached to his disciples: "A disciple is not above the teacher, nor a slave above the master; it is enough for the disciple to be *like the teacher,* and the slave like the master" (10:24; emphasis mine).

Readers seeking to evaluate Judas's guilt and repentance might exonerate him on the basis of the moral maxims and ethical discourses so frequently on the lips of Matthew's Jesus: "pray for those who persecute you" (5:44); "forgive others their trespasses" (5:14); "Do not fear those who kill the body but cannot kill the soul" (10:28); "those who lose their life for my sake will find it" (10:39). Whereas William Blake's Milton—who by his own account set out to justify the ways of God to men—aligned himself unconsciously with Satan, Matthew involuntarily supports a Judas who ultimately aspires to Jesus' instruction in a Gospel that opened the way for later interpreters wishing to take up Judas's cause.

LUKE'S DEMONICALLY POSSESSED
TRAITOR

In every change Luke made to the biblical narrative, Jesus becomes more mystically powerful and Judas more satanically evil, even as their story recedes into "an orderly account" of a more distant past (Luke 1:3).[27] Whereas Matthew's Jesus foresees his fate, at times Luke's seems in control of events that he affirms as necessary (9:22, 44; 13:33; 17:25). In between his conception, when the angel Gabriel announces that Jesus will be the Son of God, and his self-revelation after walking down the road to Emmaus with two disciples, Luke's Jesus is associated with miraculous healings and authoritative parables that stress his intimate relationship with the Holy Spirit (4:1) and his concern not just for the poor and for women but also for such outcasts from the Jewish community as tax collectors, Samaritans, and Romans, for he is animated by a universalism that will shape the church's mission to the Gentiles.[28] Judas, the director of nefarious Jewish authorities who do not comprehend the evil they are enacting, begins to become unforgivable.

Luke's initial listing of the twelve presents two Judas apostles, the first being Judas, son of James, and the second Judas Iscariot, who is described not as the betrayer but instead and starkly as "a traitor" (6:16): thus an all-pervasive identity (rather than a single action) defines him as a renegade, a defector from the collectivity of the apostles as well as their Lord. After Luke's Jesus goes into the wilderness for forty days to triumph over the devil's temptations, Luke explains, "When the devil had finished every test, he departed from him *until an opportune time*" (4:13; emphasis mine). That time occurs as the festival of unleavened bread approaches: "Then *Satan entered into Judas* called Iscariot, who was one of the twelve; he went away and conferred with the chief priests and officers of the temple police about how he might betray him to them" (22:3–4; emphasis mine).[29]

The logic that moves Satan-in-Judas to deliberate not only with the priests but also with the "temple police" confirms Jesus' earlier lacerating attack on the Pharisees, who are "filled with extortion and wickedness" (11:38). In addition, the story of the woman with the alabaster jar no longer precedes this event; neither the exorbitant cost of the ointment nor the thirty pieces of silver are mentioned in Luke's version of the story (see 7:36). Unrelated to spiritual, political, or mercenary considerations, Judas's motivation is quite simply satanic possession. During the Last Supper, Judas receives a portion of the loaf given as Jesus' body and a sip of the wine as a covenant of his blood, after which Jesus sees that "the one who betrays me is with me, and his hand is on the table" (22:22). Jesus then announces the determined course of the Son of Man and pronounces, "woe to that one by whom he is betrayed" (22:22). That he does so expressed to the early church father Tertullian (ca. 155–230) "the imprecation and threat of an angry and incensed Master" against a Judas who "was of course to be punished by Him against whom he had committed the sin of treachery" (354).

A manuscript illumination from the Stuttgart Psalter, composed at Saint-Germain-des-Prés (around 820–830 C.E.; illustration 2.3), depicts Christ giving Judas the eucharistic chalice and bread accompanied by a black bird that, according to Gertrud Schiller, "illustrates Paul's words in 1 Corinthians 11:29 that 'he that eateth and drinketh unworthily, eateth and drinketh damnation to himself'" (34). The writing clearly alludes to Psalm 41: "Even my bosom friend, whom I trusted, / who ate of my bread, has lifted the heel against me" (9).[30] The line may bring to mind "the primordial associations between the sharing of bread and fidelity, between the secular codes of trust referred to by King David and the ultimate trust, modeled on the secular, in the bread of transubstantiation" (Steiner, *No Passion Spent* 413). Like a contemporary cartoonist, the illustrator has managed to capture Judas's hypocritical duality as he faces toward Jesus to receive the host (orally, physically), while his feet move him quickly away to do the evil bidding of the dark spirit about to possess him (orally, physically). This Judas just might be the first casualty of restless leg syndrome.

2.3. Judas with black bird, manuscript illumination from the
Stuttgart Psalter, composed at Saint-Germain-des-Prés
(ca. 820–830 C.E.). Source: Württembergische Landesbiblio-
thek, Stuttgart, Cod. Bibl. fol. 23, 97v.

Next, in Luke, the apostles all ask which one of them would betray
Jesus. The devil appears again here when Jesus predicts Peter's denial:
"Simon, Simon, listen! Satan has demanded to sift all of you like
wheat, but I have prayed for you that your own faith may not fail"
(22:31). But Luke's Jesus must not have prayed for Judas, whose guilt
increases as that of the other eleven decreases. Luke, unlike Mark
and Matthew, never has Jesus chastise Peter with the phrase "Get
you behind me, Satan" (8:33, 16:23). Asleep on the job, the apostles
on the Mount of Olives are not viewed as especially derelict, for
their slumber occurs only once (not three times) and is attributed to
grief. As for the approaching Judas—who here is depicted "*leading*"
crowds and "the chief priests, the officers of the temple police, and
the elders" (22:47, 52; emphasis mine)—Jesus confronts him with so
much apprehension or foreknowledge that the contaminating kiss
may be avoided entirely: "[Judas] approached Jesus to kiss him; but
Jesus said to him, 'Judas, is it with a kiss that you are betraying the

Son of Man?'" (22:47–48). Neither the word "Rabbi" nor the kiss itself definitively is part of this story. As a sign of his mystic power, Jesus immediately touches and thereby heals the ear of the slave who is struck. Before being led away, Luke's Jesus bleakly concludes, "this is your hour, and the power of *darkness*" (22:53; emphasis mine), a pronouncement that contributes to Judas's subsequent representation as a shadowed or black man controlled by the devil. The black bird in the Psalter prefigures innumerable black insects, bats, dogs, and other animal totems aligned with Judas in later visual and written representations.

Nothing more is reported about Judas in Luke's Gospel; however, at the start of Luke's Acts, which is traditionally read as an integral part of his Gospel, Peter begins the account of the end of Judas,

> "who became a guide for those who arrested Jesus—for he was numbered among us and was allotted his share in this ministry." (Now this man acquired a field with the reward of his wickedness; and falling headlong, he burst open in the middle and all his bowels gushed out. This became known to all the residents of Jerusalem, so that the field was called in their language Hakeldama, that is, Field of Blood.) "For it is written in the book of Psalms,
>
> 'Let his homestead become desolate,
>   and let there be no one to live in it':
>
> and
>
> 'Let another take his position of overseer.'" (1:16–20)

As Matthew had done in his efforts to explain a place called the Field of Blood, Luke links the location to Judas, but to a decidedly less penitential Judas.[31] Unlike Matthew's repentant suicide, who throws away the money subsequently used by the Jews to purchase the property, Luke's Judas falls "headlong" on the land he bought with the priests' money, a phrase that evokes not only the fall of Adam and Eve in the garden but the earlier mythological fall of the rebellious Lucifer from the angelic throng: Luke's Jesus had "watched Satan fall from heaven like a flash of lightning" (10:18).

Where might Luke have gotten the idea that "all [of Judas's] bowels gushed out"? It accords with the "horrible death" visited upon villains like an ungodly man in 2 Maccabees whose "body swarmed with worms, and while he was still living in anguish and pain, his flesh rotted away, and because of the stench the whole army felt revulsion at his decay" (9:9).[32] In Acts 12:23, Herod Agrippa is struck down by an angel and eaten by worms. Evocative of Jesus' teaching that it is "what comes out of a person that defiles"—namely, the evil accompanying "fornication, theft, murder, adultery, avarice, wickedness, deceit, licentiousness, envy, slander, pride, folly" (Mark 7:20–22)—the gushing bowels may also derive from the source Luke quotes.

To prove that Judas's fate constitutes a fulfillment of scriptural prophecy, Luke echoes the curses in Psalm 69: "May their camp be a desolation; let no one live in their tents. / For they persecute those whom you have struck down, / and those whom you have wounded, they attack still more" (69:25–26).[33] In this passage from the Hebrew Bible, the psalmist cries out against those who hate him without cause, those who have set out to destroy him. Luke likens Judas to the enemies of the psalmist, who "accuse [him] falsely" (69:4). These foes, he hopes, will be shamed and dishonored; since his persecutors gave him poison to eat and vinegar to drink, he prays for their punishment: "Let their eyes *be darkened* so that they cannot see, / and *make their loins tremble continually*" (69:23; emphases mine). Did Luke recall the darkened eyes and the trembling loins the psalmist conjures, transforming them into "the power of darkness" and the "bowels gush[ing] out"? What the psalmist wishes upon his enemies is clearly what Luke seeks to accomplish with and for Judas—specifically, to add guilt to his guilt so that Judas may "have no acquittal from you" (69:27). The Field of Blood effectively blots Judas out of the book of the living, while his excremental eruption proves he can never be enrolled among the purified. Jesus' uplifting spiritual eschatology has been set against Judas's debasing scatology. According to Luke in Acts, then, Judas is expelled from and by the eleven, who replace him with Matthias.

Within Luke's Gospel, the apostles are not characterized as deserters, as they are in Mark. In stark contrast to the abandonment of God that suffuses Mark's and Matthew's Jesus on the cross ("My God, my God, why have you forsaken me?" [Mark 15:34; Matthew 27:46]), Luke presents a tranquil Jesus: "Father, into your hands I commend my spirit" (23:46). All secular authorities are blameless: both Pilate and Herod find Jesus innocent of the charges brought against him and want to release him (23:14–16). But Jewish religious leaders are shrewd, dishonest, and materialistic (16:8–9). That the obdurate Pharisees are hypocritical and self-exalted (12:1, 18:13–14) appears particularly important in light of some additional references to the Temple that Luke supplied in a number of the early and final episodes of his version of Jesus' biography: Jesus is first recognized as the Messiah in the Temple (2:36–38); there his parents offer a sacrifice (2:25, 39); there, in what he calls "my Father's house," the adolescent Jesus visits and enters into discussions with Jewish authorities (2:49); and after the resurrection he is seen returning to the Temple (24:50–52).

More than Matthew, according to Paula Fredriksen, Luke presents "a Jesus who harmoniously realized God's most fundamental promises to Israel" (193), but the scribes, chief priests, and Sadducees harass him in the Gospel and vindictively plot against the apostolic church in Acts. To the extent that Jewish leaders conspire with Judas to bring about Jesus' death, they insult the messianic foundation of their own tradition and thus become implicated in cosmic evil. In Acts, we have seen, Peter is said to have announced to a crowd of 120 that "the scripture had to be fulfilled, which the Holy Spirit *through David foretold* concerning Judas, who became *a guide* for those who arrested Jesus—for he was numbered among us and was allotted his share in this ministry" (1:15–17; emphases mine). As far back as the time of King David, then, it was foreknown that Judas would perform his nefarious deed. After Satan enters into Judas and he schemes with the officers of the temple police, "They were greatly pleased and agreed to give him money. So he consented . . ." (Luke 22:5), with the result that both the chief priests and Judas are contaminated by this unspecified sum. Nor does satanic possession cancel Judas's responsibility, for he is accused in Acts of "wickedness."

Many commentators have noted that Luke's revisions transform the crucifixion from a divine sacrifice atoning for the sins of humankind into the Jewish murder of an innocent being imbued with the Holy Spirit. On the cross, Luke's Jesus (and only Luke's Jesus) does ask his "Father" to "forgive them; for they do not know what they are doing" (23:34). But forgiveness has little force against the evil of this injustice, which, Luke makes clear in his sequel, will be fathomed not by murderous Jews but by Gentiles who have been saved through the acknowledgment of guilt that spurs repentance. Repeatedly in Acts, Bertil Gärtner has pointed out, the Greek words for betrayal and betrayer apply to the Jews who killed the prince of life (24–25; see Acts 2:23, 3:12–15, 4:10, 5:30, 7:52, 13:27).

JOHN'S DEVIL-TREASURER

What happens to Judas when John's exalted Jesus becomes the "Word of God," "the light of the world," "the resurrection and the life" (1:1, 9:5, 11:25) in a narrative that retains the Passion sequence, but eschews most of what prefaces it in the three earlier synoptic Gospels? During a ministry of three years (rather than one), John's Jesus repeatedly defines himself openly (through a succession of lengthy speeches) as divine: "No one comes to the Father except through me" (14:6). Gone are the temptation in the wilderness, the agony in Gethsemane, the cry of anguish on the cross (recorded in Mark and Matthew). Even the miracles up the ante in this Gospel, since Jesus

changes water into wine and raises Lazarus from the dead. The height
of the elevation of John's Jesus to the divine—"I and the Father are
one" (10:30)—equals the depth of the degeneration of John's Judas
into a deicidal devil, and that of "the Jews," who play a more prominent role here than in earlier accounts.[34] Although many Jews must
have resented the ruling high priesthood and although "faithful Jews
could be very much against the temple" (Borg and Crossan 43), John
tends to lump all Jews together with the Jewish priesthood and the
Temple. Just as demonic as Luke's Judas, John's is given a quite distinct character (he is a thief) and profession (he is the apostles' treasurer, a keeper of their purse) in recounted political events that make
him representative of the Jewish people as quislings, collaborationist
toadies to their pagan Roman rulers.

Judas Iscariot enters the Gospel of John at a moment when many
are finding it difficult to accept the words of Jesus. Surrounded by
skeptics, John's Jesus intuits the place from which his opposition
comes and also immediately knows it to derive from one source.
From the very beginning, Jesus realizes who is predetermined to
betray him, as well as that agent's satanic character or origins: "Jesus
knew from the first who were the ones that did not believe, and
who was the one that would betray him" (6:64).[35] After Simon Peter
pledges faith in him, Jesus answers, "'Did I not choose you, the
twelve? Yet one of you *is a devil.*' He was speaking of Judas, son of
Simon Iscariot, for he, though one of the twelve, was going to betray
him" (6:70–71; emphasis mine). According to Henry Ansgar Kelly,
"This is the first and the last time that anyone is called a *diabolos* in
the Gospels" (110).

The devil furnishes the link John forges between Judas and the
Jewish populace. In chapter 8, not the chief priests or the Pharisees
but "the Jews" claim to "have one father, God himself," but Jesus
disagrees:

"If God were your Father, you would love me, for I came from
God and now I am here. I did not come on my own, but he sent

me. Why do you not understand what I say? It is because you cannot accept my word. You are *from your father the devil,* and you choose to do your father's desires. He was a murderer from the beginning and does not stand in the truth, because there is no truth in him. When he lies, he speaks according to his own nature, for he is a liar and the father of lies." (8:41, 42–44; emphasis mine)

Jesus' subsequent claim—"before Abraham was, I am" (8:58)—causes the Jews to begin stoning him in the Temple. Judas, "a devil," shares a demonic bond with the Jews, whose "father [is] the devil" and "the father of lies."

In John's Gospel, the disbelieving Jews gain agency, organizing a delegation that goes to the Pharisees:

> So the chief priests and the Pharisees called a meeting of the coun-
> cil, and said, "What are we to do? This man is performing many
> signs. If we let him go on like this, everyone will believe in him,
> and the Romans will come and destroy both our holy place and
> our nation." But one of them, Caiaphas, who was high priest that
> year, said to them, "You know nothing at all! You do not under-
> stand that it is better for you to have one man die for the people
> than to have the whole nation destroyed." He did not say this on
> his own, but being high priest that year he prophesied that Jesus
> was about to die for the nation, and not for the nation only, but
> to gather into one the dispersed children of God. So from that day
> on they planned to put him to death. (11:47–53)

The leaders of the Jewish religion here produce ersatz prophecies manufactured to ensure the survival of Judaism under Roman rule; Jesus represents "a threat to the priestly, temple authorities and to their concordat with the Romans" (D. Smith 220).[36]

Fearful of imminent destruction, John's occupied Jews never confront punitive or potentially vindictive Romans heroically, but instead strategize with cunning deceit that involves human sacrifice. Of course, historically the Jews distinguished themselves from pagans by banning human sacrifice, but John's Jews plan to put Jesus to death in order to preserve their holy place and their nation.[37] Thus, according to John, a brewing political conspiracy hatches the murder plot. From his point of view, the scheme reeks with irony because, unbeknownst to the Jews, the lie they fabricated—"that Jesus was about to die for the nation, and not for the nation only, but to gather into one the dispersed children of God"—precisely predicts what will happen.

Does Judas share an ideology with this faction, or does he merely capitalize on their designs? This question arises out of the revision John provides of the episode involving the costly ointment, here perfume used to anoint Jesus' feet. "Judas Iscariot, one of his disciples (the one who was about to betray him)," objects, "Why was this perfume not sold for three hundred denarii and the money given to the poor?" (12:15). The question echoes earlier variants; however, it is attributed only to Judas by John, who then immediately offers a parenthetical explanation: "(He said this not because he cared about the poor, but because he was a *thief;* he kept the common purse and used *to steal* what was put into it)" (12:6; emphases mine). With this aside, John isolates Judas from the other apostles and simultaneously cancels any interpretation that would propose a more legitimate basis for Judas's alliance with the Pharisees.

According to John's Jesus, none of his apostles will be "lost but the *son of perdition,* that the scripture might be fulfilled" (17:12; emphasis mine). The expression "son of perdition" appears again in the New Testament when Paul describes the "man of lawlessness" who reveals himself before the final coming of Christ (2 Thessalonians 2:3): the Antichrist, like Judas, is a human being, but one who works Satan's will.[38] Not theology but thievery or Satan drives Judas, just as John's Jews are motivated not by religion but by political expediency, though some of them, even those in positions of authority, act out of panic: a number of Jews believe in Jesus, but so dread reprisals from the chief priests that they hide their faith out of "fear that they would be put out of the synagogue" (12:42). Clearly, the Christians of John's day felt embattled within their Jewish communities; demonization of Judas and the Jews may have served as a protective reflex on the part of this persecuted, defensive minority.[39]

At the last meal, before John's Jesus decides to wash the feet of his beloved apostles, we are informed that "*The devil had already put it into the heart of Judas* son of Simon Iscariot to betray him" (13:2; emphasis mine). For this reason, John's Jesus declares the apostles "'clean, though not all of you.' For he knew who was to betray him; for this reason he said, 'Not all of you are clean'" (13:10–11). The dirtiness of Judas, like his allegiance to the devil, relates him to the Jews, for John (unlike the synoptic authors) places the Temple cleansing "at the beginning of Jesus' ministry . . . to suggest that his ministry was in general designed to cleanse Judaism" (Kysar 6). Jesus' assertion—"I know whom I have chosen. But the Scripture will be fulfilled" (13:18)—has been read two ways: Jesus knew "the *kind* of men—i.e. Jesus chose Judas knowing full well the sort of fellow he was"—or Jesus knew "'*whom* I have *really* chosen—and Judas is not among them'" (Carson 131). Whether or not Jesus knowingly picked an evil Judas so as to actualize his own messianic destiny, he attempts to clarify the disciples' ability to understand his message by qualifying again that he is "not speaking of all of you" (13:18). Because they want to know who will betray him, Jesus gives a clear sign by saying at table,

> "It is the one to whom I give this piece of bread when I have dipped it in the dish." So when he had dipped the piece of bread, he gave it to Judas son of Simon Iscariot. After he received the piece of bread, *Satan entered him.* Jesus said to him, "Do quickly what you are going to do." Now no one at the table knew why he said this to him. Some thought that, because Judas had the common purse, Jesus was telling him, "Buy what we need for the festival"; or, that he should give something to the poor. So, after

receiving the piece of bread, he immediately went out. And *it was night*. (13:26–30; emphases mine)

There are a number of fascinating alterations here, beginning with the fact often noticed that this is not a seder, for John clearly makes the event occur "before the festival" (13:1)—probably, many interpreters surmise, so that the subsequent crucifixion will occur at the moment the Passover lambs are slaughtered ritually at the Temple, and Jesus can thereby represent the sacrificed Lamb of God. As in Luke, in John Judas suffers a demonic possession, here achieved through the bread Jesus gives him. In contrast to the account in the synoptic Gospels, John's Judas has not plotted earlier but decides on betrayal during the supper. Whereas Jesus is the "true light, which enlightens everyone" (1:9), Judas inhabits the epistemological and spiritual darkness of even well-meaning Jews. (Perhaps the tension between "The devil had already put it into the heart of Judas" [13:2] and "After he received the piece of bread, Satan entered him" [13:27] relates to the multiple authorship or levels of redaction attributed by scholars to the Gospel of John.)[40] According to J. Albert Harrill, "possession" might not be the proper term for what happens to John's Judas, "because Satan merely enters into a person who already belonged to him (his child)."[41]

In all three of the synoptic Gospels, Judas shares the sacramental bread and wine with the other apostles, and therefore many readers have associated the meal with the line from the Psalms illustrated by the pseudo-cartoonist of the ancient Psalter: "Even my bosom friend, whom I trusted, / who ate of my bread, has lifted the heel against me" (41:9). But in John's Gospel, where Jesus so early intuits Judas's evil nature and where this psalm is quoted (13:18), Judas does not receive the bread proclaimed to be Jesus' body or the cup of wine proclaimed to be his blood. Jesus does not institute the Eucharist at the last meal. Instead, Judas alone eats and in eating is consumed by the devil. At the front of the cathedral of Volterra's pulpit (twelfth century; illustration 2.4), a kneeling Judas appears on one side of the table, while

2.4. Judas with dragon, pulpit in the cathedral of Volterra
(ca. 1100–1200). Source: Alinari Archives, Florence. © Alinari/
Art Resource, New York.

all the other apostles are seated at the other: as in John, his satanic
nature is emphasized, here by the winged dragon at his feet whose
mouth seems ready to devour and whose tail coils snakelike in knots.
In opposition to the seated eleven, Judas kneels in supplication, a sign
of deceit that will earn his fate: after he eats from the hand that feeds
him, he will be gobbled by the devil. His lower position—as in many
of the illustrations of the Last Supper discussed in the next chapter—
signifies Judas's debased state, which is contrasted with that of the
beloved disciple, whom Jesus favored and who blissfully nestles on
Jesus' bosom. Unlike the god who is eaten to bring about spiritual
consummation, a dwarfed Judas with an oversized head and his devilish familiar-father—both with wide-open mouths—gorge to destroy
and damn.

Yet John's Jesus instructs Judas to do quickly the task that sends
him into the allegorical night. And the other eleven do not comprehend, because here for the first time Judas is not merely an avaricious

crook but professionally a sort of treasurer. It is hard, though, to claim that love of money plays a major part in motivating Judas's betrayal, for in John's Gospel Judas never negotiates with the Jewish priests for money. Simply "a thief" by nature (12:6) and by virtue of his devilish character, John's Judas exhibits an evil not fully attributable to material need, greed, or anger.

After Judas's departure, Jesus goes on to warn the eleven through the so-called Farewell Discourses: lengthy speeches and prayers about the persecution his disciples will suffer, as well as attestations of his identity as "the true vine," commandments of love, and even a reference to one "Judas (not Iscariot)."[42] Prophesying their weeping and mourning, Jesus also promises his apostles ultimate joy as he petitions "the Father on your behalf" (16:27). Without a shadow of the doubt he had shown in the first Gospels, John's Jesus proclaims to God, "The glory that you have given me I have given them" (17:22), before going to a garden that "Judas, who betrayed him, also knew . . . , because Jesus often met there with his disciples" (18:2). According to Graham Stanton, "Judas takes the initiative, leads the way, and hence is fully culpable" (116); and here he brings not crowds but "*a detachment of soldiers* together with police from the chief priests and the Pharisees," all of whom confront Jesus (18:3; emphasis mine). Roman troops—"a cohort" (of six hundred Roman soldiers) or "a maniple" (of two hundred)—appear (along with the temple guards of the priests and Pharisees) at this last view of Judas in John's Gospel, setting up the more political, ideological denouement (Brodie 524).

No greeting of "Rabbi" and no kiss occur in a scene that stresses not only Jesus' foreknowledge but also his effort to protect the eleven from harm's way so as to "fulfill the word that he had spoken, 'I did not lose a single one of those whom you gave me' " (18:9). In this confrontation, an oddly silent Judas stands with those to whom Jesus twice says "I am he," thereby identifying himself for arrest, while also causing the arresting party to fall to the ground. For many biblical commentators, the repeated "I am he" statements echo God's identification of himself to Moses: "I am who I am" (Exodus 3:14). After

Simon Peter cuts off the right ear of a slave, here given the name Mal-chus, Jesus rebukes him: "Put your sword back into its sheath. Am I not to drink the cup that the Father has given me?" (18:11).

Just as there is no wish to remove the cup, there is no trial before the Sanhedrin in John's Gospel, no charge of blasphemy. Instead, Pilate repeatedly rejects the case against Jesus, and hands him over only because of the Jews' hectic shouts for crucifixion. Indeed, when the charge against Jesus, that he called himself "the Son of God" (19:7), becomes clear to Pilate, he is sufficiently anxious about the possibility of its truth that he pleads with Jesus, explaining that he has the civic power to release him:

> Jesus answered him, "You would have no power over me unless it had been given you from above; therefore the one who handed me over to you is guilty of a greater sin." From then on Pilate tried to release him, but the Jews cried out, "If you release this man, you are no friend of the emperor. Everyone who claims to be a king sets himself against the emperor." (19:11–12)

The high priest is "guilty of a greater sin" than Pilate, and so, accord-ing to John, Pilate is forced by the Jews to crucify Jesus.

Just as important, John's Jews are deeply political beings, conniv-ing collaborators with the imperialists who have colonized them not just politically but also psychologically. When Pilate asks, "Shall I crucify your King?" the chief priests answer, "We have no king but the emperor" (19:15). The Jews, rejecting anyone who claims "to be a king" in their feigned fealty to the Roman emperor, have shockingly saved their skins by losing their souls: John intimates that in their conformity to pagan rule, they have betrayed their own faith, with its long history of preparation for a messiah. Passive-aggressive, Judas in John's account hardly speaks or acts autonomously, but instead represents the hypocrisy, servility, and cowardice of the dirty and dev-ilish Jews who frame and then murder Jesus not as a spiritual leader but as a trumped-up rebel against imperial Rome, a scapegoat to ensure Jewish colonial survival. Well suited to nothing but servitude, John's Jews deserve the captivity they endorse.

A BRIEF INVENTORY OF KNOTS

Should we, by way of summary, review lines and scenes from Mark, Matthew, Luke, and John together (rather than separately), inconsistencies and incongruities swirl around the twelfth apostle and his story. From antiquity on, people did not dissect and pull apart each of the discrete Gospels in the way I have just done. Until relatively recently, in fact, Mark, Matthew, Luke, and John were assumed to be reliable eyewitnesses, whose accounts needed to be aligned and combined to comprehend the truth.[43] Even today, according to Marcus J. Borg and John Dominic Crossan, "we most commonly hear the story of Jesus's death as a composite of the gospels and the New Testament as a whole" (139). The list of divergences below is meant not to discredit the Gospel authors but rather to demonstrate that *when taken together or considered harmoniously* their *composite* portraits of and plots about Judas generate a number of mysteries. Anyone attempting to integrate the accounts of Mark, Matthew, Luke, and John must confront manifold discrepancies. Judas the imagined character was launched into life by these obscurities and puzzles, which acted like a magnet, attracting numerous interpreters. Such enigmas begged to be solved by subsequent artists in almost all media and by theological thinkers of all stripes, as the rest of this book demonstrates.

Here, then, is a brief summary of the multiple perplexities that have to be tackled when we interpret the united Gospels in concert, rather than singly, and that were recurrently addressed while the four canonical accounts of the betrayal congealed in various formations as they were retold. It includes clear and simple differences of opinion about the events in the various narratives, inexplicable decisions or consequences, and paradoxes. Organized chronologically to keep Judas's narrative intact, each item on this list could and did become a question, prefaced by the phrase "how can it be that . . ." or "why is it the case that . . .":

* Jesus chose Judas as a disciple, giving him the power to cure the sick and preach a message of love, even though the Son of God knew from the start that Judas had been or would soon become inhabited by the devil.

* A thief, the twelfth apostle was nevertheless appointed treasurer and entrusted with the common purse.

* Judas, along with several or all the disciples, objected to the costly spikenard used to anoint Jesus; or he alone objected because he was a thief.

* Judas conceived the treachery early in Jesus' ministry; or during a visit to the high priests before the Last Supper; or during the last meal, when given the sop by Jesus; and it was foretold by King David.

* Though a thief, Judas was not motivated by greed, for he did not ask for money from the Temple authorities; or, when he did ask what they would give him, was offered and accepted a pittance.

* Judas attended a Passover seder on Thursday night; or that Thursday occurred the day before Passover and he left the table during the meal, while the other eleven remained.

* Judas received all the benefits of Jesus' solicitude for his disciples' eternal life, including the holy Eucharist or the foot washing; however, he remained committed to treachery.

* At the moment when Judas began to enact the devil's plot, Jesus instructed him to go and execute it quickly.

* Judas arrived in Gethsemane with crowds from the chief priests and elders; or he led the crowd; or he brought a detachment of Roman soldiers, along with police from the chief priests.

* Judas used a kiss to reveal Jesus to the Temple authorities in the garden; or he attempted a kiss; or he instead watched the soldiers he had brought fall down.

* The only disciple Jesus specifically called "friend" in the synoptic Gospels performed the role of enemy.

* Judas repented, returned the money, and hanged himself; or he burst open on the field he used the money to buy; or he simply disappeared.

* Jesus explained that he would lose no soul given into his care, but his twelfth apostle ended by hanging or exploding or disappearing.

* Though Satan controlled his activities, Judas was judged to be personally wicked.

* Jesus informed his disciples that it would have been better for the betrayer not to have been born; however, Jesus also explained that he knew who he had chosen for the scripture to be fulfilled.

* An agent of God's will—instrumental in the crucifixion and resurrection—was regarded by Jesus as an unclean sinner.

  * Jesus assured the twelve that in the coming kingdom they
    would sit on thrones to judge the twelve tribes of Israel, but
    he called Judas a lost son of perdition.

  * Judas's evil was Jesus' good; his rejection resulted in human-
    ity's election.

As should be evident to most readers, it remains difficult, if not
impossible, to take full account of the totality and specificity of *all*
these jostling details in a coherent narrative about a harmonized
Judas.[44] Part II of this cultural biography demonstrates that widely
divergent Judas characters sprang from attempts to position various aspects of the New Testament in the background or foreground,
interpretive efforts that proliferated because of the sheer number of
its tough textual knots. It was easier to repress or forget some features of the Gospel stories, given their contradictory testimonies. If
Judas's thievery would be emphasized, for example, his participation
in the Eucharist or the foot washing tended to disappear; in stories
in which Jesus asks Judas to perform the betrayal quickly, spontaneous explosion may drop out. While some artists and thinkers, teased
by gaps in the Gospel accounts, set out to fill in absent information,
their tensions and inconsistencies spurred others to provide coherent
explanations—usually by elaborating on some details, occluding others. Before we turn to postbiblical spin-offs of the Passion, though, it
makes sense to explore exactly what the escalating rhetoric against
Judas in the four successive Gospels signifies in terms of the earliest
formations of Christian identity.

A JUDEO-CHRISTIAN INTERMEDIARY

Truncated though it was, my account of the Gospel writers' dissimilar
approaches to the betrayer in the Passion story suggests that as Jesus
ascends in spiritual power to become Christ, Judas plummets spiritu-

ally and morally. In other words, when and while Jesus becomes more divine, Judas devolves into a satanic figure. The mechanism depends on the figures with whom he is conjoined. For Mark, Judas remains closely aligned with the all too fearful and faulty apostles, especially Peter. For Matthew, Judas gains an interiority that eventually causes him to embrace a self-sacrificial fate, one that powerfully certifies and reflects Jesus' innocence. For Luke, Judas works in Satan's thrall only to suffer a deservedly filthy end. For John, Judas is a devil, and his collaboration with the equally demonic Jews buttresses their servile allegiance to the occupying Romans through a deicide. This biblical transmutation means that the speculations of thinkers who doubt Judas's historical identity and whom I mentioned in the first chapter illuminate different Gospels: Frank Kermode's theory—that the betrayal plot required a betrayer—holds true for the earliest Gospel, whereas Hyam Maccoby's and John Shelby Spong's view—that Judas enabled Christians to define themselves against the "Jews as a Judas-nation"—gains credibility with respect to the later Gospels.

Most biblical scholars attribute the increasing vilification of Judas and the Jews to the persecution of Christian communities, specifically to their expulsion from the synagogue during the period when John was writing. Earlier Gospel authors considered themselves Jewish; however, later authors and the communities they addressed would have defined themselves as Christians antagonistic to the non-Christian Jews who, after the devastating defeat of the Jewish-Roman War and the destruction of the Second Temple in 70 C.E., had begun labeling them heretics and harassing them. "The gospels were written in full knowledge of the fact that Jesus' own movement was spreading better among Gentiles than among Jews," E. P. Sanders has explained. "Thus," he continues, "in some ways they de-Judaized the scheme by emphasizing Israel's partial rejection of Jesus and his acceptance by a few Gentiles" (80). More pointedly, Rosemarie Radford Ruether argues that the writers of the New Testament "shift the blame for the deaths of Jesus and his disciples from Roman political authority to Jewish religious authority" (88).[45] To lesser and greater degrees, in other words, the rhetoric of all the Gospel narrators hints that the crucifixion should be blamed on Jews (religious leaders), not Romans (political rulers). With lesser and greater emphases, their authors propose a fundamental division and friction between Jews and Jesus, between the Jewish authorities and the followers of Jesus, even as they hold out the promise of Christians living peacefully among Romans and Gentiles.

Yet Judas's role subverts precisely this authorial intent by making manifest the interconnectedness of Jews who did and did not follow Jesus. The twelfth apostle's participation with Jewish believers in Jesus (the apostles) and his initiative in placing Jesus in the hands of nonbelieving Jews (the chief priests and Pharisees) function as an impediment to or break in the Gospel narrators' overarching message. Regardless of who tells the story and how, the Gospel authors all admit that Jesus was not simply arrested, charged with being "King of the Jews," and killed by either Roman or Jewish authorities. Instead, they all concede that Jesus was doomed by one within his own inner circle, and by doing so they inevitably blur any hard-and-fast distinction between those who accepted Jesus' spiritual authority and those who did not. The betrayal that baffles, bruises, torments, the most shocking and distressing abandonment, comes not from known enemies but from trusted friends or enemies within.

The indistinct boundary between faithful apostle and fugitive apostate reflects the blurry or inchoate division between Jew and Christian in the ancient world: this is what the composite portrait of Judas in the New Testament delineates. He serves as a prototype, therefore, of the scandalous melding or permeability of Judaism and Christianity, the difficulty of disassociating Christianity from its Jewish origins. A go-between, Judas hands over (transmits, gives, delivers) Jesus or information about Jesus' whereabouts (or political mission or religious identity) to the Temple authorities; Judas also mingles with the crowds around Jesus at the parables and the healings, and with Jesus' chosen disciples and traveling companions at intimate meals, teachings, miracles, and rituals. Indeed, he proclaims the message, anoints the sick with oil, heals them, and casts out demons. (Only in John is Judas seen with Roman soldiers, and in this context he does not speak.) An evocative essay titled "Framing Judas," by Kirk T. Hughes, emphasizes how Judas "fits between the priests on the outside, and Jesus and the disciples on the inside," how he "crosses the boundaries" and "crisscrosses back and forth from world to world," weaving between the apostles and the priests (225).

Judas travels recurrently between the small band of those devoted to Jesus and the larger social world regulated by the Temple and its officials, wavering in his allegiances and bound to both groups. He is the hyphen between those who would later be marked Christian and those who would later be designated Jewish. The sense of confusion Judas may rouse in readers of the Gospels illuminates what it might have felt like to be a Jewish Christian or a non-Christian Jew before the two terms became starkly opposed. Judas thus grows ever more alone and anomalous among the disciples, yet he might be said to stand for the throngs of people who first crowd around Jesus in awe and wonder, but soon turn against him in skepticism and anger. Judas's vacillations epitomize those of the multitudes now celebrating, now castigating Jesus in the Gospels. Singular Judas may be among the apostles, but he exemplifies the bafflement of the populace depicted in the New Testament: assemblies of anonymous people who hang on Jesus' every word, bring their infants to be touched, and shout "Hosanna!" but who also mock Jesus, swear false witness against him, call him crazy, spit on him, or cry out for the release of Barabbas rather than Jesus. Like the Jewish crowd around Jesus, Judas becomes increasingly vilified during the succession from Mark and Matthew to Luke and John.[46]

As Saul/Paul does differently, Judas illuminates the intricate fusion of and friction between Judaism and Christianity.[47] John's Jesus knew that "many of his disciples" found his teaching "difficult" to accept (6:60), and one verse of the Johannine letters mentions defectors from Jesus' community: "They went out from us, but they did not belong to us; for if they had belonged to us, they would have remained with us" (1 John 2:19). Julie Galambush attributes "much of the rancor [about the Jews] in John's gospel" to such schisms (279), which also illuminate mounting hostility toward Judas. Difficult though it may be to conceive of Christianity before it became an established religion, in this confused time Judas can be imagined as a sort of everyman, incapable of knowing—or embodying the difficulty of knowing—in whom he should place his trust.

In Roman-controlled Palestine during the intertestamental or Second Temple period, Judaism was an eclectic mix of ordinary peasants unfazed by the heated theological debates of Pharisees, Sadducees, Essenes, the rabbinate, the priesthood, and the Zealots, all of whom disagreed about the meaning of the Torah and the oral Torah, the centrality of the Temple in worship and of fellowship meals, and the proper connection between spiritual and political practices, between humanity and divinity.[48] With diverse definitions and expectations of who the messiah would be and what he would bring about, all these factions disputed with each other, vying to resuscitate the spirit of Exodus—God's covenant with the Jewish people and their liberation from Egypt. Amid such intense and complex disagreements, the sort of indecisions, vacillations, or reversals that characterize Judas's mind frame and actions could not but illustrate the reactions of many, if not most people. It was a chaotic period when, as Matthew's Jesus predicted, "Brother will betray brother to death" (10:21).

An atypical apostle, Judas typifies the society in which Jesus first lived and then the communities in which Jesus' story was prized and preserved. Up until the end of the fourth century, Daniel Boyarin has argued,

> Judaism and Christianity were phenomenologically indistinguishable entities, not merely in the conventionally accepted sense, that Christianity was a Judaism, but also in the sense that differences that were in the fullness of time to constitute the very basis for the distinction between the "two religions" ran through and not

between the nascent groups of Jesus-following Jews and Jews who did not follow Jesus. (89)

He goes on to explain: "there were non-Christian Jews who believed in God's Word, Wisdom, or even Son as a 'second God,' while there were believers in Jesus who insisted that the three persons of the Trinity were only names for different manifestations of one person" (90). Boyarin calls these "differences *within*" and distinguishes them from subsequent "differences *between*" (90). When Judas is viewed as "one of us," we can see the differences *within* a complex community of Christian and non-Christian Jews; when Judas is viewed as "one of them," we glimpse the differences *between* Christians and Jews.

What does it mean that the more historically accurate and benign account of Judas, in the earliest Gospel, was to be the least influential? Maligned, neglected, or marginalized until the mid-twentieth century, the Gospel of Mark was superseded by all the others, while the highly influential Gospel of John fueled anti-Semitic theology and artistry for two thousand years. Only in John's version does Judas not partake of the sacrament at the Last Supper that conveys to him in the synoptic Gospels the body and blood of Jesus.[49] According to John (and only John), Judas is definitively denied the resurrection Jesus promises; for, as John's Jesus explains, "Those who eat my flesh and drink my blood have eternal life, and I will raise them up on the last day" (6:54). Giotto's *Pact of Judas,* on the side of the chancel arch in Padua (ca. 1303–05; plate 2), encapsulates the fate he would encounter in the premodern period, in large part because of Luke and John.

Unlike the long-bearded and white-haired conniving patriarchs of the Temple, Giotto's yellow-robed and red-headed Judas evinces the youthfulness and perhaps some of the ardor or intensity of Jesus' other apostles; however, he also exhibits the squeezed-in forehead and long, slanting nose that were conventionally attributed to Jews (Barasch, *Giotto* 160–61). As in the ivory plaque, the Stuttgart Psalter, and the Volterra pulpit, his appearance in profile emphasizes his two-faced infamy. Behind his back and also profiled, a satanic creature with a dog's or wolf's head lurks to claim him for the devil. Giotto has departed from tradition, for "here the money has already been exchanged," the "pact has been sealed," and thus the devil's placement of his hands on Judas's shoulder "is a legal gesture signifying confirmation of an offer" (Derbes and Sandona 279).[50] Probably the dark blotch above Judas's head derives from discoloration, but it casts a sinister aura over him. The twinning of the demon behind him and Caiaphas before him—Satan and the Jewish priest—sandwiches a Judas doomed to do the devil's bidding, especially in antiquity and the Middle Ages.

Yet even the moment of bribery depicted by Giotto could be thought to invoke the betrayer's betrayal, for the money bag he clutches in his left hand might bring to mind Matthew's insistence that Judas later flung it back at its original owners. Not only is Judas outnumbered, but all the conspiring hands that Giotto portrays point toward Judas, fingering him as the fall guy. And even the harshest book in the New Testament can be used to explain why Judas could be understood to have been unfairly used as an instrument of forces beyond his control. For instance, when John's Jesus explains to Pilate, "You would have no power over me unless it had been given you from above," might not John be intimating that Judas "would have no power over" Jesus either, "unless it had been given [him] from above"? Or earlier in John's Gospel, at the meal Jesus shares with his disciples, what does it mean that Satan enters Judas after he receives bread from Jesus' hand? Might not John—whose Jesus had earlier proclaimed, "I am the living bread" (6:51)—be suggesting here that Jesus provides the yeast to leaven (or the fuel to feed) Satan's vigorous advance into Judas? Read in this way, as a sort of anti- and ante-Eucharist devised by a complicit Jesus, some of the illustrations of Jesus offering the sop to Judas in the next chapter might be thought to connect the hand of Jesus with the mouth of Judas, for John's Jesus does advise Judas, "What you are going to do, do quickly" (14:28).

These interpretive possibilities are, of course, what make the New Testament so compelling to the many book illustrators, painters, musicians, and creative writers whose works later reinvented a figure who gained in charisma from a number of doubles and foils in the Hebrew Bible—especially Cain, who murdered his brother Abel, and the patriarch Judah, who sold his brother Joseph into slavery—for Judas even in the ancient texts can be construed as Jesus' treacherous sibling or relative. Indeed, in the New Testament Jesus does have a brother named Judas (not Iscariot), and the names Jesus and Judas seem to echo each other. Still, such analogies and evocations ultimately fail to convey the magnetism of an apostate apostle whose perplexity dramatizes the confusion Jesus' ministry must inevitably have spawned and whose propinquity served as a catalyst of crucifixion and also therefore of resurrection.

The title of this chapter derives from Marina Warner's study of the virgin mother, *Alone of All Her Sex*. My allusion has been used to argue that Judas—presented as growing more nefarious and isolated from the other disciples in the later Gospels—actually exemplifies the confused reactions Jesus encountered from most people in Jerusalem. It is also meant to suggest that in the earlier Gospels Judas somewhat surprisingly resembles Mary not only in singularity but also in the act of delivering God's son. Pointing to his twelve disciples, Matthew's Jesus proclaimed them not only his "brothers" but also his "mother" (12:49), thereby drawing attention to the fact that the Greek word for "betrayal" could be translated with the phrase *give over* as well as with the word *deliver*. "I am the first that betrayed him," Robinson Jeffers's Mary declares in the early twentieth century, when she ponders the inexorable connection between the womb and the tomb.[51] "The mothers, we do it" (47), she adds, referring to children brought into the world only to be made hostages to fortune. When in a contemporary work Jamaica Kincaid's protagonist Lucy has to separate herself from a confining past, she associates its limitations with the betrayals of her mother, a mother she calls "Mrs. Judas" (130).

Numerous medieval stained-glass windows and manuscript illuminations depict Mary embracing and kissing Jesus, as Judas does in Mark and Matthew. Like Mary at the Annunciation, Judas registers the shock of the new messianic being born in the New Testament. In one *Daily Missal of the Mystical Body*, worshippers are informed about the link between Mary and Judas: "Among those closest to our Lord were many who loved and served Him sincerely and devotedly. But there was one, a thief, who became a betrayer of his indulgent Master. Both the anointing by Mary and the treachery of Judas prepared for the holocaust of God's Son, a holocaust that was to merit the grace for every act of love and for every forgiveness of sin" (303). Without the labors of Mary and Judas, Jesus could never have become Christ. But whereas Mary's name exonerated women from the curse incurred by humanity's first mother, Judas's branded a demonized race accused of precisely the carnality Eve was thought to embody.

Complex as Judas's trajectory would be, he began his hectic career by incarnating evil. When in the premodern period Judas disowns allegiance where it is most owed, the vulnerability or frailty of trust underscores Jesus' generous magnanimity. What would have to be repressed in the ancient pariah Judas were all those contrary attributes or circumstances that would later surface to exonerate or differently excoriate his name.

PART II

EVOLVING INCARNATIONS

3

DAMNED MISCEGENATION: A FIENDISH ADOLESCENCE FROM ANTIQUITY ON

During premodern times, Judas became a physical and moral monster whose punishments fit his abominable crimes. While the church established its theological doctrines and emergent capitalism its commercial enterprises, Judas personified racist folklore about the anal and oral degeneracy of Jews. Yet popular legends, ballads, and plays in the Middle Ages frequently translate his damnation and despair into an Oedipal doom that begins to grant Judas a human dimension.

WERE IT NOT FOR the prospect of an ungainly table of contents, the subtitle of this chapter would take an antiquated form: "wherein Judas acquires a series of bodily ailments (replete with very decided odors), a mother and a father, a wife and a sister, as he travels far and wide throughout various mythic realms, exhibiting a proclivity for crimes that range from cannibalism to incest and patricide, while intermittently submitting to the fate befitting his fiendish adolescence." During the establishment of the early and the later church, Judas goes through a fiendish stage in his historical development. From antiquity on, a number of stories and images circulated to fill in the biographical blanks in the Gospels' account of Judas's life and death or to resolve their multiple paradoxes. Two related portraits— one of a demoniac Judas and one of a doomed Judas—emerge from the meditations, paintings, narratives, and plays that survive as elaborations on or illuminations of the New Testament. I have organized this chapter in an episodic sequence around diverse incarnations of the demoniac and then the doomed Judas, although in fact they circulated simultaneously. Such a picaresque approach suits the Gothic plots in which Judas finds himself embroiled, and does so without unifying, homogenizing, or flattening his diverse features.[1]

Of course, the chapter title I did choose suggests that there is one enduring feature in all the early manifestations of Judas: namely, his association with the devil and with a diabolical confusion of orders that ought to be kept quite distinct. In the Gospels, chapter 2 proposed, Judas typifies the complex fusion of Judaism and Christianity. Afterward, Judas confuses a number of primary categories. Specifically, he blurs or crisscrosses traditional divisions between the living and the dead, and between human beings and satanic or animal species, as well as distinctions between male and female bodies, between fraternal and aggressive as well as filial and sexual activities. Because of this outrageous amalgamating of domains, Judas had to be and was repeatedly excoriated. The process actually occurred in reverse order: in order to revile Judas, he was made to embody a chaotic, indecent hodgepodge of the living dead, the human-animal, the hermaphroditic, the incestuous. Viewed from either perspective, Judas functioned as a warning against miscegenation—a perpetually tortured bogeyman deployed to police the borders of Christendom.

"He must be wicked to deserve such pain": this resonant line captures Judas's development in post-Gospel cultures.[2] For early Christians, the terrifying contradiction between the redemptive grace of God (available to all), on the one hand, and, on the other, Judas's ordained role and fate in the Passion could be dealt with by proving the twelfth apostle absolutely irredeemable. The unnerving logic of Augustine's intuition that "Delivering up was done by the Father, delivering up was done by the Son, delivering up was done by Judas" had to be rigorously countered by his assertion that "one act should be loved, the other condemned": "we bless the Father, we detest Judas," Augustine insisted; "We bless love, we detest iniquity" (*Tractates* 222). To bless the Father, to absolve God of blame for the crucifixion, Judas was assigned culpability.[3] Many thinkers repressed the fearful idea that Judas advanced the Passion without attaining salvation by divorcing him from the eleven and arguing that he had never eaten the bread or drunk the wine at the Last Supper, or that he had never had his feet washed by Jesus.[4] Luther, predictably, was harshest in wrapping him in treachery: "Every Abel has his Cain; every Isaac, his Ishmael; every Jacob, his Esau; and Christ, His Judas, who was against his soul, especially in those things which pertain to the soul, namely, faith and righteousness" (*Selected Pslams* 197). Premodern thinkers and artists visualized the antispiritual inequity of a fully and foully embodied Judas by dwelling on the images most viscerally prominent in the New Testament: lips that kissed to kill or opened to eat the sop, bowels that gushed and soiled.

Judas's bodily orifices fascinated the ancient and medieval imagination. Related to the porous "Judas ear" (the common name for a mushroom once thought to poison the tree upon which it grows), oral and anal or intestinal cavities link the permeable borders of the body with Judas's violation of normative boundaries. As Christianity grew from a marginal Middle Eastern cult to the official religion of the West, the physical and moral monstrosity of Judas polluted church and state precincts that had to be patrolled against the shameful sinners he exemplified: impious foreigners, heretics, and usurers. To his orality (eating the bread, kissing to kill) and his anality (bursting bowels) are attributed transgressions that justly earn reprisals. During a period when most people did not read the Bible but instead watched biblical pageants or heard sermons or often-recounted biblical legends and ballads, a biting, exuding, or excreting Judas functioned as an admonition against heretical religious and economic practices that were irresistibly proliferating in premodern societies. The only unclean apostle also served as an emblem of Jewry.

In an early linkage of Judas with the Jews, Pope Gelasius I (492–496), who argued that "the whole is often named from the part," asserted that "Judas, concerning whom it was said: 'One of you is a devil' [John 6:70] for he was the devil's workman, without any doubt gives his name to all the race" (Synan 32). Even earlier, Saint Jerome had explained that "Judas is cursed, that in Judas the Jews may be accursed" (262); and by the eleventh century, a Benedictine monk named Othlon de Satin-Emeran was alleging that the crimes of Judas "extend to the entire Jewish people" (Nirenberg 62). Not surprisingly, then, Judas quickly came to stand for an entire people who were condemned by association. According to the medieval historian Lester K. Little, "All of the standard forms of dress for identifying a Jew were applied to Judas, while at the same time he absorbed the attributes of avarice as well" (53). Excavated medieval toys, in the form of tiny figurines with pointed Jewish hats, have recently been featured in museum catalogues as probable replicas of Judas Iscariot. Jews forced by Christian mandates into the role of moneylenders were thereby required to reenact Judas's role and assumed to be treacherous keepers of the purse (see Forsyth and Egan 142).

Between 1215 and 1434, the church enforced systematic segregation through laws prohibiting Jews from participating in most employment and social activities and through shameful uniforms: conical hats and yellow circular badges. Jews were expelled from England and southern Italy in 1290, from France in 1306 and again in 1394, from most of Germany by 1350, from Spain in 1492, and from Portugal in 1497 (Langmuir 303). Through elaborations on selected details in the Gospels and suppression of others, the charges against Jews as Christ-killers and usurers could be combined in the figure of Judas, who was demonized and thus enlisted as an instrument to punish the people he was said to typify. Although unspecified in three of the Gospels, the sum that Matthew marked as patently insufficient accrued in value to emblematize Judas's greed, which was conflated sometimes with his filthy, smelly anality, sometimes with his voracious, vicious orality. In addition, we will see that his figure reflected the rampant anti-Semitism that produced accusations of Jewish pestilence, animality, assaults on the consecrated host, and ritual murder, charges that, though discredited by twentieth-century historians, resulted in the recurrent torture and slaughter of Jewish men and women.

Extant early texts about Judas were recycled in various popular forms, and their subsequent pictorial elaborations buttressed prevailing stereotypes that explain the actual fate of Jewish people: "By the end of the Middles Ages," Rosemary Radford Ruether has succinctly declared, "Western Jewry was ruined" (213). Ghettoization, routine massacres, and expulsion were the historical backdrop for the demonization of Judas. Might these ruinations express a series of crises in Christianity, recurrent attempts to stifle doubts about rituals and controversies about dogma that also took the form of multiple heresies in this period?[5] A definitive answer to such a complex question remains elusive, but even a speculative "yes" cannot fully account for what Judas does and who he becomes during premodern times, when a macabre magnetism was added to his character.

In the absence of real Jews, or at least inside the dream of a Jew-free world, a Christian-authored Judas-Jew incarnates what everyone loves to hate: Luke's Satanic "traitor" (6:16), John's devilish "son of perdition" (17:12). At and after the start of his postbiblical career, the relish with which he was denounced lends the Judas-Jew a kind of antic energy as he progresses (in a nonnormative fashion) from the anal and the oral to the genital phases of development. Indeed, perhaps the gusto with which the pariah was damned led to the emergence of some awareness that Judas may have been destined to play (or manipulated into playing) the role of designated villain. For whatever reason, in due course the demoniac Judas pops up as doomed or duped in literary texts that draw on the Oedipus story in such a manner as to grapple with the fearful fate of an individual trapped inside a preordained script. Whether damned by his revolting body (his dirty bowels, his greedy maw) or doomed by sexual rapacity (his phallic crimes), however, the scapegoat Judas had to be disavowed, for otherwise his miserable fate might cast suspicion on the mercy of God and God's Son. Through Judas, we will see (as we travel into the bowels of Judas's hell and the hell of Judas's bowels), Jews are assigned an unredeemable carnality that exculpates or absolves more spiritual Christians.

FILTHY ENDS

Given the conflicting accounts in the Gospels of Judas's demise, how exactly did he deteriorate before his end? In antiquity, this question claims the attention of authors intent on dramatizing Judas's allegiance to the devil. Early stories about the twelfth apostle conflate his moral degeneracy with his physical degeneration. Although it might seem counterintuitive to begin with Judas's ends—the end of his life and the end of his alimentary canal—many of the early accounts focused obsessively on his fetid dying. Whether commentators followed Luke, by showing Judas's bowels bursting, or Matthew, by depicting him hanging on a tree, they emphasized stinky deformity, bloating, exploding excrement, bloody intestines, and hemorrhages. Curiously feminized by all these bodily outpourings, in poems and in paintings a leaky Judas frequently holds a sack that presumably contains the thirty pieces of silver. Given his physical seepages, though, it begins to look weirdly like a uterus or a colostomy bag. What Judas had nefariously hugged or hoarded to himself during his life—his own self-interests and conspiratorial thoughts, the money from the Temple authorities—disgorges as he loses control over everything, even his own innards. In a classic instance of poetic justice (to which Albert Tucker's portrait also alludes), the thief who secretly concealed, connived, and coveted is flagrantly and filthily turned inside out.

A fragmentary account by Papias, an early leader of the Christian church who wrote around 130 C.E., elaborates on the demonic possession of Judas, even as it illuminates an emerging cultural consensus about the pathological effects of Judas's iniquity on his body.[6] Papias's *Exposition of the Lord's Sayings*—which survived only in part, through subsequent quotation—enlarges on Luke's description of Judas's self-bursting in the Field of Blood:

> Judas was a dreadful, walking example of impiety in this world, with his flesh bloated to such an extent that he could not walk through a space where a wagon could easily pass. Not even the huge bulk of his head could go through! It is related that his eyelids were so swollen that it was absolutely impossible for him to see the light and his eyes could not be seen by a physician, even with the help of a magnifying glass, so far had they sunk from their outward projection. His private parts were shamefully huge and loathsome to behold and, transported through them from all parts of his body, pus and worms flooded out together as he shamefully relieved himself. He died after many tortures and punishments, in a secluded spot which has remained deserted and uninhabited up to our time. Not even to this day can anybody pass by the place without shielding his nostrils with his hands! Such is the afflux that goes through his flesh [and even pours] out on the ground. (Ehrman, *Apostolic Fathers* 105, 107)

Papias translates Judas's spiritual blindness into actual blindness, both his inability to see and other people's inability to perceive his organs of perception. If seeing is believing, blindness signifies apostasy. As Papias literalizes thickheaded solipsism, the afflictions of a humongous Judas recall a passage from Isaiah loosely quoted by John to debunk the Jews who refused to believe in Jesus, despite all the signs he performed: "He has blinded their eyes / and hardened their heart, / so that they might not look with their eyes / and understand with their heart" (12:40; see Isaiah 6:10). Not darkened (as he is at times in paintings), Judas is nevertheless in the dark.

Since Luke's Judas "burst open in the middle and all his bowels gushed out" (Acts 1:16–20), toward the end of his life he must have blown up like a blimp before popping. Papias emphasizes the swelling that presumably occurred before the spontaneous explosion. Having grown larger than a cart and thus eventually having been immobilized, flabby Judas—drenched in his own effluvia—sprouts enlarged genitals. Yet unlike the Greek god Priapus, who is endowed with a huge erection, Judas gains no phallic potency. Instead, a bad case of erectile dysfunction renders him pestilent, contaminated with a contagious malady and thus pernicious. His extremities bloated by a disease (which Victorian interpreters diagnosed as elephantiasis),[7] he anticipates "parallels in the development of the persecution of heretics, Jews and lepers" in the Middle Ages (R. Moore 66). During medieval times, the phrase *mal de Judas*, which signified measles, reflects the perceived sickness of Jews (Hand, *Dictionary* 354). While alive, Papias's Judas is dead matter, his body carrion for the pus and worms he emits. An obese corpse before his death, Judas probably cannot be resurrected. Since he dies on his own property, he obviously has not repented by returning the money to the scribes, as in Matthew. Because of his swelling and smelling and relieving himself, the land he purchased is laid waste by his stinking remains. The uncanny echo of his inability to pass through space and the incapacity of anyone else to pass by his place hints that there is no exit for Judas or those who stray into his malodorous domain.[8]

Even early commentators and artists who relied on Matthew's account of Judas's suicide tended, like Papias, to enlarge on the stench of Judas's swelling flesh. Many extrabiblical legends combined Matthew with Luke by having Judas hanging *and* exploding with bloody, wormlike intestines.[9] Jerome's Latin translation of the Greek Bible in the late fourth century allowed them to do so: Jerome blended Matthew's and Luke's accounts of Judas's death by changing Luke's Judas "falling headlong" into Judas "hanging" before he burst open.[10] As a cautionary lesson about heresy, usury, and avarice, Judas's end— when Matthew was harmonized with Luke and the explosion combined with the hanging—reflected prevailing ideas about suicide not just as a grievous spiritual wrong of despairing of God's grace, but also as a divine punishment for evil. From antiquity through the Middle Ages, the suicide of Judas was considered a dire but appropriate retribution for a bad conscience as well as a signature of the devil's influence. According to Jerome, "Judas offended the Lord more by hanging himself than by betraying Him," for "His prayer should have been repentance, but it turned into sin" (259). Not a sign of contrition, suicide was believed to resemble homicide in its compounding of guilt.[11]

According to Augustine, too, "Judas by hanging himself heightened rather than expiated that crime of dastardly betrayal—because by despairing of God's mercy he abandoned himself to an impenitent remorse and left no room in his soul for saving sorrow" (*City of God* 46). In the fourteenth century, Heinrich der Teichner's didactic poem "On Human Despair" argued that "Judas [who] received the body of God from God himself was damned"; therefore "Those who despaired had no more chance of seats in Heaven than those spirits whom Lucifer loaded with despair and dragged down with him," for "God still maintains this principle: he will not accept those who despair" (Ohly 38). Similarly, in the sixteenth century John Calvin declared that "Judas was touched with repentance" but did not reform; instead, he was plunged "into despair, that he might be an example of a man banned from the grace of God" (175). An allegorical personification of despair, Judas was thought to have "confessed his sin, [but] he did not hope for pardon and therefore did not obtain mercy" (Voragine 77). From the medieval perspective, then, the ancient ivory casket discussed in the previous chapter (illustration 2.2) does not establish any parallelism between Jesus and Judas, but instead contrasts the hanging Judas as "the symbol of total despair" against the crucified Jesus as "the symbol of hope for ultimate salvation" (Barasch, "Despair" 569). The so-called sin of Judas was the sin of suicide, the sin of despair. "Despair," the literary historian Lee Patterson reminds us, "is, after all, the inability to repent—the inability, that is, to change: the man in despair cannot get rid of the self of illicit desires in order to assume the reborn self of innocence" (414).[12]

As the laity saw it, the desolate Judas killed himself *and* his bowels

burst out: the exploding bowels were the climax of the suicidal hanging. In Germany, the actor playing Judas in the Passion plays was
stuffed, along with sheep intestines and a live blackbird, into a cow-
hide costume so that the guts and the bird would belch out during the
popular hanging scene (Weber 182). Innumerable stone carvings on
medieval church façades throughout Europe portray the rope around
Judas's throat and the ropes of his bulging intestines as he hangs
suspended between heaven and earth, his broken neck strangling his
own breath, his innards polluting his own corpse. One architectural
frieze, on the thirteenth-century Münster church in Freiburg, displays
a hanging Judas with his wormlike bowels spilling out, while silver
coins slip out of his hand. Since Matthew's Judas flings the money
back and Luke's uses it to buy the Field of Blood, "the money at the
moment of death contradicts the Gospel accounts" (Weber 168) to
affix him with the sin of avarice.[13] Devils—in the Münster church,
two of them carry off Judas's damned soul—appear in many depictions of the hanging Judas with his spilling bowels. Sometimes, as on
the stonework of Autun Cathedral, one of France's national monu-
ments, gaping devils engaged in what looks to be a sort of tug-of-war
pull at each end of the rope looped around the naked Judas's neck.

In the Church of Saint-Sébastien de Névache, a devil extracts a
baby-Judas from a Judas hanging with his intestines pouring over
his robe (ca. 1530; illustration 3.1). The horror of Judas's bowels
gushing out apparently has less to do with their visibility than with
the degradation of spontaneous eruption, for one biblical character named Razis certifies his heroism by falling upon his sword and
then tearing out his entrails, hurling them at a crowd of witnesses as
he calls on the Lord to return them (2 Maccabees 14:41–45). Antithetically, Judas, as in Acts, involuntarily witnesses his own corporeal explosion, experiencing a deserved torment without the hope
of bodily transfiguration. But what about the baby almost fully
emerged from his chest cavity? In other contexts, the infant often
functions as a symbol of innocence; sometimes in death scenes depicting the eternal judgment of souls, the infant soul is exhaled through

3.1. The death of
Judas, Church of
Saint-Sébastien
de Névache (ca.
1530). Courtesy
François Darbois.

the lips and associated with the spirit of life.[14] Not blown out from
the down-turned mouth of the swinging corpse in the Church of
Saint-Sébastian, Judas's eternal psyche is instead abdominally excised
from the inert, dead weight of his mortal remains. Disemboweled
and bloody, a dying or dead body, sightless, Judas confirms Steven F.
Kruger's point that in Christian medieval polemics "we find Jews
depicted as excessively corporeal and concomitantly less spiritual
than their Christian counterparts" (*Spectral Jews* xxiv). An energetic
demon grasps the left arm of Judas's emerging spiritual afterlife, the
demon's doppelgänger.

Why did Judas deserve a double dying, with the hanging noose
replicating the tangled cords of his exploding intestines or bowels? In
the twelfth century, Petrus Comestor argued in his *Historia Scholas-*

tica that first Judas hanged himself, then his bowels burst because his noxious soul could not leave a mouth that had kissed Jesus:

> For he was not worthy of touching the heavens or the earth; but he perished between them, because he had betrayed the Lord of both. . . . And his intestines were spilled, but not through his mouth, in order to spare the mouth with which he had kissed the Saviour. (quoted in Weber 169)

Others believed that Judas burst after the suicide attempt was unsuccessful "either because the rope broke . . . or because the Devil bent down the branch . . . or because . . . the trees themselves refused to take him" (Braswell 305).[15] Unburied, the hanged man might bring to mind the church's denial of Christian burial to usurers (in 1179) and suicides (ca. 1240). The Church of Saint-Sébastien's Judas has a halo, but its dark hue reflects his damnation as he swings—twice killed between the domains of earth and sky, as befits his mixed-up character—off a gibbet variously assumed to be a fig (which bows down), an elder (which bears bitter fruit), or an aspen (which quivers).[16]

A number of the characteristics attributed by Papias and later visual artists to an eviscerated Judas forecast or reflect anti-Semitic features often ascribed to stereotyped Jews. Certainly his wanderings and hangings typify the rootless, peripatetic Jew: nomadic or ungrounded, Judas is an outcast like the fratricidal Cain, whose sins cannot be pardoned and who pledged allegiance to no civic authority.[17] Just as Cain is contaminated by the blood of his brother crying from the ground, some translate the "pus" of Papias's account into "blood" flowing all over the body of Judas in the Field of Blood, as it does over the hanging Judas.[18] The bloodstains bring to mind Matthew's Jews ("His blood be upon us and on our children" [27:25]) and also, in medieval times, the red hair, hat, or beard that were used to represent Jews on stained-glass windows and on stage. A founding member of the red-headed league of Jews in Western painting and

literature, Judas in the Field of Blood—with his often ruddy or freck-
led complexion—presumably smells as well because of his physical
decomposition before and after death.

Throughout the medieval period, Lester Little has shown, the
correlation of Jews and filth "places Jews in the company of that
foul-smelling creature, the devil": "At a critical moment when a converted Jew was baptized, that is, when he abandoned his allegiance
to the devil and became a servant of Christ, he was thought to lose
his foul smell in the purifying waters of baptism" (53). By 1646 Sir
Thomas Browne reproved the widespread "received opinion" that
"Jews stinck naturally" (201): such an assumption may be related
to an emphasis on Judas as decomposing carrion before and after a
death that makes the Field of Blood uninhabitable, his flesh emitting
the *foetor Judaicus* or Jewish stench.[19] A character in Shakespeare's
The Winter's Tale (ca. 1608–12) offers as an established fact that he
who "did betray the Best" emanates the stink of mortality, "a savour
that may strike the dullest nostril" and was "shunn'd, / Nay, hated
too, worse than the great'st infection / That e'er was heard or read"
(1.2.419, 421, 423–25).

The rank-smelling "afflux" flowing from Judas's flesh also relates
to another curious medieval belief, namely that Jewish men menstru-
ated. According to Joshua Trachtenberg, Jews in the Middle Ages
were believed by Christians to suffer all sorts of leaky troubles: most
often mentioned was "menstruation, which the men as well as the
women among the Jews were supposed to experience; close seconds,
in point of frequency of mention, were copious hemorrhages and hemorrhoids (all involving loss of blood)" (50).[20] With his huge genitals,
Papias's Judas seems grotesquely male; however, his bloated, bloody,
and smelly body also calls to mind taboos against menstruating
women. Similarly, his worm-encrusted torso recalls Eve, allied with
the crafty serpent, as well as Medusa with her snaky ringlets. A place
of gender anarchy for the living dead, the Field of Blood with its Jewish stink constituted a sexual and ecological wasteland.[21] Emblematic
of sexual misrule, the Church of Saint-Sébastien's Judas—giving birth

to an infant Judas-soul—is figuratively a man hung in the throes of a posthumous childbearing. A demonic afterlife springs from a dead man who himself brings to mind a stillborn, since the rope wrapped around hanging Judas looks like a strangling umbilical cord.

On an Alsatian painted-glass panel, a hanging Judas (without a halo) actually undergoes a sort of caesarean section, further affirming his unnatural transgendering. A speckled and bat-winged devil acts as midwife, extracting his soul (1520–30; plate 3).[22] Both these hanging Judases display lowered eyes, embodiments of the belief that heretics die with downcast eyes in the sorrowful realization that they can never rise to heaven.[23] A satanic creature receives the soul of Judas, reflecting the view that God did not create him; the devil did, and so to the devil he ought to be consigned.[24] Emerging from a slit in Judas's side, the Judas-soul on the Alsatian panel recalls both Eve, created out of Adam's spare rib, and also an iconographic tradition that depicted the Antichrist's caesarean birth, where devils act as midwives or attendants.[25] With the psyche of Judas springing up just above the area of his genitals, the image also calls to mind Freud's notion of the baby as phallus (or more homely designations of the penis as a "little man"). The taut and serpentine tongue of a spotted Satan (possibly afflicted with the *mal de Judas*) as well as his kneeling posture, the baby ejaculated out of the incised male belly: what might Satan's act of oral stimulation have meant to the early modern artist or viewer? Caught in the act of diving, the baby looks properly filled with consternation about the fate awaiting him. With laboring Judas in limbo, obstetrical devils midwife a soul rightly delivered into their eternal possession.

Gender anarchy may be precisely the idea Giotto sought to convey when, on either side of the chancel arch in the Arena Chapel, he juxtaposed his *Pact of Judas* (see plate 2) to the *Visitation*'s depiction of the meeting of Mary and Elizabeth, both pregnant. According to two art theorists, not only do the frescoes' settings, figures, and colors draw attention to the pairing, but "even the placement of Judas's money bag, at his abdomen, seems to echo the pregnancy of the women in the *Visitation"* (Derbes and Sandona 279). Judas is cast "in the female role" because "the plot has been conceived, but in a sense, Judas himself has also conceived, as Mary and Elizabeth have," which is why later "Judas's belly splits open in a grim inversion of childbirth, the inevitable result of the sinister conception shown on the chancel wall" (280). In the context of a child-birthing (and thus feminized) Judas, it is significant that the yellow of Judas's traditional garb is a color he shares with prostitutes.[26]

From Aristotle to Aquinas, philosophers and ethicists touted the natural and spiritual benefits of fecundity, fertility, and biological reproduction over and against the unnatural and sterile breeding of coins, and many preachers judged usurers as guilty as sodomites and prostitutes—which was why moneylending was relegated to Jews, forced to reenact Judas's role as treasurer.[27] In the Last Judgment depicted in Giotto's fresco in the Arena Chapel, the damned hang suspended by the strings of money bags tied around their necks, while a pregnant Satan displays his bloated belly as he gives birth to a monstrous sinner. This image seems to illustrate Judas's fate in *Meditations on the Life of Christ,* a popular biography dating from the end of the thirteenth century whose narrator intones, "Woe to you, wretch, hard-hearted one! What you have conceived, you will bear" (313).

The bag near the abdomen of Giotto's Judas and the hanging Judas's protruding bowels or psyche as placenta, abortion, fetus, or miscarriage signify more than the sterile breeding of money, however. They evoke early modern ideas about usury as blood money, as do Judas's swelling and smelling: parasitic, the usurer who bleeds people of their money is equivalent to the one who made money by spilling Christ's blood. The ill-gotten gains of blood money besmirch its holder most graphically in Valentin Lendenstreich's *Christ on the Mount of Olives,* part of the Wüllersleben Triptych (1503; illustration 3.2). The artist has created a sort of composite of Jesus praying in Gethsemane with his sleeping apostles (all with halos in the foreground), while a yellow-robed, red-headed Judas approaches from the

3.2. Valentin
Lendenstreich,
*Christ on the Mount
of Olives*, part of
the Wüllersleben
Triptych (1503).
Source: Toledo
Museum of Art.

background, leading the soldiers with their lanterns, flags, and spears. Tightly hugging himself, Judas does not gaze at Jesus but instead is shown in three-quarter profile, looking away, as if he shirks recognition of the direction he is taking. Just as the position of his arms might bring to mind a straitjacket, his turned-away face speaks less of the duplicity of the two-faced profile than of the divided consciousness of a madman. In his crossed left hand, he holds the white money pouch with a red drawstring. Ruth Mellinkoff has pointed out how uncommon the red paint on the third finger of Judas's blood-tainted finger appears (*Outcasts* 52). Blood stains the hands that handed over Jesus for thirty coins. The bleeding bag of money appears, here and in many other paintings, dangling very close to Judas's waist, stomach, or intestines. As in depictions of his evisceration, blood and guts, feces and hemorrhoids apparently adhere to Judas's currency.

When not full of blood money, the pouch of a constipated and then evacuating Judas symbolizes filthy lucre, which ends up besmirching (rather than enhancing or enriching) its erupting owner.[28] Around the mid-thirteenth century, the Anglo-Norman author Walter of Wimborne wrote a poem protesting a rising commercial economy for which Judas was taken as the entrepreneurial role model. "Of Simony and Avarice" dwells on Judas's betrayal of Jesus in exchange for "wretched coin," connected in the following section of the verse with entrails, lawlessness, and poison:

> The traitor lives again who once rattled,
> By which excrement Judea was soiled;
> Having been scattered, the venom and entrails are entangled again
> That previously polluted the worthless world.
>
> The unhappy traitor, who previously was wretched
> Discards the burden of the bag of entrails,
> It scatters that uncleanness which it swallows down again,
> And in turn it discharges the destructive poison.
>
> Being born again, the traitor captures the poison
> And the rank burden which he once scattered;
> Nevertheless, the most recent bile overcomes the first bile,
> The poison that thrusts in is worse than the poison it discharges.
>
> Reviving, the traitor resumes his impiety
> Impiously and more venally;
> Now however he discharges copious poison
> That now has been scattered widely and harmfully.[29]

The phrase "bag of entrails" and the idea that venom, excrement, and poison were scattered and then entangled again, swallowed and then discharged, connect usury in particular and commerce in general

3.3. The Master of the Housebook, *Last Supper*, panel from the Speyer Altar (ca. 1480–85). Source: Art Resource. © Alinari/ Bildarchiv Preussischer Kulturbesitz/Art Resource, New York.

with Judas's gushing body, with the ill-gained money he first hoarded, then expelled.

Often the money bag dangling from the hands or belts of early Judas figures becomes a symbol of his bowels, entrails, or feces. In a painting of the Last Supper, a panel from the Speyer Altar by the Master of the Housebook (ca. 1480–85; illustration 3.3), a hook-nosed Judas—seated on the wrong side of the table—attempts to hide his shameful poop-pouch behind his back, where it hangs down like a dropping near a basket on which sits an insect, a sign of waste, stink, pollution. All the other diners resemble the apostles described in Jacques Prévert's witty poem "The Last Supper":

> They are at table
> They eat not
> Nor touch their plates
> And their plates stand straight up
> Behind their heads.

Only Judas has no halo. The right hand of the Master of the House-book's Judas strokes the left in a masturbatory gesture of self-absorption (very much related to his turning away from the table) that contrasts with the prayerful hands of the other apostles. The full face of Jesus stands out against the profile of Judas, which, as is often the case, signifies a duplicity that allows the painter to connect his chin with his nose so as to evoke a witch or sorcerer.[30] More didactic than the Master of the Housebook, Walter of Wimborne argues in "Of Simony and Avarice" that whereas in biblical times Judas polluted Judea, in the poet's own day his entrepreneurial offspring defile the whole world, for "Christ is sold every day" by merchants dedicated to "foolish commerce."

To one of the few critics who have studied Walter of Wimborne's "Of Simony and Avarice," the feces of Judas resembles "a *virus,* a slimy, stinking liquid poison, that infected first the homeland (*patria*) and then the Church (*ecclesia*) with avarice" (Nirenberg 62). Judas's diarrhea or dysentery can be comprehended by juxtaposing it to the putrid odors emitted by crooked statesmen:

> Of old, when Judas died by hanging,
> the flow from his guts polluted Judah.
> Today, an effusion of shit more fetid stinks
> than the smell of a sufferer from the king's disease.[31]

The "king's disease," a virus thought to afflict corrupt rulers as a punishment sent by God, connects the dishonest monarch with lepers and Jews (Nirenberg 60). But it was specifically Jews whose filth directly threatened the icons of Christian piety. As R. I. Moore has pointed out, "In the middle of the twelfth century Peter the Venerable, abbot of Cluny, warned King Louis VII that Jews would subject sacred vessels which came into their hands to disgusting and unmentionable indignities, and a hundred years later Matthew Paris produced his tale that Abraham of Berkhampstead used his privy as a place of storage for a picture of the Virgin and Child lodged with him as security" (38–39).

A strange quotation at the start of this book can now be contextualized. As I mentioned in the introduction, the only way Martin Luther could comprehend Jewish interpreters of the Bible was to "think that when Judas Sharioth hanged himself, his intestines burst, and, as it happens to the hanged, his bladder burst: perhaps the Jews had their servants there with gold and silver jugs and basins which caught the Judas-piss (as it is called) together with the rest of the holy things, thereafter they mixed it into the excrement and ate it among each other and drank it so that they developed such sharp eyes" (Luther, *Vom Schem Hamphoras* 214).[32] Composed in the sixteenth century, Luther's gruesome travesty of the Last Supper—"the Jews, bad and mendacious as the devils," eating Judas's shit and piss (*Vom Schem Hamphoras* 215)—raises a simple question: how and why did a polluted Judas dislodge a pure Judas who can be found in a few (though certainly not all) ancient texts?

Distinct from the aesthetically powerful tradition of a dying or dead Judas cursed by bloody, fecal, and urinary corruption are portrayals of Judas in a number of noncanonical gospels (discovered in 1945 at Nag Hammadi) in which he appears as a pious, devoted apostle, just like the other eleven.[33] In Dialogue of the Savior, for instance, Jesus enters into a (now fragmentary) series of Socratic conversations with three of his disciples: Matthew, Judas, and Mary.[34] In stark contrast to Papias's gross Judas, he exclaims in the Dialogue of the Savior, "We [w]ish to understand the sort of garments in which we shall be clothed [when] we leave the corruption of the [f]lesh" (310). Even when Judas has sinned, as in an eighth- or ninth-century

Coptic text titled the Acts of Andrew and Paul, he appears penitential as he pleads with Jesus for forgiveness, and "Jesus sent him to the desert to repent, bidding him fear no one but God" (J. Elliott 304).[35] As part of their determination to refute Gnostic sects and doctrines, however, the church fathers rejected such depictions in favor of an unredeemed, unredeemable Judas.

In early sectarian wars, Judas functioned as a flag or a hostage: if he was championed by, for example, the Gnostics, he had to be desecrated by their victorious adversaries. Irenaeus, considered by some to be the founder of Christian theology, makes an allusion in his *Against the Heresies* (ca. 130–200 C.E.) that explains how and why Judas became more closely associated with demoniacs, animals, and deviancy in the medieval period. According to Irenaeus, the Gnostic heretics he attacks "say that Cain comes from the Supreme Authority," as do "Esau, Core, the Sodomites": "Also Judas, the traitor, they say, had exact knowledge of these things, and since he alone knew the truth better than the other apostles, he accomplished the mystery of the betrayal. Through him all things in heaven and on earth were destroyed. This fiction they adduce, and call it the Gospel of Judas" (102–3). Irenaeus identifies the Gnostics and Judas not just with treachery (underscored by the mention of "Core," who is probably Korah, a rebel against Moses in Numbers 16:1–50) but also—by means of exiled Cain, hairy and disinherited Esau, and especially the doomed Sodomites—with evil abhorrent to God. In his conclusion, Irenaeus castigates the Gnostic Judas as a "wild beast" whom he has managed to "expose" and whom he also wishes to "wound" (104). Another thinker who linked Judas with Cain, the Sodomites, Esau, and Korah was Epiphanius of Salamis (ca. 310–402): he also ascribed to the Gnostics the view that Judas ought to be praised.[36] Theologians and orators would follow Epiphanius's and Irenaeus's diatribes against what the former called "the mischievous ignorance" of the Gnostics (134) so as to position Christians as antagonists to Judas, who quickly became a prototypical heretic.

Early Christian thinkers vehemently denounced Judas, making the Gnostic view untenable. In a long poem called the *Paschale Carmen* (ca. 425–445), for instance, Sedulius ranted against Judas, the "blinded one [who] bore so much wickedness," exclaiming "If only that damned one had, on account of a sterile womb, / Been unable to experience a birthday" (ll. 43, 50–51). In other words, this epic, which was "required reading in schools throughout the Middle Ages and a source for Latin and vernacular biblical epics well into the seventeenth century" (Springer 1), agrees with Mark's and Matthew's Jesus that the betrayer would have been "better" unborn (14:21; 26:24). Outrage at Judas's perfidy motivates Sedulius to ask,

> Are you not blood-spotted, proud, audacious, mad,
>   rebellious,
> Treacherous, cruel, deceitful, bribable, unjust,
> A harsh traitor, a wild traitor, an impious mercenary,
> A standard-bearer leading the way, accompanied by terrible
>   swords? (ll. 59–62).

Just as irate, the brilliant rhetorician St. John Chrysostom lambasted the demoniac Judas in his fourth-century homilies on Matthew.

To John, Judas's greed, treachery, and suicide figure as symptoms of a satanic bestiality that accords with the animalized devils serving as the horned, bat-winged, or spotted obstetricians to Judas's soul in the Church of Saint-Sébastien de Névache and on the Alsatian Panel. Judas's lawless desire for riches "drops human gore, and looks murder, and is fiercer than any wild beast, tearing in pieces them that fall in its way, and what is much worse, it suffers them not even to have any sense of being so mangled" (*Homilies* 61). Likening Judas's "extremity of wickedness" to that of "the demoniacs," John fears that those who "imitate him, like fierce wild beasts escaped from their cage, trouble their cities, no man restraining them" (193). Judas serves as a clear warning against greed:

Harken, all ye covetous, ye that have the disease of Judas; hear-
ken, and beware of the calamity. For if he that was with Christ,
and wrought signs, and had the benefit of so much instruction,
because he was not freed from the disease, was sunk into such
a gulf; how much more shall ye. . . . For terrible, terrible is the
monster, yet nevertheless, if thou be willing thou wilt easily get
the better of him. For the desire is not natural; and this is manifest from them that are free from it. . . . [T]he vice and disease of
covetousness, wherein Judas, being entangled, became a traitor,
is contrary to nature. (483)

Against those who would argue that Judas effected a crucifixion
that ultimately saves, John Chrysostom states flatly, "Not so" (487),
for Judas was "seized by covetousness, as by some madness, or
rather by a more grievous disease," and therefore "He poured not
forth foam out of his mouth, but he poured forth the murder of his
Lord. . . . Wherefore his madness was greater, because he was mad
being in health" (488). Despite all the instruction and kindness of
Jesus, Judas "became fiercer than any wild beast" (499).

BITING MAWS

Was Judas a fierce wild beast from the cradle? What sort of baby was
he, and how soon did his iniquity first make itself known? The Arabic Infancy Gospel, dating from the fourth or fifth century, answers
these questions by attributing a fierce bestiality to the infant Judas. It
builds not on the Dialogue of the Savior's pure Judas but rather on
Papias's contaminated Judas. Whereas Papias's fragment gives Judas
a problem (the loss of bodily fluids), the Arabic Gospel of the Saviour's Infancy hints at a solution (blood lust) that motivates the oral
crimes attributed to the race he begins to represent, for it portrays
Judas as an obsessive flesh eater or bloodsucker. To the extent that it

sustains John Chrysostom's condemnation of the evil that pours from the betrayer's mouth, the Arabic Gospel supplies a suitable beginning to the grotesque end visited upon Papias's Judas, one that attributes his character to an unnatural nature, not to nurture.

According to the Arabic Gospel of the Saviour's Infancy, the miracles performed by the amiable baby Jesus, who heals children as well as adults, set him in contrast with the exceptionally irritable baby Judas in perhaps the first extant description of infant colic or (worse yet) of Lesch-Nyhan syndrome (obsessive self-mutilation):

> Another woman was living in the same place, whose son was tormented by Satan. He, Judas by name, as often as Satan seized him, used to bite all who came near him; and if he found no one near him, he used to bite his own hands and other limbs. The mother of this wretched creature, then, hearing the fame of the Lady Mary her and her son Jesus, rose up and brought her son Judas with her to the Lady Mary. In the meantime, James and Joses had taken the child the Lord Jesus with them to play with the other children; and they had gone out of the house and sat down, and the Lord Jesus with them. And the demoniac Judas came up, and sat down at Jesus' right hand: then, being attacked by Satan in the same manner as usual, he wished to bite the Lord Jesus, but was not able; nevertheless he struck Jesus on the right side, whereupon He began to weep. And immediately Satan went forth out of that boy, fleeing like a mad dog. And this boy who struck Jesus, and out of whom Satan went forth in the shape of a dog, was Judas Iscariot, who betrayed him to the Jews; and that same side on which Judas struck Him, the Jews transfixed with a lance. ("Arabic Gospel" 116–17)

Like Cain and Abel, Judas and Jesus seem destined to contend, with innocence the ultimate victim. As elsewhere, Judas in the Infancy Gospel is aligned with a subhuman species: Satan's seizure, which takes the shape of a dog reminiscent of Cerberus, the monstrous hound of

the Greek underworld, turns Judas into a snapping animal. The bites
of someone infected by this demonic beast rouse the specter of rabies,
though Jesus goes unbitten (to keep him clean).

The episode of the biting Judas is prefaced by a story about another
unfortunate, a young woman "afflicted by Satan; for that accursed
wretch repeatedly appeared to her in the form of a huge dragon, and
prepared to swallow her. He also sucked out all her blood, so that
she was left like a corpse" ("Arabic Gospel" 115). Happily for this
vampirized victim, Lady Mary gives her the Lord Jesus' "swathing-
cloth" (115), and it drives the devil out and away. But Jesus is struck
before he can cast Satan out of Judas and, we must assume, the exor-
cism when it does occur is only temporary; Judas's case is terminal.
Unlike innocent but possessed creatures, the sinful Judas deserves his
demonic possession.[37] Just as the infant Jesus' magic tricks predict his
later messianic miracles, so the baby Judas's attack on the boy Jesus
forecasts the Jews' piercing of Jesus' body, even though in the synoptic Gospels, Jesus is not transfixed with a lance; and in John, it is not
Judas or the Jews but a Roman soldier who "pierced his side with a
spear, and at once blood and water came out" (19:34).

The biting Judas of the Arabic Gospel directs our attention to
Judas's gaping greedy mouth and to recurrent medieval pictorial
depictions of his teeth. Jerome's homily on Psalm 108 established
Judas's and the Jews' orality by emphasizing "the malicious mouth,"
"the lips," and the "lying tongues" in "the story of Judas[, which]
in general . . . is that of the Jews" (255). Many illustrations of the
Last Supper exemplify a decidedly mouthy Judas. In the Winchester
Psalter (ca. 1150; illustration 3.4), a twisted and reclining Judas (not
merely on the wrong side of the table, but beneath it) fingers a plate
with a fish: with his wide-open mouth, he would consume or steal
the symbol of Jesus, while eleven other apostles in halos attend duti-
fully to their teacher's lamentations.[38] In the Hours of Elizabeth the
Queen (ca. 1420–30; illustration 3.5), a red-haired but black-bearded
Judas opens thick lips to show teeth that might bite the sop or the
hand feeding it to him: without a halo, on the wrong side of the table,

3.4. *Last Supper*, detail from Winchester Psalter (ca. 1150). Source: British Library, MS Cotton Nero c.iv, fol. 20r. © The British Library Board.

robed in gold, using the tablecloth to conceal the money bag, his profile exhibits a wolfish look, just as the confusion of black beard and red hair hints at an aberrant miscegenation. Although clearly depicted as a communicant, the kneeling Judas in many depictions— for example, in Master Bertram's panel (from a Passion Altar, late fourteenth century)—looks less pious than slithery as he frequently displays his teeth to bite the wafer being handed to him by a resigned Jesus; abstemious, the other apostles rarely show their teeth, as they face Judas en masse, aware he is not of their company.

In illustrations of John 13:26 (where Jesus identifies the betrayer at table by saying, "It is the one to whom I give this piece of bread . . ."), Judas epitomizes overindulgence, addiction, and gluttony. According

3.5. *Last Supper*, detail from Hours of Elizabeth the Queen of England (ca. 1420–30). Source: British Library, Add. 50001, fol. 7. © The British Library Board.

to Leo the Great (ca. 395–461), love of money, the "root of all evil," motivated "Wicked Judas, drunken with this poison, [who] went to the noose while thirsting for profit" (263). When Luther castigated the Jews as "the devil's children damned to hell" (*Vom Schem Hamphoras* 167), he explained that the "devil's filth comes from them": "Yes, that tastes good to them, into their hearts, they smack their lips like swine" (171). Moreover, Luther's astonishingly vitriolic *On the Jews and Their Lies* (1543) clearly means to call to mind stone carvings that, from the fourteenth to the sixteenth century, were built into churches and civic buildings.

The so-called *Judensau*, a German architectural sculpture, riffs on Judas's bestiality and greedy orality by depicting Jews sucking on the teats of a sow, or eating and drinking its excrement, competing with piglets beneath the belly or anus of their pig mother (see Shachar).[39] Like demoniacs and wild beasts, the Gadarene swine in the New Testament could be related to Judas not only because they were demonically possessed but also because they committed suicide, in their case by rushing into the sea (Matthew 8:28–34). One seventeenth-century screed glossing an illustration of the *Judensau* conflates a cast of characters called "the gallows-worthy thief" and the "fart-glutton" with "Judas [who] betrayed Christ swiftly"; they all soon burned in hellfire, as surely they should (J. Cohen 208). Luther, who believed "David composed [Psalm 109] about Christ, who speaks the entire psalm in the first person against Judas" (*Selected Psalms* 257), argued that "next to the devil, a Christian has no more bitter and galling foe than a Jew" (278): cited in the passage from Acts about Judas's explosion, Psalm 109 curses "wicked and deceitful mouths" that speak "against me with lying tongues" (109:2).[40] To Luther, "Judas was an apostle and yet not an apostle" because rightfully reviled throughout the history of Christendom, along with "the Jews, Judas' people" (*Selected Psalms* 308, 263).

Although there is no Eucharist at John's last supper, it would be and indeed is easy to confuse or conflate John's sop, which instigates the devil's entrance into Judas, with the sacramental bread that Jesus distributes in the synoptic Gospels.[41] In the combined stories circulating about the last meal, the anti-Eucharist that John's Jesus offers Judas shadowed the Eucharist that Mark's, Matthew's, and Luke's Jesus celebrated with the twelve. A toothy Judas chomping on the consecrated host consolidated beliefs not only about the greediness of Judas and the Jews but also about their harming, desecrating, or stealing the host.[42] As late as the seventeenth century, the vituperative author Abraham a Sancta Clara easily moved from an attack against "some Jews who mauled the most holy Host with knives in a very shameful way" to a curse: "O rogue Judas, what are you doing? Don't you fear that the earth will swallow you whole?" (127).[43] He frequently warns Christians against Judas's "filthy tongue" (138):

3.6. *Last Supper*, detail from stained-glass window at King's College, Cambridge University (ca. 1500). Source: By permission of the Provost and Scholars of King's College, Cambridge.

"when one takes this highest good [the host] unworthily, that means one has followed the godless Judas Iscariot, that means one has mocked Jesus . . . that means one has spewed [or spit or vomited] together with the Jewish functionaries into the most holy face of Jesus" (140). The charge of host profanation—"that Jews got hold of a consecrated wafer and then subjected it to some iniquitous treatment" (Little 52)—may reflect anxiety about eucharistic doctrines that became dogma only in 1215 and around which controversies continued to swirl. In a stained-glass window at Cambridge University (ca. 1500; illustration 3.6), a red-haired, red-bearded Judas—profiled with a hook nose—opens his lips to receive the morsel, displaying his teeth as well as his tongue.

Did pictures of Judas biting the consecrated bread that is the body of Jesus morph into images of Jews conspiring to eat the flesh or drain the blood of innocent Christians? Given his debased carnality, does the anemia suffered by a Judas dying from blood loss combine with the image of a toothy Judas to lay the foundation for accusations of Jewish ritual murders?[44] According to the historian Gavin Langmuir, "From 1150 to 1235, the ritual murder accusation against Jews was that they annually crucified a Christian boy to insult Christ and as a sacrifice. In 1235, a second type of ritual murder accusation appeared: . . . that Jews killed a Christian child to acquire blood they needed for their rituals or medicine" (240).[45] In one infamous case, the purported murderer was said to have paid the victim's mother three silver shillings, meant to recall "the thirty pieces of silver paid to Judas" (J. Cohen 97). In *The Jew and Human Sacrifice* (1909), perhaps the first exhaustive study of this topic, Hermann Strack debunked firmly believed rumors that Jews performed the long list of ritual murders that he enumerated, many of which were followed by the torturing of Jews for confessions.[46] Jews, of course, were forbidden not just human sacrifice but also the intake of animal blood.[47] Why, then, were they accused of cannibalism—and not only in the medieval period? "[T]he Jews must have been in the habit of eating human flesh," Voltaire later argued about "the most abominable people upon earth" (88).

Strack suggested that "Christians, after the Christian religion had become dominant, directed against others the calumny once directed against themselves" (283). In the second and third centuries, "the mention of partaking of the body and the blood of the Lord" led to the persecution of *Christians* as cannibals engaged in ritual sacrifice or, as Tertullian put it in his defense against such charges, "the secret practice of killing and eating children" (Strack 281, 283).[48] But popular iconography about Judas may have also contributed to the accusation. Throughout Tudor times, according to James Shapiro, "exorbitant moneylending was often referred to as 'biting' usury, and the elision of Jews as economic exploiters and literal devourers of Christian flesh was easily made" (*Shakespeare* 110). During an era rapidly moving from an agriculture- to a commerce-based economy dependent on business practices that conflicted with many of the church's teachings, the usurer would be likened to a lippy leech or a toothy beast, sucking the blood or gnawing the flesh of its host. Judas trying to steal or bite the sacrament threatens to bite the hand of his host, who proffers it.

Significantly, then, Shakespeare's Shylock persistently demands his legal pound of flesh after his first words on stage—"Three thousand ducats"—which echo blood money exacted in factors of three: Shylock is a "cut-throat dog" (1.3.106), one whose "desires / Are wolvish, bloody, starv'd and ravenous" (4.1.137–38), who goes "in hate, to feed upon / The prodigal Christians" (4.1.394).[49] That Shylock—who hates Christians and who is compared to the devil incarnate—forfeits his life and wealth because the laws of the land forbid the shedding of Christian blood helps explain why *The Merchant of Venice* was so popular in Nazi Germany and occupied France. The biting Judas baby, the Jews shown lancing Jesus on the cross, the bites of usury: all these wounds relate to Judas "accompanied by terrible swords" (the words are Sedulius's) in manifold illustrations (discussed in the next chapter) that raised the specter of Jews (wearing pointy hats and wielding spears) threatening to castrate or cut up Christ or his followers.[50]

Just as Jesus' divinity did not abrogate his humanity, so Judas's demonism did not abrogate his. After Nicaea (325) and the Chalcedonian Definition (451), the church promulgated the view that Jesus was human and also godly: not part human and part divine, not sometimes human and sometimes divine, not only human or only divine. In stark opposition to the God-man Jesus stands the Devil-man Judas, who is not part human and part Satan, not sometimes human and sometimes Satan, not only human or only Satan, but human and also Satan. Yet here, as with the accusation of cannibalism, Christians may have deflected accusations once directed against themselves and in this case also against Jesus. For in the New Testament, it is Jesus who is accused of being possessed by Satan. Disbelieving crowds watching Jesus cure the sick wonder if Beelzebub, "the ruler of demons," bestowed power upon him (Mark 3:22; Matthew 12:24; Luke 11:15); a mob responds to Jesus' preaching first by claiming "You have a demon!" (John 7:20), and then by asking, "Are we not right in saying that you are a Samaritan and have a demon?" (8:48).

What better way to defend Jesus' inspiration as God-given than by lambasting Judas's as Satan-driven? Jesus' miraculous feeding (of vast throngs of people) stands in opposition to Judas's bleeding (of his victims), a crime not unrelated to what James Shapiro calls the "feminized male Jew's leaky body" or his periodic menstruation (*Shakespeare* 108).[51] Jesus provides, whereas Judas destroys or drains; Jesus heals, while Judas wounds; Jesus' wine purifies, but Judas's blood pollutes; Jesus' bread saves, but Judas's flesh damns.

The effort to sustain this sort of opposition can be traced back to the first or second century, when a number of works severed Judas's connection to Jesus altogether. The author of the Narrative of Joseph Arimathea, for example, claims of Judas, "He was *not a disciple* before the face of Jesus; but all the multitude of the Jews craftily supported him, that he might follow Jesus, not that he might be obedient to the miracles done by Him, nor that he might confess Him, but that he might betray Him to them" ("Narrative" 238; emphasis mine). A secret agent of and for the Jews, Judas responds to the plundering of the Temple sanctuary with trumped-up charges against Jesus, hatched with the help of Caiaphas the priest; and in this version, Judas is the son of Caiaphas's brother! Having been paid thirty pieces of *gold,* Joseph's Judas hands over an innocent man to a manifestly "unjust trial" (239–40).[52] Similarly, in the Acts of Thomas, the same serpent who tempted Eve, who "inflamed and fired Cain to kill his own brother," and who "hardened Pharoah's heart" is "he who inflamed Judas and bribed him to deliver the Messiah to death" (J. Elliott 460). That the snake subsequently swells and bursts led one scholar to connect him to Papias's Judas (J. Harris 509). In the Book of the Resurrection of Jesus Christ by Bartholomew the

Apostle, Judas is punished by thirty sins ("a clear but unstated link to the 'blood money' ") that become the snakes sent to devour him (Cane 146).

Bursting, bleeding, biting, and also bargaining, Judas emerges from antiquity as a transgenic organism, human and satanic, person and animal. While some church fathers emphasized how convertible the Jews could be, Judas the Antichrist cannot be converted but must instead be fought, expunged, for he is a member of an altogether different species from that to which humanity belongs. A repository of anal and oral excess, Judas typifies the fate of those who refuse to conform to the church's tenets, though he helps to bring organized Christianity into being. Jeffrey Kahn, who has studied the role of Judas in fourteenth- and fifteenth-century French Passion plays, describes some versions in which devils hatch the conspiracy and afterward appear beside Judas to advise him to hang himself or, in scenes of low comedy, stuff his soul into a witchy cauldron (66). Perversely and inexplicably revolted by Jesus' sanctity or avariciously bickering with Jews over each and every coin, a frenzied Judas in other plays despairs because he has sold his soul to the devil, before he is caught and boiled in the cauldron so that Satan can eat him (95). As Kahn notes, "The moral link between the traitor and the Devil is clearly indicated" (97).[53]

No wonder, then, that the demoniac Judas lent his name to an instrument used to regulate and chastise heretics. Amid the equipment routinely used on people being tested and found wanting during the Inquisition, the Judas cradle or chair appeared in Italy as *culla di Giuda* and in Germany as *Judaswiege* (Held 50). The suspected culprit was stripped naked, hoisted up by ropes or belts, and lowered onto the point of a pyramidal block fixed onto a stool, pedestal, or tripod. Some of the victim's weight rested on the top point of the pyramid, which was positioned in the anus or vagina, or under the scrotum or coccyx (illustration 3.7). Rocked repeatedly or made to fall back over and over again, the accused would experience the painful stretching of a body cavity or impalement with a pressure that

3.7. The Judas cradle or chair (ca. 1680). Source: Robert Held, *Inquisition: A Bilingual Guide to the Exhibition of Torture Instruments from the Middle Ages to the Industrial Era* (Florence: Qua d'Arno, 1985).

could rise to his or her total body weight. Precisely the despoilment of the body is what the victim of the Judas cradle shared with Dante's earlier portrait of Judas in *The Inferno*, though the former emphasizes anality and the latter orality.

At the end of Dante's magisterial travelogue through hell, the poet, attended by Virgil, descends into Judeccea, the lowest realm at the center of the earth, named after Judas and the Jews. Amid sinners literally frozen in grotesque postures in the *anus mundi* (rectum of the universe), Dante and his guide encounter an immobilized and gigantic Lucifer (some 817 feet tall, according to one commentator).[54] Endowed with six mighty wings, resembling sails at sea or massive bat pinions, the *Inferno*'s emperor rises from the ice below his breast to display one yellowish face (impotence but also Asia?), one red face (anger but also Jewish blood lust?), one black face (ignorance but also Africa?):

> Out of six eyes he wept and his three chins
> dripped tears and drooled blood-red saliva.

> With his teeth, just like a hackle
> pounding flax, he champed a sinner
> in each mouth, tormenting three at once. (XXXIV, ll. 53–57)

The "soul up there who bears the greatest pain," Virgil explains, "is Judas Iscariot, who has / his head within and outside flails his legs" (XXXIV, ll. 62–63). Once again drenched in bloody efflux, here Lucifer's, Judas is only partly swallowed by his fiendish progenitor in a sort of imagistic antibirth. Silenced, half in and half out of the death canal of Satan's front and central red mouth, gnawed (while the two main conspirators against Julius Caesar occupy the other two jaws), Judas is clawed until "his back was left with not a shred of skin" (l. 60).

The linchpin in an unholy trinity of traitors, the cannibalistic biter finds himself eternally bitten. As early as the Latin *Voyage of Saint Brendan* (written in Ireland around 800 C.E.), Judas gains a respite from hell, which "devours the souls of the impious," a temporary reprieve from being "eaten by the demons," for (on Sundays and certain holidays) Jesus granted him "a place of refreshment" on a bare rock exposed to winds and ocean waves. Demons protest Saint Brendan's adding a few hours to Judas's holiday from hell because the godly voyager has "taken our mouthful away from us" (58, 29). On a nave roof in Southwark Cathedral in the fifteenth century, an amiable devil appeared, chewing with relish on the head and torso of a partly eaten Judas, whose legs stick out (illustration 3.8).[55] Judas half engorged inside the masticating toothy mouth of Lucifer; the Judas-culprit impaled upon a pointed apparatus penetrating anus, vagina, or scrotum: these punishments fit the oral and anal crimes

3.8. *The Devil Devours Judas,* ceiling boss, Southwark Cathedral (ca. 1400). Reproduced by kind permission of the Dean and Chapter of Southwark. Photograph by Martin Brewster.

attributed to Judas throughout premodern times and forever after. As late as Thomas Harris's *Hannibal* (1999), a cannibalistic killer operates under the sign of the twelfth apostle: Hannibal Lecter lectures a group of scholars on "Judas hanging with his bowels falling out" and "the matter of chewing in Dante," before he arranges the hanging of a pursuing policeman who spins posthumously "with his bowels swinging below him in a shorter, quicker arc . . ." (196, 197, 203).

Judas the demon had a long life in Western letters. From Charles Dickens's red-haired and fanged Fagin, despoiling Christian boys by training them in thievery, to Anthony Trollope's bloodsucking Melmotte, driven by his own iniquity to commit suicide, Judas's greed combines with his avarice and his self-destruction to shape the Jew's depiction in British literature.[56] Significantly, at a glimpse of the protagonist of Bram Stoker's Victorian novel *Dracula* (1897), a reliable witness describes the foreign Count "with a red light of triumph in his eyes, and with a smile that Judas in hell might be proud of" (72).[57]

Man yet demon, human yet bat or wolf, the foreign Count at "reple-
tion" trickles blood from the corners of his mouth "like a filthy leech,"
cringes before a crucifix, and cannot pass over ground sprinkled with
the crumbled host (73). Picking up on these associations, Wes Cra-
ven's movie *Dracula 2000* (2000) presents the Transylvanian vampire
as a reincarnation of Judas whose aversion to silver, the Bible, and
the cross date from his role in the Passion and whose fanged teeth
puncture to bite human flesh in a murderous Judas kiss. In James
Rollins's novel *The Judas Strain* (2007), the fictive virus named for
the twelfth apostle stimulates an insatiable appetite, the "flesh-eating
disease" of cannibalism (293). Yet if, like Count Dracula's acolytes
or the victims of Rollins's exterminating organism, Judas had been
infected by demonic forces that in turn propelled him to consume
and contaminate others, this one sick guy might have suffered a destiny he had no power to combat.

JUDAS-OEDIPUS HEXED

Whether erupting anally or incorporating orally, a transgenic Judas
seems conceptually irreconcilable with the more fated, less fetid Judas
who simultaneously emerges through a folkloric response to a series
of questions: who were Judas's parents, where did he come from,
what sort of work engaged him in young adulthood, and how did he
eventually become the twelfth apostle? The answers to these blanks
left by the Gospel accounts are furnished by an Oedipal version of
Judas that circulated from the eleventh century on in popular narratives and ballads throughout almost every European country and
that moved Judas out of the anal and oral phases into a decidedly
phallic one. Because parents, provenance, profession, and motives
tend to humanize a character or because such features may factor
into stories depicting Judas himself as a victim, Judas-Oedipus began
to shed his demoniac persona as he modulates into being the bearer
of a horrific but nevertheless poignant because preordained doom.[58]

Given that Oedipus (as he vows to root out the plague afflicting his subjects) is generally associated with impulsive generosity, Judas with selfish deliberation, the idea of conflating Judas with Oedipus may seem odd; however, the amalgamation occurred as early as the third century. Once Judas is viewed through the prism of tragedy, his fate addresses two disturbing ideas: that an individual may be destined to perform unintentional wrongdoing and that the extermination of such an individual may not free a society from the calamity he is thought to exemplify. Within legends, plays, and ballads that provide imaginative insight into the mechanisms that produce a pariah, Judas becomes what René Girard (writing about Oedipus) once called "the repository of all the community's ills," "a prime example of the human scapegoat" (77). When patricide and incest join the accusations leveled against Judas, when he is pictured with an embarrassingly visible erection (at a highly inappropriate moment), one might suppose that the phallic phase clinches his villainy. As so often with the twelfth apostle's progress, however, the Oedipal Judas who kills his father and sleeps with his mother defies logical expectations by expressing repentance and meriting some commiseration for his wrongdoing.

The issue of free will or determinism that the story of Judas raises caused him first to be linked with Oedipus by Origen in the philosopher's *Contra Celsus* (third century C.E.).[59] Celsus was a Platonic critic of Christianity against whom Origen defends his religion and whom he quoted extensively in fashioning his argument (here Celsus's words are italicized to set them off from Origen's). To Origen's consternation, Celsus had argued that there was something wrong with the idea that what Jesus *"foretold must assuredly have come to pass. A god, therefore, led his own disciples and prophets with whom he used to eat and drink so far astray that they became impious and wicked"* (84). According to the skeptic Celsus, then, Christianity constructed a perverted divinity, for *"God himself conspired against those who ate with him, by making them traitors and impious men"* (84–85), a point that can be argued on the basis of the synoptic Jesus predicting his betrayal and John's Jesus giving Judas the sop that allows the devil's entrance. In order to disentangle prophecy from causality, to clear Jesus of culpability and establish Judas's free will, Origen refutes Celsus by quoting the oracle who warned Laius: "Beget no children against the will of the gods, / For if thou dost produce a child, thy offspring shall slay thee, / And thy whole house shall pass through bloodshed" (86). The Greek oracle's and Jesus' predictions do not, the Christian theologian argues, make them responsible for the subsequent impiety and wickedness of Oedipus and Judas. Yet the recurrent recycling of the Judas-Oedipus story can suggest quite the opposite; namely, that Judas, like Oedipus, had become ensnared in an inexorable script advanced by all those with whom he came into contact and about which he could do nothing.

Oedipal accounts of Judas's life circulated throughout medieval Europe in almost every language; I will draw on Jacopo da Voragine's *The Golden Legend* for a composite that includes many of the most often reworked motifs (167–69).[60] Dated around 1260, it was compiled by the archbishop of Genoa and was so popular that some one thousand manuscript copies were made; once printed editions began appearing, translations multiplied. The story, encapsulated within a chapter devoted to Judas's successor, Saint Matthias, recounts the betrayer's birth to Ruben and Cyborea after she dreamed that they would "bear a son so wicked that he would bring ruin upon our whole people" (167). Horrified at the thought of killing their baby, the parents launch him in a basket out to sea, where he is carried to "an island called Scariot" (from which he took the name Iscariot; 167). When Judas is found there, the childless queen of Scariot pretends to be pregnant while she has him secretly nursed. "When the time came, she lied by announcing that she had borne a son" (167), and word spread throughout the joyous kingdom. The queen does finally conceive a legitimate son with the king, but this royal boy is mistreated by his cruel brother. After Judas's origins are revealed, he murders the queen's biological son and flees to Jerusalem, taking service in the house of Pilate, governor of Judea: "Pilate noticed that Judas was a man after his own heart and began to treat him as a favorite, finally putting him in charge of his own domain; and Judas's word was law" (167–68).

Indubitably a sinner, Judas nevertheless seems helpless against those who sin against him. His parents, Ruben and Cyborea, recall Laius and Jocasta, a father and mother so fearful of their child's bringing destruction that they abandon the infant, though in this version Judas is not left wounded on a mountain but instead is floated like Moses in a basket on the water. While the ritual murders attributed to Jews depended on charges of infanticide, *The Golden Legend*'s Judas is himself the victim of an attempted infanticide by his biological parents. And once the baby Judas floats to the island Scariot, thereby obtaining a patronymic, the foundling-pauper can be made a prince because of the fictionality of paternity: that is, only the princess knows lineage and legitimacy for sure. As in the Arabic Infancy Gospel, the spiteful boy quickly exhibits the violence of a nature that aligns him with the fratricidal Cain, but the tale hints at collaborative wrongdoing. For on Scariot his adoptive stepmother stages a fake pregnancy, lying to her husband, to the populace at large, and to the boy about the parentage she has fabricated to gain an ersatz heir to the throne.

In addition, Judas's murder of the true heir results not in nomadic exile, such as Cain suffered, but in his immigration back to his hometown, Jerusalem, and his landing a job with a man simpatico in temperament: he becomes Pilate's right-hand man, and (perhaps predictably for some readers) a kind of lawyer. Logically, the legend could then directly recount Judas's meeting with Jesus and his apostles. Yet instead what follows in Voragine's version (and in many others) is patricide and incest, both of which (though clearly meant to vilify) oddly generate sympathy, for agency accrues not to Judas but to Pilate. It is he (shades of Eve) who spies forbidden fruit in a nearby orchard, enlisting Judas to obtain it for him: Pilate, seized with desire, orders Judas into Ruben's garden; there Ruben, discovering Judas picking apples, confronts the thief, who ends up killing him. After Pilate awards all of Ruben's possessions, including his wife, to Judas, she is troubled and so recounts her history, which informs Judas that "he had taken his mother to wife and had killed his father" (168). She persuades him to repent, and at this point he turns "to our Lord Jesus Christ" (168). To the extent that a manipulated Judas feels remorse, he cannot but gain the reader's pity: after all, he seeks forgiveness for a succession of crimes instigated by everyone with power over him. Like his mother-wife, Judas—who returned to Jerusalem as a "part of a tribute payment" (in other words, a gift or tax; 167)—functions as a passive object of exchange between empowered agents. Thus, he himself has been unwillingly and unwittingly "handed over" to fratricide, patricide, and incest. In any case, Jesus presumably forgave Judas, because Jesus made Judas a disciple in full knowledge of the patricide and incest.

Still, the heinous crimes of incest and patricide are clearly meant to reflect on a familial level the same horrific transgression that occurs in the state as regicide and in Christianity as deicide. A man capable of betraying his beloved teacher must be culpable of everything, even killing his father and marrying his mother, "extreme transgressions of the fifth, sixth, and seventh commandments" (Archibald 108–9). Because the Oedipus plot represents phallic activity gone awry—a son contentious with his father, libidinal with his mother—it recalls Judas with the shamefully huge private parts of Papias's description. The horned, hairy, bat-winged, and pinion-footed devil from the Church of Saint-Sébastien de Névache proves that demonic animalism was often conflated with sexual perversion: witness the devil's second set of eyes at the level of his intestines, the second and lower mouth at his crotch (illustration 3.1). On the Alsatian panel, too, the emerging Judas-soul sprouts like a protuberance on Judas's body that incites the devil into what looks to be an act of fellatio (plate 3). Yet there is, to my knowledge, only one painting from the early modern period that explicitly presents the phallic Oedipus-Judas: Jörg Ratgeb's *Last Supper,* part of the Herrenberg Altar in Stuttgart (ca. 1519; illustration 3.9).

Flagrant defiance of chastity and poverty characterizes Ratgeb's

3.9. Jörg Ratgeb, *Last Supper*, part of the Herrenberg Altar in Stuttgart (ca. 1519). Source: Staatsgalerie, Stuttgart.

Judas. In his hurry to eat the sop handed to him by Jesus, Ratgeb's Judas overturns a wine jug by his feet, as well as a chair. The Herrenberg Altar is typical in its presentation of a red-haired and yellow-robed Judas, stigmatizing him as the only Jew at the meal. Also common is the relative isolation of his figure at a table where all the others seem connected in pairs or in their devotion to Jesus, here (as so often) holding the beloved sleepy disciple in an embrace. Equally standard is Judas's wide-open mouth, his teeth showing (in contrast to his small eyes) in a profiled face that proves him two-faced, as is the deceitful groveling posture of his body. That Judas, unlike the others, wears sandals proves that he disobeyed Jesus' instruction (Matthew 10:10). But what distinguishes Ratgeb's Judas is the erection exhibited amid the folds of his robes.[61] To draw attention to that unseemly excitation, Ratgeb presents playing cards and dice falling from Judas's midriff, another sign of his profligacy. Like the fly beneath the Master of the Housebook's Judas and the worms on Papias's Judas, the insect just below Ratgeb's host intimates that the devil will inhabit the body of Judas so as to punish him for his unpardonable sins. These parasites signify Judas's relationship to his host.

Several centuries before Ratgeb but in keeping with his painting, *The Golden Legend* disavows the circumstantial story it retells ("it is better left aside than repeated") in its punitive conclusion. Judas's death increases his guilt "*because* the first part [consisting of Jesus' pardon] could have served as a counter-example to show that even the worst of sinners can be forgiven" (Ohly 26). Although Jesus made Judas a disciple and loved him dearly, Judas as treasurer stole alms, protested the price of the ointment, and betrayed his Lord for "thirty pieces of silver, each coin being worth ten pence, and so he made up the three hundred pence lost over the ointment" (Voragine 168). Sorry for his sins, Judas throws back the money, hangs himself, and bursts asunder. The piling up of vengeful reprisals signals how the entire community bands together in "violent unanimity" (Girard 78) to dispel its own guilt by projecting it onto that of the individual, a harmonized Judas who steals from the treasury (as in John), hangs himself (as in Matthew), and also explodes with gushing bowels (as in Luke). The crimes of Ruben, Cyborea, the queen of Scariot, and Pilate pale as "the surrogate victim" meets the demons to whom he is eternally consigned, to borrow a term from Girard's analysis of Sophocles' Oedipus (79). The unbearable and unjust violence of Jesus' death can be attributed to the evil of an individual who deserves to be expunged.

Yet the generalizing logic of Freud's reading of the Oedipus myth—
the idea that all boys desire their mothers and resent their fathers—
suggests of this version of Judas that all of Jesus' followers harbored
a secret wish to become apostates; all the devout were tempted to
lapse into doubt or self-interest. More to the point, in light of Jesus'
predicament on the cross—of feeling abandoned by a father who
requires his death—the Oedipal Judas rebels in rage against the
despotic father. Is it the disavowal of this shocking possibility that
earns him defamation? Oedipus-Judas's rebellion against the paternal
death sentence to which Jesus submits: centuries later, this symmetry
would open the door to meditations on their commonality.[62] Even in
Ratgeb's painting, hectic energy as well as passionate attentiveness to
Jesus distinguishes Judas from the other self-absorbed disciples. And
there is an uncanny doubling between the red-bearded Judas looking
up to Jesus in the foreground and the red-bearded Jesus looking up
to God in the background.

What of the supposition in *The Golden Legend* that Judas "sold
his Lord for the tenth part of the lost sale price of the ointment"
(Voragine 168)? The idea that Judas calculated what he considered
his fair or at least usual share of Jesus' purse places a limit on his
avarice.[63] It is precisely this downplaying of Judas's cupidity within
an incestuous narrative that links Voragine's legend to the earliest
Middle English ballad, "Judas," where the twelfth disciple is sent by
Jesus with thirty coins of silver "to beg our meat" but is robbed by
his temptress sister.[64] Judas in the ballad, encountering his "deceitful"
sister, is reproved for following a "false prophet," and then unfortunately heeds her seductive instructions—"Lay your head in my lap,
sleep thou anon"—only to awaken to the shock of the silver gone:

> He pulled at his hair, so that it ran all bloody.
> The Jews out of Jerusalem believed he was mad.

> Before him came the rich Jew that was called Pilate:
> "Would you sell your lord that is called Jesus?"

"I will not sell my Lord for any kind of riches,
Unless it be for thirty coins that he entrusted to me."

"Would you sell your lord Christ for any kind of gold?"
"No, unless it be for the coins that he would have."

Less a sign of damnation or pollution than of intense anguish, the blood-drenched hair of the ballad protagonist registers his shock at having been robbed of his Lord's entrusted coins by a sort of *belle dame sans merci* or femme fatale. As in *The Golden Legend,* in the "Judas" ballad the fault lies not in the stars, not in Judas's self, but in the wiles of others. In this case, the sinister sister lures him to sleep (is sleep a euphemism for sex here?) so that she might steal from him and then force him into a cover-up that clearly destroys his beloved Lord, but that has nothing whatsoever to do with any desire for wealth: Judas "will not sell my Lord for any kind of riches"; he wants only to return to Jesus what belongs to Jesus. That Pilate is a "rich Jew" and that he hatches the plot further exonerates Judas, who seems less doomed than duped (though of course the Jews are still to blame). The ballad's emphasis on a wronged and frightened betrayer adumbrates the relatively sympathetic treatment accorded Judas in a number of English mystery plays.

The Wakefield Mystery Plays, composed during the fourteenth and fifteenth centuries and presented yearly in English villages of that region, showcased a Judas who reacts as might a CPA to the money squandered on Jesus' anointment, for the payment of thirty coins is quite rationally the tenth part Judas takes as his standard fee:

The tenth part, truly to tell,
To keep by me was my intent;
For of the treasure that to us fell,
The tenth part ever with me went;
And if three hundred be right told,

> The tenth part is just thirty;
> Right so he shall be sold[.] (339)

Judas raises the prospect not exactly of the profit motive but of expectations about conventional tithing. As Richard Axton puts it, "The relationship between three hundred pence and thirty pence had been lurking in the gospels, waiting to be discovered by medieval minds, which loved pattern and which were also recurrently preoccupied with the problem of usury" (184). In one Provençal Passion, Axton explains, the thirty pence or tenth part are promised to Judas by Jesus to help take care of Judas's two children (189)! Even in the English version, the betrayal is motivated by what Judas takes to be an unjust business practice: "He made me lose what was my share; / Now are we even for once and ay" (*Wakefield* 340). Before the crucifixion scene, moreover, Judas speaks his (incomplete) monologue of Oedipal remorse:

> Alas, alas, and welaway!
> Accursed caitiff I have been ay;
> I slew my father, and after lay
> With my mother;
> And later, falsely, did betray
> My own master. (390)

In a different cycle, *The York Cycle of Mystery Plays,* Judas again appears less avaricious, more protective of his assets. He explains, "'Twas all pain for my tenth part" that caused him to protest the ointment that would have brought three hundred pennies and thus thirty pence for himself (191).[65] He sells Jesus because he is convinced that Jesus defrauded him of his rightful compensation. Recently, one scholar of the plays in the York cycle has pointed out that they "depict Judas as a servant who wrongly, flagrantly, illegally, and greedily acts as a trader on his own behalf rather than in relation to the greater needs of the community" (Pappano 320–21). In other words, to become a trader on one's own behalf is to be a traitor to God; cheating one's master is like betraying Jesus, a Judas-act.[66] The plays, seeking to resolve local economic tensions, castigate Judas as an uppity servant to teach real apprentices to stay in their appointed station. Paradoxically, though, as they stage Judas's ambitious decision to put personal gain over community needs, Judas might be said to articulate the quite understandable aspirations of some of the cooks and bakers who played him in the pageants.

The unusual "Remorse of Judas" scene in *The York Cycle*, when Pilate and his cohorts conspire to turn Jesus over to Sir Herod, features Judas's soliloquy expressing deep compunction at his role in the capture—"Shameless myself thus ruined I, / So soon to assent to his slaying" (251)—before he determines to save Jesus, offering his own life in exchange for his master's: "I pray you, good lord, let him go; / And have of me your payment plain" (252). After offering himself as a bondman or indentured servant to save his master, Judas curses, throws back the money, and determines to kill himself: "I loathe all my life, so live I too long; / My treacherous turn torments me with pain" (256). A market economy certainly gets Judas nowhere quick, as if to reprove servants who think they can play fast and loose with their masters; however, the suicide is an admission of his conscious atonement for the error of his ways. That we hear his expression of frustration and repentance from his own mouth further humanizes him.

One can even catch a glimpse of efforts to exonerate not the Jews but Judas in early texts. The ninth-century long poem *Elene*, for instance, recounts the journey of the mother of the emperor Constantine to Judea, where she finds the true cross through the offices of one Judas. Not only does this later-day Judas reveal the location of the cross; in the process, he is converted, baptized with a name meaning "the Saviour's revelation," and becomes a bishop to minister to other Jewish converts (191).[67] A more explicit effort to vindicate the biblical Judas appears in a fifteenth-century Middle English dialogue, *Lucius and Dubius*, in which the doubting Dubius makes a claim for the twelfth apostle as an instrument of providence, an agent of God:

> God willed that his son Jesus
> Should be dead for man's sake:
> Therefore, I want to know, what did Judas do amiss
> Who would betray him?
> For because God willed that he should be dead,
> And Judas did the same,
> And Judas was not to blame,
> It seems they worked by the same measure
> For no man may murder
> Who carries out God's will.[68]

Can an instrument of divinity be condemned as a murderer? Despite a name meant to make his position dubious, Dubius's theological speculation vindicates Judas in a manner more sophisticated than the redemption of Judas allegorized in the Croxton *Play of the Sacrament*.

When it becomes possible to imagine Christians playing the role of Judas, the twelfth apostle predictably becomes redeemable. In the Croxton miracle play, probably composed late in the fifteenth century, a merchant named Aristorius sells the host to five Jews who proceed to torment it. Aristorius stands in for Judas because he accepts a bribe and gives over the host to the Jews, who put it through what the scholar Ellen MacKay calls "a second passion," which convinces them that it is indeed the body and blood of Jesus.[69] In all images of Jews attacking a wafer or a piece of bread, "violence is directed at the very body of God" (Greenblatt 100): "The Jews are inevitably guilty in such stories [of host desecration] because they do not believe and because at the same time they are made to act out, to embody, the doubt aroused among the Christian faithful by eucharistic doctrine" (Greenblatt 104). At the happily-ever-after end of the folkloric and somewhat farcical *Play of the Sacrament*, the Jews have converted to Christianity and the *Christian* Judas-Aristorius relinquishes his wealth, becoming a mendicant penitent by the play's end.

If Christians could perpetuate Judas's cruelty or selfishness, then his punishment and damnation have not solved the problem of human depravity. For George Herbert, too, Judas represents the propensity of all people to fall into the sin of avarice. Herbert's "Self-Condemnation" (1633) conflates the sins of Judas with the sins of the Jews, but it also affirms that materialism constitutes a snare for Christians as well:

> He that hath made a sorry wedding
> Between his soul and gold, and hath preferred
>   False gain before the true,
> Hath done what he condemns in reading;
> For he hath sold for money his dear Lord,
>   And is a Judas-Jew. (150)

To the extent that early modern writers insist that Christians are capable of committing Judas's crime or that a penitential Judas ascertained something valuable from Jesus' teachings, they drew on unusual thinkers in antiquity who imagined suicide not as the sin of despairing in God's mercy but as a desperate act of contrition and even a sign of wisdom. Origen, who first associated Judas with Oedipus, believed that "the teachings of Jesus had been able to put into [Judas] some capacity for repentance, and were not utterly despised or abominated by the traitor" (76). According to Origen, "By condemning himself he showed what effect the teaching of Jesus could have even on a sinner like Judas, the thief and traitor, who could not utterly despise what he had learnt from Jesus" (76–77). Similarly, a ninth-century commentator named Paschasius Radbertus speculated that Judas's suicide might have been motivated by the hope of meeting Jesus in the next world, where he could ask and receive pardon (Murray 2:196, 363).[70] Suicide, though labeled a sin by a good number, could be envisioned as penitence by a few.

3.10. Willem van Swanenburg, *Judas*, engraving after Abraham Bloemaert, from *Sinners of the Bible* (1611). Source: Michael Cavanagh, Kevin Montague. Copyright © 2006 Indiana University Art Museum.

IVDAS ISCARIOTH.

A 1611 engraving of Judas by Willem van Swanenburg (after Abraham Bloemaert) depicts a noble-looking Judas before and after the hanging: in the foreground, his money bag unattended, Judas sits at the base of a blasted tree, tying the rope around his neck, while at a distance in the background we see him hanging from the tree (illustration 3.10). At its base, Judas is quoted bemoaning his own hard lot ("alas") with perplexity ("I . . . unwittingly lost myself"; "What should I do?"); the Latin script concludes with his hanging "the sad burden" of his body "on the branches."[71] Relinquishing the heaping bag, a man hangs on a tree. That the series in which this picture appears—*Sinners of the Bible*—includes Judas with such figures as King Saul, Saint Peter, and Saint Paul indicates that the twelfth apostle no longer stands for aberrant demonic embodiment.

A repentant act of suicide had been imagined by thinkers besides Radbertus and Swanenburg. The historian Alexander Murray quotes a late fourteenth-century memorandum about a sermon delivered by a Dominican, one Vincent Ferrer (d. 1419). According to Ferrer, throngs of people made it impossible for Judas to get to Jesus on Mount Calvary, and he "therefore said in his heart

> "since I cannot get near Christ with my corporeal feet at least I shall meet him on Calvary by journeying in my mind, and once there I shall humbly beg pardon from him"; and that he did this by hanging himself with a noose, and his soul flew thence to Christ on Calvary aforesaid, and therefore he begged for pardon, *which Christ granted at once;* and that from thence Judas rose with Christ into Heaven, where *his soul is blessed* with those of the other elect. (Murray 2:361; emphases mine)

Noting the eccentricity of Radbertus's and Ferrer's views, Murray persuasively points out that "nearly all medieval theologians" refused to believe that Judas atoned (364). From the point of view of most ancient and medieval thinkers, Judas remained the epitome of evil.

Varying from nation to nation, as from period to period, figures of Judas from antiquity through the Middle Ages do not develop in a single, coherent manner, which is why I have eschewed a single historical trajectory. Yet despite stray exceptions, his anal, oral, and phallic excrescences were mercilessly penalized, as they would be in later times. Throughout Czech and German towns, a wooden or straw Judas effigy was burned in consecrated bonfires on Easter Eve, the Saturday before Easter Sunday. Thought to preserve the community and its agricultural produce from harm, the celebration with its chanting of *Pálíme Jidáše!* (We are burning Judas!) occurred on mountaintops or inside churchyards (Chudoba).

Understandably, then, ancient Jewish storytellers reacted with some vehemence to Judas's demonization by producing portraits of Jesus that were as offensive to Christians as Christian depictions of Judas must have been to Jews. One Jewish-authored effort that matched Christian mythologizing (if not in influence or in popularity, at least in weirdness) is assumed to have arisen in the fifth or sixth century. It countered the demoniac and doomed Judas with an obscene and farcical attenuation of Jesus' spiritual potency through what can only be interpreted as Judas's punitive act of airborne sodomy. Indeed, this Jewish-created Judas seems to be a sodomite on crack.

Sepher Toledoth Yeshu (*Life of Jesus*), a legend recycled during the Middle Ages and one that particularly infuriated Luther, tells the story of an illegitimate bastard named Yeshu who learns the letters of the Name of God, proclaims himself the Messiah, cures lepers, brings the dead to life, but convinces "the Sages" only that he has been practicing "sorcery and was leading everyone astray" (Goldstein 151).[72] Judah Iskarioto, hired by the sages and thus a sort of "intrepid undercover agent" (Maccoby 98), discovers the letters of the Ineffable Name, just as Yeshu had, and, like Yeshu, acquires the ability to fly. When Judah cannot bring Yeshu down from the heavens (because both have obtained the Ineffable Name), "Iskarioto defiled Yeshu, so that they both lost their power and fell down to the earth, and in their condition of defilement the letters of the Ineffable Name escaped from them. Because of this deed of Judah, they weep on the eve of the birth of Yeshu" (Goldstein 152).[73] A blurb for a book advertised on an American Atheists Web page calls Jesus in this rendition "the aerially sodomized victim of a flying Judas" ("Jesus"). Eventually, Judah apprises the sages that Yeshu can be found in the Temple and points him out by bowing or prostrating himself.

As good a trickster as Yeshu, if not better in some versions, Judah has liberated the people from chicanery, while the sages end up trying to hang Yeshu from a tree, though his pronouncement (by means of the Ineffable Name) that no tree should hold him leads to his finally swinging from a carob-stock, "for it was a plant more than a tree, and on it he was hanged" (Goldstein 152). Here, inverting the usual equation, Judas and the sages triumph, while Jesus becomes a doomed false prophet who led people astray. This unusual reversal—

Judas victorious over an abject Jesus—had a negligible effect on the overwhelming number of representations that it sought to dislodge. Just as important, this turnabout and the representations it tried to displace obscure another dynamic of cultural importance: namely, a tradition envisioning not one triumphing over the other's abjection, but instead the two, Judas and Jesus, welded in bondage or wedded and bonded together.

4

ARRESTING KISSES: COMING OF AGE, ESPECIALLY DURING THE RENAISSANCE

Kissing brings Judas and Jesus together. From the medieval period to the Renaissance, some visual artists depicted the betrayer as a stereotypically African or Semitic sadist. Yet many others presented Jesus and Judas as brothers, friends, or lovers. These representations of the kiss reveal a range of responses to a sometimes soulful, sometimes sexy Judas and to the love scene he stages.

WHAT DOES IT MEAN THAT the most public, communal image we have of two men kissing and embracing derives from Judas's act of betrayal? Or that Mark and Matthew, who generally deploy the Greek word *phileō* to describe a kiss, use *kataphileō*—an intensive verb meaning "to kiss warmly, effusively, or intensely"—in their account of Judas's sign in the garden of Gethsemane?[1] The placement of Judas as far away as possible from Jesus in so many illustrations of the Last Supper makes perfect sense in terms of Judas's contaminating odors, filthy ordure, and perverted appetites. But his physical proximity to Jesus at the crisis of the Passion narrative could never be avoided—not only because of the kiss in Mark and Matthew but also because Jesus had chosen Judas as a disciple, taught him how to heal and preach, included him in the Eucharist or the foot washing, called him "friend," promised that none of the disciples' souls would be lost, and predicted that Judas would rule with the eleven in the coming kingdom.

Such details in the New Testament, as well as traces of Gnostic veneration for Judas, made it possible for some early interpreters to imagine a cherished twelfth apostle. Significantly, an intimation of Judas's spiritual proximity to Jesus is evident even in early representations on stained-glass windows or in Psalters. At this point in my narrative, therefore, it makes sense to retard the pace of Judas's development, to concede that he never morphed in a direct historical path from biblical anomaly to medieval pariah; then, thanks to the Enlightenment, onward into a nineteenth-century heroic comrade of Jesus; and finally into the twentieth century's savior of Christianity's savior. In other words, it seems feasible here to suspect the quaint biographical fiction of a subject starting out bad and getting good, to remind ourselves that Judas's history is more complicated than such a teleological bildungsroman might suggest. A hateful kiss—an oxymoron—has proved Judas's duplicity in centuries of sermons, but even in medieval times some artists have imagined a kiss motivated by adoration and fealty.

From the perspective of most of the material presented in the previous chapter, Judas's betrayal kiss reeks of exactly the hypocrisy expected of a demonic creature: what other sort of being would exploit a gesture of love—signifying affection, loyalty, union, consummation—to camouflage an act of hate? In a religious context, of course, kisses should be sacrosanct, not sacrilegious. During the first five centuries of the Common Era, the Greco-Roman kiss of public greeting was reinvented by Christian "brothers" and "sisters," who kissed each other to "produce a new kind of family, a community formed not by biological relationship but by a kinship of faith" (Penn 37). Up till today, in eucharistic celebrations, worshippers are invited to "offer one another a kiss of peace" or a handshake, using a shortened version of the greeting in the Christian Bible: "Peace to all of you who are in Christ" (1 Peter 5:14; cf. Romans 16:16).[2] At

Saturday services, orthodox Jews kiss the tallith or the book they extend to touch the Torah, and on Good Friday Catholics kiss the crucifix. Numerous illustrations of the New Testament present prostitutes kissing the feet of Jesus in adoration, or Mary cradling either her beloved baby or her crucified Son. Within secular or erotic paintings such caresses are usually heterosexual: the rapturous desire of Cupid and Psyche or Mars and Venus springs to mind, or later Gustav Klimt's ornately blanketed and intertwined lovers.[3]

In Judas's same-sex kiss, though, a gesture of fidelity melds with malice aforethought. Attributed to Judas—and only to Judas—in the New Testament, the idea of using a kiss to target someone for destruction does not simply dramatize hypocrisy; it manifests perversity, an almost theatrical setting of the most unlikely and deceptive of scenes. Judases—whom Shakespeare describes as "Villains, vipers, damned without redemption"—kiss their masters, crying "All hail!" whereas they mean "all harm."[4] In contemporary times, such a venal clinch conjures images of the Mafia kiss of death, a treacherous kiss that—rather than deluding an unwitting victim—brings about precisely what the guilty party (presumably a Judas to the godfather) deserves. Much more disturbing is the kiss in the garden, which horrifies because it exploits previous intimacies to destroy a trusting intimate. Harms unintentionally inflicted by allies (such as so-called friendly fire) can be endured; however, mortal shock attends a consciously murderous embrace: "Well meant are the wounds a friend inflicts, but profuse are the kisses of an enemy." Often connected by interpreters to Judas, this puzzling line (from Proverbs 27:6) is prefaced by the statement, "Better is open rebuke than hidden love." Yet these last words may also trip one up, given the excessive guile of Judas's kiss, for how could his spiteful kiss-and-tell be said to be motivated by "hidden love"?

Curiously, it is precisely Judas's "hidden love" that Emily Dickinson proposes in a dramatic monologue that can be understood as spoken by Judas.[5] In Dickinson's verse, a masochistic betrayer asks to be disciplined by God, who has accepted his Son but rejected the speaker whose love equals or surpasses that of Jesus. As always with Dickinson's fractured syntax, the meanings are obscure and multiple. If we take Dickinson's speaker to be Judas, however, in the first stanza he seems to defend his actions by explaining that he was motivated by love—perhaps for Jesus, "The Real One"; perhaps for "Thee," God. Yet Dickinson's Judas understands, even accepts, the need for his own punishment:

> 'Twas Love – not me –
> Oh punish – pray –
> The Real One died for Thee –

Possibly Dickinson's Judas is attempting to exonerate himself at the start, to suggest that not he with his betrayal but Jesus with his love led to the sacrifice on the cross.

Equally convoluted, the second stanza extends Judas's guilty self-reproach, but relates it to the overpowering strength of his love as well as to his wish to be eventually forgiven:

> Such Guilt – to love Thee – most!
> Doom it beyond the Rest –
> Forgive it – last –
> 'Twas base as Jesus' – most!

Dickinson concludes her short poem with Judas emphasizing his resemblance to Jesus and readying himself for chastisement (which perhaps will allow him to be reunited with "The Real One" or "Thee"):

> Let Justice not mistake –
> We Two – looked so alike –
> Which was the Guilty Sake –
> 'Twas Love's – Now strike! (Fr. 562)

The last two words recall a passionate sentiment voiced in John Donne's "Batter my heart, three-personed God": a bereft Donne longs to be struck so as to be opened by and to the Divine because "dearly I love you, and would be loved fain" (i.e., gladly). Dickinson's Judas feels exiled from God, but also left behind by the "Real One" (Jesus) who loved "Thee" (God), as he did and does. What competition existed within this trinity?

Dickinson's line "We Two – looked so alike –" establishes a commonality between kin whose resemblance to each other makes them appear to be siblings. Perhaps the bereaved Judas sought to rival his brother Jesus in exhibiting the greatest love of God, or perhaps he feared that God loved Jesus more than himself. Or, as so often happens in love triangles, perhaps Judas competed with Jesus for God's love in order to pursue his desire for Jesus. Difficult as the opening and closing phrases remain, the repetition of "'Twas Love" and "'Twas Love's" hints that just as Jesus loved God and sought to love him "most," so did Judas. If guilty, then, Judas is guilty of loving too much. His betrayal, like Cain's violence, may have been motivated by sibling rivalry: Cain's or Judas's desire for paternal approbation or jealousy of the favored son. With Jesus judged the "Real One," a despised and rejected Judas has become acquainted with the grief of being deemed unreal and secondary, inauthentic and belated. Since Jesus has risen to join his maker, an isolated and lonely Judas is doomed "beyond the Rest" or asks to be doomed "beyond the Rest" in order to be forgiven at last.

The phrase "'Twas Base" that appears between "'Twas Love" and "'Twas Love's": does it mean that Judas's love was as sordid as Jesus' love was pure (which would be a normative reading)? Or might it signify that Judas's love was as basic, as foundational as Jesus' love? The word *base* can mean "corrupt, vile," but it can also mean "central, indispensable." "Forgive it – last –": the son forgiven last might be—or perhaps ought to be—the first in God's favor. In this complaint to God, Judas argues that it would be a miscarriage of justice—and this verse is addressed to "Justice" on high—to label wicked an act of consummate (though unconsummated) love. Dick-inson's miserable Judas longs to attain his righteous place alongside "Thee" (God) and "the Real One" (Jesus), a position he did at times achieve in the history of European art.

The story told in the previous chapter of Judas's evolution in postbiblical literature from antiquity to the Renaissance has eclipsed this aspect of the loving identification behind his sibling rivalry with Jesus: insight into Judas's adoration of God's Son and of God pre-dates Emily Dickinson's poem. Intriguingly, this perspective, which is rarely supplied in the words of early fictive narratives and theologi-cal meditations, can be found in premodern pictures, specifically in illustrations of the betrayal kiss. Why does Judas's love story appear earlier and more frequently in visual art than in written texts, and what does it mean? To answer such questions, this chapter stops the chronological progression, as I step back to trace the iconography of a bonding between Jesus and Judas that subverts the prevalent vilification at work in many textual representations of Judas, though it never dislodges the demonic imagery.

Quite predictably embellishing the familiar degrading caricatures, a number of visual artists recoil against Judas's perverted sadism, depicting the kiss as a form of oral aggression on the part of an African- or Semitic-looking assailant. Because such racist images so clearly turn the betrayer stereotypically black or Jewish, as Jesus glows whiter, they contribute to Judas's bad reputation in the medi-eval period. However, this chapter also emphasizes earlier and later visual artists who—at times viewing the relationship between Jesus and Judas in isolation from the battalions surrounding them—imbue their embrace not just with physical but also with spiritual fervor. Possibly frustrated in Luke and entirely absent from John's account, the betrayal kiss nevertheless became a principal motif in art, appear-ing as early as the fourth century and often replacing or eclipsing depictions of Christ's seizure (as noted by Schiller 2:52). That in illu-minations and paintings the kiss used by Judas to get Jesus arrested is arresting recalls many other words—*stunning, striking, seizing, captivating*—all of which convey the shockingly coercive power of eros, as does the phrase *the Passion* itself. "Passion," from the Latin *passio*, literally means "suffering," but in everyday English it designates "any consuming interest, dedicated enthusiasm, or concentrated commitment" (Borg and Crossan viii). Keeping this in mind, I have organized my approach to pictorial representations of the betrayal kiss around three perspectives in which Jesus and Judas look, first, like dedicated soul mates or kin; then, like mortal enemies engaged in a consuming life-and-death combat; and, finally, like committed partners victimized by a miscarriage of justice.

The relationship between the soul mates or twinned Jesus and Judas brings to mind the friendly love of the Greek word *phileō*; the connection between the battling Jesus and Judas recalls the more tangled emotions clustered around the erotic life-and-death struggle signified by the Greek words *erōs* and *thanatos*; and the rapport between the entangled partners Jesus and Judas evokes the compassionate love conveyed by the Greek word *agapē*. Yet just as sharp distinctions cannot be drawn between the Greek words for love, so too all the visual images studied in this chapter ask us to consider the ways in which affection, desire, and compassion blend and blur with each other. Ultimately we will see that the most brilliant representations of the kiss in art—the scenes envisioned by Giotto and Dürer, Carracci and Caravaggio—crystallize the fearful but also fascinating power of an arresting (glamorous) same-sex encounter that compels arrest (capture).

While in ancient and medieval legends and plays Judas was turned inside out (with his bowels spilling over the surface of his body), in a number of visual images he is outed as his clasp evokes the "hidden love" that dares not speak its name. Albeit shocking (to some) in its own right, such a claim might sound (to others) anachronistic. It appears to collide with histories of sexuality influenced by the thinking of Michel Foucault, who dated the emergence of the concept of homosexuality to modern times.[6] But Foucault was arguing that the identity category *homosexual* originated in the nineteenth century:

before that period same-sex acts of affection, desire, and compassion obviously did occur, though the people engaged in them were not categorically or ontologically defined by them. Representations of the betrayal kiss ask us to consider a homoerotic embrace between two men who need not be categorized as homosexuals.

This same-sex act that is *not* a homosexual identity: what does it mean in religious and spiritual terms? And how might it have shaped secular images of men intensely bonded with each other in passionate face-to-face encounters? From the medieval period to the Renaissance, Psalters, stained-glass windows, altar cloths, woodcuts, and oil paintings intimate, as Emily Dickinson did, that the resemblance of Judas to Jesus may have fooled the Gospel authors and even God about who was the real and most loving Son. Indeed, Dickinson's most ambiguous line—"Which was the Guilty Sake –"—might make viewers of a wedded Jesus and Judas wonder, which was the guilty one forsaken, and exactly by whom or for what?

SOUL KISSES

If we consider a kiss just a kiss, the fond bonding of Judas and Jesus puts a decided spin on folkloric speculations that date Judas's birthday as either April 1 (April Fool's Day) or February 14 (Valentine's Day).[7] Maybe Judas was just a fool for love—love in the most all-encompassing sense of that word. Some visual representations in the early medieval period emphasize the twinning of Judas and Jesus in a kiss that looks very much like other kisses that are both physical and spiritual—the holy kiss of peace in the Mass, for instance, or the joyous and sensual kisses of the Song of Solomon: "Let him kiss me with the kisses of his mouth! / For your love is better than wine" (1:2); "Your lips distill nectar, my bride; / honey and milk are under your tongue" (4:11); "His lips are lilies, distilling liquid myrrh" (5:13); "O that you were like a brother to me, / who nursed at my mother's breast! / If I met you outside, I would kiss you, / and no one would despise me" (8:1). Ancient and medieval theologians often interpreted the Song of Solomon as an allegory of God's love for the children of Israel, or of Christ's love for the church, or of the mystic's adoration of Christ. Odd though the claim might sound, at times the pictorial kiss of Judas—visually juxtaposed to the violent seizure—also seems to meditate on the confluence of human accord and mystic concord.

Perhaps the *Kiss of Judas* in the Rheinau Psalter best exemplifies the kinship of Judas and Jesus already apparent in Byzantine mosaics (like the one discussed in chapter 2; see illustration 2.1), though here the foot of Jesus does appear over the foot of Judas to signify Christ's supremacy (1250; plate 4). Jews (in conical hats) can be glimpsed behind the two central figures, and behind them are upright flaming torches as well as the tops of staves. These staves find a parallel in the upturned sword Peter holds in his right hand, while with his left he grasps the hair on the head of a kneeling Malchus, whose cut right ear bleeds profusely. Peter's violence against Malchus stands in stark contrast to Judas's gentle embrace of Jesus. Exactly the same height, Judas and Jesus both have long auburn hair and short auburn beards; Judas's hands encircle Jesus, while Jesus' hands rest serenely crossed, also on his body. Judas is seen in profile, but his visage is just as noble as Jesus' and their moods or temperaments seem harmonious. Not clothed in distinctive yellow, Judas wears green and rose robes, Jesus blue and red, and, unlike those of the other figures, their naked feet are visible. While Peter looks out at the viewer and Malchus casts his eyes down, Judas and Jesus gaze intently at each other, and only at each other. Their stasis and concentration highlight the bustle behind and adjoining them. Has the kiss already taken place? And does Malchus's cut ear predict the bloody end of Jesus, after his ears have received Judas's address ("Rabbi") and he has accepted Judas's lips on his own? Under the lantern held up by a Jew in the background, the betrayer and the betrayed are conjoined.

Given a Jesus encircled within Judas's arms, the tender intimacy of mouths that might have just met suggests reciprocity. A number of medieval thinkers assumed that the Gethsemane embrace culmi-

1. Albert Tucker, *Judas* (1955). SOURCE: NATIONAL GALLERY OF AUSTRALIA.
COURTESY OF THE ALBERT TUCKER ESTATE AND BARBARA TUCKER.
© BARBARA TUCKER.

2. Giotto, *Pact of Judas,* on the side of the chancel arch in Arena Chapel, Padua (ca. 1303–05). SOURCE: ART RESOURCE. © ALINARI/ART RESOURCE, NEW YORK.

3. Alsatian or Southern German, *The Hanging of Judas*, ca. 1520. Glass, vitreous paint and silver stain, 57.2 × 44.6 cm. SOURCE: BUCKINGHAM FUND, 1949.494. REPRODUCTION, THE ART INSTITUTE OF CHICAGO.

4. *Kiss of Judas*, Rheinau Psalter (1250). SOURCE: ZENTRALBIBLIOTHEK, ZÜRICH, MS RH. 167, FOL. 52V.

5. Copy of Ludovico Carracci's *The Kiss of Judas,* by a follower of Carracci (ca. 1589–90). SOURCE: PRINCETON UNIVERSITY ART MUSEUM. MUSEUM PURCHASE, FOWLER MCCORMICK, CLASS OF 1921 FUND. PHOTO CREDIT: BRUCE M. WHITE. © TRUSTEES OF PRINCETON UNIVERSITY.

6. Caravaggio, *The Taking of Christ* (1602–03). SOURCE: NATIONAL GALLERY OF IRELAND AND THE JESUIT COMMUNITY, LEESON ST., DUBLIN, WHO ACKNOWLEDGE THE GENEROSITY OF THE LATE DR. MARIE-LEA WILSON. © THE NATIONAL GALLERY OF IRELAND.

7. Rembrandt, *Judas Returning the Thirty Pieces of Silver* (1629). Oil on panel. Source: Private collection, England.

8. *Last Supper* by unknown Ottonian artist, Regensburg (ca. 1030–40). Tempera colors and gold leaf on parchment, 9 1/8 × 6 5/16 in. SOURCE: J. PAUL GETTY MUSEUM, MS LUDWIG VII 1 FOL. 38.

nated in a mutual kiss. Saint Bonaventure (1217–1274), for instance, insisted that both Judas's and Jesus' lips were involved:

> in the very hour of his betrayal
> this most mild Lamb did not refuse to apply
> with a sweet kiss
> his mouth *in which no guile was found*
> to the mouth which abounded in iniquity
> in order to give the traitor every opportunity
> to soften the obstinacy
> of his perverse heart. (141)

What is remarkable about the Passion is the compassion and trust of Jesus, regardless of the trustworthiness of the recipient. Even though a few medieval commentators thought that the kiss was on "the foot, the hand, or on the hem of [Jesus'] robe" (Hughes 231), so profound or widespread was belief in the sanctification of Judas's lips (through their touching of Jesus') that many thought Judas's contaminated soul had to pass through another orifice upon the demise of his body, as one preacher quoted in the previous chapter surmised.

The presumption of a reciprocal embrace has significant consequences, if one accepts the idea proposed by the psychoanalyst Adam Phillips: "Kissing on the mouth can have a mutuality that blurs the distinctions between giving and taking" (97). An entry in the Coptic Gospel of Thomas conveys Jesus' thoughts on this subject: "Jesus said: 'He who drinks from my mouth will be as I am, and I will be he, and the things that are hidden will be revealed to him'" (Cartlidge and Dungan 28).

In some thirteenth-century representations of the betrayal kiss that stress affinity and mutuality, Judas is not in profile. Instead, the two heads of Jesus and Judas tilt toward each other, as Jesus' cheek is laid against Judas's cheek, their doubled lips close together. In order to make the close contact between bodies visible to viewers, the artists accomplish what so many later directors do with actors in staged or

4.1. *Betrayal and Arrest of Christ*, Chichester Psalter (ca. 1250). Source: John Rylands Library, University of Manchester.

filmed love scenes: they compel the figures "to face each other and to face front" simultaneously (Williams 293). In the *Betrayal and Arrest of Christ* from the Chichester Psalter, for example, a blackened and animalized Malchus as well as a group of blackened and animalized arresting soldiers are juxtaposed against a very youthful Judas upon whose face Jesus leans his own (ca. 1250; illustration 4.1). The eyes of Judas and Jesus, their noses, mouths, and chins, are aligned in loving union. These two lips join together and speak to each other. Gazing directly at us, Judas clasps Jesus' robe with his left hand, while his right seems to be clasping the hand of another man, an enemy—or perhaps he is restraining this proximate attacker.

The *Betrayal and Arrest of Christ* in St. Peter's Church—the two
heads of Judas and Jesus with eyes, noses, and chins aligned—also
emphasizes the intensity of their union as well as their commonality
(1280–90; illustration 4.2). The Chichester Psalter and the St. Peter's
Church images stress a protective Jesus' command over the scene,
for in both a taller Jesus bends down to the shorter and instrumental
Judas who does his Lord's bidding by leaning or reaching up to meet
him.[8] As did Bonaventure's imagining of the "Lamb" applying his
lips to the traitor's, this portrayal troubles and revises the traditional
idea that Judas was the kisser, Jesus the kissed. Thus the visual artists
resemble a number of earlier Christian thinkers who "marveled that
even though Jesus knew Judas planned on betraying him, Christ still
kissed his betrayer in a last effort to save him" (Penn 65). Violence
congregates around each couple, but not within it. Mouth joined to

4.2. *Betrayal and
Arrest of Christ*, St.
Peter's Church,
Wimpfen in
Tal, Germany
(1280–90). Source:
Hessisches
Landesmuseum
Darmstadt. Inv.
Nr. Kg 54:34.

mouth, the kiss (detached from the arrest) signifies precisely what it does in other and quite numerous iconographic settings: physical as well as spiritual reciprocity.

In all three of these thirteenth-century representations, Jesus and Judas are attached to each other bodily, like conjoined twins, facing pages (recto and verso) in an open book, or a face and its mirrored image. With their lips closed, their intimacy seems chaste but charged, public as well as private, and a sign of their cohesion.[9] Soul mates, Judas and Jesus accept their narrative entanglement, as well as the fearful fate it will mete out to both. Not self and Other but two selves neither different from nor opposed to the other appear to coexist amicably. As in the philosophy of Emmanuel Levinas, the face-to-face relationship, in which "the Other is not known, he is *greeted*," institutes a "moral relationship of equality": "To look at a look is to look at something which cannot be abandoned or freed, but something which *aims* [*vise*] at you: it involves looking at the *face* [*visage*]" (242). In the pause of action stopped before violence, it remains possible to entertain Levinas's proposition that "To see a face is already to hear 'You shall not kill,'" for the perceived face reveals the sovereignty of the other self and thus announces an ethical prohibition against murder (243).

The extraordinary visual doubling of Judas and Jesus calls to mind early Gnostic views preserved in the writings of Epiphanius, who explained that some of the Gnostics believed that Judas betrayed because "he was good," and

> because of his [Judas's] *knowledge of heavenly things*. For, they
> say, the archons knew that if Christ were given over to the cross,
> their weak power would be drained. Judas, knowing this, bent
> every effort to betray him, *thereby accomplishing a good work
> for our salvation.* We ought to admire and praise him, because
> *through him the salvation of the cross was prepared for us* and
> the revelation of things above occasioned by it. . . . (Epiphanius
> 134; emphases mine)

If Jesus must die so that he (and his followers) can live eternally, Judas joins him in accomplishing the task at hand; quite a few scholars believe that just this message is conveyed in the ancient Coptic Gospel of Judas.[10] Should we take as a moral guide Jeremy Bentham's utilitarian definition of "the Good"—the greatest benefit for the greatest number of people—we can perceive Judas's prolonged embrace to be serving the good of Jesus' sacrifice, as the two devotedly unite in a common purpose.

The twinning of Jesus and Judas surfaces in a number of noncanonical gospels to stress their commonality. As early as the Coptic Gospel of Thomas, which some scholars consider the most important fourth-century addition to the New Testament, a figure named Judas appears as a double of Jesus. The 114 sayings of Jesus recorded in the Gospel of Thomas are written down by one Didymus Judas Thomas. "Both 'Didymus' and 'Thomas' are words that mean 'twin,'" according to Bart Ehrman, so "Judas is his proper name," and in the Acts of Thomas "he was a blood relation of Jesus" (*Jesus* 72). Later, in an Islamic-influenced Gospel of Barnabas that could have been read by or to medieval or early modern Italians and Spaniards, Judas is actually mistaken for Jesus, taken to Herod, mocked, scourged, and finally crucified instead of Jesus because of their uncanny resemblance.

The Gospel of Barnabas's Judas—traitorous to the godly Jesus, who here proclaims Muhammad the true messiah—received "thirty pieces of gold" from the Pharisees to betray his teacher into their hands (*Gospel of Barnabas* 253); but Jesus is hidden away by Nicodemus and then spirited "out of the world" by God's angelic servants, while God "acted wonderfully, insomuch that Judas was so changed in speech and in face to be like Jesus that we believed him to be Jesus" (262, 263). With Jesus in heaven, not only the high priest but even "all the disciples" believed "Judas to be Jesus": "the voice, the face, and the person of Judas were so like to Jesus, that his disciples and believers entirely believed that he was Jesus" (264, 268).[11] Because the Gospel of Barnabas's Judas has been turned into a Jesus lookalike, the twelfth apostle actually suffers the nailing onto the Calvary cross. In stark opposition to orthodox Christian preaching, the narrator of the Gospel of Barnabas rejects the assertion that Jesus died and rose again. Readers are instead informed that the disciples "stole the body *of Judas* and hid it, spreading a report that Jesus was risen again; whence great confusion arose" (269; emphasis mine).

Within orthodox Christian thinking, early as well as late, one can also discern theological assertions of the kinship of Jesus and Judas. At the beginning of the seventeenth century, John Donne delivered a sermon to affirm that Judas, like Pilate, could not possibly have given Jesus away. Only "the unexpressible and unconceivable love of Christ"—his "willingnesse, a propensnesse, a forwardnesse to give himselfe to make this great peace and reconciliation, between God and Man"—empowered him to give himself away as a "free, and absolute" gift (*Sermons* 122–23). Meditating on the handing over ("*Tradidit*") that absorbed Augustine, Donne attributed the betrayal to Christ himself:

> The word which the *Apostle* uses here, for Christ giving of himselfe, is the same word, which the *Evangelists* use still, for *Judas* betraying of him: so that Christ did not onely *give* himselfe to the will of the Father, in the eternall Decree; nor onely deliver himselfe to the power of death in his Incarnation, but he *offered*, he exhibited, he *exposed*, (we may say) he *betrayed* himselfe to his enemies; and all this, for worse enemies; to the *Jewes*, that Crucified him once, for us, that make sinne our sport, and so make the Crucifying of the Lord of life a Recreation. (122–23)

According to Donne, Jesus *betrayed himself* (to be killed, Donne more typically insists, not by the Romans but by the Jews).

Whereas Donne intimates that Judas has been credited with a power belonging only to Jesus, one modern theologian has reflected on their strange cohesion: Karl Barth asks, "For all the dissimilarities, is it possible to overlook the likeness in which Judas alone of the apostles stands face to face and side by side with Jesus?" (*Doctrine*

479). Barth notes not only "the proximity of Judas to Jesus" but also "the resemblance to Him, which he alone knows of all the apostles" (480). Even a twentieth-century creative writer who emphasized the monstrous duplicity of Judas could contrast the confused impotence of the eleven at the arrest with the twelfth apostle's passionate engagement, as the Russian author Leonid Andreyev did in a story titled "Judas Iscariot" (1920):

> [Judas's] heart was set aflame with bitter anguish not unlike the agony which had oppressed Jesus a short time since. His soul transformed into a hundred ringing and sobbing chords, he rushed forward to Jesus and tenderly kissed His windchilled cheek, so softly, so tenderly, with such agony of love and yearning that were Jesus a flower upheld by a slender stem, that kiss would not have shaken from it one pearl of dew or dislodged one tender leaf. (103)

The same-sex partnership in a number of visual representations of Judas "face to face and side by side with Jesus" emphasizes the tenderness of union: physical but profoundly spiritual, it connects like to like, breath to breath, contrasting Jesus and Judas to the animalized Others who threaten to overtake them.

Such an image—of two men from decidedly different backgrounds, and with entirely different perspectives, about to unite in an intensely emotional as well as spiritual attachment—suits a narrative tradition in the Hebrew Bible. Jonathan loved his father's enemy David, "loved him as his own soul" (1 Samuel 18:3); and David mourned Jonathan's death because "greatly beloved were you to me; / your love to me was wonderful, / passing the love of women" (2 Samuel 1:26). But the Song of Solomon played a more central role in the rhetoric of Christian mysticism than did either of the books of Samuel, and early in Western civilization the Song was often interpreted to articulate the longing of one man for another.[12]

"Let him kiss me with the kisses of his mouth": so begins the

Song of Solomon, where the sometimes stiff-necked people of Israel become the enraptured brides of a divine and divinely masculine God. In the Hebrew Bible, male as well as female supplicants long to be embraced by the divine husband, just as the New Testament explicitly specifies that "in Christ there is neither male nor female, but we are all one in Him" (Galatians 3:28). As Stephen D. Moore has shown, early church sages could allegorize the Song to describe "the mutual attraction between two males" (*God's Beauty Parlor* 27). In a meditation on the Song of Songs, quoted by Moore, Bernard of Clairvaux (1091?–1153) wants to kiss Jesus on the mouth in order to satiate his desire for spiritual consummation. Desire has everything to do with knowledge of and longing for the divine and with same-sex intimacy:

> Of what use to me the wordy effusions of the prophets? Rather let him who is the most handsome of the sons of men, let him kiss me with the kiss of his mouth [Song 1:1]. . . . [E]ven the very beauty of the angels can only leave me wearied. For my Jesus utterly surpasses these in his majesty and splendour. Therefore I ask of him what I ask of neither man nor angel: that he kiss me with the kiss of his mouth. (quoted in *God's Beauty Parlor* 23)

The bride's yearning for union with her beloved groom conveys Bernard's longing for a kiss from "the most handsome of the sons of men."

Would it have been possible for Bernard or for Denis the Carthusian (1402?–1471), meditating on this same passage in the Song of Songs, to perceive in Judas's embrace the mystic's pining to kiss Jesus? Absolutely not, a historicist would probably answer. Yet when Denis asks, "Did he not himself create me so as to receive that happy kiss of his mouth in the homeland of the Blessed?" (quoted in S. Moore, *God's Beauty Parlor* 26), he provides a route for reading the illustrations against the grain of the Passion narrative they are meant to adorn but that they also interpret. In other words, these images resonate differently if we view them as illustrative not of the Gospels but of the Song of Solomon. One justification for doing so: the only person in the Passion who received what the mystics longed to obtain was Judas.

The erotic words that St. John of the Cross (1542–1591) used to elaborate on his craving for union with God have nothing to do consciously with the betrayer's kiss; however, they curiously gloss visual images stressing the doubling of Jesus and Judas:

> I shall see you in your beauty, and you will see me in your beauty, and I shall see myself in you in your beauty, and you will see yourself in me in your beauty; that I may resemble you in your beauty, and you resemble me in your beauty, and my beauty be your beauty and your beauty my beauty: wherefore I shall be in your beauty, and you will be me in your beauty, because your very beauty will be my beauty; and thus we shall behold each other in your beauty. (*Spiritual Canticle* stanza 36, 5)

The balancing of "you" and "me" in John's chant bespeaks the rhythmic giving and taking of interidentification. If the femininity of the bride in the Song could serve as a mask for the mortal mystic's desire for the immortal Jesus' kiss, perhaps the villainy assigned the betrayer could function as a camouflage or excuse for some visual artists' portrayal of the union of the enamored Judas and Jesus. In addition, if we detach Judas's kiss from the Roman soldiers and Pharisees, as visual artists can and do, we might read it as a variation on the *osculum pacis* (kiss of peace), which was a physical gesture reflecting or effecting the spiritual reception of Jesus in the supplicant's soul. After baptism, as part of a wedding vow, during High Mass, or bestowed on the dead, the kiss of greeting, of promise, of prayer, and of farewell communicates a silent vow of amity. Depictions of the loving union of Jesus and Judas recall the "friend" whom Jesus instructed to go quickly on his mission.

Yet even the most soulful depictions of Judas's kiss hint at enmity to come. A detail from the *Capture of Christ* (ca. 1280) by Cimabue presents the profile of a noble Judas next to a haloed Christ in order to emphasize their unity and their shared seriousness of intent. Still, Cimabue's Jesus looks a bit suspicious of the embrace he accepts. And all the thirteenth-century illustrations discussed thus far place Jesus on the right side, often associated with good luck, the pure, and the holy, and Judas on the left, often associated with bad luck, the impure, and the profane: already in Latin, the word *sinister*—literally, "on the left"—had taken on the meanings "perverse," "unlucky." Moreover, the patience of Jesus evident in the Rheinau Psalter, the Chichester Psalter, and the image in St. Peter's Church may signify not acquiescence in the embrace but acquiescence to God's will and to his own ghastly fate on the cross.

In Fra Angelico's *Kiss of Judas* from *Scenes from the Life of Christ* (ca. 1450–53; illustration 4.3) the isolation of an older Judas and Jesus is emphasized by the positioning of the Jewish authorities and the Roman soldiers on the ground, where they have fallen as they do in John's Gospel account.[13] Judas has a halo here, as does Jesus. Even though it is darkened, the halo clearly connects Judas to the apostles standing to Jesus' right, and differentiates him from the Pharisees and soldiers knocked out by a thoughtful, powerful Jesus, who meditates—as he is embraced—with crossed and limp hands that register his resignation. Fra Angelico's reconciled Jesus reminds us of John's hint that Jesus is complicit in Judas's act: after John's Jesus says to Judas, "'Do quickly what you are going to do,'" we are informed: "Now no one at the table knew why he said this to him" (13:28)—no one except, of course, Judas and Jesus.

The proximity, intimacy, and repose of the pair put into question but do not directly contradict prevailing written interpretations of the kiss, such as the fourteenth-century meditation once attributed to Saint Bonaventure. *Meditations on the Life of Christ* explains,

It is said to have been the custom of the Lord Jesus to receive disciples He had sent out with a kiss on their return. Therefore the

4.3. Fra Angelico, *Kiss of Judas*, detail from panel three of the
Silver Treasury of Santissima Annunziata (ca. 1450–53).
Tempera on panel. Source: Bridgeman Art Library.

traitor gave the kiss as the sign. Preceding the others, he returned
with a kiss, almost as though to say, "I have not come with these
soldiers but, returning, I kiss you according to custom and say,
'Ave Rabbi, God save you, master.' " O real traitor! Pay care-
ful attention and follow the Lord as He patiently and benignly
receives the *treacherous embraces and kisses* of that wretch whose
feet He had washed but a short time before and to whom He
had given the supreme food. *How patiently He allows Himself
to be captured, tied, beaten, and furiously driven,* as though He
were an evil-doer and indeed powerless to defend Himself! (325;
emphases mine)

As if loath to depict "treacherous embraces and kisses," Fra Angelico takes a cue from John and refrains from depicting the actual kiss.

Reflecting on the kiss as a sign of love, Saint Ambrose (ca. 339–397) wondered whether Judas's act of hate could be considered a kiss at all:

> What kiss could the Jew have, seeing that he has not known peace, has not received peace from Christ who said: "My peace I leave with you." . . . So the Pharisee had no kiss, except perhaps the kiss of the traitor Judas. But *Judas had no kiss either;* and that was why, when he wanted to show the Jews the kiss he had promised them as the sign of betrayal, the Lord said to him: "Judas, betrayest thou the Son of man with a kiss?" He meant, do you offer a kiss when you have not the love which goes with a kiss, do you offer a kiss when *you know not the mystery of the kiss?* . . . A kiss conveys the force of love, *where there is no love, no faith, no affection, what sweetness can there be in kisses?* (quoted by Perella 28; emphases mine)[14]

"[B]ecause Jews have no love," Michael Philip Penn explains about this passage from Ambrose, "they cannot exchange a sign of love" (62). In many early Christian commentaries, Penn has reasoned, the ritual kiss provoked allusions to Judas because "the ritual kiss could become like Judas' kiss; a deceitful Christian could, like Judas, kiss with his lips, but not his heart" (117). Augustine and many of his successors sought to distinguish the profane and deceitful kiss of Judas from the sacred kiss of peace and reconciliation. Precisely the effort to differentiate proves that each of these mouth-to-mouth encounters inevitably recalls the other.[15]

Fear or loathing of Judas's "treacherous embraces and kisses" may explain why some early Catholic thinkers questioned the symbolism of the liturgical kiss of peace and why a number of clerics active in the Protestant Reformation removed it entirely from religious services. Since the betrayer's kiss conveyed the bitter force of hatred, the kiss of peace was soon omitted from the Mass on Maundy Thursday, and in some places on Easter. By the end of the fifteenth century, the face-to-face kiss of peace had often been supplanted by a pax-board, a rounded or rectangular tablet of wood or precious metal bearing an image of Jesus that was kissed; however, even the pax-board came under attack by Protestant reformers who objected to the idea that the body and its gestures could reflect or effect a spiritual transformation (see Koslofsky). Those worshippers who kissed each other or the pax-board were in danger of following in the footsteps of the traitor: "By omitting the kiss of peace, the early Protestants suggested liturgically that all kisses were in fact Judas kisses" (Koslofsky 26).

LIP SERVICE

Not a kissing kin, the villainous Judas gives a kiss that cozens, as do his precursors in the Hebrew Bible. Absalom, for instance, manages to steal the hearts of the people of Israel with a kiss: to enlist support for his rebellion against his father, David, "he would put out his hand and take hold of them, and kiss them" (2 Samuel 15:5). Isaac is deceived into blessing Jacob by a deceitful kiss, and the general Joab kisses Amasa while sticking a sword through his ribs (Genesis 27:26–27; 2 Samuel 20:9–10). Like Absalom especially, Judas uses a hypocritical kiss to incite violence against his Lord. Artists who emphasize the sadism of Judas's kiss tend to use two central devices: they racialize Judas and Jesus—making Judas black or Semitic, while Jesus becomes whiter—and they link Judas to the advancing battalions of aggressive Jewish authorities and Roman soldiers coming to capture, tie, beat, and furiously goad Jesus.[16]

These two representational decisions tend to render the embrace of Judas and Jesus disgusting, for the black-white, Semitic-Caucasian couple signifies racial miscegenation, as well as a repulsive amalgam of love and war. The confused gendering of the pair also contributes to their degradation: to some viewers a passive but chastely virtuous Jesus brings out the hypermasculinity of a grotesquely aggressive Judas, while to others a stalwart Jesus produces the parodic femininity of a clingingly parasitic Judas. Whether the twelfth apostle looks too male or too female, his embrace involves excessive and volatile sexuality. Highlighted in early modern times, most famously by Giotto and Dürer, the nasty physical encounter between Judas and Jesus reveals the abhorrent proximity of a sinner to the most sacred of beings.

When Judas undergoes a race change in a number of fourteenth-through seventeenth-century stained-glass windows, altar pieces, wall paintings, and woodcuts, he emerges as an African, Middle Eastern, or Semitic creature whose features verge on the Neanderthal. Backed by spear-carrying soldiers, a barbaric and bestial Judas embracing a pallid Jesus brings to mind invasive armies, aggressive heathens, or Orientalized cannibals threatening Christendom itself. Sedulius's popular biblical epic *Pascale Carmen* (ca. 425–450) puts into words the sacrilegious aggression of the twelfth apostle's kiss:

> When you shake both the sacrilegious blade and the
>   projecting one
> By means of swords and stakes, do you both press your
>   mouth to the honey and implant the potion,
> And flattering the lord, come forth under that image?
> What friend do you represent and with what friendly deceit
>   do you greet him?
> At no times does that agreement conspire against the terrible
>   swords
> Nor does a savage wolf extend kisses to a pious lamb.
>   (Sedulius ll. 63–68)[17]

Judas's fatal attraction to the innocent victim plants a poisonous "potion" or "savage" bite, sexualizing the violence of his biting of baby Jesus in the Arabic Infancy Gospel. With an implicit threat (of cutting, circumcising, and castrating), "sacrilegious blade[s]" and "terrible swords" abound around the dark and fleshly "wolf" whose mouth would savage the white and ethereal "pious lamb."

Decrying cross-species contact, innumerable poets after Sedulius cursed the creepy traitor's kiss in lines not unlike those Robert Stephen Hawker published in 1841:

> Hail! Master mine!—so did the viper hiss,
> When, with false fang and stealthy crawl, he came
> And scorched Messiah's cheek with that vile kiss
> He deemed would sojourn there—a brand of shame.

The physical touching of Judas, a fanged viper, and Jesus, a divine Son, inspires painters with revulsion, but also with a titillating voyeurism in dwelling on the twelfth apostle's malicious pleasure at inflicting pain.[18] To emphasize horrific miscegenation, dark skin pigmentation and coarse features are bestowed on a negroid and profiled Judas in the Passion window in the church at Walborch near Hagenau (1451) and a painting in the Church of the Dominicans of Colmar by Martin Schongauer (1480–90; illustration 4.4).

In the church of the Dominicans of Colmar, the thick lips and curly or tightly cropped hair of a passionately intent Judas contrast with the pale, pensive submission of a doomed Jesus, whose eyes look away from the shameful betrayer. As innumerable scholars have shown, the whitening of the image of Christ equates whiteness with virtue and beauty, here highlighted by linking the betrayer to people endowed with stereotypically African features.[19] An African Judas makes sense of Othello's reference to himself as a "Iudean" who threw a pearl away, especially because Shakespeare's Moor eventually murders his white, innocent wife with a kiss.[20] Yet Othello achieves a heroic stature denied Judas, whose malicious treachery recalls Iago's. And Iago's betrayal of his trusty leader also involves a kiss, indeed a same-sex kiss that he fabricates to churn up Othello's jealous suspicions about his wife.[21] Judas looks aggressively masculine in the church of Colmar. For the barren garden scene created by Martin Schongauer—

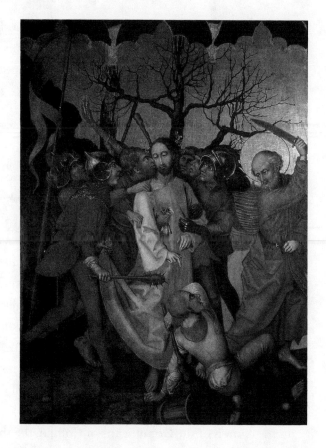

4.4. Martin Schongauer, *Betrayal and Arrest of Christ*, Church of the Dominicans of Colmar (1480–90). Source: Musée d'Unterlinden, Colmar. Photo courtesy of O. Zimmermann.

with a downcast Jesus mute in his white robe—features villainous persecutors in the hyperbolic manner of melodrama, rendering Jesus passively resistant and piously feminine.[22]

In other attempts to make Judas repulsive, his hooked nose and red hair incarnate the stereotypical Jew. Two illustrations of the betrayal and arrest—one by Johann Koerbecke on the Marienfeld Altar in Munster (1457; illustration 4.5) and the other by Gaspard Isenmann in the Church of St. Martin in Colmar (1462–65; illustration 4.6)—present a caricatured Semitic Judas. The color of sin, of agitation, of Satan, and of blood, red on head and chin was linked by one of the most vituperative writers about Judas with the name "Iscariot," which Abraham a Santa Clara defined as "ist gar rot" or "is all red" (Dinzelbacher 26). Intent on bringing a pale Jesus down,

4.5. Johann
Koerbecke, *Betrayal
and Arrest of
Christ*, panel from
the Marienfeld
Altar in Munster
(1457). Source:
Westfälisches
Landesmuseum.

the darkened Judas featured in Koerbecke's brilliantly balanced composition exhibits a markedly hooked nose. Because he seems decades
older than Koerbecke's youthful Jesus, his embrace looks pedophilic
as well.[23] Also in profile (because he is two-faced, a hypocrite), also
endowed with a prominent hooked nose, Isenmann's Judas lunges at
a forward-facing and pale Jesus, who is simultaneously threatened
on his other side by a simian soldier, either a member of the Temple
police (Luke 22:52) or a Roman (John 18:3). The light emanating
from the heads of both Jesus figures, their sorrowful mien, the fact
that Isenmann's Jesus reaches down to heal the cut ear of Malchus,
the metal armature of the soldiers: all highlight the martyrdom of
Jesus, brought about by an alliance between Judas, the Jews, and the
imperial powers of Rome.

4.6. Gaspard Isenmann, *Betrayal and Arrest of Christ*, Church of
St. Martin in Colmar (1462–65). Source: Musée d'Unterlinden,
Colmar. Photo courtesy of O. Zimmermann.

In still other depictions, Judas is shown looking deranged, either
bald or in a tightly fitting helmet, mashing his face onto Jesus'.[24] At
times, the melee surrounding Jesus at the arrest—entangled in ropes,
encircled by armored troops—can obscure Judas: in the Sforza Hours
Betrayal and Arrest of Christ (ca.1490; illustration 4.7), it is difficult
to surmise which (or whether) one of the grinning, open-mouthed
tormentors might be Judas. Thick-lipped and gesticulating, the black
Roman or Temple police in this picture look like grinning minstrels,
stereotyped stage blacks (traditionally played by white men) whose
capture of the sorrowful, limp, blond-haired Jesus cannot but bring
to mind the hapless heroine of melodrama whose steadfast virtue
is tested by villainous men. Perhaps Judas's is the smiling face in
profile, positioned between Jesus and the dark tormentor who ropes
Jesus around the neck and hands. The Sforza Hours image evokes
the specter of cannibalism in the depiction of a scene that occurs

after the kiss, for in the upper right-hand corner one can glimpse the kiss of Judas that earlier occurred. In the foreground, the cutting of Malchus's ear plays an important role in depicting the depravity of Judas's treachery. Set against the spears and knives, it summons the threat of castration—the slicing off of any body part generally does raise fears of the unkindest cut of all; at the same time, it intimates that eventually the sadistic abusers of Jesus will be avenged, as indeed they are by such a debasing caricature.

Giotto's famous depiction of the Judas kiss best captures the castration threat that Judas poses. In profile without a halo, dressed in yellow with red hair, a youthful Judas puckers up, as his robe shrouds a profiled, haloed Jesus (ca. 1305; illustration 4.8). Also with a halo, St. Peter on the left side of the wall painting parallels Jesus, just as Malchus parallels Judas. Like the slave Malchus, Judas

4.7. *Betrayal and Arrest of Christ,* Sforza Hours, Milan (ca. 1490). Source: British Library. MS Add. 34294, fol. 147v. © The British Library Board.

4.8. Giotto, *Betrayal of Christ*, Arena Chapel, Padua (ca. 1305).
Source: Bridgeman Art Library.

is enslaved by the Jewish authorities who control him. But whereas
Peter reacts violently against aggression by knifing off Malchus's ear,
Giotto's Jesus turns his cheek to the viewer, accepting the affront
while simultaneously staring intently into Judas's eyes, as if forcing
Judas to acknowledge his crime. Pressing behind and around the two
central figures are the soldiers, guards, and Temple authorities whose
lighted torches, spears, clubs, and halberds bristle in the night air like
the spines of a gigantic hedgehog. The plump face of Judas, as well as
his corpulent frame beneath the enveloping robe, warns that the kiss
might be an incorporating bite, as wounding as the upright knives
and spears of the amassed crowd.

In Giotto's fresco Judas seems swollen beneath his billowing robes, especially when compared to the erect, slender Jesus. Jesus' beard, as well as his noble forehead, set against Judas's beardless face and his reduced forehead, contributes to the idea that the twelfth apostle belongs to a different, effeminate race. Besides Malchus, Judas's double in this painting is the hooded captor with his back to the viewer: an anonymous (but sinister because faceless) executioner, he reaches, with his cape draping in a manner similar to Judas's, to catch hold of the cloak of a deserting disciple—perhaps the young man who fled Jesus in such a rush that he left behind the linen cloth (Mark 14:51). The disciple's absence from the scene underscores Jesus' presence of mind as he refuses to run away but instead confronts head-on his multiple antagonists: Judas, the high priest accusing him with outstretched hand on the right, the mob pressing around in such great numbers that they spill over the edges of the representation.

"Kissing is eating without devouring," Adrianne Blue has reasoned (140), but behind Judas's lips lurk the teeth of the law. The bites of the law and the sword, as well as the horrifying suffering of Jesus, are everywhere apparent in the six cycles produced by Albrecht Dürer about the Passion, all of which place kissing and cutting side by side. In their approach to Judas, three of these exceptionally popular and influential depictions are particularly important: *The Betrayal of Christ,* from the Small Passion (1508; illustration 4.9); *The Taking of Christ,* from the Small Passion (1509; illustration 4.10); and *The Betrayal of Christ,* from the Large Passion (1510; illustration 4.11), all created after the legal expulsion of the Jewish community from Nuremberg.[25] Interpreting the Gospels' narrative spatially, Dürer repeatedly places the kiss above the lower image of Peter slicing off Malchus's ear, as he successively heightens Jesus' helplessness. To the extent that these works foreground Peter wielding his sword and the Temple slave Malchus cowering in fear at his mutilation, they stop the action before Jesus enjoins his followers to "Put your sword back into its place; for all who take the sword will perish by the sword" (Matthew 26:52).

The biblical connection between Peter and Judas had been estab-lished by Mark, first when Jesus rebukes Peter—"Get behind me, Satan! For you are setting your mind not on divine things but on human things" (8:29, 32–33)—and later when Jesus predicts Peter's betrayal: "before the cock crows twice, you will deny me three times" (14:30). In the apocryphal gospel of Nicodemus, or Acts of Pilate, a repentant Judas returns home to get a rope, but his wife scoffs at the idea of Jesus' resurrection, likening it to "this cock that is roasting on the fire of coals" crowing: "And immediately at her word that cock spread its wings and crowed thrice. Then was Judas yet more con-vinced, and straightway made the halter of rope and hanged himself" (James 116). In Acts, we noted, it was Peter who prefaced the descrip-tion of Judas's exploding in the Field of Blood (1:15–19). The name of Judas's father, Simon, further links him to Peter, formerly Simon (see Matthew 16:18).

From the Middle Ages on, the nighttime denial of Peter and the suicide of Judas on the next day encouraged thinkers to weigh the eventual repentance of the elected Peter against the despair of the rejected Judas.[26] An evil anti-Peter, unrepentant Judas enacts through the Passion kiss an injury that Dürer revenges through the righteous apostle who would go on to found the church. Peter's swift, violent, and fully justified retaliation: does it prophesize or emblematize the church's future and triumphant victory over wretched Jewish mis-creants? Does it rationalize the legal expulsion of the Jewish com-munity from Nuremberg? In Dürer's woodcuts and engraving, Peter emerges as Judas's major adversary, as if to suggest that the church he would build fortifies itself through hostility to the people represented by Judas, Malchus, and the Temple authorities they serve. By means of Peter's act, the servant of the high priest, Malchus (a name mean-ing "king"), will become as deaf as his Jewish masters are deemed blind.

In the somber 1508 engraving by Dürer, a contorted and fallen Malchus struggles to use his club to ward off Peter's avenging sword. Above them, a profiled and dark-faced Judas thrusts himself at

4.9. Albrecht Dürer, *The Betrayal of Christ*, from the Small Passion (1508). Engraving. Source: Michael Cavanagh, Kevin Montague. Copyright © 2006 Indiana University Art Museum.

Jesus, as Dürer pinpoints the exact moment of the kiss. It almost seems as if the force of the crowd and of the avenging Peter presses Judas onto Jesus' nonresisting figure. An avid Judas, whose lips and eyes fix on Jesus, hints at the sort of sexual perversion with which Judas-Oedipus was associated in the previous chapter. One colorized version of the 1508 image features a dark-haired, swarthy Judas pressing against a blond, fair Jesus.[27] Despite "the commotion" of the arrest, Jesus appears to Erwin Panofsky to be "Unconscious of the noose which threatens His neck": "He bends His head and closes His eyes to receive the kiss as though He and Judas were alone in the

4.10. Albrecht Dürer, *The Taking of Christ*, from the Small Passion (1509). Woodcut. Source: Indiana University Lilly Library. Courtesy of the Lilly Library, Indiana University, Bloomington, Indiana.

universe" (146). Behind Dürer's antagonists, as in Giotto's painting, flaring torches and pointed spears bristle vertically in the gloomy nocturnal air. Not only the volatility of the marauding troops but also the avid gaze of the kisser—savoring the sight of his prey, wanting to see the humiliation he activates—lend the scene a sadistic, raw power. Although overwhelmed by the torments inflicted around him, an older, white-haired Christ almost seems to control the embrace, as he submits to the in-your-face bravado of his personal tormentor. In Judas's right hand, one can glimpse the bag of coins with its dangling drawstring.

Just as violent, the 1509 woodcut again pinpoints the exact moment of the kiss, again foregrounds the sword Peter uses to strike an already-fallen Malchus, again features lassos, swords, spears, and flaming torches to stress both the physical and the psychological anguish Jesus suffered at the hands of Judas and his minions. Here on the left side of Judas, Jesus does not look particularly feminine in these depictions that nevertheless present the thoroughly discredited—ghoulishly sadistic—masculinity of Judas. Asymmetry rules in the woodcut, as in the engraving: Jesus does not know or see what Judas knows or sees; Jesus is vulnerably singular, whereas Judas is multiplied by the overpowering mob he leads. Judas holds the money bag in the hand resting on Jesus' back, a clear sign of mercenary motives that cannot fully explain the febrile excitement that his features register. Dürer's face-to-face encounters are shocking, because the vision of the face does *not* register the sacred autonomy of the Other. A monster of violent and selfish sovereignty, Judas—by gazing directly at Jesus—abrogates the faith in which humanity puts its trust: namely, as Emmanuel Levinas put it, that "murder is possible, but it is possibly only when one has not looked the Other in the face" (244).

The 1510 Large Passion woodcut moves the avenging foregrounded Peter to the right corner, but also adds a number of Gothic elements that heighten the horror. Especially in the Large Passion woodcut, where Jesus is roped around the waist and the neck, he looks vulnerable as the darkened face of Judas battens on his upturned lips. The ropes pulling Jesus yoke him to a foe he would resist, if he could. The gnarled limbs of the tree on the right, the blasted stump next to it, the diagonal swords and spears, the countless number of anonymous assailants, the soldier binding Jesus' hands behind his back: all these heighten a nightmare from which we are more removed. In the background, two tiny figures in flight can be detected: a soldier tearing linen cloth from a frightened follower. Again, a voyeuristic traitor ghoulishly gazes at his prey, as if schadenfreude has engulfed Judas: a warped delight derived from observing the torment of the Other. But here Jesus tries to absent himself at least mentally or spiritually by looking up to the heavens for support. Malchus groveling on the

4.11. Albrecht Dürer, *The Betrayal of Christ*, from the Large Passion (1510). Woodcut. Source: Albrect Dürer, *Die grosse Passion: eine Holzschnittefolge* (Zurich: Arche, 1946).

ground brings to mind earlier pictures we have seen of Judas on the wrong side of the table during the Last Supper.

Taken together, Dürer's woodcuts and engravings dramatize the passionate ferocity of a Judas paying lip service to Jesus while consciously serving the malevolent violence he unleashes. Putting on display the inscrutability of why treachery occurs, Dürer, like Giotto, dramatizes the unnerving confluence of spiritual exultation and fleshly mortification in an arranged, enforced marriage of heaven and hell. Whether Jesus looks feminine in his chaste resistance to seduction or masculine in his steadfast resolution against aggression, Judas appears either hypermasculine (the ruthless leader of armored soldiers) or parasitically feminine (swollen and clutching). In either case, Judas's excessive and therefore grotesque gender underscores the deviance of a same-sex embrace that must be read in Schongauer's, Koerbecke's, and Isenmann's works as an act not just interracial but interspecies, between two beings from entirely different orders of creation. A vicious Judas entrapping Jesus exhibits a sinful or sick ardor that threatens to destroy all the sons in the family of man.

What interpretation of the Passion might give rise to the visual work I have clustered under the rubric of a passionately murderous lip service? Could the image of a hateful kiss be related to a twisted or rancorous rivalry between Judas and Peter for Jesus' love? In Mario Brelich's *The Work of Betrayal* (1975), an oddly discursive novel, "a triangular romantic relationship between Jesus, John and Judas" is postulated to explain John's peculiar hostility to Judas (41): Brelich's investigator attributes "the calumnies and perfidies" of John's Gospel to "John's jealous soul," which sensed "mysterious ties" between Jesus and Judas (42). Inadvertently—in an extended aside—George Steiner laid the groundwork for a related and "flagrantly unorthodox" construal of the Gospels by positing Judas's jealousies of John (*No Passion Spent* 415). The twelfth apostle, from this unusual perspective, "loved the Nazarene most vehemently, albeit with a love flawed by this excess," but his vehement love was warped by "Seeing the beloved disciple so manifestly (so scandalously?) preferred" at the Last Supper, a sight that plummeted Judas into "murderous jealousy" (415). Stung by John's preeminence—he is often assumed to be the beloved disciple reclining next to Jesus or in his arms at table—Steiner's Judas feels impelled to hurt the one he loves.[28]

The sculpture in the cathedral of Volterra (illustration 2.4) and a number of depictions of the Last Supper do contrast Judas and the beloved disciple. But the pictures in this section hint that a comparable competition or rivalry over Jesus existed between the elected Peter and the rejected Judas. Was Judas goaded by rivalry with Peter into a punitive or murderous passion? Perhaps Peter's enmity against Judas and Malchus served as the foundation of his subsequent church building. Yet it is possible to postulate, antithetically, that the cutting

action works not to contrast but to link or conflate Peter's vengeful enterprise, clearly not countenanced by his teacher, with Judas's
treachery. Like Judas, after all, Peter denied Jesus and disobeyed his
precepts: those who "take the sword will perish by the sword" (Matthew 26:52).[29] Brandishing his weapon, Peter continues to set his
mind "not on divine things but on human things," as Jesus put it in
his rebuke of Peter (Mark 8:33). Ironically, then, Peter's righteous
vengeance would impede the good outcome that will result from
Judas's evil embrace.

KISMET

By translating the betrayal kiss into destiny or fate, two Italian artists
produced astonishingly provocative meditations on violence and the
sacred, both of which depict the arrest of Christ as a miscarriage of
justice administered by civic authorities over which Judas had little or
no control. Lodovico Carracci, the premier sixteenth-century painter
of Bologna, and his now even more famous younger contemporary
Caravaggio eschewed earlier stylized portrayals of the kiss. Instead,
they used realism to create the illusion of powerful human bodies in
crowded and fraught situations. Whereas earlier artists maintained
a great distance between the viewer and the Passion, Carracci and
Caravaggio position us quite close to the actions taking place. Rather
than presenting Jesus and Judas from top to toe, they paint the upper
halves of their protagonists' bodies in life-size proportions. Within
large horizontal formats, Carracci's The Kiss of Judas (ca. 1589–90)
and Caravaggio's The Taking of Christ (1602–03) zero in on a singular moment of enormous emotional intensity. These justly famous
representations of the betrayal kiss, both of which were lost for
nearly two hundred years, jettison any sequential narrative; remove
Malchus, Peter, and the Jewish authorities from the picture; and center attention on eroticism (in Carracci's painting) and aesthetics (in
Caravaggio's). Judas emerges through such depictions as a complex

character whom it is difficult to judge, with whom it is easier to sympathize.

Possibly the most startling re-creation of the Passion scene, Ludovico Carracci's *The Kiss of Judas* encircles Jesus and Judas with a ring of hands, as does the later copy of the original painting reproduced in this volume (plate 5).[30] On a canvas meant to be placed over a door, Carracci tightens the noose around his two central figures, drawing the eye from the yellow-robed arm of Judas, with his fingers near the hand of an unseen soldier on the left; up to the hand holding a lantern toward the upper left; then toward the two hands holding a hanging rope that functions like a halo at the top of the canvas; next to the two hands on either side of the helmeted soldier on the right (also cut off); and finally down at the bottom right to Christ's limp, grasped wrist. The bodies of the soldiers, who appear mostly as faceless helmets, are radically chopped out of the painting. For this reason, when I first saw Carracci's *Kiss of Judas* in a book reproduction, I thought I was looking at a blown-up detail. Only later did I realize that the painter had used a kind of zoom effect to rope off the ropers, to excise the removers. But why the emphasis on their ungloved, naked hands? The Greek word used for Judas's action in the garden, *paradidōnai* (to hand over), assigns Judas alone the task of handing Jesus over to the authorities; however, Carracci emphasizes the number of human hands involved in a conspiracy ring.

At the center of the canvas, we find the pallid, pensive Jesus and the stereotypically African Judas of earlier times totally transformed. With his full lips open to receive the kiss, Carracci's Jesus looks almost expectant, his eyebrows raised and eyelids partly lowered; the pinkish shadows serve to highlight the smooth and pearly texture of his bared shoulder. On closer inspection, his right and left eye do not seem to be focusing together, as if he is dazed, drugged, or perhaps entranced. Swarthy in complexion, Judas—with glossy black hair as well as a long nose that appears more aquiline than hooked— looks down on the mouth his lips are about to touch. An interracial or interethnic couple, Jesus and Judas seem transported, oblivious in their physical intimacy to the ring of violence surrounding them: Jesus because of his unworldly fervor, Judas because of his fleshly ardor. Rather than grasping, like the guards in the painting, Judas simply reaches his left hand out to touch with open palm the space where the robe slips down Jesus' chest. Judas's body, behind Jesus', is pressing forward as he strains to place lips on lips.

There are no demarcated Jews present in Carracci's depiction of the betrayal kiss—at least no stereotypical Jews. Yes, Judas wears the traditional yellow robe, but it is so beautifully painted in its luxurious thickness and amplitude that it reflects the light from the lantern much as does Jesus' bared shoulder. The soft drape of the golden fabric, like the soft and vulnerable texture of Jesus' illuminated skin, contrasts with the sinister sheen on the hard helmets that protect but also dehumanize the police.

The ropes, the clutching hands of jostling guards who manage to slip Jesus' clothing off his shoulder, and especially the lighting and the kiss itself charge the picture with a frisson not unlike what one may experience when looking at Robert Mapplethorpe's homoerotic photographs. A breastplate on the guard on the right, the rope around Jesus' extended left hand on the bottom right, the lasso above his head, and the martial uniforms and gleaming helmets: all this paraphernalia we could read today as sadomasochistic equipment. Also lending an atmosphere of theatricality found in scenarios of sadomasochism are the open mouth of the guard on the left; Jesus' limp wrist and slender, exposed neck; and Judas's absorption in the midst of violent voyeurs who dramatically light up the dark scene. The circular noose above Jesus' head has led one art critic to argue that Carracci's painting was "inspired" by Dürer's 1508 engraving (Fiore 26), but Carracci's painting eroticizes the violence over which Dürer's broods. Carracci's Jesus, with his enticing partial nudity and languorous posture, and his Judas, with his taut concentration, appear intent on abrogating the boundaries of their individuality in a quest for exactly the sort of transgression Georges Bataille associated with eroticism. "What does physical eroticism signify," Bataille asked and then answered, "if not a violation of the very being of its practitioners?—a violation bordering on death, bordering on murder?" (17).

Fully clothed, Judas engages in such a passionate kiss that it could be interpreted as a prelude to further physical intimacy.[31] Should this suggestion sound anachronistic, keep in mind that homosexual activity in Renaissance Italy "seems not only to have been common but, despite its illegality, less stigmatized and shameful than we might suppose" (Prose 44). Consider, too, the early founders of Christian theology (discussed in the previous chapter), whose attacks against the Gnostics recurrently placed Judas in the company of the Sodomites, as well as the medieval legend told in *Sepher Toledoth Yeshu* (*Life of Jesus*), in which Judah Iskarioto physically defiles Yeshu. Centuries later, D. H. Lawrence pondered the repercussions of Judas's embodied desire for Jesus, specifically through an analysis of his Jesus' ashamed reflection that he had offered "only the corpse" of his love to his followers: "If I had kissed Judas with live love," Lawrence's Jesus speculates, "perhaps he would never have kissed me with death. Perhaps he loved me in the flesh, and I willed that he should love me bodylessly, with the corpse of love—" (90). Also attuned to the impact of physical contact on spiritual relatedness, the openly gay Judas in Terrence McNally's recent Passion play, *Corpus Christi,* responds to Jesus' avowal of love—"I did love you, you know"—by exclaiming, "Not the way I wanted" (8). In Gethsemane, McNally's Jesus character responds to Judas's kiss: "JOSHUA *kisses him back, hard*" (72).

Is the domain of eroticism at the center of Carracci's *Kiss of Judas* the domain of violence, of violation? In *Visions of Excess,* Bataille argues that erotic desire shocks us at the very core of our being; it moves us out of our individual separateness into dissolution, paving the way for a fusion or mingling of two previously self-contained beings. But how does this linking of the extreme experiences of loving and dying relate to Carracci's interpretation of the Passion? The intensity of Judas wanting to seize, to become one with, to have and hold God's Son as a personal beloved: this astonishing hubris seems most shocking about the painting. On the one hand, it recalls the noble friendship between men expressed in one of John Dryden's plays, *All for Love* (1677): "I was his Soul," Dryden's Antony proclaims about his comrade, "he liv'd not but in me: / We were so clos'd within each other's brests, / The rivets were not found that join'd us first" (3.1.92–94). On the other hand, it turns Judas into an impassioned figure imbued with the spirit of a poet like Shelley who feels himself to be interfused with his beloved

> As mountain-springs under the morning Sun.
> We shall become the same, we shall be one
> Spirit within two frames, oh! *wherefore two?*
> *One passion in twin-hearts,* which grows and grew
> 'Till like two meteors of expanding flame,
> Those spheres instinct with it become the same,
> Touch, mingle, are transfigured; ever still
> Burning, yet ever inconsumable[.] ("Epipsychidion"
>   ll. 572–79; emphases mine)

Judas's transgressions pertain to the impossibility of fusing two into one and also to the immorality of turning the sacred into the sexual, his transposing Jesus' message of divine love into a license for sensuality. Instead of channeling his physical desire into an ennobling spiritual mysticism, Judas is driven to possess physically, individually, for himself, on his own terms, in his own way the Son of God, who came to bring love to humankind. Neither a blessed saint nor a demonized sinner, a possessed Judas betrays Jesus in a moment when he is himself betrayed by his own overwhelming and impossible desires; he initiates the Passion because of his own unendurable passion for Jesus. In yielding to it, he gives himself up to death, for the noose looming over Jesus' head also forecasts the rope on which Judas himself will hang. In that way, the connection between sexual excitement and death that Bataille postulates infuses Carracci's painting with its unnerving juxtaposition of the ardor of union, the anguish of individuation.

But of course other transgressions can be read on a canvas that also breaks the taboo against same-sex love. This prohibition, which may be stronger in modern times than it was in Carracci's, could be circumvented through the figure of the androgyne by artists who associated androgyny with "effeminacy and therefore bisexuality and homosexuality" (Bersani and Dutoit, *Caravaggio's Secrets* 10–11). Does Carracci portray Jesus as an androgynous ephebe, a sensuous youth before his fall into gender, into a rigidly constricting masculinity; or, like Mapplethorpe, does Caracci instill the homosexual couple with the brutal glamour of cruelty? Looking at the painting with admittedly and unavoidably contemporary eyes, I am tempted to interpret the central male couple in terms less of sadomasochism than of androgyny and the policing, the criminalizing of homosexuality. As applied by the claustrophobic and callous soldiers, after all, the s/m equipment of a titillating theater of cruelty will divide, not unite, the lovers. And the intertwined central pair stands quite apart from the conspiratorial violence.

Indeed, it is Judas's right hand that gives the picture its extraordinary poignancy, for the fingers hold Jesus' neck with delicacy, the brush of Judas's fingertips barely touching Jesus' skin. Although the painting's most authoritative interpreter judges the embrace "horrible" and the couple "ill-matched" (Feigenbaum 12), I linger on the glamorous lassitude of the ephebe or androgyne and his rapt mate. In their abandon, they remain so absorbed as to be indifferent to the vicious clamor surrounding them. Neither heterosexualized nor feminized, both men are bearded, youthful but poised, enraptured by distinct visions of excess, and vulnerable to the torments that await them.

For Caravaggio, as for Carracci, there is no need to demonize Judas. Also decreasing the distance between viewers and characters by bringing the represented action to the forefront of the canvas, Caravaggio's *The Taking of Christ* (plate 6) has received much more critical attention than Carracci's rendition of the kiss, in part because the figure presented at the extreme right, holding up a lantern, has been taken to be one of Caravaggio's self-portraits, in part because of its dramatic vibrancy, and in part because of the story of its (astonishing) rediscovery.[32] The power of this complicated painting has everything to do with the pivotal role it plays in Judas's evolution. Less concerned with eroticism than with the ethics of his own aesthetics, Caravaggio stresses that there is an abiding need to comprehend humankind's complicity in and commonality with Judas and his deed. Instead of absolving us from the guilt of betrayal (by exonerating, demonizing, or eroticizing Judas), Caravaggio dramatizes his own and his viewers' collusion in the sheer momentum that hurtles everyone from the right side to the left side of the canvas, as if tossed by a storm from paradise, driving them into a fearful future.

The only full face in the picture—and even it is half in shadow—is Jesus'. Unlike Carracci's Jesus, Caravaggio's tilts his head away from Judas with lowered eyes. On the extreme left and physically attached to Jesus is a shocked man gaping in horror. Four other men surround Jesus on the right: moving out from Jesus, first Judas, then two Roman soldiers, and finally the lantern holder identified with the painter, all in profile. The frenzy surrounding Jesus emphasizes his stasis, as do his lowered eyes and his clasped hands, the arms extended out and the fingers intertwined. But the powerful momentum of the figures on the right threatens to topple Jesus, while the terror of the open-mouthed man on the left provides him no ballast. Each of these five profiled figures deserves closer attention. For the crucifixion, according to Caravaggio, depends on a collusion between Jesus' followers and apostles, the legal powers of the civic state, and the aesthetics that drive Western artistry, including his own.

If we identify the horrified man on the left as the anonymous young follower at the Gethsemane arrest whose shock led him to leave off his linen cloth and run away naked (Mark 14:51), his physical union with Jesus (back melded to back, hair to hair) makes sense because he is a believer.[33] Yet in this case the adherent—replacing the usual figure of Malchus—is poised in flight from Jesus, moving toward the left and out beyond the represented scene; his left arm and hand actually extend invisibly outside the picture's frame. As in Mark's Gospel, where all the apostles flee in fear, an irony is italicized: the aghast follower does not follow, but instead turns his back on a Jesus doomed to reconcile himself to an inescapable fate. The anonymous runaway's cascading cape forms a sort of arc or dome of drapery over the heads of Jesus and Judas. It calls to mind Jewish weddings, when the bride and groom stand beneath an awning made of fabric or flowers, called a *chuppah*. Tentlike, the red billowing canopy over Jesus' and Judas's heads unites them as a couple.

However, Judas does not appear as Jesus' fraternal twin here; nor is he demonized or eroticized. Instead, worry lines are etched on Judas's forehead; his head shows the hint of a skullcap (or perhaps he is tonsured); his left arm is gently laid on Jesus' shoulder in an embrace. One commentator has viewed Judas with his "big, squat red nose and coarsely furrowed forehead" as "the most unattractive and most uncouth face in the crowd of faces" (Mormando 182). Another has pointed out how Caravaggio's painting, like Dürer's 1509 wood-cut, "makes use of the horizontal barrier created by the overlapping arms of Judas and the soldier in armour" (Fiore 24). But the veined hand and somewhat coarsened features of Judas's face may reflect the wear and tear of a street-smart man as battered by nighttime brawls as was his creator. And the soldier's arm constrains Judas as well as Jesus. Indubitably, no stereotypical red hair, hooked nose, or money bag appears on a canvas that propels Judas, along with all the other figures, toward the left.

Given the forces besieging Jesus, Judas's arm might be viewed as propping his teacher up, to keep him from toppling over. Jesus and Judas are the same height, equals in age, although Jesus seems wan and troubled, Judas anxious. Neither looks at the other. And their disturbance is understandable, because the left arm in which both are caught gleams like a robotic tentacle or gigantic claw, though it is the prosthetic arm of the law. Indeed, what takes up the very center of the canvas is the polished carapace of the soldier's body armor. Its metallic sheen glitters, as the Roman tightens his hold on Jesus and

Judas—both victims of the coercion of civil, secular forces invisible except for the uniformed policemen, who are only following orders. Where did Caravaggio get the idea of replacing Judas's ardor with Roman armature?

Numerous depictions, like Jan Joest of Kalkar's *Betrayal and Arrest of Christ* (1505–08), prove that the kiss and the seizure could be combined not to displace but to double the figure of Judas with the Roman or Temple troops. Often mirroring is effected with rigorous symmetry, as Jesus is nabbed by two grotesque and parallel figures in profile: Judas's witchlike pointy chin can be exactly replicated by the pointy chin guard on the armored soldier. In such renditions as Joest's, Judas and the Roman soldiers or Temple guard work hand in glove. Consider how differently Caravaggio uses this sort of assemblage in *The Taking of Christ*. Almost faceless, the military figures in Caravaggio's painting stage and compel the confrontation between Jesus and Judas, the betrayal itself. With the individuality of their facial features and bodies hidden by steel helmets, visors, and bodices, fixed by leather straps and buckles, they represent the impermeable authority of the nation-state. Less a double of Judas than a captor of him and of Jesus, the inviolable Roman soldier at the center of the painting grasps Jesus' neck and also threatens to choke Judas's throat.[34]

Judas's more profound double in Caravaggio's painting is the profiled figure holding the lantern: Caravaggio himself. Judas's kiss clarifies Jesus' identity and presence for the arresting soldiers. Leo Bersani and Ulysse Dutoit point out that the witness Caravaggio has a similar purpose: "witnessing here is figured as an illumination, a spectatorial lighting up of the scene analogous to Judas's treacherous 'lighting up' of Jesus as the one accused of being the self-proclaimed Messiah" ("Beauty's Light" 17). But given that "the lantern he carries shines only into his own eyes while the rest of the scene is lit from other sources" (Varriano 202), what does this doubling signify? Since Caravaggio sheds more light on himself than on the scene, the self-portrait questions the efficacy of, say, his or any other painter's ability to elucidate the biblical Passion. The Romans direct the production event, and Caravaggio calls out, "Lights! Action!"—or, more precisely, "Brush! Paint!" The painter, peering intently at the scene, hints at the complicity not simply of a bystander but of a complicit voyeur who takes as his subject the betrayal of innocence. Does Western art depend on the consumption of trauma, the recycling of human sacrifice, an obsession with painful betrayal that is perpetuated through its recurrent representation?[35]

More, do we as viewers crave the destruction of innocence? Do we wish to see disaster dramatized over and over again, for our own delectation? Perhaps Caravaggio meditates on the disequilibrium of the sublime, on how the mystery of unjust suffering prompts feelings of terror and awe, a vertiginous confusion about our incapacity to comprehend the moral and mortal matters of experience. Terror and awe here relate to the sublime paradox of the crucifixion itself. Christians believe that they will be saved by Jesus' death on the cross. When demonized, Judas, who accomplished the task of salvation, must shoulder the burden of guilt for a human sacrifice benefiting all, guilt that all must therefore share: namely, the shame that his worshippers' everlasting spiritual gain depends on Jesus' grievous physical loss. Instead of being demonized, Caravaggio implies, Judas should be understood as part of a disastrous human sacrifice in which all conspired. To the objection that such an advance hardly equals the more deeply ethical progress of abolishing human sacrifice altogether, Caravaggio's painting proposes a stinging challenge.[36]

For the mystery of unjust suffering (ritualized or not) hovers not only inside but outside the frame, an intimation that human sacrifice cannot be eradicated. To confirm the sacrifice not shown, Caravaggio uses another surrogate. The gesture of the unheard but screaming follower in flight also replicates the artist's self-portrait: on the extreme left and right of the canvas, both the shocked runaway and the painter have an illuminated right hand extended high in the dark air. Thus far, we have assumed that the deserter is fleeing the scene, putting it behind his back. But he can also be interpreted as looking outward at another traumatic conflagration before his very eyes, one we cannot see but toward which all are inexorably propelled. The painting thereby suggests that just as Caravaggio witnesses the disaster of Jesus' arrest, so too the frightened follower is flinging his hands up in horror at an oncoming disaster he cannot ward off. Such a repetition compulsion hints that there will be an infinite succession of witnesses to an infinite number of catastrophes toward which humanity is being hurtled. From this perspective, Judas's betrayal—enforced by the invisible authorities of the nation-state as well as their physical pawns—figures a disastrous postbiblical history.

To sum up: two oddities in *The Taking of Christ* drive home its subversive message. First, the eccentricity of its dramatic lighting, for which Caravaggio is justly famed. At thirty-one years of age, Caravaggio depicted himself holding up a lantern whose function is "purely compositional as it appears to throw no light, the true light source being high on the left, beyond the scene depicted" (Benedetti 738). Second, and placed at the very center of the canvas, "the highly polished, that is, mirror-like sleeve of the arresting solder," a "quasi-mirror . . . inviting his viewers to see themselves reflected in the behavior of Judas and the other tormentors of Christ" (Mormando 183). These two features of the painting function self-reflexively. On the one hand, the artist (who portrays himself shedding no light on the scene he seeks to illuminate) admits the inefficacy of the only means at his disposal to deal with the suffering he seeks to witness, the insufficiency of his own artistry. On the other hand, much as the painter takes his place in the line-up of perpetrators, the armor-mirror at the center of the painting invites viewers to comprehend their own complicity in betrayal. When, through these two techniques, Judas becomes a prototypical everyman, we are made conscious of our inability to pass judgment on his actions.

No kiss occurs in *The Taking of Christ*. The space between the faces of Jesus and Judas on Caravaggio's canvas means either that the kiss will occur next or that it has just occurred. Or perhaps, as in Luke and John, it has been or will be forestalled. Because of the consternation on Judas's face, the flight of the follower, the intervention of the law's arm, and most especially Jesus' abstraction, face averted, as he concentrates not on the actions or the actors but on keeping his arms braced, his fingers entwined, it might well capture the moment *after* the kiss, along with dawning consciousness on Judas's part that he holds in his arms an innocent man condemned to death. The painting therefore brings to my mind a perfect line of iambic pentameter by James Wright: "I held the man for nothing in my arms." Put into Judas's mouth (about a victim who is not Christ), it is a strangely inconclusive concluding sentence for a poem, since it might mean "I held the man [for no personal gain] in my arms," or "I held the man [for no ulterior motive or reason] in my arms," or "I held the man [who was nothing to me or would become nothing] in my arms" and thus "I held [nothing] in my arms."

Wright's sonnet "Saint Judas" (1959) opens as Judas goes out to kill himself, but then happens to witness a "pack of hoodlums beating up a man." It closes with Judas's response (in the first person) to this anonymous casualty of casual street violence:

> Banished from heaven, I found this victim beaten,
> Stripped, kneed, and left to cry. Dropping my rope
> Aside, I ran, ignored the uniforms;
> Then I remembered bread my flesh had eaten,
> The kiss that ate my flesh. Flayed without hope,
> I held the man for nothing in my arms.

As Wright, like Caravaggio, refrains from further judgment of Judas, he balances the "bread my flesh had eaten" against "The kiss that ate my flesh." The phrase recalls the assertion of Jesus in the Coptic Gospel of Thomas that "'He who drinks from my mouth will be as I am, and I will be he, and the things that are hidden will be revealed to him'" (Cartlidge and Dungan 28).

By envisioning a Judas graced by the kiss, just as believers are by the Eucharist, Wright suggests that the kiss must have had a profoundly transformative impact on Judas, that it might have gotten Jesus under Judas's skin, might have betrayed the betrayer into ministering to the "beaten, / Stripped, kneed, and left to cry," and thus into sainthood. Wright's poem dwells on the moments in Judas's life after the kiss revealed hidden things, a revelation that in turn changed him into a replica of the one he kissed. Perhaps, "Saint Judas" intimates, only a person "Banished from heaven"—cognizant that he is capable and culpable of betrayal—can attain sainthood. The rest of us righteous types would quickly pass by the nameless victims of assaults in our own neighborhoods.

A Web search will find more recent images of the kiss at the heart of the Passion, but I have chosen those I found most compelling. Taken together, the images assembled here raise a question: did medieval and Renaissance depictions of Judas's betrayal contribute to or reflect a homophobic suspicion or loathing of amorous gestures or kisses between men? Put another way, when we see two men kissing, do we think of Judas and treachery? That the central act of betrayal is repeatedly imagined as a same-sex kiss might lead to facile conclusions about ongoing and obsessive fears of men who love men. Whereas heterosexual kisses signify "the logical consummation of the heterosexual encounter," Phillip Brian Harper has explained in a very different context, same-sex kisses and in particular same-sex kisses *in public* function as a "signal" speaking about identity "in a much more highly charged way" (9, 22). Perhaps the Judas kiss first registered the high degree of social danger faced or posed by a man whose open embrace of another man turns him into a dangerous criminal. Or maybe it is only the hindsight conferred by a long and gruesome history of homophobia that now makes visible an invidious connection between men who love men and what some painters render as Judas's rapacious molestation.

For it would be hard to make the case that Judas's kiss reflects homophobia, given the number of homophilic representations discussed in this chapter (even though, significantly, the word *homophilic* has no currency). What Stephen D. Moore proposes of decidedly queer interpretations of the Song of Songs holds true for many pictures of the Judas kiss: namely, that they bespeak, indeed presuppose, "a lack of homosexual panic" ("The Song" 349). To be sure, in frescoes and woodcuts that emphasize a sadistic alien or foreigner overwhelming Jesus, depictions of Judas may have fueled dangerous stereotypes of the homosexual predator. Yet in a curiously counterintuitive manner, representations of Judas's betrayal kiss—when spiritualized as a sign of fraternal kinship or eroticized as a passionate encounter—provoke meditations not on its malevolent eccentricity but on the disturbing infidelity or treachery always inherent or potential in any and all acts of affection or love. In doing so, such images give the contemporary viewer an opportunity to challenge assumptions about the homophobia consequent to the historical impact of Christianity, and thus to contest homophobia in the present.

Adam Phillips once considered Freud's insight into the nature of desire—"always in excess of the object's capacity to satisfy it"—in order to explain why Freud associated kissing with a "grudge at the root of sexuality": always disappointing and thus frequently returned or repeated, "the kiss," according to Phillips, "is a symbol of betrayal, and of the revisions that betrayal always brings in its wake" (100). In other words, all kisses are Judas kisses. The New Testament itself underscores such a view, or so a supposition of Jack Miles suggests. When John the Baptist characterizes Jesus as a bridegroom (John 3:29), he does so, Miles explains, to elaborate on passages in the Hebrew Bible where "God, as the bridegroom of Israel, is a betrayed bridegroom" (*Christ* 73). Although God's spouse is continually unfaithful, the bridegroom insists that he will remain faithful.

Regarding the marriage of untrue, as of true, minds, visual images of the kiss admit impediments, alterations, and removals. Yet even when Judas engages in a biting kiss, painters for the most part give him a human, not a demonic, form. That the most benevolent and numerous glimpses of a humanized Judas occur first in the pictorial arts, rather than in theology or creative literature, may be related not only to the centrality of human figures in representational art but also to the ways in which paintings arrest the arresting betrayal scene, detaching it from the Passion narrative. Even so-called narrative paintings stop the plot, frame a moment or series of moments in isolation, leaving us in doubt about the causes and consequences of conflicts, their beginnings and endings. Especially when Judas and Jesus are contrasted with the Temple authorities in depictions of the betrayal kiss, they set the stage for writers who start to endow Judas with interiority. On the canvases of Carracci and Caravaggio in particular, we see Jesus as well as Judas overwhelmed by repressive modes of social control that define *both of them* as delinquent, criminal, outcast, anathema to the morally bankrupt but highly effective policing authority of the civic state.

Needless to say, greater liberties are taken by philosophers and authors living in subsequent ages, during more secular periods of history. But from the thirteenth through the seventeenth centuries, visual artists focused on a sign of love's treachery that the Irish poet Brendan Kennelly recently approached through the subjective perspective of Judas:

> I come to him
> I kiss the tired legends in his eyes
> I kiss the pleading lepers in his face
> I kiss the mercy flowing through his skin
> I kiss his calm forgiveness of sin
> I kiss the women hovering at his side
> I kiss the men who make him their cause
> I kiss the money made and lost in his name
> I kiss the murders committed by his children
> I kiss the mob adoring him
> I kiss the treachery of men
> I kiss the ways they will remember him
> I kiss the ways they will forget him
> I kiss his words his silences

4.12. The kiss—Judas played by Otello Sestili and Jesus by
Enrique Irazoqui—in Pier Paolo Pasolini's *The Gospel According to
St. Matthew* (1964). Source: Photofest.

I kiss his heart
I kiss his caring daring love
                    He seems relieved. (239)

According to one of Kennelly's finest interpreters, the kiss in this passage is "an act of mirroring, of replication, a moment in which Christ
is forced to own, not his singularity, but what he shares in common
with fallen humanity" (Roche 93).

A close-up from Pier Paolo Pasolini's movie *The Gospel according to St. Matthew* (1964)—with the stubble on Judas's chin and the
extension of his neck clearly evident—similarly emphasizes our propinquity to Judas, as well as Judas's to Jesus: their reciprocal inter-
subjectivity (illustration 4.12).[37] If read in an allegorical manner that
the images certainly do not compel or always countenance, the pic-

torial relationship of Christ to Judas, of Christians to Jews, displays the friendly admiration of *phileō*, the ambivalent struggle of *erōs* and *thanatos*, and the compassion of *agape*. Medieval and Renaissance visual artists prefigure Enlightenment thinkers brooding on the common humanity of Judas, for later poets and dramatists would go on to imagine a heroism born of the daring vision Kennelly's Judas possesses when he declares, "Knowledge belongs to one, it always will / Who dares to recognize, to kiss and kill his god" (136).

5

IN A MODERN
GLASS DARKLY:
THE ISSUE OF SACRIFICE

*The rehabilitation of Judas during the Enlightenment was facilitated by
authors who imagined him first as a redeemable sinner, then as a heroic
rebel. An idealistic Judas enabled nineteenth- and early twentieth-century
writers to ponder the benevolent intentions of the betrayer. Even when this
rebel is robbed of his cause, a woeful Judas elicits sympathy as he suffers
the limits of redemption, prompting his creators to question the justice of
God as well as the efficacy of God's Son.*

To the extent that Caravaggio's Judas shares with Jesus apprehension about a moment that may not resolve the grievous upheav-
als of history, his *Taking of Christ* can serve as an introduction to
Judas's maturation from the eighteenth century on, when intensifying
secularism diminished the cultural prominence of the Passion narrative, along with faith in its literal truth, even as it increased Judas's
heroic stature. During and after the Enlightenment, while Jews of
every conceivable background were being assimilated into European
and American societies, Judas matured into a militant who works
to establish Christ's reign, and who does so comprehending that he
would pay a price beyond the tormented death demanded of a Jesus
rewarded with resurrection. This twelfth apostle knows that Jesus
gave him the powers and benefits of the other eleven, but at times

he wonders whether Jesus can deliver on his promise to save all the souls given into his care. Indeed, in these renditions a valiant Judas realizes that he can help issue God's providential plan only by losing his most cherished friend, his own life, his soul, and his repute in perpetuity.[1] At his gloomiest, the twelfth apostle grieves over the implacable forces that produce a supremely ironic juxtaposition: his instrumental agency with respect to God's plan, on the one hand, and his own damnation, on the other.

Paul Peter Rubens's painting *The Last Supper* forecasts the tragic stature of this conflicted but noble Judas (ca. 1630–31; illustration 5.1). Even more than Daniele Crespi's rendition (see illustration 1.1), which it recalls, Rubens's canvas presents a Judas looking anxious, fearful about what he will be called on to effect. Some viewers may find Rubens's Judas ashamed or embarrassed, as he should be if he is thought to resemble the greedy dog gnawing a bone by his feet. However, to my eyes he appears apprehensive. And the bright halo behind Jesus' head is matched by the nimbus of the candle behind and surrounding Judas's head. While the other apostles look soulfully upward with Jesus, who is clearly consecrating the eucharistic bread and wine, Rubens's meditative Judas—hardly the most unattractive at the table, not red-haired or hook nosed, with no money bag— keeps his left hand on the table, his right before his mouth. Along with Peter on Jesus' right and John on his left, Judas is the only other apostle who can be identified. He and Jesus are the major players in a narrative that explains why Jesus exults in the light with his eyes upraised, whereas pensive Judas glowers in apprehension at the dire prospect of having to carry out God's will.

Inside the candle-lit but dark, cavernous room, the tightly knit band of apostles are hardly distanced from each other or from Jesus, as they are at a rectangular table (such as the one Leonardo da Vinci's *Last Supper* depicts, for example). Elevated upon a monumental chair, Judas with his dangling feet (like a child's) has been placed in a position beyond his control. The doubling between Jesus and Judas—not physical but ethical or temperamental—seems to balance expectant

5.1. Paul Peter Rubens, *The Last Supper* (ca. 1630–31). Pushkin
Museum of Fine Arts, Moscow. Source: Art Resource. © Alinari/
Art Resource, New York.

faith against anxious cynicism, serene self-renunciation against edgy
self-assertion. Does Judas's hand over his mouth signify a vow of
silence, a sign that his side of the story will never be told? Rubens's
troubled protagonist appears to ruminate, glowering at the viewer or,
like the betrayer in William Rayner's *The Knifeman* (1969), at "God
in the role of cruel jokester," as though to ask, "If this was God's
work, then what kind of God ruled the affairs of men . . . ?" (151).
Everyone else surrounding Jesus at the table looks absorbed in the
matters at hand, and their confidential circle excludes the observer.
But Judas seems to catch the beholder's eye as he comprehends and
ponders the cost of his future dealings with the Temple authorities.

Through this connection with the viewer, does Rubens intimate that we have more in common with Judas than with any other player in the Passion? In John's account Judas alone eats and is consumed by the devil, but Rubens's Judas sits far removed from the bread, with his mouth shut, his lips covered. His familiar is not a devil, demon, dragon, bat, or insect—only a companionable dog beneath his chair. Payment is not part of the picture.

The idea that a radical Judas entered into a conflicted partnership or covert operation with Jesus for the salvation of humanity might derive from the New Testament itself, specifically from John's accounts of "Judas, not Iscariot" and of Jesus' brothers. These shadowy and importunate characters have much in common with each other and with the twelfth apostle. After foot washings at the last meal, after Judas Iscariot leaves to perform his appointed task, John's Jesus explains to the remaining eleven that he will eventually return to those who keep his commandments, but "Judas (not Iscariot) said to him, 'Lord, how is it that you will reveal yourself to us, and not to the world?' " (14:22). Hyam Maccoby persuasively connects "Judas (not Iscariot)" to John's portrait of Jesus' brothers, when they earlier tell him not to skulk at home in Galilee but instead to pursue his pedagogic mission in Judea (148–49): "for no one who wants to be widely known acts in secret. If you do these things, show yourself to the world" (John 7:3). In Mark (6:3) and in Matthew (13:55), Jesus actually has a brother named Judas. Like Judas (not Iscariot) and Judas (the sibling of Jesus), an eager Judas Iscariot often functions in modern times as Jesus' zealous brother-in-arms, urging him to divulge the messianic secret, to manifest himself to the world.

This is not to say, of course, that the demonized Judas disappears during the wide swath of time I associate with his maturation. Priests as well as educators and novelists lambasted the sterility, rapacity, debauchery, and sneakiness of Judas as well as the people he represents, the Jewish race.[2] "What hast thou done?" Algernon Charles Swinburne asks Judas and, before consigning him to "the filth and flame . . . in the clefts of hell," answers, "Thou hast made earth faint, and sickened the sweet sun, / With fume of blood that reeks from limbs that rot" (350). As the nineteenth century was ending, innuendos about the guilt of Alfred Dreyfus, a Jewish officer in the French army accused of collaborating with the Germans, were circulated in a spate of anti-Semitic French books and articles invoking Judas's name.[3] But even as such defamations proliferated, Judas advanced from a repentant sinner to a militant revolutionary, complicating cultural understanding of the Passion story.

If, as all the Gospel authors hint, the fleshly Son could not become the spiritual messiah without Judas, shouldn't the twelfth apostle be honored as a foundational actor who risked his own self-interests and his neck to serve as a tool of humanity's redemption? Judas may have accepted the dipped morsel and departed into the night in order to fulfill God's will, "to compel the Passion and Resurrection of his master who might otherwise, at this last hour, have flinched from unendurable agony, who might have fled into Galilee" (Steiner, *No Passion Spent* 415). Especially in the nineteenth and twentieth centuries, an indispensable Judas confronts the double bind of loving the man he must endanger, fully aware of his own painful lack of mastery and how it mirrors that of Jesus, but refusing to allow it to stymie his determination to act in and for the world.

Secular writers pondering Judas's role speculate on his perspective, much as Howard Nemerov does in his poem "The Historical Judas" (1980):

> He too has an eternal part to play,
> What did he understand? that good has scope
> Only from evil, flowering in filth?
> Did he go smiling, kissing, to betray
> Out of a fine conviction of his truth,
> Or some original wreckage of our hope?
>
> If merely mistaken, at any rate,
> He had a talent for the grand mistake,

The necessary one, without which not,
And managed to incur eternal hate
For triggering what destiny had got
Arranged from the beginning, for our sake.

Let us consider, then, if not forgive
This most distinguished of our fellow sinners,
Who sponsored our redemption with his sin,
And whose name, more than ours, shall surely live
To make our meanness look like justice in
All histories commissioned by the winners.

"The Historical Judas" asks us to "consider, then, if not forgive" a figure who might be one of "our fellow sinners," or a militant rebel acting "out of a fine conviction of his truth," or an instrument "triggering what destiny had got / Arranged from the beginning, for our sake." Most intriguing about Nemerov's verse is the idea that the normative notion of a demonized Judas could not have been universally held in biblical times, that it did not originate and would not accord with the perspectives of the Roman or Jewish authorities or even Jesus' circle in Jerusalem, and that it has been used by later Christians in a morally suspect way: that is, "To make our meanness look like justice."

The rehabilitation of Judas's "distinguished" character coincided with a proliferation of historical and literary critical approaches to the past, even the remote biblical past. In particular, David Friedrich Strauss's *Life of Jesus* (1835) and Ernest Renan's *Life of Jesus* (1863) spurred interest in the mythic or legendary significance of the Gospel narratives.[4] While the biographical details of Jesus' life were being investigated by biblical scholars and excavated by archaeologists, they could also be imagined by creative writers who proposed what we would today call alternative histories: sometimes probable and sometimes improbable counterhistories of what might or could have happened.[5] Taken together, the alternative histories of modern men (and at least a few women) of letters engage the baffling questions that perplex Nemerov. What does it mean that flowering requires filth, that sin sponsors redemption, they wonder. Two sorts of alternative histories emerge in this chapter: one in which new perspectives challenge and change received interpretations of the Gospel narratives, another in which inventive suppositions generate entirely new characters and events that challenge and change the accounts offered by the Gospel narratives. By means of both types of counterhistories, Enlightenment writers ingeniously rehabilitate Judas through a process that first commutes or at least shortens his guilty sentence, then defends his ethical activism, and ultimately mourns the painful fate of a man whose sacrifice sponsored redemption.

When an absolved Judas seeks to conquer sin, injustice, and death itself in a partnership demanding the supreme sacrifice, he begins again to look and sound a lot like Jesus. Yet since Jesus jeopardizes his body while Judas endangers his soul, the hatred incurred by the twelfth apostle raises the question, who suffered the worst injury in the Passion? Indeed, under some circumstances, a Judas inexorably denied grace embodies the wreckage of hope suffered by the followers of "Judas (not Iscariot)"—better known as Saint Jude—for he comes to represent those miserable lost souls who take Judas Thaddeus or Jude as their patron saint. Especially in this stage of Judas's career, the betrayal and subsequent suffering of Judas raise disturbing issues about the justice of the Passion and the limits of Christ's mercy. To arrive at these complicated issues expeditiously, this chapter sketches first Judas the redeemable wretch and then Judas the brave rebel in such a manner as to increase momentum toward its concluding sections. There—in keeping with his disorderly evolution—the woeful "grand mistake" that modern Judas becomes resonates in sometimes much earlier and sometimes much later representations that ponder what it might mean to inhabit an existence better unborn.

A WRETCH LIKE ME

The repair of Judas in the eighteenth and nineteenth centuries eventually emphasized his human fallibility and the amazing grace of Jesus. Human fallibility would be imagined in many counterhistories that stress humanity's propensity for grievous sins and mistaken actions or the powerful feeling of repentance that in their wake might lead to atonement, though some popular stories judged Judas to be himself betrayed by powerful sexual drives over which he had little control. In all these cases, Jesus proves himself to be the messiah by extending his unconditional compassion to the most fallen of sinners. However, the process of repair began less with a vindication of Judas's character than with barbed diatribes against contemporary villains whose pitch of evil makes his crimes pale in comparison.

Satirists have always delighted in excoriating clergymen and statesmen said to exceed Judas in their guile and cupidity. Jonathan Swift's "Bishop Judas" (1731), for example, attacks hypocritical church authorities by insinuating that their lies and abuses of power propagate the hypocritical spirit of Judas:

> Judas betrayed his master with a kiss:
> But, some have kissed the gospel fifty times,
> Whose perjury's the least of all their crimes;
> Some who can perjure through a two-inch board;
> Yet keep their bishoprics, and 'scape the cord.
> Like hemp, which by a skilful spinster drawn
> To slender threads, may sometimes pass for lawn.
>   (ll. 10–16).[6]

Without receiving their just punishment, the people Swift calls "a new set of Iscariots" repeatedly get away with the crime for which Judas paid with his life (l. 19). Even more vitriolic about spinsters (or spin doctors) who cheat and defraud, Charles Lamb's epigram "To

Sir James Mackintosh" (1801) curses the sort of blackguard who is as wicked as Judas, but lacks his guts:

> Though thou'rt like Judas, an apostate black,
> In the resemblance one thing thou dost lack:
> When he had gotten his ill-purchased pelf,
> He went away, and wisely hanged himself.
> This thou may'st do at last; yet much I doubt,
> If thou hast any *bowels* to gush out![7]

Unlike the villainous hollow men of Charles Lamb's own day, Judas with his gushing bowels proved himself all too human.

The nefarious deeds of Judas's offspring exceed the corrupt practices of their progenitor, who did, after all, relinquish his unjust rewards: "More just was *Judas,* who his Saviour sold"; John Dryden explained, "The sacrilegious bribe he cou'd not hold, / Nor hang in peace, before he render'd back the gold" ("The Hind" 182; 3.715–17). Contrasting the singularity of Judas's one act of betrayal with a contemporary penchant for building careers on an extensive portfolio of shady deals, a short poem published by Catherine Jemmat in 1766 sets the record straight—it was silver, not gold that Judas held—but nevertheless concurs with Dryden's larger point:

> The traitor Judas stands upon record,
> For selling to the Jews our blessed Lord;
> But he, in traffic, will a novice seem,
> To all who hear how we've improv'd his scheme.
> He to the Jews but once his Lord cou'd sell,
> How often we may do't no man can tell;
> And (to his shame, and our renown, be't told)
> He made but silver of him, we make gold.

Jemmat echoes Swift's excoriation of "a set of new Iscariots" whose materialism far exceeds that of Judas in its excessive rapacity (not in silver but in gold) as well as in its multiplying scale (not a single bribe returned but a perpetual getting and spending).

Such deployments of Judas castigate an age imbued with the profit motive, as did the thirteenth-century diatribe of Walter of Wimborne. Yet the pronoun "we" in the last line of Jemmat's poem intimates that if Judas represents all sinners, then like all sinners he can be redeemed through Christ. Morally superior to those sinners who get away with their crimes, a repentant Judas can also be pardoned and saved. John Wesley's hymn "God's Sovereign, Everlasting Love" (1868) addresses Jesus as "all-redeeming Lord" to conclude that he brings grace even to the most fallen:

> Thou dost not mock our race
>   With insufficient grace;
> Thou hast reprobated none,
>   Thou from *Pharaoh's* blood art free;
> Thou didst once for all atone—
>   *Judas, Esau, Cain,* and me. (ll. 43–48)

Unless one keeps in mind the number of times Judas's name appears throughout Renaissance and Restoration plays, poems, and sermons prefaced by "perfidious," "vile," and "false," the identification in Wesley's last line of himself, of ourselves (as singers of the psalm) with Judas will not sound as astonishing as it is.

The celebrated painting *Judas Returning the Thirty Pieces of Silver* (1629; plate 7), by Rembrandt, anticipates Wesley's identification with a penitential Judas. In a scene less frequently rendered than the kiss, shame has Rembrandt's Judas in its thrall, or so his bloodied scalp, tightly clasped hands, kneeling posture, torn robe, and averted eyes suggest. In contrast to the richly clothed priests and elders, a plainly clad Judas—"shut off from human sympathy or help"—weeps in agony (Durham 92–93).[8] Especially telling is the contrast between the bulky seated priest, his wide girth encircled by a golden belt, and an emaciated Judas, whose roped belt droops over his genuflecting legs. The pieces of silver on the floor look paltry in comparison to the golden robes and turbans of the Temple authorities as well as to the brightly illuminated but unattended sacred book. Seven Temple authorities, some in shadows, refuse to gaze at the skinny, cringing penitent, and the central seated priest raises his hand, while averting his face, as if to banish this abject Judas from the cavernous Temple and the human community. The Hebrew letters on the open book are only partially legible, but one art historian suggests two possible interpretations of the lettering: "to know your blindness" or "to know your mistake (ruin)" (Durham 94). Whereas the scornful Temple authorities spurn the ruined Judas, Rembrandt places Judas's piteous figure at the center of his canvas and in the process emphasizes how his guilt and also his sorrow over it epitomize the human condition.

Eight lines of verse from the Middle Ages can serve to emphasize the shift in perspective made manifest by Rembrandt's wretched penitent and Wesley's concluding line:

> O Judas and o Cain also
> And o such sinful many more,
> Who, because of their sin, gain
> Never to win mercy,
> And be assuaged for their despair,
> They fall without recovery.
> For there is no man who may have mercy
> Who does not ask and beg for it.[9]

In earlier times, Judas and Cain personify despair that does not seek mercy and therefore earns eternal damnation, but Wesley imagines Judas and Cain receiving clemency through the sufficiency of Christ's grace, just as Rembrandt's painting conveys sympathy for the twelfth disciple's miserable contrition. If Judas, who committed the worst possible sin, sincerely atoned and obtained forgiveness, he holds out hope for all human beings.

Robert Buchanan depicted the magnanimous love of Wesley's

Christ as it comes to encompass Judas Iscariot in a hallucinatory narrative poem reminiscent of Coleridge's "Ancient Mariner"—and of its concluding maxim "For the dear God who loveth us, / He made and loveth all" (ll. 620–21). Throughout most of Buchanan's "The Ballad of Judas Iscariot" (1874), the desperate soul of Judas Iscariot carries its own postmortem body, looking for a place to bury it. Icy to the touch, with its teeth rattling in its jaw, the corpse is lifted and taken to a succession of inhospitable burial grounds: a windy place, a stagnant pool, a cross upon a hill, a "Brig of Dread" full of bloody torrents that "splashed the body red" (11). For "months and years, in grief and tears, / He wandered round and round" (11), until the exhausted soul comes upon a mystic hall full of wedding guests, bathed in moonlight, and hosted by a "Bridegroom in his robe of white" with "a light in his hand" (14). The "black, and sad, and bare" soul of Judas explains his appearance—"There is no light elsewhere"—causing the wedding guests to cry out, "'Scourge the soul of Judas Iscariot / Away into the night!'" (15).

But Buchanan's Jesus proves himself to be Christ by refusing to scourge the soul of Judas. Instead, the Bridegroom, calling forth snowflakes and doves with his waving hands, makes the dead body float away, even as he beckons the live soul to enter the hallowed hall:

> "The Holy Supper is spread within,
>> And the many candles shine,
> And I have waited long for thee
>> Before I poured the wine!"

> The supper wine is poured at last,
>> The lights burn bright and fair,
> Iscariot washes the Bridegroom's feet,
>> And dries them with his hair. (16)

Apparently, the Last Supper was not really the last supper; the meal described in the conclusion of Buchanan's ballad features the redeemed soul of Judas rejoining his beloved Bridegroom with a fully resurrected body (complete with hair). An 1846 pamphlet by one W. A. Darby, arguing that "Judas Iscariot was saved," similarly envisions the twelfth apostle standing "in the Church triumphant as the highest monument of THE AMPLITUDE OF THE MERCY OF THE CROSS!" (quoted in Cane 144). The theologian Anthony Cane's comments about Darby pertain to all these visions of the salvaged Judas: "For him there is no question of Christ being defeated, and therefore Judas must be saved" (144–45).[10] Albeit a sinner, the man who helped bring about the eternal life Jesus tendered must not be excluded from its rewards.

Judas's commonality with fallen but redeemable humankind could be represented not only through his ultimate redemption but also through his all-too-human failings. For this reason, counterhistorians of the wretched Judas in the twentieth century elaborated on his fall and his redeemability by focusing on his erotic perplexities. Perhaps, they suggested, Judas's treachery was motivated by his inability to maintain an apostolic vow of celibacy. The protagonist of T. Sturge Moore's turgid long poem *Judas* (1923) remains convinced that "Jesus in [Judas] found what no other gave. / They had been brothers, not by condescension . . . But like in kind" (46).[11] Yet sexual frustration contributes to the delusions that cause him to betray Jesus: in youth Judas had shamefully committed the "semblance" of acts that left him self-disgusted at masturbatory lapses, followed by stringent efforts at abstinence. Unlike the incarnations of Judas studied more extensively in these chapters, a promiscuous Judas hinges on no extant verses in the New Testament, which is why I accord this variant so little space. Because narratives about Judas's sexual exploits did continue to proliferate, however, it needs to be mentioned that in mediocre but popular stories too numerous to recount, betrayal predictably translates into sexual betrayal: a wretched Judas frequently falls in love or lust with Mary Magdalene or with some other nubile Judean nymph who alienates him from his teacher.

Greedy wives or erotic entanglements with Mary Magdalene promote the sexual confusion that plagues a host of pathetic Judas characters in romantic films and fictions. For example, Cecil B. DeMille's silent movie *King of Kings* (1927) begins with a half-naked Magdalene enamored with the twelfth apostle: she rides a nifty zebra-drawn chariot to confront Jesus about Judas's defection before she herself becomes a Christian convert. Not uncommon, the triangulation of desire between Judas, Mary Magdalene, and Jesus could devolve into Judas duping Jesus simply in order to win a woman. In Sybil Morley's narrative poem, Judas accepts the thirty pieces of silver in order to buy "a robe of the sweetest blue" for a fickle wench; Morley's Judas temporizes, "So to buy her a robe I sold my Lord" (57). Up until the 1970s, novelists suggested that a banal (but not necessarily venal) Judas was tempted by seductive fiancées, call girls, and temptresses.[12] Caught between the demands of body and spirit, the fleshly bride and the soulful bridegroom, the tormented sinner in sexy renditions of the betrayal hardly stands a chance. Familiar as Judas's erotic lapses are, he tests and through his eligibility proves God's mercy.

Even artists who refused to stray so markedly from the accounts in the New Testament could endow Judas, especially Matthew's Judas, with penitential sorrow. "I have done wrong by betraying innocent blood," Judas laments in Bach's *St. Matthew Passion* (1727). Because the solo voice is immediately answered by a chorus of male and female singers vigorously retorting "What's that to us? See to it yourself," an isolated Judas gains in pathos that increases as the bass singer giving voice to Judas identifies himself as "the prodigal son" and repeatedly pleads, "Gebt mir meinem Jesum wieder!" (Give me back my Jesus! no. 42). At the close of the work, a bass voice is heard again in what constitutes the final solo aria: "I want to bury Jesus myself. / From now on he shall find / Sweet rest in me" (no. 65). The injunction—"let Jesus in!"—constitutes the last words listeners are left to hear and heed before the closing recitatives and choruses.[13] Judas's despondency and contrition are precisely what begin to reflect many people's fearful awareness of their own wrongdoings: by 1926, in a poem tellingly titled "*Our* Thirty Pieces" (emphasis mine), Harry

Kempe asked, "who has not betrayed enough to know / How Judas drank immeasurable woe / Of broken love, with one most hapless kiss?" (ll. 12–14).

During the period between Bach and Kempe, a number of poets imagine the temporary reprieve of a fellow reprobate.[14] "The Feet of Judas" (1895), by the African American poet George Marion McClellan, does more than commute Judas's sentence. For McClellan opens every one of his five stanzas with the line "Christ washed the feet of Judas!" (which also closes the poem), because

> if we have ever felt the wrong
> Of trampled rights, of caste, it matters not.
> What e'er the soul has felt or suffered long,
> Oh, heart! This one thing should not be forgot:
> Christ washed the feet of Judas! (178)

The lyric recalls Buchanan's Judas, who "washes the Bridegroom's feet / And dries them with his hair," as well as Moore's Judas, who believes that he and Jesus are "brothers, not by condescension . . . But like in kind," and Bach's Judas, who pleads, "Give me back my Jesus!" All of these phrases intimate some desired and desirable union between Jesus and Judas. Given his devotion and repentance, might Judas have been led astray not by financial greed or sexual lust but by well-intentioned plans to further his teacher's goals? Judas evolves from an object of pity or forgiveness (a wretched but loving and beloved disciple) into an icon of nobility and Jesus' champion when they are envisioned as comrades-in-arms within an occupied territory, co-conspirators in an anti-imperialist plot.

REBEL WITH A CAUSE

Recently, a number of biblical historians have hypothesized that Jesus was an apocalyptic Jewish leader, preaching the imminent climax to and conclusion of the history of the world within his own lifetime.[15] Such scholars follow in the steps of Romantic and Victorian thinkers whose treatises and poetic meditations present just such a radical Jesus envisioned and supported by a Judas equally or even more fervently committed to the Temple's destruction. By that act, Jesus and Judas seek to usher in a new era when the faithful will suffer neither death nor disease, neither poverty nor oppression, but will instead witness and celebrate the arrival of God's kingdom on earth. Judas, trying to assist in a revolutionary transformation of his society, works gallantly with Jesus to overthrow both the Temple authorities and the Roman colonizers. Previously disgraced, in the nineteenth century Judas gains the dignity of a hero. Heroism, according to the sociologist Philip Zimbardo, should be attributed to an individual engaged in a voluntary but risky act incurring the possibility of injury or death, one "conducted in service" to other people or the community "without secondary, extrinsic gain anticipated at the time" (466).

During an age grappling with the repercussions of the French and American revolutions, Judas Iscariot is seen as voluntarily risking himself in service to Jesus' daring message, and doing so without the anticipation of any personal gain. In this scenario, if and when Jesus harbors doubts about his radical enterprise, a militant Judas urges him on not only for Jesus' good but for the sake of the peaceful and just millennium they were determined to bring into being together. Key for this approach is the biblical phrase "kingdom of God," which can register both religious and political meanings. "Religiously, it is the kingdom of *God*," Marcus Borg and John Crossan explain; "politically, it is the *kingdom* of God" (25). In texts about the conflicting claims of the desired spiritual kingdom (of Jesus) and the desired political kingdom (of Judas), betrayal signifies Judas's allegiance to a higher ethical ideal that necessitates his creative rebellion against whatever might impede it: a militant Judas seeks to ignite a cautious, tentative Jesus. A number of English-language writers attribute a coherent political motive to Judas and thereby relate him to headstrong Adam and Eve, who challenged the divine prohibition against eating the fruit from the tree in the garden, for their Judas seeks to assist Jesus in his effort to "be like God" (Genesis 3:5).

In a spirit of clemency similar to the absolution at the close of Wesley's hymn and Buchanan's ballad, Thomas De Quincey reminds the readers of his 1857 essay "Judas Iscariot" that "it must always be important to recall within the fold of Christian forgiveness any one who has long been sequestered from human charity and has tenanted a Pariah grave" (184). Fully crediting German thinkers, De Quincey further argues of the false translations and interpretations of Judas that "we ought not to revise merely, or simply to mitigate his sentence, but to dismiss him from the bar" (184). Judas should be exonerated, according to De Quincey, because he was a Hebrew patriot, a passionate and sincere revolutionary impatient with "the Roman yoke," who believed that "Christ contemplated the establishment of a temporal kingdom—the restoration, in fact, of David's throne" (178, 179). What he confronted was Christ's indecisive and doubtful character, which resembled "Shakespeare's great creation of Prince Hamlet" (179). Judas, guilty of presumption but not of treachery or avarice, mistakenly assumed that he comprehended Jesus' mission to overthrow the Romans: he dared to hope that "when at length actually arrested by the Jewish authorities, Christ would no longer vacillate" (181). Thus, Judas "sought to the last the fulfillment of his master's will, but by methods running counter to that master's will" (194). He mistook Christ's spiritual mission to establish a new world order for a political enterprise.

De Quincey blames "the somnolence of copyists, or their blind stupidity, or rash conceit" for the contradictory accounts of Judas's death in Matthew and Luke (195). To resolve the issue of how Judas died, he traces an etymological history of the term "bowels," and then contends that Judas died of a broken heart: "in saying that the *viscera* of Iscariot, or his middle, had burst and gushed out, the original reporter meant simply that his heart had broke" (197). If

Judas "fell headlong," it was not from a tree but instead into "fierce despair" at the ruin of the democratic movement (197). No hanging rope, no exploding intestines, no scatological fluid, but simply suicide (as a result of despondency) was Judas's end. Thus "a deep and heart-fretting Hebrew patriotism" (184) led Judas "not to thwart the purposes of Christ, still less to betray them—on the contrary, to promote them," if only "by means utterly at war with their central spirit" (186). De Quincey believes "that neither any motive of his, nor any ruling impulse, was tainted with the vulgar treachery imputed to him" (177). If Judas was guilty of "spiritual blindness," so were "most of his brethren" on whom "the true grandeur of the Christian scheme" had not yet dawned (181). To the extent that De Quincey rejects the mistaken zealotry of Judas's project, his depiction plays into a general critique of the political extremism of earlier Romantics who supported the French Revolution; but his essay nevertheless "recall[s] within the fold of Christian forgiveness" one who had "tenanted a Pariah grave" (184).

Before and after De Quincey published his meditation, British and American poets linked a hesitant Jesus to an agitated and agitating Judas, and they did so in attempts to "disabuse the world of one of its incongruous 'monsters,'" as Richard Hengist Horne put it in the preface to his "Scriptural Tragedy," a verse drama titled *Judas Iscariot* (1848). Horne's Judas, who ardently believes that Jesus "shall have dominion over all the earth" (120), seethes with rage at the taunts and lies of the scribes and Pharisees, and in a hectic soliloquy declaims against the passivity of Jesus: "Why moveth not his work / More rapidly and widely," he worries; "Why doth he wait?" (124–25). Seeking to ignite his tentative Jesus into action, Horne's Judas decides to help Caiaphas not because of any mercenary motive but to "force the lightning," to see Jesus topple the corrupt Temple "And in the place a mighty Temple erect / To the true Spirit" (144). After Jesus is arrested, after Jesus' mother and Mary Magdalene rebuke Judas, his final soliloquy in the first act reflects his confused but optimistic commitment to his apocalyptic scheme:

Wherefore be miserable? Why should I feel
Thus heavy and cast down? Reproachful words
Were certain—natural—and they will change
To praise and hosannas, when my deed
Shall justify itself, and the Messiah
Compelled his power and terrors to reveal,
Shall burn to stubble all their armed hosts,
And sit enthroned. (154)[16]

With Jesus silent and generally offstage in Horne's verse drama, Judas understandably remains convinced that "Our Lord, Christ, hath two kingdoms, one in heaven, and one upon earth" (166). Despite reports of the scourging, Horne's Judas clings to the delusion that "It was *not* blood! No blood have ye seen—neither shall Christ be crucified" (168–69). When it becomes clear that Jesus will not ascend in his lifetime to become king of the world, Judas enjoins "monstrous Hell" to "be a friend" and "swallow him up—and from the eye of heaven" (174). Even as he decides to die, Judas attests, "I never thought of death to him— / Nor believed in it—I dreamed of nothing / But power's surpassing glory" (189). Judas, as in De Quincey's rendition of the Passion, always loved Jesus, but he mistakenly believed his God could not be killed, would instead reign supreme in the present moment.

Frederick William Orde Ward's dramatic monologue "Judas Iscariot" (1897) also reads like a gloss on De Quincey's approach to the Gospels. When Judas acts, he seeks to awaken an indecisive Jesus to the urgency of wielding his sword so as to liberate Judea: "And so I played the traitor, I who meant, / Only to force His hand, and on Him leant. . . . I would compel Him thus to make us free" (ll. 143–47). Judas performs the masquerade of the traitor role merely to set the stage for an apocalyptic confrontation that would lead to Jesus wielding his scepter, becoming Lord of a secular realm. Like De Quincey's and Horne's Judas, Ward's conceives of himself as a patriotic rebel: "They thought me thief when I with patriot thrill / Preferred my country and God's righteous will" (ll. 179–80). Neither treachery nor self-interest motivated him—"Myself I never served" (l. 187)—but an anti-imperialist, insurrectionist fervor:

> No pulse of gain, no dream of traitorous greed
> Moved me one moment to the daring deed
> So gravely planned, and all without offence;
> I thought the armies of Omnipotence,
> The hierarchies of the heavens and Space
> Would at his bidding in their bright embrace
> With Cherubim and Seraphim in hosts,
> Fall on the city and its vantage posts,
> And seize the Temple and the towers and cast
> The tyrant out with one consuming blast. (ll. 195–204)

At the conclusion of Ward's "Judas Iscariot," his faithful and fond speaker watches Jesus die on the cross, reads his own pardon in Jesus' look, but admits, "now I cannot live apart from Christ, / And thus I go to keep a wedding-tryst" (ll. 261–62). A soldier or sailor dying with his captain, a loyal subject joining his dethroned king, Judas embraces death as a union with his beloved ruler. Suicide here constitutes a loyalty pact.

If Judas's history were not commissioned by the people Nemerov calls "the winners" (that is, the Christians)—if it were composed, for example, by the Romans—we would have gotten a different vantage on his character, or so W. W. Story proposes. Story's long poem *A Roman Lawyer in Jerusalem: First Century* (1870) can be seen as encapsulating the tradition that vindicates a prophetic, brave Judas, the only one of the apostles who did *not* betray Jesus, who cleaved to his ministry.[17] To the soldiers coming to arrest Jesus in the garden, Story's visionary Judas explains how hopeful he is about opening "the gates of glory to his Lord" (80); immediately, however, he is disabused and so shocked that strong convulsions drop him to the ground, where he lies twitching and protesting what his eyes have seen:

You could not seize him—he is God the Lord!
I thought I saw you seize him. Yet I know
That was impossible, for he is God!
And yet you live—you live. He spared you, then.
Where am I? What has happened? A black cloud
Came o'er me when you laid your hands on him. (21)

Judas's seizure, occurring when Jesus is seized, dramatizes their doubling. Haggard and blasted, Judas remains loyal, despite the appalling reversal of his expectations, and thus is soon found hanging from
a cedar tree. A Judas fired by glorious dreams of his Lord's material apotheosis becomes quite simply a tragic hero: "rash if you will,
but grand" (29). Judas represents the most passionate, idealistic, and
loyal, if the most traumatized, of believers.[18]

When a rebelliously valiant Judas is depicted as prompting a wavering Jesus, the central couple in the Passion impels literary artists to
mull over conflicting definitions of the messianic kingdom: Judas's
kingdom being political and conceived in the present apostolic time,
Jesus' spiritual and meant for the future. By portraying Judas's intentions as well meant but ironically reversed by providential events,
De Quincey, Horne, Ward, and Story lend him the stature of other
Romantic heroes, ambitious visionaries such as Prometheus, Man-
fred, Cain, and Faust. Misguided these mythic protagonists might
be, but they seethe with an ontological energy that endows them
with a kind of hyperreality, a superhuman energy. Indeed, Ward's
poem closes by explaining that Orestes fared better than Judas since
the "Furies were appeased," whereas "Judas perished, tortured unto
death, / Unpardoned, unappeased, unpurified" (31). Sincere in his
devotion to Jesus, a fervent Judas believes himself to be working on
Jesus' behalf, but his name bears "the brand of infamy, / The curse of
generations still unborn" (31).

To the extent that the two agonists in this approach to the Passion evince antithetical temperaments, they form a whole: Judas the
desirous id and Jesus the restraining superego, Judas emotive anima

and Jesus intelligent animus, Judas bold willfulness and Jesus brave restraint. Therefore, Judas and Jesus form a composite but split personality, making it inevitable that the death of one will lead to the death of the other. Since, as John's Jesus explains to the eleven after Judas has left the table, "No one has greater love than this, to lay down one's life for one's friends" (15:13), in all of these texts the suicide of a rash but earnestly devoted apostle epitomizes Judas's "greater love" of Jesus. Yet because Jesus and Judas mirrored each other, their characteristics could be flip-flopped. Especially in the twentieth century, when modern authors dedicated their art to iconoclasm or heterodoxy, the two agonists in the Passion could and did exchange roles, with Judas exhibiting peace-loving compassion and devotion to the spiritual kingdom (characteristics previously associated with Jesus) and Jesus articulating conflicted aggression and allegiance to the political kingdom (previously identified with Judas). Both the pacific Jesus, who turns the other cheek, and the apocalyptic Jesus, who urges children to rise up against parents, can be found in the Gospels.

Unlike De Quincey, Robinson Jeffers joins a pacific Judas to a rebelliously militant Jesus in a verse drama that nevertheless continues to justify the righteousness of Judas's actions as well as the purity of his intentions. According to Jeffers in *Dear Judas* (1928–29), a play that elicited protests from the Catholic Church, Judas righteously rejects Jesus' arrogant and suicidal determination to "bring not peace but a sword" (24). Within the shifting time frames of a Noh-style dream play, Judas's alienation from Jesus springs from an exceptional sensitivity to suffering.[19] Exquisitely attuned to the pain of others, an empathic Judas argues with his master in terms that sound very much like those of Jesus as conventionally portrayed: "It would be salvation," Jeffers's Judas explains, "To think that I could willingly bear the suffering—if it were possible—for all that lives, I alone" (17). He cleaves to a Jesus who originally called for a "bloodless" victory of people rising up against Roman rule; however, Judas soon worries that Jesus' ministry will lead "to sudden bloody destruc-

tion" (20). Like De Quincey's Judas, in other words, Jeffers's Jesus is
headstrong and deluded.

From Judas's perspective, according to Jeffers, Jesus preaches but
one message in the Temple: "I destroy, I destroy" (22). That Jesus
has praised a woman for pouring perfume "Over his hair and his
clothes, enough in value to have saved many from misery," proves
to Judas that Jesus has "changed indeed," while the escalating violence of Jesus' rhetoric reflects not only his selfishness but also his
exploitation of "the dreadful key" to people's hearts: he preaches the
destruction they secretly crave (23). The arrogance of this anarchic
Jesus, who defines himself as "God / Himself to God" (24), and his
contempt for the cold priests, lying scribes, and mocking rabble lead
a fearful Judas to guard against what he foresees—namely, Jesus'
death and the death of his dream: "If Jesus should persist in Jerusalem, preaching destruction, rousing the looting street-people," Judas
frets, "Roman vengeance" will retaliate with massive "suppression"
(27). Apprehensive of imperial reprisals that will increase suffering,
Jeffers's Judas decides to go to the priests, advising them quietly to
take Jesus at night. For, he thinks, "What harm can they do him, but
keep him / Three or four days for the city peace and dismiss him?"
(27–28). By providing Jesus a cooldown, the priests will cure him of
his destructive ambitions, return him to his original humility. "And
he'll forgive me," Judas thinks, "he'll let me follow him, we'll walk
together" (28). Judas is driven to save Jesus from an overweening and
dangerous pride that can only destroy himself and his followers.

Yet Jeffers complicates his unorthodox interpretation of the Passion by raising doubts about Jesus' parentage, leaving it unclear if
he was fathered by God or by a mortal man.[20] The consequences of
this ambiguity are multiple. On the one hand, Mary becomes a figure
similar to Judas: "Without my sin," she exclaims, Jesus would "not
have been born, nor yet without my falsehood have triumphed" (39).
Toward the end of the play, she adds, "I will not curse you, Judas,
I will curse myself. I am the first that betrayed him. The mothers,
we do it" (47). On the other hand, Jesus himself worries that "I am

either a bastard or the son of God" (30). To allay those anxieties, he passionately dedicates himself to God as his Father, knowing that "Only a crucified / God can fill the wolf bowels of Rome" and that "the cross will conquer" (37). At the work's close, Lazarus judges Judas to be Jesus' "tool" and promises that his "name shall couple" with Christ's "for many centuries: you enter his kingdom with him" (48). Given Judas's empathy for those who suffer, Jeffers's apostle expresses the compassion usually assigned to Jesus, while Jeffers's Jesus in his conflicted relationship to a God who might or might not be his father articulates the anger and the divided loyalties generally associated with Judas.

In what attempts to be a more orthodox rendition of the Passion, Dorothy L. Sayers also imagines a Judas devoted to peace and therefore fearful about a Jesus who brings a vengeful sword. Sayers's *The Man Born to Be King* (1943), a series of radio plays produced for the BBC, features a pacific Judas who follows Jesus because "he laid our burden upon us—sorrow and humility and torment, and shame and poverty and peace of heart" (134), and because "he is the Messiah, not of an earthly but of a spiritual Kingdom" (167). Soon, though, he suspects that the Son of God has begun planning a political coup with the Zealots, a revolt that can only bring ruin through oppressive Roman retaliation against Israel. Sayers's Judas thus questions Jesus' integrity: "For God's sake, Master, are you honest? Or do your words say one thing and your actions another?" (189). The notes to the fourth play in Sayers's cycle explain that Judas "is passionately sincere. He means to be faithful—and he will be faithful—to the light which he sees so brilliantly," though that light is only a "reflection in the mirror of his own brain; and in the end that mirror will twist and distort the reflection" (101). Eventually, Judas—a man with "brains and imagination" (254)—begins to comprehend the wrongful death he has conspired to bring about. That he loves Jesus is also made manifest in Sayers's commentary, for she compares Judas not to the deceitful traitor Iago but to the credulous lover Othello—"Rather like Othello, he can only believe in innocence after he has killed it"—suggesting, first, that Judas does eventually believe in Jesus' innocence and, second, that Judas "in the mood of a jealous husband, whose suspicions would only be confirmed by protestations of innocence," adores the man against whom his tormenting suspicions turn (175).[21]

Different as they are, the writers who envision Judas as a political insurrectionist and those who view Judas as a spiritual pacifist concur on the grievous losses he suffers during and after his lifetime, contrasting them to the triumph of Jesus' messianic resurrection and often also to the villainy of the targeted Christ-killers, the Jewish authorities. The sign of the kiss in the garden comes not from a demon or demoniac, not from a self-identified Jew, not from a thief or an avaricious collaborator with the Temple officials, but from an intimate apostle devoted only to preserving Jesus or his teachings, a loyal comrade who attempts to propel Jesus into manifesting himself as God of a forthcoming kingdom or to protect Jesus from the danger of such a manifestation. All these reconfigurations of Judas, as well as others less congruent, implicitly have him think the utopian thoughts entertained by Gregory A. Page's narrator in *The Diary of Judas Iscariot* (1912): "Though I have done that which seemeth evil, yet shall it turn unto good; and men shall bless me because I had boldness and was not afraid, but went right onward and did this thing" (196). Judas the rebellious hero judges his betrayal to be a collaborative act done for Jesus and thus an ethically beneficial, morally righteous undertaking.[22]

Along with Harry Kempe's central character in his play *Judas* (1913), most nineteenth- and early twentieth-century representations of the twelfth apostle express heroic intentions, ironically undermined by what needs must happen:

For the glory of the Kingdom of God what would I not dare? I would cast my soul into the balance for it. And, after it is over and done with, ages to come will glorify me for the faith of my boldness—my name will live unto all generations of men! I shall be known as the Right Arm of the Messiah—greater than Peter, greater than John—because I dared! (182)

Similarly, in *The Gospel of Judas Iscariot* (1902), Aaron Dwight Baldwin's protagonist finds his heavy task to be "part and parcel of God's plan; that it will provide the means for completing the Lord's great work" (363). Judas in this retelling knows of his relationship with Jesus, "I am surely his familiar friend" (365). When confronted by the subsequent recriminations of Peter and John, Baldwin's Judas makes his case by pointing out that Jesus chose him to become one of the twelve, entrusted him with money for the poor, endowed him with the power to heal the sick and cast out demons, gave him the gifts of body and blood, and washed his feet. Such public pledges of trust are ratified when Judas sees the resurrected Lord, who promises their ultimate reunion.

During "the most anti-Semitic period in American history" (Herman 13), DeMille's *King of Kings* portrays Judas receiving the counted-out coins from the Pharisees, but then clearly distracted and distressed at the Last Supper, anguished by his belief that Jesus would fail to bring about an earthly kingdom (illustrations 5.2 and 5.3). The deicide engineered by Caiaphas (played by the Yiddish stage actor Rudolph Schildkraut) fueled hatred of the Jews, for he displayed more wicked and stereotypically Semitic traits than did Judas (played by his son, the youthful and good-looking Joseph Schildkraut, who went on to perform Otto Frank in the movie version of Anne Frank's life-in-hiding).[23] Joseph Schildkraut's broody Judas looks like nothing so much as a charismatic movie star. Cinematic cross cutting between Jesus' and Judas's final agony—Judas commits suicide with the very rope that had bound Jesus—emphasizes their commonality as well as Judas's passionate engagement in Jesus' fate (see Reinhartz 167). By the beginning of the twentieth century, glamorous Judas must have been all the rage. Why else would Sarah Bernhardt have learned the main role in John de Kay's *Judas,* which she performed in New York in 1910?[24] De Kay's Judas—determined to "give the world instead of

5.2. Judas, played by Joseph Schildkraut, receiving the coins from Caiaphas, played by Rudolph Schildkraut, in Cecil B. DeMille's *King of Kings* (1927). Source: Photofest.

5.3. The Last Supper in DeMille's *King of Kings*. Source: Photofest.

Rome's gospel of force our better gospel of kindness"—cares nothing for money and identifies Jesus only because of his great love for Jesus and Mary Magdalene and because he is convinced that "no harm will come to the Nazarene" (10, 25).

"WOE TO THAT ONE"

Regardless of his valiant intentions, the heroic Judas often submits first to a frightful reversal of his expectations, then to an unpardoned death, and ultimately to the curses of future generations. What would such a fate mean to an altruistic (albeit misguided) Judas seeking to serve his teacher and his teacher's cause? Just as important, what would it signify, should Judas be a rebel *without* a cause—without an apocalyptic or pacifist agenda? Howard Nemerov, who wonders if Judas betrayed "Out of a fine conviction of his truth," does not rule out another possibility: perhaps, Nemerov speculates, the treachery sprang from "some original wreckage of our hope." If humanity's salvation depends on the damnation of one individual, it seems to speak about that singular soul's wrecked hopes. The character I call Judas the Obscure registers his creators' wary anxiety about unfairness at work in the Passion narrative, for the one most explicitly working God's will becomes the one most explicitly condemned by God.

"Woe to that one" is the phrase from Mark (14:21), Matthew (26:24), and Luke (22:22) pertaining to Judas's despondency at the gruesome role he finds himself having to perform in the Passion. On the one hand, it might be predictive (like a warning): Jesus could be meaning to say that at some future date, "Woe to that one" will eventuate. On the other hand, it might be performative (like a curse): Jesus' meaning could be that with the speaking of these words, "Woe to that one" now comes about. In either case, the full verse—"'woe to that one by whom the Son of Man is betrayed! It would have been better for that one not to have been born'" (Mark 14:21; Matthew 26:24)—is uttered by Jesus and heard by all the disciples. To the twelfth apostle, it could have been nothing but a crushing life-in-death sentence. As Jesus promises others election, redemption, and salvation, he bequeaths to Judas the woeful vantage of exclusion.

If we view Rembrandt's painting *Judas Returning the Thirty Pieces of Silver* (plate 7) in terms of a wrecked Judas who knows he cannot be saved, it illuminates Judas's development in modern times, for this Judas may have cast down the silver and then himself in a tortured act of contrition that (he realizes) will not earn him absolution. His is a rejected repentance. Consider the shadow that fills the lower left of Rembrandt's canvas. Just as the seated central priest averts his face and raises his hand against Judas, the seated elder in the left foreground turns his back to the viewer, blocking light in a manner that epitomizes the obstructing world that the penitential Judas inhabits, as we do too. Spectators, then, share not the communal aversion to Judas but his blocked situation. His ruin registers somewhat differently, in other words, if perceived not from the community's point of view, as in many premodern representations, but instead from broken Judas's vantage. By the end of the nineteenth century, when ethical and psychological considerations predominated over religious or political approaches to the Gospels, novelists and dramatists examined the quandaries raised by Judas's woe as well as its source.

Ought the inherent demands of the Passion narrative be blamed for Judas's wretchedness, or does the fault lie in the treachery of his character? If the plot requires a betrayer, Judas suffers within a deterministic trap: to ensure an ultimate good, he must do an evil earning him eternal damnation. If his treacherous character is the cause, he may suffer within a different deterministic trap: a compulsive psychic impulse overmasters him, triggering his eternal damnation. Here, dwelling on the problem of determinism, thinkers enter a realm in which either nature or human nature does betray the trusting heart. Judas's actions might have sprung from or resulted in repugnance—revulsion at a universe in which salvation for all necessitated damnation for him or disgust at some inexplicable but implacable subjective urge. Conceived as a dissident without any volitional rationale, Judas has been imagined as the hapless victim of a grotesque economy that hinges the well-being of humanity on his iniquity, or he has been viewed as a neurotic or psychotic casualty quite unaccountably but obdurately antagonistic to grace. In modern times, Luke's and John's ascription to Judas of demonic possession translates into fateful external or internal powers that predispose the twelfth apostle to treachery or compel him to betray.

A number of artists dwell extensively on what they imagine must have been the consciousness of a woeful Judas during a brief segment of his life in Matthew's Gospel—Thursday night, after the kiss, and Friday morning, when he sees Jesus condemned by the priests and elders, returns the coins, and decides to commit suicide. Whether his predicament is attributed to external or internal causes, what comes into full focus after the Victorian period is the isolation of a tormented Judas. As he incurs eternal hatred, this miserable creature causes some modern writers to mistrust providence or the efficacy of divine compassion. Judas with his infirm purpose of amendment becomes an afflicted soul who—taking to heart Jesus' stern judgment—internalizes the verdict that "It would have been better . . . not to have been born." When hatred spills back into self-hatred, a profound sorrow at having to endure a mistaken life reviled or abjured, Judas the Obscure suffers dysphoria, the restive depression that plagues the petitioners of Saint Jude or "Judas, not Iscariot." Pulverized by irremediable pain, Judas in this mercy-bereft state apprehends what or who is anathema—what or who is left out or excluded.[25]

An odd singsong poem titled "Handicap" (1966), by Anthony Hecht, deftly maps the genealogy that connects Judas to Jude. Not a devilish cloven foot but a disabling cloven palate and an anxious, hesitant, or immature voice characterize Hecht's twelfth apostle:

> Higgledy-piggledy
> Judas Iscariot,

Cloven of palate, of
Voice insecure,

Mumbler and lisper, was
Hypocoristically
Known to his buddies as
"Jude, the Obscure."

From the Greek *hupo* and *koristikos,* the word *hypocoristic* means "called by endearing or pet names," though the multisyllabic "hypocoristically" sounds a bit like *hypocritically* and *hypochondriacally.* Rarely called by endearments, an intimately known Judas is impeded by telling symptoms of his own ailments and straitjacketed in double dactylic verse (because of the double dactyls of his full name).[26] According to Hecht, this handicapped Judas needs to be understood as a reincarnation of Jude Thaddeus, Jesus' cousin who became the saint of hopeless causes, and Jude the Obscure, the eponymous hero of Thomas Hardy's last novel.[27]

Hecht links Judas to Jude to consider who had more reason than Judas to judge himself a lost cause. Enmeshed in a plot antagonistic to his well-being, did Judas chafe against a universal good that could not be divorced from his own personal wrongs? Wouldn't he have reason to question the goodness of such a good? It may be a stretch to link the biblical Judas to Saint Jude and to Jude Fawley, the central character of *Jude the Obscure* (1895), but Anthony Hecht encourages us to do so, presumably because Hardy explores the despair that arises when every expectation of grace is frustrated by overwhelming forces that rule a handicapped world devoid of a personal or benevolent God. *Jude the Obscure* is the only text discussed in this book that does not contain sustained commentary about the twelfth apostle or the Passion. I include it because in Hardy's novel we can glimpse the logic that connects Judas not only with Jude, the patron saint of lost causes, but also with Job, who loathed a life accursed because of

God's capricious bet with his satanic adversary. Hardy's insight into the shadowy kinship of Judas Iscariot, Saint Jude, and Job affords a perspective that, we will see, illuminates a number of powerful paintings and poems about Judas and the Passion.

In *Jude the Obscure,* the forces that control Hardy's universe recurrently work against the welfare of his miserably betrayed and self-betraying protagonist, whose son, little Jude, kills himself and the two other children in the family, much to the shock of the father, who gazes on the scene:

> At the back of the door were fixed two hooks for hanging garments, and from these the forms of the two youngest children were suspended, by a piece of box-cord round each of their necks, while from a nail a few yards off the body of little Jude was hanging in a similar manner. An overturned chair was near the elder boy, and his glazed eyes were staring into the room; but those of the girl and baby boy were closed. (404–5)

Both the murder of innocence and the death by hanging relate little Jude to Judas. Jude Fawley comprehends the consequences of this massacre of his children in terms of "the beginning of the coming universal wish not to live" (406). Like the ropes on which medieval Judas hangs, the cords wound around the necks of the baby and the two children bring to mind the umbilical cord strangling stillbirths. During a period of time associated with Nietzsche's proclamation of God's death, the suicide and infanticides express futility about hopeless causes and desperate cases generally attributed to the malignant fates butchering Hardy's universe.[28] Hardy's characters are miserably disappointed by a world of material appetite, folly, and vice that stymies any spiritual faith.

Within Hardy's plot, religious rituals and spiritual longings only torment humanity, as Christ's Passion did Judas in most formulations. Thus, the novel's bleak epigraph suggests that the biblical "letter killeth." Of course, given Hardy's criticism of damaging social institutions, *Jude the Obscure* should not be reduced to a statement about the Passion.[29] However, it does focus on an outcast who can never find fellowship in Christminster, which he associates with the heavenly Jerusalem. When Jude Fawley first hears about the existence of little Jude and then again at the end of his life, he repeats Job's lament: "Let the day perish wherein I was born" (330, 488; Job 3:3). The words echo little Jude's last expressed wish that he had not been born, as well as the dire warning of Jesus that "It would have been better for that one not to have been born." As Matthew's Judas might have fretted before the hanging, Jude Fawley and little Jude worry, as did Job, "*Wherefore is light given to him that is in misery, and life unto the bitter in soul?*" (488; Job 3:20). Father and son achieve pathos as sinned against sinners never to be compensated for their suffering, as Job eventually was. Job's lament—"I would choose strangling and death rather than this body. / I loathe my life" (7:15–16)—could gloss and thereby interpret earlier depictions of Judas's act of self-destruction, like the one in a series by Willem von Swanenburg (see illustration 3.10).[30]

Just as Judas might have realized that Jesus' saving resurrection of humanity could be guaranteed only by his own personal damnation, the youthful Jude Fawley broods that "mercy to one set of creatures was cruelty toward another" (15). Similarly, cadaverous and ghostly little Jude—an embodiment of negativity—acts on the proposition that cruelty toward one set of creatures constitutes mercy toward another: he kills himself and his siblings to rescue his adopted mother and father from penury. The antiprovidential power that scourges all the characters in Hardy's novel proves that human existence inevitably devolves into acts of betrayal, which is why little Jude is hypocoristically called Father Time. An "enslaved and dwarfed Divinity" (332), the boy with his octogenarian face allegorizes temporality itself as both destructive and self-destructive.[31] Up against the overwhelming hostility of the forces ruling the universe, the ravages of Father Time might be interpreted as asymmetrical warfare. Little Jude cannot triumph over or strike back against insurmountable odds (illegitimacy, physical ailments, poverty, social ostracism), but he can at least put an end to the struggle by taking himself out of it.[32] Not redemption or resurrection but calamity marks each individual's and each epoch's duration: in this sense, Hardy's novel belongs under the sign of a Judas condemned to suffer the horror of the role demanded of him in the Passion. Jesus' providential ascent depends on Judas's antiprovidential descent. When a miserable Judas, like Job, experiences the impenetrability or inscrutability of God, he insists, as Job did, on the personal meaninglessness of his physical and mental anguish.[33]

Regarding treachery, Hardy suggests, the fault is in the stars, the malignant fates that rule human destiny. Antagonistic to such a supposition, W. B. Yeats approached the central issue of the Passion by ascribing treachery not to the stars but to ourselves, the obstinate subjective forces that drive the human psyche. Whereas Hardy's Jude and little Jude act with good intentions horribly twisted by a treacherous chain of events that tricks them into becoming betrayers, Yeats's traitor operates out of a contrary impulse within himself. In Hardy's novel, human enmity arises against what is perceived to be a graceless universe; in Yeats's short and highly stylized Passion play *Calvary* (1920), in contrast, Judas expresses gratuitous antagonism toward grace. Whether attributing the "original wreckage of our hope" to forces outside or inside the self, Judas the Obscure figures the great divide between humanity and God: divinity's indifference to human welfare or humanity's inexplicable but implacable hostility toward divinity. This last and difficult topic is investigated by Yeats, who envisions an isolated Christ.

Yeats's *Calvary* stages the Passion, as Christ encounters Lazarus, Judas, and three Roman soldiers, all masked as in Noh drama. Here Judas, like Lazarus and the soldiers, typifies people committed to private lives quite removed from the spiritual ambitions of God's Son. Indeed, all three encounters emphasize humanity's recalcitrance or indifference to God's providential plan and thus to Jesus' attempt to redeem the world. For example, Lazarus, who describes himself as "the man that died and was raised up" (289), rebukes Jesus: "You dragged me to the light as boys drag out / A rabbit when they have dug its hole away" (290). Christ declares that he has conquered death, but Lazarus feels violated, for "I was free four days, four days being dead," and now he is "Death-stricken and death-hungry still" (291). Similarly alienated, Judas has "not doubted" Christ, but betrayed him "Because you seemed all-powerful" (291). Driven "wild" that all men are in Christ's power, Judas "could not bear to think you had but to whistle / And I must do" (291).

Not wanting to be converted into God's image, Judas views Jesus' messianic rule as a form of servitude or indoctrination. Judas, stubbornly clinging to his own identity, resists God's possession. While submitting to the narrative in which he must inevitably be interpolated, Judas insists on succumbing in his own way, on his own terms:

> It was decreed that somebody betray you—
> I'd thought of that—but not that I should do it,
> I the man Judas, born on such a day,
> In such a village, such and such his parents;
> Nor that I'd go with my old coat upon me
> To the High Priest, and chuckle to myself
> As people chuckle when alone, and that I'd do it
> For thirty pieces and no more, no less,
> And neither with a nod, a look, nor a sent message,
> But with a kiss upon your cheek. I did it,
> I, Judas, and no other man, and now
> You cannot even save me. (292)

Notoriously elliptical, Yeats's play only hints at what the three Roman soldiers also seem to suggest, that some remain unmoved by Christ's Passion. How make sense of this unwillingness or inability to be born again?

Yeats's play opens with a refrain, "God has not died for the white heron." It closes with another, "God has not appeared to the birds."[34] Some human beings—seeking the freedom of the heron, of the birds, of the specificity of an indifferent natural world—do not doubt Christ's power, but nevertheless resist it. Indeed, when he planned the betrayal, Judas was near "no live thing, . . . but a heron / So full of itself that it seemed terrified" (292). Judas decides not to follow Jesus; he chooses instead to be full of a vital sense of his own singularity, of his own individuated existence. To that extent, Yeats's Judas typifies humanity, our inevitable and embodied alienation from a spiritual perfection that would erase our unique or eccentric subjectivities. Yeats therefore illuminates Kierkegaard's diagnosis of the despair he names "sickness unto death," and in particular "the despair of wanting in despair to be oneself—defiance" (98): in the clutches of this defiance, the "self wants in its despair to savour to the full the satisfaction of making itself into itself, of developing itself, of being itself" (101). Not saved, Judas in Yeats's play nevertheless insists on retaining a sense of his inviolate being and thereby attaining the freedom of the herons. He acts on the assumption that "Whatever man betrays Him will be free" (292)—free, that is, to be himself, a self that cannot be saved.

To grapple with Judas as a personification of spiritual recalcitrance, the theologian Karl Barth at one point considered the relationship between Jesus and Judas "a heightened form of the situation between Jesus and *all other* men—between God's election of man, and his necessary rejection" (*Doctrine* 476; emphasis mine). Barth here focuses not on Judas and the Jews but instead on a disturbing mystery: namely, the "hostility of [every] man toward grace," a compulsive enmity that "is absolutely immovable" (477). Since Judas's hostility "makes manifest" Jesus' unlimited love, "it would be an unspeakably hard affirmation that there was no forgiveness of sins for Judas" or "that Jesus died in vain for him" (475). Kierkegaard and Barth approach the problem of human defiance and despair theologically, but it can of course also be understood psychologically by artists seeking to comprehend the feelings of compulsion and shame that accompany wrongdoing and guilt.

Calvary keeps Judas's motives murky. After Yeats's Jesus explains

"My Father put all men into my hands," Judas's response—"That was the very thought that *drove me wild*" (291; emphasis mine)—raises questions about his sanity. When Judas imagines going to the Temple police and chortling to himself "As people chuckle when alone," he may bring to mind the madmen of Edgar Allan Poe's stories, and in particular the insane narrator of his "The Imp of the Perverse" (1845).[35] This murderer judges perversity to be the first principle of the human soul. Paradoxically, it is a motive without motive: the unconquerable force of perversity, according to Poe's incarcerated speaker, makes irresistible just those verbal and physical deeds not in our best interests—"we persist in acts because we feel we should *not* persist in them" (1221). If viewed as a personification of the "imp of the perverse," Yeats's Judas—encased in his own interiority—acts in a manner antagonistic to his own ultimate well-being. Without regard to the utility or consequence of his actions, he feels compelled to do what he does precisely because he knows that he ought not to do what he does.

Whether sponsored by external or internal agencies, the woe of Judas the Obscure registers perplexity at the tangle of an incomprehensible existence ordained by the Passion: of being deemed a disciple, but then inhabited by evil forces; of being named a thief, but given control of the common purse; of being controlled by Satan, but held personally accountable; of being promised a throne in the kingdom, but cast as a son of perdition; of being prompted to perform a liberating act that shockingly ricochets against oneself. Mulling over the stubborn persistence of injury or the unredeemability of Judas, creative artists resemble Christian theologians, who worry that "the role of Judas in the economy of salvation represents a defeat for Jesus" and who ponder the intractability of moral evil, "resistant to every effort (even by God in Christ) to overcome it" (Cane 76).

BETTER UNBORN

Like Simone Weil, Judas the Obscure stands for those who identify with the barren fig tree. "I never read the story of the barren fig tree without trembling," Weil once explained; "I think that it is a portrait of me. In it also, nature was powerless, and yet it was not excused. Christ cursed it" (*Waiting for God* 52). Based, as this accursed and better unborn Judas is, on biblical passages—the sole evidence that might possibly be adduced from the Bible to legitimize abortion—he cannot be the exclusive brainchild of modernist writers. By surfacing in their work, he affords an approach to much earlier and much later pictures and poems about the twelfth apostle that meditate on the sickening dysphoria of self-loathing. A Judas without a cause or with a lost cause feels shunned as well as self-spurned, since he is the victim of forces beyond his control. For a number of premodern and contemporary painters and writers, Judas's condition of being better unborn speaks to his victimization and thereby illuminates the blurring of blame or accountability. Himself betrayed, he betrays, but how could he not? In addition, a Judas better unborn illustrates the inadequacy of the categories I have been employing—specifically, the clear demarcation between the anomaly and the pariah—since Judas the Obscure is an anomaly because he feels himself to have somehow *been made to become* a pariah. In other words, a shift in perspective—from that of the eleven to that of the twelfth—alters our comprehension of the social outcast.

Hardy's tormented Judes and Yeats's intractable Judas put a weird spin on very early depictions of the Last Supper. One unknown Ottonian artist from ancient Regensburg, for instance, places all the apostles and Jesus in halos on the far side of the table, while a solitary Judas eats alone in the forefront (ca. 1030–40; plate 8). As in so many depictions, his mouth is open and over the sop appears a black bird, an omen or icon of the demonic possession he is about to suffer. Bringing to mind Satan's entrance into Judas (Luke 22:3) and Jesus' injunction "Do quickly what you are going to do" (John 13:27), the placid faces of Jesus and the eleven disciples hint that they take satisfaction in witnessing an event that will soon display God's determinative will. But—especially because Judas here looks as if he is trying to make himself regurgitate—what might it mean for Judas that he alone must gag on evil to perform the nefarious act that will bring about that event? If indifferent or malignant omnipotent powers enlist or force Judas to swallow sin, Hardy would have us ask, why should we hold him accountable? If Judas—inexplicably and against his own best interests—cannot stop himself from needing or craving to swallow sin, Yeats would have us ask less conclusively, can we hold him accountable?

Even apparently anti-Semitic paintings of Judas can be interpreted from the point of view of a trapped or mysteriously sick and sickening Judas the Obscure. Consider, for example, Hans Holbein the Younger's *Last Supper* (1524–25; illustration 5.4). With his hook nose, his hunched back, his overgrown red hair, yellowed garb, and sandals (the others, in keeping with Jesus' instructions, do not wear footgear), Holbein's Judas looks Neanderthal, an unredeemable offense without virtue. Reduced in growth, with coarse features and poorly proportioned limbs, he provides a case study of cretinism (hypothyroidism). With one hand clenching the bench upon which he sits and the other his chin, far removed from the bright blue sky outdoors, he might bring to mind a resentful and disabled misfit unwelcome at the feast, a desolate figure of grievance and grief. Like Hardy's Father Time, he resembles "Age masquerading as Juvenility" or "an enslaved and dwarfed Divinity" (332). Those who are not elect do not participate in the community or fellowship of the faithful. Holbein's tense Judas, sunk within his own thoughts, suffers the indignities of a wizened cripple so misshapen that none of the relaxed and convivial apostles can bear looking at him. Nor does his misery allow him the freedom to gaze on any of those in (but avoiding contact with) his company.

As do the painters of the Last Supper discussed in chapter 3, Hol-

5.4. Hans Holbein
the Younger,
Last Supper
(1524–25). Source:
Kunstmuseum,
Basel.

bein emphasizes the isolation of Judas, who is contrasted with eight apostles avidly engaged with their teacher or each other. What justifies my placing his painting in the context of Judas the Obscure is the evident misery his Judas suffers, without any visual evidence that it is deserved (no money bag, despairing suicide, incriminating eating, teeth, demon, or weapon).[36] Just as the God-forsaken plaintiff of Psalm 22 feels himself to be "a worm, and no human; / scorned by others, and despised by the people" (6–7), so Holbein's miscreant might be thought to sense that

> all my bones are out of joint;
> my heart is like wax;
> it is melted within my breast;
> my mouth is dried up like a potsherd,

and my tongue sticks to my jaws;

you lay me in the dust of death. (14–15)

That this lament derives from the psalm famously beginning "My God, my God, why have you forsaken me?" hints at the torment Judas the Obscure paradoxically shares with the criminalized, ostracized, and ultimately sacrificed Christ.

Not empathy but aversion or indifference is sparked by intense suffering, our dread and horror of the incurable. Nailed to the cross of himself, from Kierkegaard's perspective, Judas suffers an afflicted incarnation that inspires dread among Holbein's eight healthy disciples, who put up with his presence, yet avoid any potentially contagious or contaminating interaction.[37] With downcast eyes, Jesus looks self-absorbed, while the other apostles intensely engage with each other. At least to twentieth- and twenty-first century viewers, the Judas-pariah teeters toward the state of a singular anomaly, in part because of the inexplicable but sharp contrast between his physiognomy and that of all the others, in part because of his evident dejection. Earlier interpreters of Judas emphasized how his anguish was earned and in fact warranted: John Calvin, for instance, viewed Judas as a prototype of sinners "attached to their wicked desires [who] rot in the torment that they cannot escape. In this way . . . God avenges their stubbornness" (175).[38] Whereas to Calvin an irredeemable Judas justified the ways of God to man and especially to a wicked man properly "banned from the grace of God" (175), in secular times an irredeemable Judas suffers the limits of redemption or God's broken covenant.

Especially after the so-called disappearance of God at the end of the nineteenth century and then again after Auschwitz, affliction could no longer be interpreted as either necessarily deserved (as for the pariah Judas) or inevitably ennobling (as for the heroic Judas). Judas the Obscure therefore prompts questions about the inadvertent complicity *of Jesus* in Judas's treachery, a point made in the 1950s by the philosopher Paul Tillich. Because Jesus chose Judas for his intimate group of disciples, Tillich reasoned, "the innocent one [Jesus] becomes tragically guilty in respect to the very one [Judas] who contributes to his own death" (133). An "existential estrangement" in "the ambiguity of life," which cannot be evaded by any human being—even a man who is also a God—means that "Jesus was involved in the tragic element of guilt, in so far as he made his enemies inescapably guilty": "he becomes tragically responsible for the guilt of those who kill him," Tillich believes (133). An apostle doomed to "eternal perdition" after being utilized as "an important instrument in the hand of God" in "accomplishing the great purposes of his grace": such a figure provoked righteous sermons by Calvinists, but tragic meditations by the contemporary artists—Mario Brelich, Geoff Todd, and Frank Bidart—whose works I consider to conclude this chapter.[39]

The damnation of an indispensable assistant: this comes close to the complex judgment of Mario Brelich's *The Work of Betrayal* (1975), a philosophically speculative novel (originally composed in Italian). Brelich exhumes a preeminent fictive expert—Edgar Allan Poe's master detective C. Auguste Dupin, who had proved his uncanny acumen by solving the murders in the Rue Morgue, the death of Marie Roget, and, most famously, the disappearance of the purloined letter. Like many of the thinkers considered in this cultural biography, Brelich seeks to explain "Judas' behavior[, which] remains shrouded in obscurity"; he employs Poe's matchless sleuth in an investigation based on the assumption that "the actual role [Judas] played in the arrest and in the criminal proceedings brought against Jesus . . . has never been given a convincing explanation" (16). The "riddle" of the unintelligible and mysterious "Judas Case" could be solved only by someone whose unusual logical expertise might elucidate the theological implications of what the New Testament left undisclosed: "the Sacred Writ does not contain the elements needed to clarify either the 'why' or the 'how' of the wretched apostle's treachery" (17, 15)

First, through a series of elaborate philosophical suppositions, Dupin argues that Judas "was plainly and simply identical with Evil, he was Evil itself" (136). Yet later the detective claims that Jesus approached the impending betrayal by admitting his insurmountable need for the twelfth apostle as well as his sense of guilt about utilizing Judas as a means to gain his own and humanity's salvation: Dupin's dependent Jesus eventually responds to Judas's perilous sense of culpability by saying to the betrayer, "*Do I forgive you? It's I who must put that question to you*" (236). However, Jesus did not consciously set out to exploit his apostle. In the course of his investigation, Dupin entertains but quickly discards the idea of a "Machiavellian or 'jesuitical' Jesus for whom the sublime end justifies the knowingly cruel means" of using a victimized Judas, hoodwinked to carry out the necessary task at hand (33). Jesus might have picked one of his apostles to be the betrayer, might have "counted on his disciple's criminal tendencies"; yet Dupin rejects such a proposition because of the "general aversion" it must arouse in those who revere the Son of God (34–35). So as not to vilify Jesus, Dupin stresses "his human guise," for Jesus did not know his own divinity except as it "*presented itself to him as a thesis to be demonstrated*" (53).

Through a convoluted series of suppositions, Dupin imagines Judas acting the part of Satanic adversary out of love for Jesus and faith in his divinity, which had to be demonstrated to the world at large. *The Work of Betrayal* fully explicates the trap that clicks shut on the twelfth apostle. In order to carry out his Master's vocation, a miserably conflicted Judas—"the unhappiest of mortal beings" (217)—confronts a catch-22: if he goes to the Temple authorities, he will be damned for killing Jesus; but if he does not go to the Temple authorities, he will be damned because "*everyone will be damned*" (234). No wonder, then, that Dupin's dependent and thus anxious Jesus cannot simply absolve Judas after his final and futile remorse over the "*unpardonable sin*" in the garden, but must instead ask his disciple's forgiveness. For Judas had to forfeit his personal salvation to ensure a greater good. Once again, one of Simone Weil's meditations seems pertinent. "If it were conceivable that in obeying God one should bring about one's own damnation, while in disobeying

5.5. Geoff
Todd, *Betrayal 1*
(1995). Source:
Geoff Todd.

him one could be saved," Weil once surmised, "I should still choose
the way of obedience" (*Waiting for God* 6). By making it conceivable
that one might obey God and bring about one's own damnation, portraits of Judas the Obscure hint that Jesus' sacrifice was imperfect, for
it implicated God or God's Son in the twelfth apostle's transgression
and resulting doom.

With characters damned by external constraints or internal compulsions, none of the authors of Judas the Obscure subscribes to the
idea that an almighty *and* infinitely good divinity created or rules
the world. One contemporary artist conveys Judas the Obscure's
inexplicable loneliness and pain, when he stands for those to whom
divine justice and mercy do not extend. Wreckage of hope characterizes Geoff Todd's ostracized Judas. In Todd's *Betrayal 1* (1995),
the weeping or bleeding eyes of Judas recall Sophocles' Oedipus or

Shakespeare's Gloucester, blinded so they can see (illustration 5.5). Evoking sackcloth and ashes, an ascetic Judas Dolorosus breaks up the letters of his name perhaps to commit a personal act of sabotage or self-sabotage, but perhaps also to illustrate a more generalized principle of impairment disturbingly omnipresent in the human psyche or condition. With its gray and black palette, Todd's image emphasizes guilt, remorse, a conviction about one's own worthlessness. Less a demon, more a monk or mendicant, a hopeless Judas atoning in desolate silence clarifies how it feels to be John's "son of perdition" (17:12), an anathema.

What might it mean to resolve on a sacrifice enacted in such a way as *not* to cause another human being the guilt attendant upon betrayal or complicity? The contemporary poet Frank Bidart answers this difficult question, implicitly raised by Judas the Obscure. Bidart opens and closes his poem "The Sacrifice" (1983) with an injunction that Judas, composing "the history of SOLITUDE," must note the demise of the person he is elegizing: Mary Kenwood. Just as Hardy did with little Jude, the title poem of Bidart's 1983 book of verse invokes Judas-Jude-Job to focus on what might be grist for a tabloid news headline, here the fate of one "Miss Mary Kenwood; who, without / help, placed her head in a plastic bag, // then locked herself / in a refrigerator" (75). Bidart suggests that like Father Time, Mary Kenwood was driven to deal with unjust suffering by employing suicide as a form of asymmetrical warfare, in her case waged against the ravages of disease. In the elegy's second stanza, a flashback explains why her shocking demise might have occurred. It was not just Mary's witnessing her mother's painful death from throat cancer six months earlier but also watching her mother "*want* to die" that made Mary know her own helpless innocence yet feel her own profound guilt.

The third section of "The Sacrifice" attributes Mary's final act to her interpretation of the Passion:

> Christ knew the Secret. Betrayal
> is necessary; as is woe for the betrayer.

The solution, Mary realized at last,
must be brought out of my own body.

Wiping away our sins, Christ stained us with his blood—;
to offer yourself, yet need *betrayal,* by *Judas,* before
   SHOULDERING

THE GUILT OF THE WORLD—;
. . . *Give me the courage not to need Judas.* (75–76)

A Christian who ends up following the example of Matthew's Judas, Mary Kenwood uses her gruesome suicide to enact the message she takes away from the Gospels—the necessity of becoming her own betrayer. According to Mary Kenwood, Christ's sacrificed blood did not cleanse or save everybody: Jesus in the New Testament admitted about his disciples, "'Not all of you are clean'" (John 13:11); Jesus, Bidart's poem reminds us, deeded "woe for the betrayer." Resonantly named, Mary Kenwood resolves on not exploiting an accessory so as not to stain another person with her blood. Like Tillich and Brelich, Bidart ponders what it means *about Jesus* that Judas, who made possible Jesus' sacrifice, suffers nothing but harm from it.

Still, why was a plastic bag insufficient to guarantee Mary Kenwood's self-sacrifice? Why did she need to open death's door by closing a refrigerator door on herself? Just as the mother in this poem had to contend with her fierce desire to die, as she suffered a painful life, the daughter may have had to contend with her fierce desire to live, as she suffered a painful death. Guilt is a complicated matter here. Did Mary Kenwood respond to her mother's wanting to die, and did she then take her own life because she judged herself guilty of murdering her mother? Or was Mary Kenwood guilty of letting her mother suffer, of not putting her mother out of her pain, of not killing her mother? Feeling incapable of fidelity or kindness or right conduct, an anguished Mary Kenwood witnessed the grotesque misery of fleshly embodiment, of her mother's material body with all its attendant ills, and she could not master the contradictory moral imperatives it imposed on her. Any conceivable intervention or nonintervention must have felt like a betrayal. Bidart's poem asks us to ask, are there situations of extreme pathos in which murderous actions become acts of mercy, acts of intended mercy murderous?

In "The Sacrifice," Judas becomes an avatar of humanity's nonredemptive suffering. Bidart concludes by stating "that to the friend who opened / the refrigerator, it seemed // death fought; before giving in" (76). One might expect this last line to read "life fought; before giving in." Perhaps the reason it does not is that Mary Kenwood, by virtue of taking to heart the apostle of grief, somehow vanquishes death, or her fear of dying: death, for her and by her own means, is preferable to the torment either of her own or of someone else's guilt-ridden life. Another interpreter of the poem puts it this way: "Mary knew an even greater 'SECRET' than Christ's: death can be mysteriously defeated by an individual's refusal to splatter others with blood and guilt during the process of dying" (Dyer 10). By revealing this secret, Bidart approaches a disturbing issue: namely, whether the twelfth apostle was exploited in an unconscionable manner. Would a compassionate savior or omnipotent messiah permit a devoted follower to be subjected to such a sorrowful fate?[40] A preeminent ethical rule, Immanuel Kant's moral principle that each human being must be approached as an end in her- or himself—was it broken by God or God's Son when Judas endangered his soul to serve as a means or instrument of the crucifixion and resurrection?[41]

To the extent that Judas was ensnared within a narrative inimical to his own well-being or driven by psychic compulsions over which he had no control, the twelfth apostle enables writers and painters to query the fairness of the powers ruling over human destiny. In the next chapter, post–World War II artists move from baffled reservations to angry protests against the injustice of the forces governing humanity and history. During a time period noted for unprecedented catastrophes, sorrow over the limits of redemption seethes into rage against "God [who] does not forgive the sins He makes us commit," as the Portuguese novelist José Saramago ominously put it (127). The "dusangelion" or bad news that Judas teaches counters Jesus' positive promise of salvation and hope with a profoundly negative insistence on the persistence of damnation and despair in a universe ruled by a power possibly almighty, or possibly infinitely good, but not almighty *and* infinitely good. Yet, Bidart suggests, there is a stature gained by resisting the salvation story, a heroism consisting of integrity. For Mary Kenwood insists on not diluting the bleak lesson she takes away from the Passion. She seeks "*the courage not to need Judas*" in order to assimilate guilt and innocence into a shattered consciousness. Hers is an extreme and extremely fraught posture. How much easier it would be to thrive by accepting the utility of Judas.

TWENTIETH-CENTURY DEATHS AND RESURRECTIONS: WHAT WOULD JUDAS DO?

The Nazis' exploitation of the twelfth apostle and the Aryanization of Christ precipitated a crisis in Christendom that issued in the illegitimacy of the Jewish pariah. Widespread recognition of the betrayal of the Jewish people in the Holocaust stripped Judas of stereotypical traits, as he grew into a revered savior, splitting to incarnate either omniscient but vulnerable good or omnipotent evil.

THE QUESTIONS JUDAS ALWAYS RAISES—why does evil exist? why does God allow evil to exist?—teased Jorge Luis Borges into writing an oddly essayistic story titled "Three Versions of Judas" (1944). The theological speculations of Borges's protagonist, Nils Runeberg, earn him first academic refutations, then charges of heresy, and finally obscurity, madness, and death. One year before the liberation of the concentration camps, Borges illuminated Judas's evolution in a manner that summarizes the development of the twelfth apostle in the nineteenth and early twentieth centuries even as it uncannily predicts his eccentric morphing after the Holocaust.

Taking a clue from the gallant Zealot imagined by De Quincey, the first edition of Runeberg's *Kristus och Judas* argues that the twelfth, alone among the apostles, "sensed Jesus' secret divinity" and performed the ultimately redemptive role of informer so as to force Christ "to declare His divinity and set in motion a vast uprising against Rome's yoke" (Borges, "Three Versions" 164). This is the noble hero we encountered in the previous chapter, betraying Jesus only in order to urge his indecisive comrade to establish his reign on earth. Then, in a revision of this argument, Runeberg proposes instead that Judas embraced "a hyperbolic, even limitless asceticism," renouncing honor as well as salvation by electing those "sins unvisited by any virtue: abuse of confidence (John 12:6) and betrayal" (165). Runeberg's second hypothesis recalls Judas the Obscure, a figure of the pathos and loneliness haunting any soul shut out from grace. Whereas the virtue of courage may accompany murder, or the virtue of tenderness may attend adultery, the self-hating informant deems himself "unworthy of being good" in any way (164). The ascetic Judas mortifies not his flesh but his spirit through his immovable hostility toward grace: he renounces "the kingdom of heaven" (165).[1]

Borges's obsessed Runeberg eventually puts forth a third and scandalous formulation, the idea that God "stooped to become man for the redemption of the human race," one who could sin and "be condemned to damnation," that God "chose an abject existence: He was Judas" (166). This audacious conclusion—that Judas incarnates God—might well lead readers of Borges's story to doubt his narrator's sanity. Since Nils means null or naught, of course, and a rune is an ancient letter or charm (as well as a near homophone of the word *ruin*), should one assume that Nils Runeberg has lost his way and perished on the vertiginous heights of the archaic enigma of Judas? (Would his miserable fate be mine? I sometimes worried, as my mind balked at Judas's dizzying transmutations.) How could Borges or his character imagine that God would choose Judas's "abject existence," especially after the twelfth apostle and Jewry were profiled as pariahs targeted for extermination by the Nazis?

During the Holocaust, the traits of the premodern demoniac Judas provided a veritable warehouse of anti-Semitic features exploited by Nazi propagandists, or so this chapter will try to demonstrate. While

the Jews were being systematically rounded up and killed throughout Europe, we will see, the Jewishness of Jesus was systematically
denied by many German theologians. These grievous facts—the
reemergence of the Jewish pariah-Judas, the Aryanization of Jesus—
prompted deepening skepticism in conscientious people about the
moral effectiveness of established religions. During the bloodiest
century ever, the misuses to which established religions were put, in
too many totalitarian and nationalist venues to name, deepened that
skepticism. But why and how would such phenomena lead to the
apotheosis of Judas after the war, when principled postwar church
authorities finally judged Christian anti-Semitism unacceptable and
thus the Jewish Judas-pariah illegitimate? The Jewish pariah-Judas—
betrayed by having been made to personify quintessentially Jewish
betrayal—had to go; long live Judas the exalted!

Instead of expiring, the twelfth apostle was revived after the war
to become an incarnation of omniscient but vulnerable good *or* an
incarnation of omnipotent evil. For better or for worse, Judas emerged
with newfound potency in the last quarter of the twentieth century,
now stripped of stereotypically Jewish features (at least in high art).
Omniscient good: a victimized Judas joins Jesus, and together they
signify a Passion in danger of being betrayed by a history of barbarous atrocities. Omnipotent evil: personifying a universal principle
of betrayal, Judas antithetically embodies the malignant forces that
brought into being a history of barbarous atrocities. Through a complex series of manifestations, then, a reconfigured Judas asserts his
supreme authority either as a preeminently loyal apostle, one sharing
(even exceeding) Jesus' ethical stature, or as the personification of
the acquisitive materialism and deceit that put into jeopardy Jesus'
ethical vision.

From both Jewish and Christian perspectives after World War II,
the fact that the Holocaust occurred, that it was executed by the
Nazis but also stomached by the rest of the world, meant that many
Christians had been found guilty of rejecting their messiah, along
with his lessons of love. For this reason, the Passion became a vehicle

for addressing humanity's capacity for betrayal and the consequences of that betrayal. Judas, along with Jesus, began to embody the human condition in societies that allowed the Shoah to happen. "What had been unthinkable before," the poet Edmond Jabès explained, was "the almost total indifference of the German as well as the Allied populations, which made Auschwitz possible"—with the result that "Today all trust is lined with a consuming distrust" (7). As distrust intensifies, Judas gains in stature.

Eventually neither more nor less Jewish than Jesus, postwar Judas becomes a praiseworthy but pitifully defenseless savior of the savior or the blameworthy, presiding embodiment of the avarice, hypocrisy, and treachery that derailed Jesus' mission and that characterize so many private as well as public lives today. Put simply, magisterial Judas splits to register, on the one hand, the virtue of betrayed victims and, on the other, the villainy of betraying perpetrators in a succession of catastrophes that the Shoah exemplifies. Amid proliferating calamities, Judas rose to the occasion. Actually (to give credit where credit is due), his magnification licensed writers from many different backgrounds to deal with unprecedented cataclysms. Increasingly, for this reason, literary artists in the twentieth century began to generalize about the human condition by giving voice to Judas's subjectivity. This chapter will therefore argue that the regression of the twelfth apostle to his earlier pariah role during the Third Reich paradoxically propelled his evolution toward the dignity he currently possesses at the beginning of the twenty-first century.

From the point of view of his biographer, the Nazis' pariah-Judas is the least compelling of the twelfth apostle's avatars in this chapter because so predictable and formulaic, though (as in the past) it was indubitably the most destructive. More ingenious, if less influential, are subsequent inventions of a hallowed Judas who—like Janus, the Roman deity of doors—sports two faces and looks in opposite directions: one countenance is poignantly beatific, one maliciously depraved. Whether this bipolar savior displays his benevolent or his malevolent nature and effect on humanity, he enables the writers in this chapter to add "to the concept of the Son, which seemed exhausted, the complexities of calamity and evil" (Borges, "Three Versions" 157). Despite the Nazis' death sentences, in other words, Judas did not die with the six million Jews who were killed in the Shoah. On the contrary, and because of their catastrophic demise, he was resurrected as the presiding spirit of a disastrous age.

FIELDS OF BLOOD

When the Nazis decided to expunge the Jews from the face of the earth, were they inspired by noxious stereotypes of Judas promulgated from antiquity on? Judas's demonic features in the premodern period—his dirtiness, blindness, obstinacy, conspiratorial deceitfulness, greed, animalism, contaminated blood, and stab-in-the-back cruelty—certainly mesh with Nazi stereotypes of Jews, who had to be exterminated, according to German propagandists, in order to protect the physical hygiene, national security, and spiritual strength of the *Volk*, the tribal unity of the people. "The image of Judas made Hitler's crimes possible, fertilized the field of blood Hitler harvested. Hitler was merely the catalyst for the inevitable crystallization of Christian hatred": this is the outlook expressed by Hyam Maccoby (quoted in Rosenbaum 334).

"It is a straight line, 'a direct connection,' Maccoby believed, 'between Judas and Hitler.' Between the hate-filled portrait of a treacherous betrayer of the Lord . . . and the culmination of that indoctrination in Jew-hatred" (Rosenbaum 322). George Steiner has concurred: "The 'final solution' . . . is the perfectly logical, axiomatic conclusion to the Judas-identification of the Jew. . . . That utter darkness, that night within night, into which Judas is dispatched and commanded to perform 'quickly,' is already that of the death-ovens" (*No Passion Spent* 417). Even though National Socialists were as contradictory and incoherent about Christianity as about any number of other subjects, Maccoby and Steiner attribute the Nazis' genocidal imperative to their murderous hatred of Judas. Yet given the Nazi propensity to deploy a "destructive mimesis of Christianity" in the service of a "political religion" often at odds with traditional Catholic and Protestant teaching (Burrin 335), should one be wary of too quickly attributing Nazi anti-Semitism to Christian dogma?

Images of the pariah-Judas do dovetail with pernicious Nazi stereotyping of Jewry, but Judas cannot be said to have motivated or produced the Shoah. Judas's reinventions before the middle of the twentieth century qualify the twelfth disciple's usefulness in explaining why it occurred. After the publication of Friedrich Gottlieb Klopstock's *Messias* in 1748, many German fictional treatments of Judas featured a noble character, such as the passionately sincere rebel envisioned by De Quincey.[2] Curiously, too, Richard Wagner composed a play sketch and the young Goebbels wrote a play that both offered sympathetic portrayals of Judas (see Oppermann). Of course, deeply anti-Semitic descriptions of Judas continued to circulate during the twentieth century, but they appeared in England, America, and France as well as in Germany. At Good Friday services in Catholic churches throughout the world, congregants praying for "perfidious Jews" ("perfidi Judaei" and "judaica perfidia") had a clear target of blame, and thus no need for the figure of Judas. Despite the high proportion of Nazi Party members in the 1934 cast of the popular Passion plays mounted in Oberammergau, performances in which Judas asks for and receives his just annihilation, the actor playing the character of Judas was known to have strong anti-Nazi allegiances (Shapiro, *Oberammergau* 149).

More to the point, since 1951, when Hannah Arendt published her *The Origins of Totalitarianism,* many political scientists have warned against conflating modern German anti-Semitism with older forms of bigotry. Twentieth-century fascists exploited the Jew as a "cultural symbol" of modernity and emancipation against which an aggressive program of nationalism, antimodernism, imperialist expansion, and nostalgia for a preindustrial moral code (based on the *Volk*) had to contend (Volkov 25, 34, 45). Quite a few reputable scholars have documented the toxicity of Nazi genocidal propaganda containing few or no references to Christianity in general, and to Judas in particular. Instead they attribute to the Third Reich a paranoid ideology about a worldwide Jewish conspiracy that would colonize and eventually annihilate Germans and their society, unless itself rooted out and exterminated.[3] It may be possible to connect Hitler to Christian representations of the Jews, given Catholic and Protestant sermons that depicted the Jews as responsible for placing Jesus on the cross and thus accursed by God.[4] But even in this regard there is a decided gap between, on the one hand, viewing biblical Jews as worthy of divine wrath and, on the other, actively proselytizing for civic procedures that prompt their descendants' extinction twenty centuries after the fact. Historical as well as imaginative allusions to Judas's sway can, however, be found to support a modification of Maccoby's and Steiner's argument, though such written proof-texts may be few and rather eccentric.[5]

Though not the cause of the "final solution," Judas was nevertheless enlisted to facilitate the German genocide. On a German radio broadcast in January 1939, the Nazi historian Walter Frank proclaimed that

> Jewry is one of the great negative principles of world history and thus can only be understood as a parasite within the opposing positive principle. As little as Judas Iscariot with his thirty silver coins . . . can be understood without the Lord whose community he sneeringly betrayed . . . , that night side of history called Jewry cannot be understood without being positioned in the totality of the historical process where God and Satan, Creation and Destruction confront each other in an eternal struggle. (quoted in Wistrich 1)

Frank pits a negative, sneering, parasitic Judas, Jewry, Satan, and Destruction against Jesus, his Christian community, God, and Creation in a battle that can result in victory only when one party achieves a triumph over and at the expense of the other. Also fomenting anti-Semitism and also in 1939, a caricatured President Roosevelt was pictured in the pages of a German newspaper under the caption "Judaslohn" (Judas Reward), because he had been awarded a prize for his contributions to Christian-Jewish relations.[6] One of Hitler's early followers produced a poem titled "Germany Awake!" warning that "Judas appears, to win the Reich," bringing "Woe to the people," who will be subjected by the twelfth apostle to unimaginable suffering.[7]

More significant than the relatively few references to Judas in Nazi speeches and position papers is the image of the Judas-pariah informing anti-Semitic stereotypes in the influential medium of film. Two years before the Wannsee Conference, where the "final solution" was hatched, two movies—*Jew Süss* (1940) and *The Eternal Jew* (1940)—proselytized for the expulsion or extermination of Jewry by invoking the iconography clustered around Judas since ancient times. *Jew Süss*, directed by Veit Harlan, was an instant box-office hit; *The Eternal Jew*, directed by Fritz Hippler and sometimes called *The Wandering Jew*, a flop. A fictionalized narrative about a historical personage, *Jew Süss* profited from elaborate costume designs and sexy scenarios, while the purportedly documentary *Eternal Jew* suffered from the tendentious harangues of its voice-over as well as its gruesome visual footage. Yet both directors were put on trial after the war, though neither was found guilty: many people felt that their films contributed to the intensification of anti-Semitism in Germany. The movies did so by portraying the sinister economic threat that Jews posed to Aryans, a threat that utilizes the devilish treasurer in John's account along with the hypocrisy of Matthew's Judas.

Judas stars in Nazi propaganda films not because he betrayed Christ but because, having done so, he was depicted for centuries in European art with traits that became the stock in trade of anti-Semitism. The money in the purse of John's thief, the lies on the lips of Matthew's Judas: this combination constitutes the "character" that Harlan's Jew Süss and Hippler's wandering Jew share. When, after settling on his payment from the Temple authorities, Matthew's Judas attends the Passover meal and protests his innocence of any intention to injure Jesus ("Surely not I, Rabbi?" [26:25]), he exhibits the masking, camouflaging, deceitful acting skills that both films attribute to Jews in general. Dissimulation, impersonation, masquerade join with the profit motive to create a celluloid Judas who exemplifies hypocritical and avaricious infidelity and adultery. A paramount technique for conveying the adulterating infidel involves the cinematic dissolve. Whereas the hyphen is Judas's punctuation mark, the dissolve—not a clean cut but a fading in and out transition between overlapping, superimposed scenes—could be considered his best shot.

The most popular anti-Semitic film produced by and in the Third Reich, Veit Harlan's historical drama *Jew Süss* features a deceitful, Jewish Judas, specifically a scheming Joseph Süss Oppenheimer, who manipulates the decadent duke of Württemberg in the 1730s by means of loans that buy the Jew control over the treasury and over a citizenry then threatened by burdensome taxation and inflation. This costume drama, commissioned by the Nazis and cast by Goebbels, reached some nineteen or twenty million viewers in Europe, not a few of whom left the theater to engage directly in assaults on Jews.[8] A revision of *Othello*—"an evil adviser leads a military man to his doom, all the while feigning obsequious friendship"—*Jew Süss* sparked "demonstrations against the Jews" spurred by the showing of one scene in particular: a sequence in which the Iago-like Jewish counselor manages to gain the admittance of a horde of filthy Jews into a previously "Jew free" town (Culbert 146–47). If one keeps in mind that in this same period the condemned betrayer was elsewhere being compared not to Iago but to Othello (by Dorothy Sayers), his German devolution becomes patently clear.

Jew Süss recalls Judas in a number of ways. First, there are long-sustained close-ups of him opening a money bag and pouring the coins out on a table, monies granted the duke so as to ensure his dependency on and submission to the Jew. Next, Jew Süss is not only the duke's treasurer but also a paradigmatic hypocrite, fawning on

6.1. Jew Süss,
played by
Ferdinand
Marian, in Veit
Harlan's *Jew Süss*
(1940). Source:
British Film
Institute.

the duke while strategizing various ways to dupe and defraud him.
When Jew Süss spies on the duke through a peephole (or Judas hole),
the opening is the gaping mouth of a demonic gargoyle. The duke,
perplexed ("is he my friend?"), worries that "nothing is sacred" to
his most trusted acolyte ("only profit"), as the director repeatedly
shoots close-ups of the Jew furtively whispering in the ear of the
confidant he cons. Eventually, even the deluded and selfish duke gains
an inkling of the Jew's hypocritical depredations; he confides to his
minister, "I wonder how you look" and pleads, "Throw away your
mask." Jew Süss dramatizes the famed ability of Matthew's Judas
to use language not to reveal but to conceal his nefarious intent as
well as the evil of John's Judas, "the son of perdition" (17:12). The
false-talking Jew Süss is finally caged like an animal, then hoisted up
above the town square (illustration 6.1). In a manner consonant with
Matthew's Judas, he is last seen silently swinging by a hanging rope;

his feet dangle below the dropped door at the bottom of the iron cage in which he has been suspended by the righteous wrath of a united Christian community.

Yet the Judas story does not seem to account for several melodramatic characteristics of Harlan's film. The non-Jewish actor Ferdinand Marian, who played Jew Süss, managed to enthrall audiences with his menacing but magnetic charisma. What makes the actor's magnetism even more unnerving is the rape scenario with which the plot of *Jew Süss* climaxes, for the duke's finance minister schemes to seduce the Aryan maiden, Dorothea, in exactly the manner Hitler's *Mein Kampf* had warned that Jews would.[9] Jew Süss's manipulations extend to staging the seduction in physical proximity to the torturing of virginal Dorothea's brand-new husband, so that his cries of pain will force her to comply with the Jew's sexual demands. The rapid cuts after this rape—Dorothea's running to her own demise, the Ophelia-like corpse recovered by her groom from the water in which she has drowned herself, the townspeople massing ("The Jew must go!"): these recall not the Judas script but instead the first movie masterpiece in the United States, D. W. Griffith's *Birth of a Nation* (1915). In that film, the would-be rapist Gus (played by a white actor in blackface) pursues the innocent white Flora, who hurls herself down a precipice but whose reputation is redeemed by the mighty Ku Klux Klan after the recovery of her broken body. White knights with torches (like those held by the outraged *Volk* of Württemberg) revenge themselves against the bestial black polluter of Nordic blood.

Like the use of darkened Judases on art canvases, the Nazis' deployment of *Birth of a Nation* illuminates the linkage between anti-Semitic and anti-black iconography. It might appear that the producers of *Jew Süss* profited as much from American racist propaganda as from Judas legends, but one must also factor in the prominence of the major character's sidekick, his assistant Levy, as well as the other minor Jewish characters. With his scraggly hair and beard, his hook nose, his skull cap, his mathematical agility in calculating tolls and taxes to fleece the hardworking blacksmiths and millers of Württemberg, the secretary Levy embodies what Jew Süss would look like if he took off his mask. Levy thus signals the unassimilated stage of the caftan-dressed Jew before he camouflages himself into the courtier Jew Süss.[10] The bearded patriarchs keening through whiny synagogue liturgies, a ghetto butcher brandishing his bloody knife, and Rabbi Loew conniving against the duke (in exchange for Jew Süss's promise of profits for Israel): these Jewish men resemble no one so much as the pariah-Judas. From this perspective, Jew Süss's attractive exterior is the sham that hides the shameful interiority he shares with the repulsive secretary, butcher, and rabbi.

The cinematographic technique of the dissolve enabled Harlan to show his central character at the beginning transitioning from the primitive Jew with beard and caftan into the assimilated courtier who can enter the previously "Jew free" town, and then again at the end regressing from the mimic-Aryan in courtly attire back into the bearded and caftan Jew on trial. According to one critic, "the dissolve is used in order to portray Jews as deceitful and to expose their acts of trickery to the spectators" (King 29). In terms of Judas, the cinematic dissolve perfectly suits a character who (in virtually all his guises) acts the part of go-between, passer, or poser.[11] Traveling between pious Christians and the Temple authorities, Jew Süss is as ambiguous and double-dealing as Judas—an intimate but also a foe. Perhaps Jew Süss most resembles Judas to the extent that he is the enemy within: a promoter who is a traitor, a Jew who can look like an Aryan, he must be unmasked, forced to show his true nature.

By birth an outsider, the court Jew becomes an insider; and because he brings swarms of mucky Jews into the community, he (and they) must be expelled again. With his allegiance to an "eye for an eye" principle of vengeance, he represents an archaic and barbarous people. His legalism about land he owns, for instance, results in his demolishing half of the house of an upstanding citizen, with the result that the residence looks bombed. Thus he must be made to revert to type, or his dissembling will destroy domesticity itself, just as it will seduce all the Aryan maidens of the land. To the extent that Jew

Süss is seductive, his economic and erotic scheming enacts a rebellion against the strict discipline that respectability or piety must repress. According to a number of film critics, some of whom remind us that Hitler assailed the Jews as "blood-suckers," the glamorous Jew Süss resembles Dracula, much as Judas does in his long history.[12] His protean metamorphoses and the desires he embodies are contaminating, illicit, dangerous. An infidel, Jew Süss warrants the charges of sexual and marital infidelity brought against him: an adulterer, he betrays his best friend, rapes other men's wives, and also adulterates or pollutes the reproduction of a pure Christian society. The laws against intermarriage affirmed by the righteous eighteenth-century citizens of Württemberg at the end of Harlan's film buttress the Third Reich's laws against miscegenation or blood mixing. Such legislation is only needed, of course, because of the exceptional acting ability, the deceptive masking or dissolving that Judas-Jews are capable of exploiting to contaminate the bloodlines of the master race.[13]

Fritz Hippler's Nazi-financed *The Eternal Jew* does not deploy a single Judas character; however, this purported documentary hinges on the same stereotype derived from or congruent with selected aspects of Judas's role in the New Testament. With its footage from the Polish ghettoes, newsreels from the German Ministry of Propaganda, maps, statistical tables, still photographs, photomontages, and clips of Hollywood films, *The Eternal Jew* attempts to persuade its viewers that they are receiving an objective picture of the so-called Jewish problem; but this interspliced and heavily orchestrated assemblage blatantly sets out to defame Jewish men, women, and children as a race of Judas-pariahs. Several sequences in Hippler's movie dwell on the threat of Jewish mimicry that facilitates lucrative hypocrisy. Unlike the twelfth apostle in the synoptic Gospels, who casts out unclean spirits, Hippler's Judas-Jews resemble John's dirty disciple and his people, who come from and worship the "father of lies" (8:44).

Like *Jew Süss, The Eternal Jew* repeatedly exploits the dissolve to emphasize Jewish duplicity, in one instance with before-and-after shots.[14] "Before concealing themselves behind the mask" of assimilation, the film's voice-over explains, Jewish specimens are filmed lined up in a row in order to "refute liberal theories" about the equality of all beings who look human. The Polish men, wearing skull caps and caftans and sporting beards, dissolve into these same men in European suits and hats, clean-shaven. We are informed that "It is an intrinsic trait of the Jew that he always tries to hide his origin when he is among non-Jews." But Polish Jews are said to be less "comfortable" with the camouflage of assimilation than Berlin Jews, who are shot "acting like the host people." Viewers are warned that this propensity for self-serving impersonation constitutes a grave danger to Nordic citizens, because it allows "grotesquely perverse" Jewish scientists, statesmen, businessmen, and especially theater directors and movie actors to adulterate the purity and nobility of Nordic culture through their degenerative, "niggerized" influence.[15] Early in their lives, Jews "hide their murderous nature," for their Talmud teachers instruct them "always be cunning," "hate your master and never tell the truth," "religion makes cheating and usury a duty": so the voice-over intones.[16]

The charge that Jews pass as "the host people" matches another allegation stressed in *The Eternal Jew* and derived from medieval times: that Jews are "rootless parasites," gnawing on and weakening the adulterated "host"—in this case not the sacred host of the Eucharist but the secular host of the sacramental nation. Footage of street scenes in Polish ghettoes—with recurrent shots of Jewish men, women, and children counting out coins—is said to prove that wealthy Jews who have "hoarded" their money "live in bug-ridden dwellings" because it suits their "natural inclination." The narrator attributes to Richard Wagner the motto "The Jew is the demon behind the corruption of mankind." An "Oriental mixture with Negro admixture," the Jews migrated from Palestine throughout the world (maps display the spreading of cancerous growths or octopus tentacles or spiderwebs), as the rats did (shown on comparable maps). Then a picture of scurrying rats stays on the screen, as the voice-over explains their nature: cunning, cowardly, cruel, and sneaky, Jews are said to pollute the body politic by spreading disease and plague, as Judas in medieval legends was presumed to do.

In a manner consonant with the emphasis on deceit, theft, and parasitical invasion, the contrast between the infectious rats and the noble beasts sacrificed at the climax of *The Eternal Jew* exploits the Passion narrative to frame the Jews. While viewers watch a succession of steer and sheep tied up or held down and knifed in the throat by Jews, then painfully bled to death, the voice-over describes the "cruel torture of defenseless animals" prescribed by laws of koshering thankfully canceled by the Führer in 1933. The bloodletting of the animals is meant "to remind viewers of the familiar charge of blood libel, the fictional Jewish sacrifice of Christian children" (Clinefelter 146).[17] Innocent animals so cruelly wounded, bloodied, and sacrificed by the Jews bring to mind the collaboration between Judas and the Temple authorities against the Lamb of God.[18] About Judaism, whose God is said to promise dominion to Jews and destruction of the heathen, the movie's voice-over flatly explains, "This is not a religion; it is a conspiracy against Aryan peoples." The word *conspiracy*, of course, also points to Judas's intrigue with Jews against the founder of Christianity.

The proposition that the Gospels in general and Judas in particular inform Nazi propaganda obviously cannot be deployed to blame Catholics and Protestants for the nefarious and overtly non- and anti-Christian uses to which the New Testament was twisted. It does, however, suggest that the Passion narrative provided a framework susceptible to the manipulations of anti-Semites well into the twentieth century.[19] In the words of John T. Pawlikowski, a Catholic theologian active in current Christian-Jewish dialogues, "the Holocaust was in the last analysis the product of secular, profoundly anti-Christian forces and not simply the final chapter in the long history of Christian anti-Semitism"; and yet "there is no doubt that traditional Christian anti-Semitism provided an indispensable seedbed for the successful implementation of the Nazi 'Final Solution' " (*Christ*

137). Put more bluntly: allegations of Jewish deicide and of Judas's facilitating collaboration were used to justify genocide. Given the complex constellation of economic and political factors that ushered in the Third Reich, neither Judas nor the Gospels can be blamed for causing the Shoah; but the imagery they generated, especially in the premodern period, could be exploited to buttress secular ideologies and technologies of destruction.

THE EXTERMINATION OF CHRIST

Under the sway of growing fascist sentiment, many German theologians bolstered anti-Semitism by pitting Jesus and Christianity against Judas and Judaism. In the process, they legitimized genocide—sometimes consciously and in league with National Socialist goals, sometimes unconsciously and despite their disavowal of those goals. To understand how the Holocaust precipitated a crisis in Christianity that influenced the cultural progress of Judas, consider the theological maturation of Dietrich Bonhoeffer. A leader of the Protestant resistance movement within Germany, Bonhoeffer eventually came to ponder a dying God and to posit "a religionless Christianity" (*Letters* 280). However, during the early 1930s, just a few years before he joined a conspiracy to assassinate Hitler, the Lutheran pastor disseminated a number of prevailing ideas about Judaism that impaired or delayed his pro-Jewish activism.[20]

When Bonhoeffer responded to the state boycott against Jewry on April 1, 1933, his discussion in "The Church before the Jewish Question" criticized the Reich, and yet couched its punitive measures "in a very specific context for the Church": "Never in Christ's Church has the thought disappeared that the 'chosen people,' who nailed the savior of the world onto the cross, must carry the curse of its deed in a long history of suffering" ("Kirche" 49). Bonhoeffer welcomed baptized Jews or Jewish Christians into the church because "the conversion of Israel" constitutes "the end of the time of suffering of this people" (50).[21] But nonbaptized Jews, weighed down by a "curse," were destined to suffer. Ironically enough, given its context this was a liberal position.[22] In Bonhoeffer's opposition to National Socialism, his concern for non-Aryan Christians (Jewish converts to Christianity) defied Nazi clergymen who were purging Jews from churches because Judaism had been defined as a race, not a faith, making conversion inconceivable.

Whereas Bonhoeffer hoped for the conversion of Israel to Christ, other German theologians sought to detach Christianity from its Jewish roots. They did so by returning to Houston Stewart Chamberlain's turn-of-the-century denial of the Jewishness of Christ "on the grounds that Galilee had been inhabited by heathen, non-Jewish tribes" (Mosse 94).[23] By 1939, Martin Dibelius doubted Jesus' Jewish character; by 1940, Walter Grundmann tried to prove that Jesus' Galilean descent made him non-Jewish (Klein 12, 11). Since all Jews were necessarily blighted and blighting, Jesus could not possibly have been Jewish, according to advocates of Germanic Christianity, who exploited the power of the pulpit to guide their congregations toward the proposition that "We German Christians are the first trenchline of National Socialism. . . . To live, fight and die for Adolf Hitler means to say Yes to the Path of Christ" (quoted in Littell 53).[24] When Hitler's army took Christ's path, the Jews, by virtue of their rejection of Jesus as the messiah, became "*Unheilsgeschichte*—an untranslatable term that refers . . . to the suspension of God's saving activity for the Jews *until the end of the ages*" (Meeks 529).

Anti-Nazi Protestants may not have explicitly divorced Jesus from Judaism, but they did denounce Judas's quintessentially Jewish damnation. In 1937, as persecution of the Jews escalated, Bonhoeffer was posing the question "Who is Judas?" and then conflating the twelfth disciple with the Jews, much as Karl Barth would a few years later. Bonhoeffer answered his own query about Judas's identity with a speculation: "'Judas,' does he not represent here the deeply divided people from whom Jesus came, the chosen people, who had received the promise of the Messiah and nevertheless rejected him? The people of Judah, who loved the Messiah and yet couldn't love in that way" ("Predigt" 412).[25] Bonhoeffer's conflation of Judas with people who "couldn't love" the Son of God judges Jews to be deficient or perverse. Judas and the Jews have stubbornly spurned the gift of salvation offered by Jesus. Indeed, Bonhoeffer explicitly argued that "Christianity has again and again seen in Judas the dark secret of the rejection of God and eternal damnation" (412). Barth even more vigorously denounced the "dark secret" of the "eternal damnation" of Judas and the Jews.

Two vituperative quotes from one section of Karl Barth's analysis prove this point: "Judas[,] . . . in his concentrated attack upon Israel's messiah, does only what the elect people of Israel had always done towards its God, thus finally showing itself in its totality to be the nation rejected by God"; "This Judas must die, as he did die; and this Jerusalem must be destroyed, as it was destroyed. Israel's right to existence is extinguished, and therefore its existence can only be extinguished" (*Doctrine* 505).[26] The logic behind Bonhoeffer's and Barth's ruminations, called *supersessionism*, concedes that Christianity derived from Judaism, but claims that in this derivation Christianity fulfilled the promise held out by Judaism and thus definitively replaced an outdated, legalistic faith with a better, more loving one. Whether pro- or anti-Hitler, supersessionists effectively made Jews dispensable by arguing that they had completed their part in history. Bonhoeffer and Barth assume that the incarnation invalidated the Jewish religion and that the New Testament annulled the "Old" Testament. Representative of the now obsolete Jews, Judas deserved to become a casualty. Despite the heroic stature he had attained earlier, Christian detractors and supporters of the Third Reich collaborated in divorcing Judas from the other apostles and Jesus, in attaching him to the Pharisees and the Temple authorities. Judas and the Temple priests could then be viewed not as the community within which Jesus grew or to whom he addressed himself but only as his murderers.

Yet directly after Bonhoeffer stated that "Christianity has again and again seen in Judas . . . eternal damnation," he affirmed that "it has never therefore looked upon him with pride and superiority, but rather has sung with trembling and *in recognition of its own great sins:* O you poor Judas, what have you done!" ("Predigt" 412–13; emphasis mine).[27] And after the burning and looting of synagogues and shops during Kristallnacht (November 9, 1938), Bonhoeffer began to dedicate himself to a highly dangerous campaign of advocacy for endangered Jews, whether or not they had converted. In 1943, he was imprisoned for his efforts to help Jews escape to Switzerland, and in 1945, when his part in the assassination conspiracy against Hitler became known, he was hanged inside Flossenbürg concentration camp, as if he were a Judas to the German people. Because betrayal of National Socialism constitutes not simply a morally defensible but a righteous act, many people consider Bonhoeffer an honorable "Christian martyr" (Klein 118). The case of Bonhoeffer therefore clarifies how in certain extreme contexts the act of betrayal can signify a courageous ethical good, how a condemned (and in this case Christian) Judas may be Christ-like.

Bonhoeffer's evolving thoughts also illuminate why and how the Holocaust generated turmoil within Christianity. One scholar examining Bonhoeffer's late papers came upon the sentence "The expulsion of the Jews from the West must be followed by the expulsion of Christ, for Jesus Christ was a Jew." To this pointed insight, yet another thinker added another speculation: "If the *expulsion* of the Jews means [for Christians] the expulsion of Christ from the West, what is the *annihilation* of the Jews (which began as a political measure a few months later)?"[28] Had Christians, by killing the Jews or by colluding with the killers of Jews, murdered their Christ? Precisely the idea that Jesus was exterminated at Auschwitz informs Marc Chagall's painting *Yellow Crucifixion* (1938; illustration 6.2), with its crucified Jewish martyr surrounded by burning towns, stunned victims, sinking boats of immigrants, traumatized survivors, and grief-stricken refugees. In this instance of iconography, to which Chagall repeatedly returned, Jesus wears a tallith-loincloth, phylacteries on his head, and prayer straps on his arm, and a green Torah hangs alongside

6.2. Marc Chagall, *Yellow Crucifixion* (1938). Source: CNAC/MNAM/ Dist. Réunion des Musées Nationaux/ Art Resource, New York. Copyright © 2003 Artists Rights Society (ARS), New York/ADAGP, Paris Photo © Alinari/Art Resource, New York.

him, "illuminated by the candle held by an angel who blows a sho-far" (Amishai-Maisels 86).[29] Amid the tumultuous conflagration of earth, air, and water, the angelic blast of a trumpetlike horn serves to awaken consciousness of the need for human atonement.

Chagall suggests that Christians, in their complicity with fascism, have taken on the part of the betrayer by denying their messiah's origins and destroying his people. As the art historian Ziva Amishai-Maisels explains of this imagery, highly controversial among Jewish critics, "the holiest Christian visual symbol, the Crucifixion, was used to indict Christianity, and an image which had been anathema to Jews became a symbol of their martyrdom" (104). Unable to pro-tect his flock or defeat their foes, Chagall's disarmed Son of God has been nailed to the cross by the same people who set fire to the villages, branded the wailing man on the lower right, and imperiled the fleeing mother with her swaddled infant. The painting depicts an all-pervasive principle of betrayal that produces Jewish suffering and Jesus' anguish, here conflated.[30] With no promise of resurrection, Chagall's picture brings to mind Elie Wiesel's account of the boy hanged by the SS in front of thousands of prisoners at Buna, one of whom asks, "Where is God now?"—a question answered by a voice within the adolescent Wiesel: "Here He is—He is hanging here on this gallows . . ." (62).

Wiesel, remembering the first night of his arrival at a concentration camp, vowed never to forget "those moments which murdered my God and my soul and turned my dreams to dust" (32). In a 1944 meditation that illuminates Chagall's painting and Wiesel's anguished memoir *Night* (1960), the imprisoned Bonhoeffer pondered how a vulnerable and weak "Christ [can] become the Lord of the religionless" (*Letters* 280):

> The God who is with us is the God who forsakes us (Mark 15:34). The God who lets us live in the world without the working hypothesis of God is the God before whom we stand continually. Before God and with God we live without God. God lets himself be pushed out of the world on to the cross. He is weak and powerless in the world, and that is precisely the way, the only way, in which he is with us and helps us. (360)[31]

The God who has accepted his powerlessness in the universe neither washes away the sins of Christians nor works miracles, but suffers as part of the Jewish people. One contemporary Christian thinker, attempting to grapple with the evils of Christian anti-Semitism, concludes with a related point about the genocide as a cremation of Jesus and the Jews: "When the Body of Christ is discovered at Auschwitz, it will be raised from among the victims, not hidden among the Catholic and Protestant and Orthodox guards and administrators" (Littell 131).[32]

6.3. John Heartfield, *As in the Middle Ages . . . So in the Third Reich* (1934). Source: 2003 Artists Rights Society (ARS), New York/VG Bild-Kunst, Bonn. Courtesy of Stiftung Archiv der Akademie der Künste, Berlin.

Before and after Chagall produced his canvas, pictorial artists equated Jesus with murdered Jews to protest the martyrdom of humanity during the Third Reich. By collaborating with the Nazis or ignoring Jewish suffering, did Christians effectively replace the cross with a swastika? During the 1930s, one German and one American photographer implicated Christianity in the disaster of National Socialism by affixing a crucified effigy to the Third Reich's insignia. John Heartfield's *As in the Middle Ages . . . So in the Third Reich* (1934; illustration 6.3) and Paul Strand's *Skeleton/Swastika, Con-*

necticut (1939; illustration 6.4) condemn Christianity's complicity in the torment of European Jewry. Emaciated or skeletal, the sacrificed form becomes a figure of anyone or everyone whose flesh was to be wracked or unmade by Hitler's word. Whatever ideals Jesus died for—loving-kindness, mercy for the downtrodden, the incarnation of divinity in humanity, the promise of eternal life—have been corpsed in prescient photocompositions made before the war.

Jiří Anderle's later *Kiss of Judas* (1994; illustration 6.5), arranged to resemble an opened antique folio, meditates on the crisis in Christendom posed by the Holocaust: it displays, on the left page, machinery of torture, perhaps the spear that pierced the crucified Jesus, possibly a camera, and a crane; on the right, a face so scribbled over that only the crown of thorns can be clearly seen.[33] Above the threatening implements on the left, three crosses stand, with two female

6.4. Paul Strand, *Skeleton/Swastika, Connecticut* (1939). Gelatin silver print. Source: Library of Congress. Courtesy of Gale Anne Hurd, Los Angeles.

6.5. Jiří Anderle, *Kiss of Judas* (1994). With permission from the artist.

figures at the base of the central one. On the right, more than one set of eyes appears below the barbed wire crown. Perhaps Anderle's *Kiss of Judas* hints at another point the Shoah drove home: namely, that technologies of war function as a Judas kiss, entrancing us with ultimately enslaving implements of empowerment, effectively incapacitating Christ's ministry.[34] In any case, when Jesus suffers torture in Chagall's painting and Anderle's graffiti-like drawing, we are instructed that the catastrophic events of the twentieth century sabotage whichever spiritual institutions we have placed our faith in. Like the arts and the sciences, religions are barbaric after Auschwitz.

Given Anderle's title, rendering indeterminate whether the central face is Jesus' or Judas's, and his work's resemblance to a relic (one thinks of the Shroud of Turin or Veronica's Veil), his *Kiss of Judas* asks us to ponder the catastrophic fusion of Jesus and Judas, the incapacity of grace, the inextricable entanglement of grace and disgrace. Judas similarly haunts Chagall's canvas. Consider the pitiable merging of Chagall's suffering Son of God not only with the Jews but also with Judas. For just as Bonhoeffer's martyrdom as a traitor testifies to the fusion of Jesus and Judas, the universality of betrayal could presage the fragility of all of the players in the Passion as well as the salvation they sought to bring about. With the crucifixion yellowed amid scenes of Jewish devastation, Chagall evokes Judas's traditional color, the gold he reputedly steals, and the badges assigned Jews by Nazis. A Jewish Jesus, now signifying crucifixion without resurrection, brings to mind the only apostle long imagined as an unredeemable Jew and shoulders the sorrowful impossibility of divorcing good from grief or guilt in a post-Holocaust age. If, as one Jesuit put it, "Jews are not only the people of Christ but the Christ of the peoples,"[35] Judas—especially after the Holocaust—could be judged the Christ of the disciples. Bruised, repeatedly put to an appalling death, Judas, like Jesus, "was numbered with the transgressors" (Isaiah 53:12), and was used to number all Jews with blameworthy transgressors.

After 1945, Chagall's martyred figure looks like Judas, crucified on the cross of the betrayal he was said to engineer. When Chagall's sacrificed Son appears as vulnerable and God-forsaken as his defamed twelfth apostle, the two unite to expose a scandalous conflation in Augustine's early intuition: "delivering up was done by the Son, delivering up was done by Judas" (*Tractates* 222–23). Jesus and Judas, delivering themselves up as representatives of a piteously weakened God or manipulated and then abandoned by a maliciously powerful divinity, can testify only to humanity's helplessness. But testify to whom? With the Son of God and his people dying, the disaster threatens to go unwitnessed. The flimsy ladder human beings need to raise themselves up to transcendence teeters and falls awry.

In the previous chapter, I noted that Judas the Obscure resembles Job in asserting the meaninglessness of his personal suffering. On

Chagall's canvas, where Jesus' suffering is also depicted as mean-ingless, where God's Son appears God-forsaken, Jesus shockingly confirms Judas's experience of divine impotence.[36] The extremity of catastrophe put enormous pressure on the Passion story, or so the rest of this chapter will suggest: we will find a compassionate Jesus falter-ing and failing, as he and Judas converge and together acknowledge the flimsiness of the redemptive faith they seek to foster. By melding Jesus with the Jewish people and Judas, post–World War II artists rebuff the efforts of Nazi Protestants to divorce Jesus from Judaism and to attach Judaism to Judas. In opposition to the Nazi bifurcation of an Aryan Jesus and a Jewish Judas, the logic of a nonredemptive massacre of the innocent led some thinkers to a bruising proposition: that along with Jesus, it was the Jewish people and the apostle long thought to represent them who had been martyred by being typecast as traitors in the Passion narrative. Chagall's crucifixion excoriates Christianity's collusion in genocide and it does so in the name of—on behalf of—a Christ besieged.

Eventually, the Nazis' condemnation of Jewry as a Judas race led to postwar Christian efforts to eliminate or at least banish invoca-tions of the Jewish pariah. The grim postwar diaspora, so resonant on Chagall's canvas, spurred a number of theologians and then finally the Second Vatican Council to establish a moral imperative: to clarify the fact that "neither all Jews indiscriminately at that time, nor Jews today, can be charged with the crimes committed during [the] Pas-sion," and that "the Jews should not be spoken of as rejected or accursed as if this followed from Holy Scripture" ("Nostra Aetate" 741). Pope John XXIII had removed the phrases about "perfidious Jews" from the Good Friday liturgy in 1959, and the 1965 "Nostra Aetate" issued by Pope Paul VI positioned the church against anti-Semites: "Remembering, then, her common heritage with the Jews and moved not by any political consideration, but solely by the reli-gious motivation of Christian charity, she deplores all hatreds, per-secutions, displays of anti-Semitism leveled at any time or from any source against the Jews" (741).[37] Such views necessarily colored the variegated strands of Judas's life during the second half of the twentieth century. The Jewish pariah-Judas could not be obliterated from human consciousness, but he became illegitimate.

For the first time in history, the Catholic Church determined, the Jews were not to be blamed. At least in so-called high culture, Judas would become a religiously indeterminate twelfth apostle. But if the betrayal cannot be pinned on a Jewish conspiracy, what or who might have motivated the crucifixion? Regardless of how later twentieth-century writers answer this question, they depict a Judas intimate with the Jesus he seeks to save—not an eccentrically Jewish Judas but a Judas whose spiritual affiliation evinces as much volatility as that of Jesus and the other eleven. To begin with, the absolution of a nondenominational or ecumenical Judas surpasses his earlier exoneration by means of ambitious novels about his indispensable and consummate ethicality.

JESUS' MARTYRED SAVIOR

Reacting against the genocidal uses to which Judas had been put, postwar writers built on the heroic Judas configured in the nineteenth century. But no longer a deluded adherent, after World War II the twelfth apostle becomes a knowledgeable collaborator with Jesus: he acts not only for but also *with* and *at the instruction of* Jesus. As in the case of Bonhoeffer, the act of betrayal here constitutes a courageously undertaken ethical good. When a drafted Judas becomes his savior's savior, he repeatedly declares that he betrays "Not in enmity, not in selfishness," but because enjoined by Jesus himself: "He called me to do it, that the Redemption might be fulfilled," Philip Robert Dillon's eponymous Judas of Kerioth explains (57). At this climax of Judas's representational history, the twelfth apostle relinquishes all selfish or misguided concerns to facilitate the death Jesus seeks. The gravity of twentieth-century conflagrations inspired two exceptionally accomplished artists—Nikos Kazantzakis and José Saramago—to investigate the horror of human suffering by emphasizing the confederacy of Jesus and Judas. While one imagines Judas victorious with Jesus and with humankind, however, the other grieves over the defeat of Judas, Jesus, and humankind, all vanquished paradoxically by the damaged and damaging religious economy known as Christianity.

Writers who elevate the twelfth apostle do so in a manner that accords with Judas's role as a divine instrument in the Gnostic Gospel of Judas (at least as it was initially translated), for in this ancient text Jesus tells Judas, "You will be cursed by the other generations—and you will come to rule over them" (*Gospel of Judas* 33). Indeed, Gnostic Jesus informs Judas that he "will exceed" the other apostles, "For you will sacrifice the man that clothes me" (43). In the Gospel of Judas, Jesus needs the twelfth apostle to help him shuffle off the mortal coil and enlists his aid in order to become immortal. Even though twentieth-century poets and novelists could not possibly have been influenced by a Coptic codex still lost at the time they wrote, as it had been for 1,700 years, some of them tell a similar story in which Judas is tutored by and loyal to Jesus. This twelfth apostle realizes that Jesus himself proclaimed in the New Testament, "I know whom I have chosen. But the Scriptures will be fulfilled" (John 13:18). Taking a clue also from the injunction of John's Jesus—who directed Judas, "Do quickly what you are going to do" (13:27)—they bear out the promise of Jesus in the Gnostic Gospel when he tells Judas, "Lift up your eyes and look at the cloud and the light within it and the stars surrounding it. The star that leads the way is your star" (44). A poem by Countee Cullen and a theologically motivated fictional autobiography by Albert Lévitt can bracket a tradition that was mined by Kazantzakis and later, more daringly, by Saramago to celebrate the stellar savior Judas.

In Countee Cullen's poem "Judas Iscariot" (1925), a ballad about the birth, death, and resurrection of Judas, the twelfth apostle becomes Jesus' and God's right-hand man. The son of a doting mother and the playmate of Mary's son, Judas matures to hear Christ's "dream," witness his miracles, and devote himself to Christ's service even when "the death hour" approaches:

> Then Judas in his hot desire
>   Said, "Give me what you will."
> Christ spoke to him with words of fire,
>   "Then, Judas, you must kill
> One whom you love, One who loves you
>   As only God's son can
> This is the work for you to do
>   To save the creature man." (295)

Cullen's Judas, warned that he will be cursed for an act of generosity, takes on "the sorry part" assigned to him by Jesus: "And gave the kiss that broke his heart, / But no one knew or heard" (295).[38] At its conclusion and after Judas's death, Cullen's verse imagines the twelfth apostle justly rewarded for his loyalty and for saving humanity at a last supper reminiscent of the conclusion of Robert Buchanan's ballad.

Albert Lévitt's *Judas Iscariot: An Imaginative Autobiography* (1961) also depicts Judas generously bestowing "all the love he had" on Jesus, thereby placing the responsibility of the betrayal squarely on the shoulders of Jesus. Lévitt's Judas tells the story the author proposes in his foreword: namely, that "Judas kept the true identity of Jesus a secret until he was commanded by Jesus Himself to reveal that secret" (vii). A loyal comrade, Judas defends Jesus against those who wish to arrest him until Jesus insists, "Now is the accepted time": "You, Judas, must open the gate that leads to the pathway where my feet must tread," Lévitt's Jesus explains, adding "I know that you believe in me; I know that you love me. Forgive me that I put this burden of my bodily death upon you" (52). The very last words Lévitt's Jesus speaks on the cross are "Judas, Judas, it is finished," leaving the twelfth disciple perplexed at Jesus' meaning but determined to kill himself, for Judas hopes that suicide will provide a "gate" through which he will arrive at spiritual union with his revered messiah (64).

Both Nikos Kazantzakis's *The Last Temptation of Christ* (1960) and José Saramago's *The Gospel according to Jesus Christ* (1991) support the recent proposition of Slavoj Žižek that "betrayal was part of the plan, Christ ordered Judas to betray him," and so "Judas' act of betrayal was the highest sacrifice, the ultimate fidelity" (*Puppet* 17). At stake in the disagreement between Kazantzakis and Saramago is whether God's divine will saves or damns humankind, whether the Passion redeems or dooms humanity. Whereas Kazantzakis imagines Judas, along with Jesus, triumphantly enacting a benevolent divine will, Saramago mourns Judas, along with Jesus, both shockingly destroyed by a malevolent divine will. In the process of exonerating the twelfth apostle, these authors offer opposing answers to the question, who betrayed whom? Kazantzakis hints that the Son of God almost betrayed the Passion; Saramago dares to hold God the Father accountable for a betrayal that casts him in the villainous role previously played by Judas. Both agree, however, that the twelfth apostle was asked by Jesus to sacrifice himself for the good of Jesus and for what Jesus as well as Judas hoped would be the good of humanity.

In *The Last Temptation of Christ*, Kazantzakis melds the nineteenth-century character of the insurrectionist Judas with the idea that Jesus needs Judas, indeed asks Judas to help him face the ordained ordeal. From the very beginning of this novelistic rendition of Jesus' life, the Zealot Judas haunts Jesus.[39] A blacksmith and a revolutionary, savage-faced and red-bearded Judas studies Jesus, a cross maker for the Romans, and begins to believe in the carpenter's calling (9). Yet Jesus' lesson about a loving brotherhood remains too inclusive, according to Judas, for "we're not all brothers," he thinks; "Israelites and Romans are not brothers, nor are Israelites among themselves" (178). In response to Jesus' first prolonged effort to preach "Love one another—" (185), Judas sneers, "You want us to love the Romans, eh? Are we supposed to hold out our necks like you do your cheek, and say, 'Dear brother, slaughter me, please'?" (186).

Kazantzakis's Judas may be two-faced, but only because of his ambivalence and uncertainty about Jesus' character and mission. Seeking to protect Israel from "the Roman criminals" (163), Judas feels conflicted about a Jesus apparently collaborating with the colonizers, and he also seems divided: "If you looked at him from the right, his face was sullen and full of malice; if you looked at him from the left, it was uneasy and sad" (162). Following in the footsteps of De Quincey's twelfth apostle, Kazantzakis's impatient Judas remains indifferent to "the kingdom of heaven," committed instead to "the kingdom of the earth—and not the whole earth, either, but only the land of Israel," while Jesus preaches that "the kingdom of heaven is not in the air, it is within us, in our hearts": "Change your heart, and heaven and earth will embrace, Israelites and Romans will embrace, all will become one" (196). In other words, they disagree about the kingdom: Judas believes in the body's here and now, whereas Jesus believes in the soul's eternal hereafter. But what the two share is the need to know if Jesus is really the God of Israel.

Upon Jesus' return from the desert, Judas, seeing in Jesus' hand "the Baptist's ax," feels elated, enthusiastic about Jesus' new definition of himself, no longer the "bridegroom" inviting the apostles to a wedding but instead "a wood-chopper" beckoning them to war (298–99). The other eleven are afraid—but not uncompromising Judas, who "had but one great passion, and it would be a supreme joy to destroy himself for that passion's sake" (300). And although Judas continues to mistrust Jesus' dedication to the ax, the two reach an understanding. With "Judas, the sheep dog" (279), Jesus enters Jerusalem. To Judas, Jesus confides "a terrible secret": "You are the strongest of all the companions. Only you, I think, will be able to bear it" (386). The "terrible secret" joins Judas to Jesus, separating them from the other disciples and establishing Judas's indispensability in the Passion (392). Supported on and by "the redbeard's sturdy arm" (410), Jesus explains that Judas is chosen to share the messianic secret because "you're the strongest. The others don't bear up . . ." (411). Judas is ordered to arrange the garden meeting by Jesus, who urges his helper, "Try to be brave, Judas, my brother. I'm trying too" (411). Though assured by Jesus that he will rise again, Judas balks: "You tell me this in order to comfort me and make me able to betray you without rending my own heart. You say I have the endurance— you say it in order to give me strength. No, the closer we come to the terrible moment . . . no, Rabbi, I won't be able to endure!" (420–21). But Jesus insists, "You will, Judas, my brother. *God will give you the strength,* as much as you lack because it is necessary—it is necessary for me to be killed and for you to betray me. *We two must save the world. Help me*" (421; emphases mine). What Judas is being asked to do Jesus himself could not do: "No, I do not think I would be able to. That is why *God pitied me and gave me the easier task: to be crucified*" (421; emphasis mine).[40]

Clinching the heroism of Judas as a pivotal agent of God, chapters 30–33 of *The Last Temptation of Christ* famously consist of Jesus' last temptation on the cross: a hallucinogenic vision of his life expanding *after* his thirty-third year and what he takes to be the nightmare of crucifixion. A guardian angel brings him to his marriage to Mary Magdalene and along the mortal road toward immortality by means of the flesh. After her death, the angel (now embodied in a black boy) unites him with the sisters Mary and Martha, causing Jesus to rename himself Lazarus. Procreation and paternity please Jesus-Lazarus, as does the black boy who preaches a God of Ethiopia who "doesn't scold," who "does whatever he pleases" (464), and whose followers find the kingdom of heaven on earth. Despite the mobs of children and grandchildren, a number of signs warn Jesus-Lazarus of what his evasion of crucifixion signifies. Most climactic is the return of the decrepit apostles, who rebuke him for their wasted lives and point out the only one with endurance, "a colossus who stood on the threshold like a withered, lightning-charred tree. The roots of his hair and beard were still red": "Judas! He's the only one who still holds himself erect" (488).

Jesus-Lazarus defensively justifies his placid life of plowing lands and women as a means of conquering mortality, but Judas righteously accuses him in savage cries:

> "Traitor! Deserter!" he bellowed again. "Your place was on the cross. That's where the God of Israel put you to fight. But you got cold feet, and the moment death lifted its head, you couldn't get away fast enough! You ran and hid yourself in the skirts of Martha and Mary. Coward! And you changed your face and your name, you fake Lazarus, to save yourself!" (491)

Judas is outraged that Jesus-Lazarus had taken him "in your arms—do you remember?—and begged, 'Betray me, betray me' ": "I loved you so much, I trusted you so much, that I said, 'Yes' and went and betrayed you" (492). It is Judas who recognizes Jesus-Lazarus's guardian angel as Satan. Jesus-Lazarus asks forgiveness, rushing into the redbeard's arms; however, Judas evades the embrace of a man who broke his heart. As the twelve apostles chant "Coward! Deserter! Traitor!" at Jesus, he regains a sense of himself on the cross and manages to complete the final cry, "Lama Sabachthani" (495), which can be followed by the triumphant "It is accomplished" because he "was not a coward, a deserter, a traitor. No, he was nailed to the cross" (496).

Judas saves Jesus from the last temptation, the temptation to betray his betrayer by avoiding crucifixion, and he does so to bring about humanity's spiritual immortality. But how and why did Kazantzakis's Judas, committed initially to the material body and the political kingdom on earth, come to take up the soul's transcendent hereafter and the future spiritual kingdom he ultimately manages to force Jesus to bring into being? The conversion of Judas—his renunciation of the wood-chopper and embrace of the bridegroom—remains unnarrated in *The Last Temptation of Christ*. Nevertheless, the ignominy historically heaped on Judas as a coward, deserter, and traitor is clearly piled here onto Jesus before Jesus submits to becoming Christ. For

Kazantzakis in the dream sequence, unfortunately, Jesus' and ultimately Judas's conversion to immaterial transcendence hinges on the
vilification of women and blacks, associated with material imma-
nence. The temptations of the womb and of the flesh offered by both
Marys, Martha, and the black boy with his African God stand in
stark contrast to heroic Judas; this noble apostle prods a vacillating
Jesus to reject his embodiment as a biologically procreative son of
man in favor of the soul's winged rebirth brought about by the spiritually creative Son of God.

In Kazantzakis's telling, Judas shares with the patriarch Abraham
a deep realization of the need to submit to the horrific sacrifice of a
beloved son. Despite all the controversy it caused, the novel exonerates Judas without calling into question God's ultimate role in the
Passion.[41] The same cannot be said about the remarkable revision
of the Passion offered by José Saramago in *The Gospel according
to Jesus Christ,* a work that vindicates Judas but at the same time
vilifies a tyrannical God whose determination to exercise absolute
power has corrupted him absolutely. No wonder that the Portuguese
government, along with the Catholic Church, blocked Saramago's
novel from being nominated for a major literary prize, causing him to
go into exile. For Saramago indicts the ethicality not of the betrayer,
not of the betrayed, but of the power authoring the carnage that
their story subsequently authorizes. According to the most heretical
thinker about this celestial Judas, he and Jesus struggled valiantly
against becoming tools of a divinity whose sacrificial imperative is
judged to be not merely morally questionable but quite simply appalling. Saramago takes seriously the consequences of another elision
that Augustine had floated as a rhetorical question meant to sound
downright inane: since the delivering up of Christ was done by God
as well as Judas, Augustine had asked, "Is God the Father, therefore,
also a traitor?" (*Tractates* 222). Saramago goes beyond answering in
the affirmative to say that only God the Father should be blamed.

Once again, Judas here represents Jesus' right-hand man, his friend,
and partner. One Judas the Galilean wreaks vengeance as a Zealot

against the Roman oppressors, but he cannot be confused with the disciple Judas Iscariot. Indeed, the disciple plays such a small part in this novel that it would hardly warrant inclusion in Judas's biography, except for the fact that Saramago's narrative registers an upheaval in approaches to the Passion after the evils made manifest during the second half of the twentieth century. Kazantzakis's Jesus during his Lazarus phase exclaims, in a temporary moment of escapism and delusion, that he should be identified as "son of man, I tell you, not son of God" (476). On the pivotal issue of Jesus' self-identification, Kazantzakis and Saramago disagree. According to Saramago, what made Judas as well as Jesus courageous was their united effort to define Jesus conclusively as "son of man, I tell you, *not son of God*" (emphasis mine), though they both fail in their efforts to do so.

In "an awesome work" of fiction that the incomparable Harold Bloom deems "imaginatively superior to any other life of Jesus, including the four canonical Gospels" ("The One" 155), Saramago constructed a strenuous counterhistory about the circumstances of a Jesus who follows in the footsteps of his guilt-haunted and crucified father, Joseph; who finds heaven on earth in his erotic relationship with a prostitute, Mary Magdalene from Bethany; who takes her advice and refrains from bringing Lazarus back from the dead because, as Mary cautions, "No one has committed so much sin in his life that he deserves to die twice" (362). But it was Saramago's cruel and ambitious God who most disturbed readers, especially during the scene of his *Gospel* when the creator of the universe—in a becalmed boat on the Sea of Galilee with Jesus and the devil (here, ironically, named Pastor)—explains the reasons why he wants Jesus to be crucified. One passage, in particular, is worth quoting at length since it renders the curious character of Saramago's approach to dialogue and of his God:

For the last four thousand and four years I have been the God of the Jews, a quarrelsome and difficult race by nature, but on the whole I have got along fairly well with them, they now take

Me seriously and are likely to go on doing so for the foreseeable future. So, You are satisfied, said Jesus. I am and I am not, or rather, I would be were it not for this restless heart of Mine, which is forever telling Me, Well now, a fine destiny you've arranged after four thousand years of trial and tribulation that no amount of sacrifice on altars will ever be able to repay, for *You continue to be the god of a tiny population that occupies a minute part of this world* You created with everything that's on it, so tell Me, My son, if I should be satisfied with *this depressing situation.* Never having created a world, I'm in no position to judge, replied Jesus. True, you cannot judge, but you could help. Help in what way. To spread My word, to *help Me become the god of more people.* I don't understand. If you play your part, that is to say, the part I have reserved for you in My plan, I have every confidence that within the next six centuries or so, despite all the struggles and obstacles ahead of us, I will pass from being God of the Jews to being God of those whom we will call Catholics, from the Greek. And what is this part You have reserved for me in Your plan. That of martyr, My son, that of victim, which is the best role of all for propagating any faith and stirring up fervor. *God made the words martyr and victim seem like milk and honey on His tongue,* but Jesus felt a sudden chill in his limbs, as if the mist had closed over him, while the devil regarded him with an enigmatic expression which combined scientific curiosity with grudging compassion. (311–12; emphases mine)

Jesus' shock at the caprice of this power-hungry God only increases after he hears God recite a litany of the faithful—"yes, they will die for My sake"—which God tactfully lists "in alphabetical order so as not to hurt any feelings about precedence and importance," an "endless tale of iron and blood, of fire and ashes, an infinite sea of sorrow and tears" that will ensue after the crucifixion and God's "victory over other gods" in "the battles men fight" in the name of God and of his Son (320–21). Even the devil, Pastor, is so horrified by God's profiting from "the burning stakes and the darkness from great piles of bodies" that he makes a futile proposal to acknowledge God's power and return to God's heavenly kingdom so "Your son will not have to die" (331). Unfortunately, God won't accept or pardon Pastor, would "prefer you as you are, and were it possible, I'd have you be even worse. . . . Because the good I represent cannot exist without the evil you represent" (331). God, not Judas, has betrayed Jesus. Saramago extends the criticism of divine injustice launched by the authors of Judas the Obscure, for in this novel it is Jesus who is unconscionably exploited by God.[42]

This is the point where Judas Iscariot comes in, very late in the game, to foil this malevolent paternal divinity. In a poem quoted at the start of the previous chapter, Howard Nemerov presents Judas as "The necessary one," who triggered "what destiny had got / Arranged from the beginning . . ."; Saramago would take issue with Nemerov's next phrase: "for our sake."[43] In *The Gospel according to Jesus Christ,* Judas attempts to thwart a sacrifice that will only license and perpetuate subsequent sacrifices to a ruthlessly ambitious and solipsistic God, but along with Jesus he is hoodwinked. Toward the novel's close, after John the Baptist has been beheaded by Herod, Judas—who had been baptized by the Baptist—becomes enraged: "How can this be, he railed, when God Himself ordered John to proclaim the coming of the Messiah, it must have been God, because nothing can happen without His willing it" (366). The question leads to Jesus revealing not only his own future martyrdom but also the crucifixions of Andrew and Philip, the skinning alive of Bartholomew, the butchering of Matthew, the beheading of James the son of Zebedee, and so forth:

So we will die because of you, a voice asked, but no one ever identified the person who spoke. Because of God, answered Jesus. What does God want, asked John. He wants a larger congregation than the one He has at present, He wants the entire world for Himself. (368)[44]

In revolt against such an imperialistic deity, Jesus determines to replace the Son of God on the cross with a man who has proclaimed himself king of the Jews so that he may incite the people to expel the Romans from Israel. To circumvent God's bloody design, Jesus wants to die as a secular rebel (son of man), not as a divinity (Son of God).

Despite the violent reaction of the other disciples, Judas proposes to go to the Temple, and Jesus, "kissing him on both cheeks," sends Judas into the night. A roped and arrested Jesus passes Judas Iscariot "sitting in the tree with the noose already around his neck, patiently waiting for Jesus to appear in the distance before letting go of the branch, finally at peace with himself now that he had done his duty" (371). Because Jesus knows that in the past he commanded the winds, cured fevers, and fed multitudes, the idea enters his mind to resurrect Judas, but "only the son of God has the power to bring people back to life, not this king of the Jews who walks here, his spirit broken and his hands and feet bound" (371). On Judas's body is found "Not a single coin" (372); and when John declares that "he was not one of us," another "Judas, also called Thaddaeus, hastened to correct him, Whether we like it or not he will always be one of us, we may not know what to do with him, but he will go on being one of us" (372). Jesus continues to proclaim that he is not the Son of God but only the son of man, king of the Jews. Yet during his dying seconds he realizes that "he had been tricked," his "life had been planned for death from the very beginning," so he speaks his final words: "Men, forgive Him, for He knows not what He has done" (377).

To Harold Bloom, the last cry of Saramago's Jesus "testifies both to Jesus' sweetness and to Saramago's aesthetically controlled fury" ("The One" 163). It is a fury directed against the scandalous consequence of Augustine's insight (which Augustine himself had rejected): "Delivering up was done by the Father" (*Tractates* 222–23). Our sympathy for Jesus and for Judas spills over into revulsion at a sinful God who enlisted the Gospel authors to impose Christian dominance over the globe, achieved through God's horrific sacrifice of his own

Son as well as the persecution and bloodshed of his missionaries. Borrowing Nemerov's terms to understand Saramago's novel, one might say that the New Testament accounts were custom-built, made to order, to invalidate their prequel, the earlier *Gospel according to Jesus Christ*.[45] According to Saramago, not only Judas but Jesus, too, has become enmeshed in a history commissioned by the winner. Mortals are moral, but Saramago's immortal is immoral in a novel that launches a harsh and scandalous accusation against divine injustice. Both the betrayed Jesus and the betrayer Judas are forced to play parts in a story that will fuel sadistic religious warfare that is quite irrelevant, indeed destructive, to humanity's well-being, sponsored only to obtain "a larger congregation" for a divinity inexplicably hungry for celebrity, at any price.

Like Martin Scorsese's film *The Last Temptation of Christ* (1988), the novels of Kazantzakis and Saramago invalidate any interpretation of the Passion that blames the murder of Jesus on the Jews or on a Jewish Judas.[46] When Saramago attributes an "endless tale of iron and blood, of fire and ashes," to God's "victory over other gods" (320–21), when he envisions God profiting from "the burning stakes and the darkness from great piles of bodies" (331), it is hard not to read *The Gospel according to Jesus Christ* in terms of the quarrel with God—in Yiddish, *kvetchen zikh mit got*—that the Shoah inevitably prompted in many Jews as well as in some Christians, faith communities reduced by the disaster to blasphemous prayers railing against irreparable harm associated with God's broken covenant.[47] A venerated Judas warps the Passion plot to salvage (in Kazantzakis's case) or to confront (in Saramago's case) the wreckage of faith during and after the "fire and ashes," "the great piles of bodies" at and after Auschwitz.

But how does Judas as Jesus' enlisted savior relate to Borges's proposition that God "chose an abject existence: He was Judas." Saramago's mendacious divinity provides one clear rationale for such a view; however, Borges's scholar specifically alleges that God "stooped to become *man* for the redemption of the human race" (emphasis mine). A justification for that claim lurks beneath the logic of Cullen's, Lévitt's, and Kazantzakis's presentations, a logic that depends on a scandalous allegation against the treachery of God's Son. For such seemingly positive narratives implicate Jesus in the evil usually attributed to Judas. When Judas becomes his savior's recruited savior, the Son of God—dwindling in trustworthiness into what Kazantzakis's Judas calls him ("Traitor! Deserter!")—can incarnate the principle of betrayal. A martyred Judas—as confident about his innocence as Judas the Obscure was convinced of his guilt—then finds himself sacrificed by his friend for the benefit of humanity.

Because expressions of regret or acts of restitution are usually warranted after a betrayal of trust, a culpable Jesus must make amends. Often in this script, then, Jesus has to apologize to or eventually reward a trusty apostle induced to sacrifice himself (both physically and ethically) so that the Passion can be accomplished. Cullen's Jesus feels the need to compensate his apostle for accepting "the sorry part" (295) assigned to him. Similarly, Lévitt's Jesus sounds guilt-ridden when he pleads to Judas, "Forgive me that I put this burden of my bodily death upon you" (52). Judas, one might reasonably decide, takes on the suffering of another here. Kazantzakis's Jesus, we noted, admits that he could not do what he asks Judas to do on his behalf. By utilizing Judas, a morally compromised Jesus has to betray the best interests of his most loving disciple.[48]

This supposition—about a martyred Judas, a traitorous Jesus—surfaces in a succession of disturbing and at times tawdry books. For instance, Igal Mossinsohn's protagonist in the novel *Judas* (1963), composed in Hebrew, rues the conspiracy between Jesus and Barabbas that betrayed the twelfth apostle into violence.[49] A more historical interpretation of the Passion, Hugh J. Schonfield's *The Passover Plot* (1965) concurs about the betrayal of the betrayer, arguing that Jesus determined to establish his messianic credentials by fulfilling prophetic scripture and that he himself therefore engineered the Passion plot. Schonfield effectively puts Jesus in the position of Luke's devil by stating that "The tempter [of Judas] came in the guise of his Master" (136).[50] Even when Judas more knowingly and willingly becomes an agent of Jesus, as in Armando Cosani's hermetic *The Flight of the Feathered Serpent* (1953) and Morley Callaghan's meta-fictional *A Time for Judas* (1984), authors tarnish the reputation of the Son of God by implying that Jesus took advantage of his manipulated twelfth apostle. When Cosani's Judas hears Satan tell him to "Forget the light that was" (203), the demon appears to be licensed by the messiah. When Callaghan's Jesus affirms that "Someone must betray me. The story requires it" (125), a Judas pledged to secrecy knows, "I was used. Used by the Son of God, picked out to be the victim" (131).[51]

Such stories about Judas as his savior's enlisted savior attribute a Machiavellian character to John's Jesus, who is believed to have instigated and abetted his apostle's wrongdoings when he said, "'Did I not choose you, the twelve? Yet one of you is a devil'" (6:70); or when he gave Judas the sop that let the devil enter his body and then instructed his possessed disciple to act "quickly" (13:27). Michael Dickinson's *The Lost Testament of Judas Iscariot* (1994) features a loyal Judas who explains of his demanding master, "He had to have his betrayer, and he had chosen me" (94). In this counterhistory— another follower is crucified instead of and in the place of Jesus— Jesus wants to stage his resurrection with requisite realism; during a disturbingly lurid scene, he requires Judas to hammer in the nails.[52] A tradition that indicts God's Son presents Jesus exploiting a loving soul irreparably damaged by the grotesque uses to which he has been put.

All these plots compound the charges brought by authors of Judas the Obscure, who suggest that Jesus inadvertently depended on a doomed apostle. In the more irreverent approach to a Judas drafted by Jesus to facilitate the Passion, involuntary complicity turns into overt culpability as the Son of God deliberately articulates his need to take advantage of Judas the martyr. Jesus, according to this variety of retelling, fully comprehends the deleterious psychological, social, and spiritual effects Judas must suffer, but determines that his own good and the good he will bring into being justify the vile means he must make of an obedient, self-sacrificing disciple. Later twentieth-century inventions of the sacrificed apostle thereby cast doubt on the integrity, compassion, and redemption delivered by Jesus. A Judas martyred for or with and by Jesus qualifies the all-encompassing love of Christ, making suspect his ability to keep his messianic promises.

Another story by Borges, "The Sect of the Thirty" (1975), emphasizes the grim implications of late twentieth-century reinventions of the Passion that remove blame from Judas only to cast reproach on the cosmic forces that rule human destiny. Through a purportedly found tale from pseudo-antiquity, Borges imagines a curious band of believers in the land of Kerioth whose original name was "the Thirty Pieces of Silver" and whose credo consisted of the belief that "In the tragedy of the Cross . . . there were those who acted knowingly and those who acted unknowingly" (445). The Temple priests, the Jerusalem mob, the Romans all acted unknowingly; however, Judas and Jesus did not:

> Of knowing actors, there were but two: Judas and the Redeemer. Judas cast away the thirty coins that were the price of our souls' salvation and immediately hanged himself. At that moment he was thirty-three years old, the age of the Son of Man. The Sect venerates the two equally, and absolves the others. (445)

Borges's narrator comprehends the utopian efforts of this group, their refusal to create a pariah or scapegoat: "There is not one lone guilty man; there is no man that does not carry out, wittingly or not, the plan traced by the All-Wise. All mankind now shares in Glory" (445).[53] Once again in this story, then, Borges imagines a venerated Judas.

Yet just as early Christians denounced the Gnostics' idea of God, Borges's narrator strenuously rejects the sect, in this case because its central ritual involves a frightful "abomination": "upon reaching a certain age," initiates of "the Sect of the Thirty" are "mocked and crucified on the peak of a mountain, to follow the example of their masters" (445). For all to be redeemed in love, according to such an "abominable heresy" (444), all must be doomed to an early, unwarranted, and excruciating death. Borges's parable pretends to be a fragment of a fourth-century text that might be a translation from an earlier Greek work. But his musings about a cult destined to quick extinction portend a harsh message befitting a period of time when either Jesus or God was made to replace Judas as the cause of humanity's downfall: one can make do without a betrayer, Borges hints, only when everyone is betrayed. The "Glory" shared by humanity is decidedly gory.

LORD JUDAS

The Nazis' death sentence against the Jews, as well as the Vatican's condemnation of Christian anti-Semitism, led imaginatively not only to a vindication of the twelfth apostle but also to a vilification of the divine forces he served. It might be considered a small step to move from a sacrilegious defamation of God or of God's Son to a hallelujah chorus in praise of the traitorous deity Judas, king of kings and lord of lords, but the extravagance of this malignant deification and the tone of blasphemous mockery adopted by its most prominent author warrant further examination in a brief coda. When betrayal seems to be the force ruling the world in which a Jewish Jesus and his people find themselves senselessly tortured, Bonhoeffer had explained, "The figure of Judas, which we used to find so difficult to understand, is now fairly familiar to us. The air that we breathe is so polluted by mistrust that it almost chokes us" (*Letters* 11). This perspective, uncannily glossing the worldview of Saramago's novel as well as Chagall's painting (see illustration 6.2), attributes malevolent potency to a Judas-like God and a God-like Judas presiding over late twentieth-century culture.

If God can betray his own Son, if the Son of God can trick an innocent supporter into wickedness, then the traitor Judas may put on the trappings of a deity. Judas the divine stalks through the shadows of his kingdom come, delivering his perpetually restless protégés into trespasses and transgressions. The gruesome omnipresence of betrayal persuaded Brendan Kennelly to compose his capacious collection of poems *The Book of Judas* (1991), a best seller when it was published in Ireland. In keeping with the paradoxes that always multiply around the twelfth apostle, Judas ascends glorified by virtue of his iniquity, and the moral tragedy Kennelly envisions constitutes an aesthetic triumph as well as a high point in Judas's career. A pariah in polyester, more Irish Catholic than Jewish (though ecumenically minded), Kennelly's Judas takes to televangelism to preach a credo of greed and solipsism that stakes out his claim to incarnate the spirit of our times. Although the Jewish pariah-Judas had been declared illegitimate, it is harder to kill a legendary phantom than a flesh-and-blood being.[54] The demoniac Judas shoulders his modish interfaith way to center stage because he views himself as the figure most genuinely worshipped at the turn of the twentieth century. A number of Kennelly's characters realize that Judas reigns supreme in our wired and weird postmodernity.

When Judas-the-media-celebrity asks a member of his studio audience to name the best chat show host in the history of television, she enthuses, " 'You, Judas, you alone, you are God!' " (24). *The Book of Judas* proves her right, judging Judas's betrayal to be the preeminent principle shaping virtually all societal institutions today and even the artists who lambaste them. A superlative spin doctor peddling "Judaspoison" (337), the twelfth apostle metastasizes in multiple bodies and bodies politic. If—and it is a very large if, given the history—Judas can be detached from the Jews, Kennelly makes the attempt by dramatizing a series of ancient and contemporary scenes in which various Christian and non-Christian characters effectively work Judas's will or suffer from his pervasive influence. Although in some of the numerous poems within the book Judas speaks in his own voice, often his views are channeled through other personages—

most of whom determine their course of conduct by gleefully or guilt-
ily asking, what would Judas do?

Kennelly's *Book of Judas* brilliantly communicates his heartfelt
conviction that the ideologies and counterideologies contending
for dominance today contribute to the materialism, loneliness, self-
destruction, and paranoid sense of unreality plaguing the inhabitants
of contemporary Western societies. Not Jesus with his message of
hope and resurrection but a postmodern Judas with his dogma of
despair and damage is, alas, the patron saint of our sickening days
and ways. According to Kennelly, then, we live and move and have
our being in and with Judas. In a manner consonant with the Marxist
thinker Louis Althusser, the Irish poet tracks a Judas-effect in religion,
education, families, the law, politics, economics, and communication
systems.[55] These ideological apparatuses imprint human interaction
at the cost of each and every citizen's moral and physical well-being,
which makes Kennelly's Judas "smile as converts to Judasanity /
Increase in numbers hour by hour" (197).

Religion in *The Book of Judas* surfaces through a Judas Church
that has betrayed its congregants as well as the deities it worships.
Critical of male domination and hypocrisy, Kennelly more emphatically accentuates the rapacious buying and selling of the Passion by
secular as well as sacred agencies.[56] At the crucifixion, "An Expert
Lot" of international reporters "thought it might be a zippy idea /
To interview Jesus on the cross / But Christ declined. / This was a
tragic journalistic loss" (107). After the crucifixion and while Judas
is looking for a frolic, he goes on holiday with The Church (personified as a woman), who claims they have nothing in common,
but Judas assures her, "'We both betrayed an innocent man'" (141).
How this could be is explained in "Circulating Bags," where Kennelly
contrasts Jesus' anger at moneymakers in the Temple with "the sound
of money / Dropping into circulating bags / Handled by the most
faithful of the faithful" at daily Mass (178). Regarding the church's
business, Judas believes, "Circulating bags suggest money is the heart

of it" (178). The church, according to Kennelly, has profited from the most grievous calamities in Western civilization: "Out of the smashed cities / Works of art adorn the Vatican walls" (377).

In its analysis of an educational system controlled by a religion that circulates Judas's money pouch, *The Book of Judas* introduces teachers staffing Judas Schools. A poem titled "Miracles," for instance, spotlights a pedagogy of pain through a sardonic student speaker yanked "out in front of the First Communion class" by a National Teacher who "Slips down my trousers first, then my fancy / Underpants, lashes my bum till my yelling / Splits the parish. Miracles, my ass!" (118–19). Reliant on public humiliation and corporal punishment, a perverted church-sponsored education or sexual abuse may have caused one Christy Hannitty to believe "it would be a blessing / If he cut the balls off all the Bishops of / Ireland because debollicked Bishops are less / Prone to the terrible temptations of love" (329). According to Kennelly, love and learning regulated by repressive shaming techniques find outlets in sadistic and deviant activities that only further isolate human beings.

The Judas Church and its Judas Schools infect child rearing in many poems that deal with child abuse and pederasty. "When I Was Three" features a father who "said the rosary at evening / And confessed his sins to God" before going up to his three-year-old son's bedroom where he

> stuck his finger up my bum.
> He said stick out your tongue, he put his
> Tongue to my tongue in a hideous kiss,
> Shoved his finger between my thighs,
> Same thing every night, and I was dumb . . . (48)

Unable to weep, the boy who speaks this poem perceives rain as his tears; it performs the service his eyes cannot, because of his mute entrapment in a Judas Family.

When Kennelly tackles legal, political, and economic systems put into place by global corporate capitalism, Judas announces, "I got Businessman of the Year Award" (189) or "I meet myself in Houses of Parliament" (275). He does so to approach the issue of Judas Law, Judas Politics, and Judas Business. In recurrent appearances, Pontius Pilate and Herod stand for murderous statesmen who lead Kennelly's speaker "To the private but passionate conviction / They're more attractive dead than alive" (332). This view is buttressed by the politicians' victims, those classes of homeless or impoverished people who furnish statistics on unemployment, all of whom are driven to Judas's act of despair: "We have hundreds of thousands of unemployed / Potential suicides in our land of busy rain" (335). Kennelly's Pinstripe Pig, savoring and selling his own flatulence, markets it transnationally, while Judas flunkies engage in nefarious intrigues involving sneaky nationalists and their self-serving informers. In the section "Bunk," a series of letter poems addressed to "Sir" are penned by an anonymous informant who fawns on his employer ("all people met, you, Sir, shall know"); whose surveillance is vigilant; and whose protestations of innocence ring hollow ("I am the victim of some treachery, / I did not aid, abet or in the smallest degree / Promote . . ." 90, 91, 94). The letter-writing spy reports on participants in some sort of insurrection to ensnare them, promising "If these rooms have secrets, Sir, you'll possess them all" (100). Irish names and places clarify Kennelly's satire on the schemes and counterschemes of a factionalized Irish population bent on self-sabotage; however, the locale also serves as a microcosm of the global surveillance, manipulation of circumstantial evidence, and political blackmail of various nations' intelligence agencies.

Throughout *The Book of Judas,* communication industries inject sound bites of "judassperm" (150) by means of television and radio broadcasts of hyped sporting events, bomb scares, terrorist attacks, hostage hangings, supermarket slayings, coverage of the Calvary Crisis, and rap recitations of urban dropouts, drunk or drugged. Judas so very successfully populates the world with duplicates of himself that before the close of *The Book of Judas,* his "collaborator, Brendan Kennelly, who is a sick man," suffers "exhaustion and judasfatigue," causing Judas to assume authorial authority (323). Amid the proliferation of hyped betrayers, Judas himself curiously takes on a sort of grandeur, for he knows who and why he is:

> Game-players need a hero
> Someone who plays it more despicably than they
> Standard exemplar model paradigm o hang it god
> Not just adolf stalin napoleon nero
> But someone flawless absolute and sly
> (they think). Could I be that? M'mmm. I do believe I could.
>   (22)

Invented to symbolize miserly misery and secret sin, Judas nevertheless exclaims,

>   I am no
> Symbol of anything, I am not known, heard, smelt, touched,
>   seen
> By anyone but myself in my own
> Prison of flesh and bone,
> Another ordinary appalled man. (168)

As Anthony Roche puts it about Kennelly's protagonist, "there is no part of him which the world has not penetrated and stupefied. Further, since he is the one who is blamed, he is singularly free of the human habit of blaming others" (107–8).

The allusion to "adolf stalin napoleon nero" above points to a cluster of poems toward the close of *The Book of Judas* in which Kennelly grapples with the significance of Judas in the Holocaust. The Führer, who has been taught by his friend Judas how to goosestep, emerges as no better, no worse than all the other profiteers:

> Hitler tells me skin covers a lot,
> Shown only by careful peeling.
> In you go, beyond flesh, blood, bones. To what?
>
> Nothing, the study of which I find revealing
> As a warm afternoon, on my back, grassed, staring at the sky,
> Flawless, deep, unending, like a perfect lie. (231)

The colloquial "In you go" is followed by the "Nothing" contemplated by a Judas lying on the grass, or high on grass, or fatigued, but also clearly pondering the "flesh, blood, bones" trashed in gas chambers and concentration camps.

"Nothing," anatomized by Hitler and Kennelly, resonates throughout a volume in which nothing comes of nothing but speaking again of nothing: the heart of the matter is the hole in the human heart. Judas has become "the first spokesman for // Nothing," which is what he spies "in my breast, in yours" (354), a "yours" that includes anti-Semitic Jews along with Christians. After the period when "Adolf had considered it a must / To wipe my tribe off the face of the earth" (321), Kennelly presents a Jewish-identified speaker authoring a Passion play titled *The Need for Gas* with a greedy Shylock protagonist who seems to deserve gassing. The production is censured by other Jews who now engage in an act of aesthetic extermination, with the result that Judasanity spawns a Jewish community split into self-hating haters and their rancorous foes: "To spitting kin who do not know my mind. / What should one do, betrayed by one's own kind?" (321). Unredeemable, Kennelly's Jews and Christians labor "In the name of Judas / And of Judas," who "was in the beginning / Is now / And forever shall be" (240).

Whether Judas Nazi or Judas Jew, the human subjects in *The Book of Judas* sound as inhuman as material objects, like the "Thirty Pieces of Silver" that speak in a series of poems—speak, that is, about their inability to speak. One of these bits of currency proclaims, "Money talks, they say. Wrong. I'm silent, I don't even / Have a mind of my

own. All the other minds / Pour into my no-mind" (185). In other
words, all of Kennelly's characters resemble the constructed robots,
automatons, or humanoids in such movies as *Blade Runner* (1982)
and *Invasion of the Body Snatchers* (1956). To adopt the language of
the theorist Slavoj Žižek, each denizen of contemporary civilization
suffers the "paradox of the 'subject who knows he is a replicant,'" the
certainty that "everything that I actually am is an artifact—not only
my body, my eyes, but even my most intimate memories and fanta-
sies" (*Tarrying* 40). Without minds of their own, Kennelly's characters dwindle into simulacra through which acquisitive and insincere
Judasanity pours. A male Cassandra in an age of moral turpitude,
loquacious Judas cannot be heard—no one listens—though the poet
persists, since "The best way to serve the age is to betray it" (17).

Dedicated to the idea that in our troubled times none can trust the
words on their own tongues, Kennelly's *Book of Judas* proves that
Judas continues to emerge powerfully from the canonical Gospels
of the New Testament because treachery, self-sabotage, and despair
remain entrenched problems in human life, as in the institutions and
ideologies of technologically advanced societies. Kennelly's book of
verse therefore puts a decided spin on Jesus' words about Judas in
the noncanonical Gnostic Gospel of Judas: "You will be cursed by the
other generations—and you will come to rule over them" (*Gospel of
Judas* 33). Not devotion to Jesus' teachings but self-serving treachery
has become the reigning imperative, which is why Kennelly's Judas
rules over the generations, much as he did over the "smugglers, black-
market antiquities dealers, religious scholars, backstabbing partners,
and greedy entrepreneurs" who endangered the fragile Coptic text
of the Gospel of Judas during the decades that elapsed between its
discovery in the 1970s and its publication by National Geographic
in 2006 (Robinson 156). Indeed, one of its editors, Rodolphe Kasser,
explains that the "precious but so badly mistreated" papyrus codex
was "a stark victim of cupidity and ambition" (*Gospel of Judas* 47).
The manuscript was lodged in a bank vault in Hicksville, Long Island,
at one point, stowed in a freezer at another, and parts of it did not

survive. Almost destroyed by such betrayals, the lost Gospel of Judas ironically endured the very story it may have attempted to revise.

During this same time period and most probably unaware of the archaeological finding, Kennelly added new poems to his *Little Book of Judas* (2002), proving that his apostolic antihero will not go gently into the dark night of the soul that he signifies. The concluding line of the concluding new poem, "All Over Again," elaborates on the universal existence of this disciple through and for all seasons with the betrayer's admission, "I'm your man," and then, after the bleak pause of a blank line, "Let the myths begin" (224). Amid media spinning, ethnic cleansing, sexual cruelty, nationalist intrigues, fundamentalist violence, and rapacious financial fraud, Judas triumphant has penetrated, saturated, and stupefied the corrupt world he embodies and populates through us, his clones. Intensified by this cacophony, the silence of God—whose Son's life might have been "a preparation / For what can never happen" (64)—disappoints the poet or his Judas persona, though he admits, "If I'd made the world I'd keep my mouth shut too. / Especially if I'd made me, I imagine / Dialogue with me would not be my prime concern" (167).

7

JESUS, ACCORDING TO
JUDAS'S BAD NEWS:
HE WHO IS PRAISED

A skeptical Judas, delivering his "dusangelion," or bad news, doubts the Jesus with whom he is joined, and therefore challenges Jesus' messianic claims. Now, as throughout history, Jesus and Judas—progressing in step—mirror each other in an affiliation that illuminates competing attitudes toward trust, accountability, and the human condition. Ultimately Judas's long evolution explains the meaning of his name.

FOR WRITERS TODAY, the twelfth apostle frequently broadcasts bad news. Just as all the events in the various Gospel versions of Judas's life story do not cohere, so too all the crooked ways may not become straight or the rough smooth: this is Judas's perspective on Jesus' ministry at the start of the twenty-first century. Given the decidedly fallen nature of the world, neither the historical Jesus nor the crucified Christ will bring into being the messianic age, or so Brendan Kennelly's damned Judas insinuates. With its draconian judgments, *The Book of Judas* obviously cannot stand for the entire trajectory of Judas's evolution over two thousand years, but it does point to one increasingly prominent feature in his progress. Whereas Mark, Matthew, Luke, and John recount the messiah's biography in the good news or *euangelion* of the Gospels, subsequent creators of the twelfth apostle often transmit "dusangelion": Judas's bad news conveys incredulity at tidings of glad comfort and joy.

Judas in Armando Cosani's *The Flight of the Feathered Serpent* condenses the bad news he delivers: "you are the *yes*," Judas explains to Jesus, "where I will be the *no* for man" (188).[1] Cosani's novel, like Kennelly's poems and many post–World War II treatments, insists that the betrayer should not be conflated with the Jewish people. However, throughout his long evolution he can be associated with all those individuals who (for any number of reasons) eventually decide (at least at certain moments of their lives) to self-identify as unconfirmed in a faith they once embraced: those emphatically not-born-again or unborn-again. Jews, Confucians, Buddhists, Moslems, Taoists, Hindus, agnostics, and atheists obviously might fall into this category, but so too could some Christians.[2] With respect to religious belief in general, Judas repudiates a faith he accepted not once but twice or (at Matthew's count) three times: first, when he divorced himself from whatever traditional Judaism he practiced to follow Jesus; second, when he left Jesus' circle to work with the Temple authorities; and finally, in some tellings, when he repented and reasserted his loyalty to Jesus.

Skeptical, yet not necessarily cynical, Judas in current versions of his story wishes but finds it difficult to sustain belief or commitment. He becomes a figure of the convert unconverted, the lapsing soul. Uncertainty or hesitancy or vacillation—spawned by opportunism or doubt, confusion or despondency—characterized Judas earlier in his representational career. At certain moments he has evinced ardor and tenacity, but even the heroic Judas's faith could flounder at the reversal of his expectations. And certainly in many of his alternative guises he has exhibited various degrees of mistrust about himself, other participants in the Passion, and God. A far cry from Kazantzakis's and Saramago's loyal savior or Kennelly's overweening potentate in chapter 6, the skeptical Judas of the next section returns to his humble anomalous origins. A dignified character noteworthy not for his betrayal but instead for his distrust, Judas the skeptic undermines faith in any single orthodoxy, for his own convoluted textual origins ground him in a network of disjointed psychological, social, and religious circumstances.

It is precisely Judas's perplexity that continues to make him attractive to his teacher and to readers. Authors of the skeptical Judas often intimate that he played a positive role in relation to Jesus by serving as a sounding board or honest interlocutor, for "to love without criticism is to be betrayed," as Djuna Barnes once put it (79). To many of our contemporaries, it is patently clear that wealth has not and may not come to the poor, nor happiness and health to the wretched and sick, as the human species too often abides within the mournful obscurity of perpetual injustice and suffering. It seems appropriate therefore to begin this conclusion by considering a few recent reinventions of Judas's incredulous dusangelion. Through them we can glimpse a genuine (nonstereotypical) Judaism in Judas and insight into yet another plausible justification for his actions. Then, in the middle section of this chapter, I sketch the ways in which Judas's long-term evolution over twenty centuries reflects changing ideas about Jesus' character as well as moral comprehension and judgment of the betrayal. Finally, this biography closes with an elaboration on the abiding significance of Judas for people from various backgrounds.

THE FRIENDLY SKEPTIC

For centuries, a folkloric Judas spilled out of high into popular culture to license riotous festivals within diverse communities. Free of faith and all its attendant ethical demands, Judas let people take a holiday from orthodoxy at anarchic processionals regularly staged into the twentieth century. Colorful papier-mâché Judases—filled with gunpowder, paraded, and exploded at Easter carnivals—"rarely resembled the biblical Judas with flaming red hair; rather they parodied some local bureaucrat, some wayward cleric, some pompous dude, or some nabob with up-turned nose" (Beezley 4). At Mexican celebrations on Judas Day, the Saturday following Good Friday, numerous public officials were mocked and hung and thwacked, caricatures of garishly costumed bigwigs and aristocrats treated like piñatas. Judas clowns, pyrotechnic Judas effigies in the likeness of American presidents, and Judas coyotes and skeletons proliferated, possibly to defy oppressive political powers as well as death, the ultimate betrayer of life.[3] Judas Day acknowledges the fact that despite or before the Easter of the following day, the world has not yet been redeemed. During the intoxicating reversals and riotous misrule of carnivals evocative of medieval festivals, a blood-filled bladder of a slaughtered pig might be stuffed into a Judas effigy, which was then shot to make its innards spurt out.[4]

Judas—often displayed seated with a bottle of beer or whiskey—provides a temporary reprieve from honesty, abstinence, sobriety, the doctrines of just rewards and turning the other cheek. An avatar of the folk saint known in Spanish as San Simon and in Mayan dialects as Maximon, Judas in Guatemalan towns—a "patron saint of businessmen, stimulator of sales and protector of profits"—provides access to powerful but not always benign spiritual powers (Pieper 29). Paraded through the village to the Catholic church, Judas is hung by a rope on a wooden scaffold overnight; on the next day, he returns to the identity of Maximon/San Simon, whose "feast day is October 28, the commemorative day of Saint Simon and Judas Thaddeus, or Thadeo (also called Saint Jude)" (Pieper 29). Prayers, composed on slips of paper and deposited into the pockets of Judas dolls (illustration 7.1), express less than charitable requests or wishes, evidence of the universal lure of sin, backsliding, rivalry, and corruption. In the pockets of the effigy whose photograph is reprinted here, supplicants placed notes asking Judas to "Have that other woman leave Julio . . . alone" or to "bring about an accident soon" (Pieper 163).

In high cultural venues, however, an unredeemed Judas frequently reaps not illicit pleasures but painful scruples and qualms. More

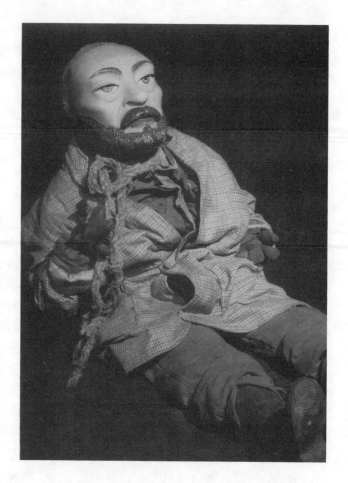

7.1. Masked Judas with severed noose, Guatemalan Highlands (late twentieth century). Source: Collection of Jim and Jeanne Pieper, Los Angeles. Reproduced with permission from *Guatemala's Folk Saints* (2002).

than Thomas, for longer than twenty centuries Judas has epitomized doubts, misgivings, reservations that cannot be placated but repeatedly return to trouble those who wish to believe.[5] For Thomas believed after and because he had been given the opportunity to see and touch the risen Christ; but Judas, who saw Jesus but not the risen Christ, may not be "blessed" as Christ wanted those to be who "have not seen and yet have come to believe" (John 20:29). To that extent, Thomas represents all the other apostles who found confirmation of Jesus' messianic stature in the resurrection that spurred faith. In Stephen Adly Guirgis's play *The Last Days of Judas Iscariot* (2006), Saint Thomas testifies that Jesus granted him what was denied Judas: "He gave me proof. I had no Faith, and he gave it to me for free. I don't know why I got the benefit of my doubt, and Judas didn't get help with his" (78).

One stage direction toward the end of Guirgis's play explains that Judas ultimately suffers in a *"frozen state of catatonia"* (102). Faced by a loving Jesus, the bereft Judas shouts reprimands: *"when I fuckin' needed you—where the fuck were you, huh?!"* (104). Broken and "unfixable," the twelfth apostle rebuffs a Jesus whose motives continue to elude him: "Why . . . didn't you make me good enough . . . so that you could've loved me?" (105, 106). At the play's conclusion, Jesus—unable to reach through the schizophrenia petrifying Judas in his psychic shell and hell—methodically bathes the feet of Judas, who, unlike Thomas, never received visible proof of the resurrection before his betrayal or its catastrophic personal consequences. Regret might be Jesus' inheritance from the history he shared with Judas, but here Judas Iscariot's middle name seems to be torment. His soul shatters in rage at a sacrifice—Jesus', but also his own—that brought an Easter from which he was excluded. Judas's skepticism pertains not only to his exclusion but also to Jesus' failure to include him in a redemption that thus fell short of its universal promise.

Unlike the eleven in the Gospels, Judas hangs, explodes, or disappears before the crucifixion, unaware that Jesus kept his promise of resurrection. The proof-deprived Judas did not live to see Jesus after he was raised from the dead. "The whole New Testament is unanimous on this point," the Catholic theologian Hans Urs von Balthasar explains: "the Cross and burial of Christ reveal their significance only in the light of the event of Easter, without which there is no Christian faith" (189). As if meditating on the consequences of Judas's disappearance before Easter, one Christian scholar calls Judas "the last man to die under the Old Law, before the dawning of the Age of Grace" (Ohly 29). Curiously, this view about bad timing was promulgated in antiquity by Leo the Great (ca. 395–461), who surmised (as if to Judas) about the suicide, "If only you had waited for the completion of your crime until the blood of Christ had been poured out for all sinners, you would have put off the gruesome death by hanging" (234). According to Leo the Great, Judas sinned because he "believed Jesus to be not God the Son of God, but only a man of our own race" (230). If the twelfth apostle had been accorded the possibility of witnessing the resurrection, his initial faith—he was, after all, a follower—would have eventually taken root in the fertile soil of confirmation.[6]

But how would doubtful Judas look to those who do *not* subscribe to the view that Jesus annulled the laws on the books, making them "Old" or obsolete by ushering in a new "Age of Grace"? From a Jewish perspective—that Jesus is "not God the Son of God, but only a man of our own race," albeit an exceptionally godly man—Judas may have ultimately dedicated himself to the law. Whereas rowdy folk rituals break or suspend local laws, Judas's theological skepticism can lead him to uphold the laws of the land of Israel. When judged guilty of nothing more than uncertainty about Jesus' claims to divinity, Judas does not necessarily undercut normative moral sanctions; indeed, he may assert them because he is troubled by suspect testimonies about a dawning "Age of Grace," or so the Jewish historian Joseph Klausner proposed in a book about the Passion composed originally in Hebrew for Jewish readers. Perhaps Judas's refusal to grant authority to the new epoch grew from his ongoing commitment to the tried-and-true old order of his origins, which (he may have believed) would not or should not be displaced or superseded.[7]

Klausner's *Jesus of Nazareth,* published in Jerusalem in 1922 and a forerunner to very recent approaches to Judas, emphasizes the brevity of Jesus' ministry as well as his steadfast commitment to the Torah. Jesus, according to Klausner, was "a humble and pious Pharisee who departed the boundaries of Jewish nationhood" (Heschel, *Abraham Geiger* 236). Susannah Heschel links the author's Zionism to his message: "to reject Jewish nationhood is to end up like Jesus, as a Christian" (236). Klausner's Judas is motivated not by satanic possession or avarice or hypocrisy, but by a propensity to question Jesus' powers: "He was gradually convinced that Jesus was not always successful in healing the sick; that Jesus feared his enemies and persecutors, and sought to escape and evade them; that there were marked contradictions in Jesus' teaching" (324). More important, "this 'Messiah' neither would nor could deliver his nation, yet he arrogated to himself the role of 'the Son of man'" (324). The dissonance between who Jesus claimed to be and what he could or did perform convinced Klausner's educated Judean that Jesus was a false messiah or prophet, not the glorious king prophesied by Daniel (7:11–14) and Ezekiel (34:23–24).

The twelfth apostle, faithful to the Hebrew Bible, followed the law commanding that anyone who led people astray should be killed. To substantiate this idea, Klausner quotes Deuteronomy (13:2–12) to ask, "Was it not, then, a 'religious duty' to deliver up such a 'deceiver' to the government and so fulfill the law: 'Thou shalt exterminate the evil from thy midst'?" (325). This chapter in Deuteronomy opens with a warning about the ethical necessity of allegiance only to the one true God: "If prophets or those who divine by dreams appear among you and promise you omens or portents, . . . you must not heed the words of those prophets or those who divine by dreams, for the Lord your God is testing you" (13:1). A solid citizen (albeit not the most endearing of fellows), Judas feels the need to disclose an imposter to the authorities.[8] Scrupulosity drives an educated but "cold and calculating" Judean, one "accustomed to criticize and scrutinise" (325). Blind to Jesus' many virtues, Judas celebrated the Passover on the thirteenth of Nisan with the other apostles and sang the Hallel (a series of celebratory psalms) before Jesus left for Gethsemane, where Jesus suffered not foreknowledge but instead tragic intimations of mortality, perfectly understandable given the power of his enemies.

"Judas had nothing against his fellow-disciples (whom he looked upon as led astray by Jesus), and in order that none of them should be arrested in place of Jesus, he himself accompanied the Jewish police and their officer" (336). The Gospel kiss is simply one of several "imaginary additions," according to Klausner, as are accounts of Pilate's opposition to the crucifixion (335, 348). Neither the Pharisees nor the Sadducees would have judged Jesus worthy of death, since "there had not been actual blasphemy" and "they would see in his words nothing more than a rash fantasy" (343). To save the community from "the cruel vengeance of Pilate," the priests handed over a suspect character to the Romans (345). Klausner concludes that "The Jews, *as a nation,* were far less guilty of the death of Jesus than the Greeks, as a nation, were guilty of the death of Socrates; but who now would think of avenging the blood of Socrates the Greek upon his countrymen, the present Greek race?" (348).

Escalating the tone and sexing up the story but nevertheless maintaining Klausner's perspective, an African American popular novelist, Frank Yerby, used fiction to set the record of the Passion straight: Yerby's historical novel *Judas, My Brother* (1968) debunks the veracity of the Gospel accounts, which were, his narrator claims, "the products of appalling ignorance combined with equally appalling spite" (474). As recounted by a thirteenth disciple—specifically, the young man who hastily fled the arrest naked, leaving his linen wrapper behind—*Judas, My Brother* depicts a despairing twelfth apostle cursing Jesus "for lifting my hopes so high, then hurling them down": "I wanted a king," Yerby's disillusioned Judas exclaims, "Not a bleating, sacrificial goat!" (433). A messiah who beguiles or deceives inevitably "leads astray" the people, causing his adversaries to assume that "the Law commands [him] to be killed without pity or compassion or forgiveness" (434). As for Judas's actions during and after the arrest, more errors abound "in Sacred Books whose every other word is wrong," "For your Gospel writers were lunatics, surely, men who couldn't even manage to tell convincing lies, because their addled pates held no seat of memory" (437, 440). The kiss, the money, the hanging, and the explosion reflect only "what [their authors] hoped would happen to Judas, their sick impotent desire for vengeance, fleshed out in empty words" (505).

In the poems, plays, and novels about Jesus (composed by Jews and non-Jews alike) that continue to appear at the start of the twenty-first century, Judas is often seen as Klausner envisioned him: an apostle committed to values that lend him some credence. Frequently in high culture Judas pledges himself to secular values—economic equity, social justice—that clash with Jesus' spiritual priorities. For instance, he briefly materializes as a Marxist agitator against the Romans in Norman Mailer's lackluster *The Gospel according to the Son* (1997). According to Mailer, Judas's hatred of the rich—"They poison all of us. They are vain, undeserving, and wasteful of the hopes of those who are beneath them. They spend their lives lying to the lowly" (138)—takes precedence over his admiration for Yeshua: the squandered pomade is simply the last straw. Yet Mailer's Son of God remains so compassionate about his well-intentioned disciple that the twelfth apostle turns into Judas lite: Jesus feels nothing but pity for a disciple emptied of any demonic or daring energy and suffering a pathetic fate.[9]

Like Mailer, Nino Ricci and Knut Ødegård recycle the familiar script of Judas the rebellious Zealot. In Ricci's novel *Testament* (2002), Judas realizes that Jesus' "kingdom was of an entirely unpolitical nature, a philosophical rather than a physical state, requiring no revolution"; the insight leads the twelfth apostle to complain "that it seemed then a mere salve to make more bearable the yoke of an oppressor" (47).[10] Is religion merely an opiate for the masses? Ricci's activist Judas worries. In a sequence of poems translated into English in 2005, the Norwegian poet Knut Ødegård also stresses Judas's alienation, here at the anointing of Jesus. Upset at the sight of the expensive balm, Ødegård's Judas determines to put a stop to this mad and "superfluous vanity": "things have reached the limit now, now things have gone far enough" (61). The three hundred denarii that the ointment must have cost should have been "given to the faithful of Judah's tribe" (61).

The specifically Jewish Judas unearthed by Klausner surfaces more clearly defined in an evocative pseudo-Gospel undertaken by the popular novelist Jeffrey Archer in collaboration with the biblical scholar Francis J. Moloney: *The Gospel according to Judas by Benjamin Iscariot* (2007). This account—purportedly written by Judas's son—

features a pious Jewish Judas, well schooled in the verses of Daniel, Ezekiel, and Isaiah. The Judas of Archer and Moloney hopes that Jesus will become "the expected Son of David, the Messiah and King of Israel" (46), but is concerned that some of his admired teacher's practices and predictions contradict the five books of Moses: "Search as he might, Judas could not find any passage in the Torah that made an association between suffering, death and the fulfillment of the messianic hopes of Israel" (40). After Peter witnesses and reports on the Transfiguration in Archer and Moloney's pseudo-gospel, Judas begins to doubt that Jesus is the messiah, for there was "nothing written or spoken in Jewish tradition" that suggested the death and resurrection of the Davidic messiah, king of Israel (50). According to Archer and Moloney, then, a worried Judas tries to save Jesus in Jerusalem, but is himself betrayed—first by a Scribe acting as a double agent and then by a guilt-ridden Peter, who is given the grave line, "It would be better for you not to have been born" (76).[11] The twelfth apostle concludes his life in exile, believing "that Jesus was a holy man, even a prophet, who followed in the tradition of Jeremiah, Isaiah and Ezekiel. But Judas no longer accepted that Jesus was the chosen one, destined to rescue the Jews from their oppressors" (83). Neither suicide nor eruption nor thievery but disenchantment marks the later life of this observant Jew.

C. K. Stead elaborates on the idea of a Jewish Judas understandably (even predictably) wary about Jesus' mission in the novel *My Name Was Judas* (2006), which puts Judas at the center of a fictional autobiography. Stead does so to envision Judas in temperamental terms: here a skeptical Judas loses faith in Jesus and eventually in God. Contrary to the report of Judas's suicide in Matthew and death by spontaneous explosion in Luke, Stead's aged first-person narrator—Judas of Keraiyot—has clearly survived to tell the tale of what he experienced with his boyhood schoolmate Jesus during his discipleship and after Jesus' crucifixion, when Judas had to flee Palestine to remake and camouflage himself as the pseudonymous Idas of Sidon. A witness and survivor of Jesus' ghastly death, Stead's Judas mourns his lost friend while remaining unconvinced of Jesus' claims to a messianic identity or destiny. Like Archer and Moloney's, Stead's work can therefore be interpreted as a rejection of the reasoning first proposed by Leo the Great (if only Judas had lived longer, he would have believed).[12]

At seventy, amid accelerating rumors of the Roman siege of Jerusalem in 70 C.E., the Greek-identified Idas of Sidon recalls the early pleasures of learning with and from an exceptionally gifted young boy and then a charismatic leader whose oratory worked wonders on crowds of people longing to be convinced that the blind will see, the lame walk, the poor prosper, the dead live again. According to Idas of Sidon—a reasonable man and a reasonably reliable narrator—the poetic prophecies of Jesus could calm the mad and soothe those in pain. But Judas, the rationalist among the apostles, questions whether these acts are literal miracles. His materialist explanations need not be correct to seem plausible, partly because he is not alone in his distrust: "Belief was what [Jesus] required of us, and it was where we all, at one time or another, failed him. We did our best, some much better than others. Temperamentally skeptical, I was clearly first among the non-achievers" (133).

Doubts continue to plague Judas about Jesus' ministry. Not only do Jesus' promises of freedom and peace beyond the grave sound like "empty promises and threats that divert attention from the horror of what men do to one another in the real world" (144), but Jesus craves attention and adulation in a way that makes Judas fear for his teacher's sanity as well as his safety. Did Jesus demand or need faith because "he himself had difficulty believing the story, even as he told it, even as he acted it out" (152)? Judas's growing skepticism is what constitutes his betrayal: "My 'betrayal' was in my refusal to affirm what I couldn't believe" (171). When the peace-loving Jesus (the lamb) turns into the militant Jesus (the lion), Judas continues to worry that "our leader suffers moments of insanity" (175). Even the pacific message of hope and trust troubles Judas, who knows "that some who asked would *not* receive, that some who sought would *not* find" (184).

Judas in the Temple—anxious about Roman retaliation and about a hectic orator rousing throngs of followers—witnesses with dread the overturning of the stalls of the money changers and of the sacrificial animals, wanting "to get Jesus out of there and save him from arrest" (205). Unable to persuade Jesus to return home, the treasurer of the disciples uses the thirty coins in their purse to book an upstairs room in a Jerusalem tavern for Passover. Although he doubts Jesus' messianic claim, Judas cleaves to his childhood friend, interrupting him during prayers in Gethsemane Gardens—"what he was doing was suicide" (216)—to warn Jesus of the impending arrival of the Temple guards, but to no avail. By the end of his account, Judas does feel tormented but not guilty, since he never sold Jesus out:

> I felt anger, the anger of frustration and despair. How could he have done this to himself? How could we, his friends, have allowed it? My anger was most of all with myself, because I'd seen what was coming, but had not been strong enough and clear enough in confronting him. I'd failed to save him from himself, or (if you prefer) from the almighty sadist, maker of heaven and earth, whose son he imagined himself to be. (229)

A cross between Robertson Jeffers's and José Saramago's approach to the Passion, Stead's *My Name Was Judas* puts friendship at the very center of the story: Judas does not accept a bribe from the Temple police; he does not kiss or betray; he is one of only two disciples who remain steadfast (the other is Simon Peter). At one point in the novel, as Jesus compares himself to Jacob, Judas worries "that Jacob was a twin, and that his brother Esau, who was a greedy good-for-nothing, had sold his half of the inheritance they shared for a plate of stew." Judas therefore asks, "Who is your Esau?" Stead's plot bears out Jesus' response: "There's no Esau" (106). Later, when Judas witnesses Jesus telling Caiaphas "you will see the Son of Man, who sits at the Lord's right hand, come down through the clouds of heaven," Judas marvels at his bravado, whether or not Jesus actually believes himself to be the Son of Man, whether or not Jesus actually is the Son of Man: "My heart leapt at the courage of it. How wonderful if only it had been true! How superb if he knew it was not and said it anyway!" (220).

On the cross Jesus' final cry of abandonment calcifies Judas's skepticism into atheism: "It's how I know there's no God" (231). A loving and omniscient, omnipotent creator could not possibly countenance the suffering of the innocent. Unable to credit evangelists who claim to have seen a resurrected Jesus, Judas understands his own sightings—"I saw him in the street . . . heard his voice coming from an open window"—to be the aftereffects of grief: "Our dead are always with us. But they are not alive" (235). Throughout the novel, Stead's Judas exhibits the confusion, the divided loyalties, the serial spiritual attachments of someone who deeply sympathizes with yet distrusts both the traditional faith of his parents and the new faith of his best friend. According to Stead, Judas stands for many people who have embraced a cherished cause and a beloved companion, but who then find that external circumstances and their own internal disposition conspire to push them toward letting down, relinquishing, or disappointing an ally. Regret might be this friendly but skeptical Judas's middle name.

Even when authors of the skeptical Judas occasionally imagine him plummeting into atheism, they base his doubts about Jesus' messianic claims on justifiable respect for the Torah. To that extent, they imagine not a stereotypically Jewish Judas but a Judas who exhibits traditionally Jewish reverence for Jesus as a spiritual teacher as well as traditionally Jewish qualms about identifying Jesus as the Son of God. Because in biblical times the messiah was assumed to be the God-chosen mortal king who would be anointed to reign over Israel, Jesus' claims to be God's Son might well have seemed bizarre to his listeners. The messiahs or prophets selected by God to rule his

people, according to Stuart E. Rosenberg, were figures such as Saul
and David: "Always, and in every biblical case, the 'anointed one' is
a human, not a divine being" (34; emphasis mine). Bart D. Ehrman
reminds us that "prior to Christianity there is *not a single Jewish
tradition* that the messiah was supposed to die and be raised from
the dead" (*Lost Gospel* 159; emphasis mine). In other words, the
overwhelming majority of people living in biblical times did not suppose that the messiah would be crucified. Instead of dying and resurrecting, instead of performing miracles, the messiah was expected to
lead God's people. In 1 Corinthians 17–24, "Paul admits that when
he preached among Jews, the terrible fact that Jesus had been crucified presented a nearly insurmountable obstacle to any who heard
him; among Gentiles, his claims about an executed criminal sounded
ridiculous" (Pagels and King 13).

The very fact that Jesus kept predicting his own death might have
prompted and intensified doubts about his messianic destiny. As Julie
Galambush has succinctly explained, "a messiah who died without
establishing *something* like peace and justice was simply not the messiah. If Jesus' painful and humiliating death provided anything, it
was that he had not been the messiah" (13). Whether or not Judas
knew that the handing over would lead to Jesus' crucifixion, he—like
generations of Jews after him—adjudicates between reverence for an
inspired and inspiring teacher, on the one hand, and, on the other,
unavoidable and logical suspicion about or rejection of Jesus' claims
to divine sovereignty. Before the inevitable vilification takes hold,
his loyalties are distressingly divided. A Jewish Judas, scrupulously
following the laws of the Hebrew Bible and exhibiting the courage
of his convictions, finds himself grievously subjected to conflicting
moral codes: he must choose between betraying his community and
betraying his friend. Fearful of the new order, reluctant to break with
the old, he mistrusts the thoroughness or authenticity of a promised
revolution. In stark contrast to the radical activism of the nineteenth-
century insurrectionist, the choice of the skeptical Judas remains fervently conservative. That this skeptical Judas frequently appears at

the start of the twenty-first century suggests how much credence a Jewish approach to the Passion has begun to gain. This end point of the twelfth apostle's intricate representational history proves again that he has evoked as much admiration as rancor among thinkers passionately engaged as they grapple with Christianity's relationship with Judaism.

FEARFUL SYMMETRY

Toward the close of *My Name Was Judas,* years after the crucifixion, Stead's loyal protagonist reveals himself to another apostle, only to be labeled a devil and cursed. To this aspersion, an aged Judas responds, "It was a new theology and gave me a certain status—very much below Jesus, of course, but a significant player in the metaphysical drama. I felt honoured in a way" (241). Throughout the previous chapters, I have followed the biographer's rule of keeping my subject at the center of numerous sightings where, even when vilified, this minor character has been honored as "a significant player in the metaphysical drama."[13] But what characterizes the overall evolution of Judas's changing figurations from start to finish, and how does that progress clarify altering attitudes toward Jesus?

At the risk of softening some of the edges on the forms of Jesus and Judas, I will generalize answers to these questions by taking a clue from a sentence Stead's Jesus speaks during his ministry: "Judas is my mirror" (174).[14] Stead hints with this phrase that even when Judas does not function as an obvious double of Jesus, the twelfth apostle does nevertheless reflect his teacher. Doubling accompanies a historical sequencing of Judas's incarnations that can now be summarized. Postbiblical art clearly starts with the pariah-Judas; then it moves to showcase successively the lover, hero, and savior, with the anomalous skeptic-Judas now reemerging most prominently. In each and every age, as I have indicated, Judas exhibits the disjunctive roles of pariah, lover, hero, savior, anomaly. But in the progression of literary and pictorial history over twenty centuries, the pariah-Judas predominates in antiquity, the lover-Judas can be detected in premodern and Renaissance times, the hero emerges most emphatically in the Enlightenment, the savior in the twentieth century, and the anomaly today. On this chronological course, despite innumerable reiterations and regressions, Judas moves from disgrace to dignity while escorting a Jesus who conventionally personifies trust.

Whether trust is a feeling or a faith, it is generally attributed to Jesus and reflects his vulnerability, his acceptance of risk—because trust invariably involves the potential of a harmful and hurtful betrayal. The first question about Jesus raised by the presence of Judas in his intimate company is, how could Jesus have possibly chosen and trusted Judas as an apostle? This age-old question tends to be answered in a similar manner by authors of wildly divergent works (many of whom dispense with the devil as a credible agent). Since trust requires an interpersonal relationship that inevitably makes participants vulnerable to the possibility of untrustworthiness, quite a few storytellers assume that Jesus may have operated on what today is termed a principle of "therapeutic trust": the assumption that trust—even when placed in a potentially untrustworthy agent (a child, an addict, a convict)—might inculcate trustworthiness.[15] According to biblical scholars, "the ancient meaning of the word 'believe' has much more to do with trust and commitment"; thus the injunction "to believe in the good news" means trusting in and committing to that news (Borg and Crossan 25).

Jesus, a teacher of trust, holds out the promise of making his followers good, better than they probably are. By virtue of this supposition, which in earlier times would have been considered a leap of faith, it is possible to understand how Jesus' trust need not have depended on his belief in the trustworthiness of all his disciples. In any case, in almost every imaginative re-creation of the Passion, the intimacy accorded Judas enabled him to come physically very close to a defenseless Jesus, who was therefore an eyewitness to his own betrayal. Such is the clear impression given by many of the representations of the New Testament discussed in this book, although contradictory approaches to Judas complicate the meaning of trust's betrayal—Judas does not always betray his teacher, or always think that he does, and in some instances it is not Judas's trustworthiness but Jesus' or God's that fails. To encapsulate the meaning of the complex evolution charted in this cultural biography, to map shifting attitudes toward trust and betrayal, the next few paragraphs sketch the evolving characters of Jesus and Judas as countless artists have represented them mirroring each other from postbiblical to contemporary times.

Put simply, the pariah-Judas reflects the pariah that Jesus had to become; the lover- and heroic-Judas highlight the lover- and heroic-Jesus; the savior-Judas accompanies the savior-Jesus; the anomaly-Judas underscores the anomaly of Jesus' ministry. Sometimes evident, sometimes hidden, commonality marks Jesus and Judas in their partnership. For to many of the painters and writers considered throughout this book, both the teacher and his student look like social menaces (pariahs), devoted servants (lovers), ambitious or ambivalent sufferers (heroes), vulnerable collaborators (saviors), or doubtful itinerants (anomalies). Once again, keep in mind that each facet of Jesus and Judas draws on only a few of the specific details in the knots or cruxes of the New Testament. As Jesus changes shape, of course, Judas's moral accountability is recalibrated, as are its consequences. Their path, outlined in the next pages, substantiates the view that "Doubt is far more insidious than certainty, and distrust may become the source of its own evidence" (Gambetta 234). For when we consider the progress of Judas's career over time, we see that it provides a vehicle to express mounting anxieties about the redeemer's or God's capacity for betrayal.

An outcast Jesus contests a pariah-Judas hardwired for selfish deceit. Targeted as a blasphemer and a social hazard, an isolated and ostracized Jesus was mocked, flogged, and tortured on the cross. Without any reference to Judas, the critic Northrop Frye observes that if we think of Jesus' "significance as prophetic rather than legal, his real significance is that of being the one figure in history whom no organized human society could possibly put up with"; "The society that rejected him represented all societies: those responsible for his death were not Romans or the Jews or whoever happened to be around at the time, but the whole of mankind down to ourselves and doubtless far beyond" (132–33). Through his torment and death, an injured and insulted Jesus submits to the realization that he can take away the sins of the world only by being dehumanized to the status of an abject criminal or a sacrificed animal. Jesus absolves humanity by demonstrating through his death how thoroughly sinful the world is.

Not merely adversaries, the pariahs Jesus and Judas pose rival principles at enmity, as seen at the beginning of the tradition in Luke, at the end in Kennelly's *Book of Judas*. When Jesus represents a prophetic temporality beyond or outside of history, Judas stands for historical time. While Jesus entrusts himself to the otherworldly values of spirit, chastity, and poverty, the untrustworthy Judas pursues worldly acquisition and aggression, related to flesh, desire, and greed. Serenity and sincerity characterize a Jesus who suffers Judas's hectic mendacity. In terms of Judas's role in the Passion narrative, what applies here is the usual model of liability: Judas was responsible because he meant to harm Jesus, or his inimical being intrinsically harms Jesus, and therefore he must be condemned. Malice aforethought motivates Judas, who becomes an emblem of humanity's unregenerate capacity for corruption. The psyche burdened by guilty knowledge divides a sinful or sick creature from those he curses, the righteous and the saved inhabiting a realm elsewhere. Yet, ironically, Jesus and Judas resemble each other. Jesus suffers the fate of an outcast in all organized societies, just as Judas suffers the fate of an outcast in eternity. Jesus was as estranged from the world into which he was born as Judas is within Christendom.

In an alternative and unorthodox approach that can be glimpsed intermittently, Jesus the charismatic lover divines the mysterious possibilities of perfect concord between himself and Judas. Eminently trustworthy, the bridegroom makes good on his bountiful promises by displaying his reciprocity with Judas—or so the relationship can be construed at the beginning of the tradition, through several verses in the New Testament; during its midpoint in paintings of the twinned couple; and in passages by, about, or influenced by the Gnostics. On the night of the betrayal, Jesus prays that his followers "may *all* be one. As you, Father, are in me and I am in you, may they also be in us" (John 17:21; emphasis mine). Great blessings are assured, too, when, at the moment of Jesus' dying in Mark, the Temple curtain is rent, symbolizing that holiness now dwells not in a segregated part of the Temple but everywhere, and thus is available to all human beings. Replete with erotic and holy love, the mystical union of a Jesus who walks with Judas and talks to Judas—during or after the betrayal— proves that Jesus rewards with joy a disciple bonded with him by the intimate embrace apparent in the Rheinau Psalter.

Matthew's compassionate Jesus had proclaimed in the Beatitudes, "Blessed are you when people revile you and persecute you and utter all kinds of evil against you falsely on my account. Rejoice and be glad, for your reward is great in heaven, for so in the same way they persecuted the prophets who were before you" (5:11–12).[16] Reviled and persecuted for his allotted role in the Passion, Judas had eaten at the Last Supper or had his feet washed, making resonant Paul's testimony that God will not reject "his people whom he foreknew," for "the gifts and the calling of God are irrevocable" (Romans 11:1–2, 29). The principle of *Tout compendre, c'est tout pardoner* applies to Judas's role in the Passion: to understand everything is to forgive everything. Just as Jesus was executed as a criminal but turned out to be not only innocent but also the Son of God, so any offender might turn out to be innocent and, if not God, then nevertheless human, godlike, a son of man. For "*everyone* who calls on the name of the Lord shall be saved" (Acts 2:21; emphasis mine). We have seen that the amazing grace of Jesus can encompass Judas the wretched penitent. Why shouldn't Judas be pardoned, John Wesley and Robert Buchanan asked, if his conscience eventually prompted contrition and repentance? The psyche burdened by guilty knowledge ultimately joins the vital fullness of being that is inherent in humanity and divinity.

Yet Jesus the heroic visionary can bring into being the kingdom of God only by incurring the disappointment and death of an apostle who is also heroic. Valiant Judas was himself betrayed by misguided if laudable ambitions, and therefore he inadvertently endangered Jesus as well as himself. The mutual trust of the two comrades-in-arms fractures when they disagree over interpretations of their goal or the methods needed to attain it. Although their conflict (over means and ends) bespeaks their common commitment to the future kingdom, the partnership of Judas and Jesus suffers a defeat, for which Judas pays with his life. Here the principle of strict liability applies to Judas and does so in a tragic way: like innocent but blameworthy protagonists in tragedies, the twelfth apostle has not done intentional harm, but his actions result in injuries and thus he is held accountable.[17] Still, the psyche burdened by guilty knowledge repudiates the nervous logic of blame shifting. By shouldering responsibility for what he could not avoid doing, the heroic Judas gains in nobility unless he wavers in his faith.

Should the strand of trust in Jesus become tangled, however, the web of faith begins to fray, and miserable Judas the Obscure emerges.[18] As seen in chapter 5, Judas, inexplicably estranged from grace, signals a growing alienation of human beings from themselves, from others, and from divinity. The distrust of Judas the Obscure inaugurates what Annette Baier calls (in a different context) "the worst pathology of trust"—namely, "a life-poisoning" illness characterized by anxiety and paranoia (129). Judas himself first succumbs to painful misgivings, but Jesus also begins to be tarnished, for he has profited by way of the resurrection from the losses incurred by his handpicked apostle. A remote Jesus finds himself enmeshed in the moral ambiguity of human existence while a woeful Judas suffers the obdurate limits of grace.

When the thread of trust in God snarls or breaks during the atrocities of the twentieth century, Jesus and Judas attest to the vulnerability of the human condition. Jesus, the enlisted savior of humanity, suffers doubts about God; Judas, the enlisted savior of Jesus, suffers doubts about the Son of God. Chapter 6 demonstrated that a reluctant and conflicted messiah—whose power is limited, whose sacrifice may be inefficacious—accompanies Judas the enlisted but reluctant and conflicted savior of Jesus. Jesus—wary of the ordeal he must undergo in order to take away the sins of the world—dreads the imminent sacrifice, but encounters a Judas who carries out the imperatives of justice and does so to his own detriment. In this phase, Judas and Jesus are not enemies, lovers, or divided heroes but accomplices. Crucial to such an approach is the sentence Jesus speaks in John's Gospel, when he explains that he knew who he had chosen so that the scripture would be fulfilled (13:18).

A needy Jesus asks Judas to sacrifice himself for the good of humanity: betrayal here, paradoxically, constitutes an act of fidelity. The resemblance of Jesus and Judas in this scenario can cause innocence and guilt to change places.[19] Even if a tenuous human filament takes up slack in the frayed web of trust, the compassion of God or his Son may be qualified. Jesus or God proves to be weak or treacherous, when Judas ironically verifies his trustworthiness through the act of betrayal. We live in a world that betrays trust, post–World War II authors seem to say: God's Son or God, having become enervated or inscrutable or antagonistic in relation to humanity's well-being, must be held accountable for suffering and injustice. Cleared of all liability, the twelfth apostle ends up a venerable martyr, whereas Jesus may turn into the willful betrayer of his preeminently trusty apostle or of a malevolent God.

Finally, at the end of the tradition in *My Name Was Judas,* as at the beginning in the Gospel of Mark, the anomalous Jesus pursues his itinerant preaching with a wavering Judas who brings into focus the astonishing singularity and radical claims of Jesus' mission. Challenging normative expectations of who the messiah would be and what he would do, Jesus preaches doctrines partially at odds with the

Torah, and thus he might be either the founder of a Jewish sect or an apostate, a lapsed Jew. In an atmosphere of uncertainty, Judas and Jesus are friendly adversaries, not accomplices. The disbelief of Judas, in this account, testifies to the widespread skepticism that Jesus knew he would have to face and did in fact face in Jerusalem when he redefined the messianic role to present himself as the suffering Son of God. Should Judas's qualms about the coming of a messianic age appear plausible, even credible, the audacity of Jesus' healings and parables can be fully appreciated. Despite the tenacity with which Jesus maintains a conviction in his messianic mission, to the wary outsider it looks like an effort on Jesus' part to convince himself and his followers of what he himself at times might have quite rationally doubted.

The words of Jesus sound quixotic at best, dangerous at worst, to the skeptic who continues to witness unredeemable pain and poverty.[20] From this vantage, Judas does not consciously seek to betray or hurt his daring teacher, but instead discovers or feels or fears that it is necessary to let Jesus down. A trusted intimate, Judas is given discretionary powers to best advance Jesus' welfare. In his own way, by his own lights, Judas judges the situation in a manner that does not accord with the assessment of his admirable friend. In terms of Judas's role in the Passion narrative, the principle of proximate but not morally responsible cause applies here: perhaps the twelfth apostle was guilty of committing an accidental injury, but he did not necessarily intend or fully understand the consequences of his actions. Whether right or wrong about persistent doubts, the psyche burdened by hurtful knowledge suffers in a joyless state of consciousness, apprehending its own conflicted course of conduct but seeing no way out. In this respect, anomaly-Judas resembles the Jesus with whom he is conjoined, who frequently expresses fearful hesitation about the mission he must undertake.

A clear index of escalating uncertainty about the goodness and power of God and God's Son, this historical trajectory also evinces the growing universality of Judas as writers increasingly inhabit his

(imagined) subjectivity to comprehend the human condition. Contradictory portraits abound. As he progresses from disgrace to dignity,
Judas sometimes appears to be a guilt-ridden victimizer, sometimes a
blameless victim; sometimes a lover, sometimes a hater; sometimes a
radical, sometimes a conservative; sometimes a keen doubter, sometimes a fervent believer. Answers to the question "Why does Judas
betray?" supply as many motives as there are avatars: the pariah's
malice or the lover's adoration, the hero's ambition or the savior's
loyalty or the anomaly's incredulity. Judas's trajectory nevertheless
repeatedly returns to a doubling with Jesus in order to deal with the
evil of injury. Why in a narrative about treachery do the antithetical
Jesus and Judas recurrently reflect each other? What does the pairing
of the two tell us about evil or injury?[21]

Mirroring allows one to glimpse the commonalities shared by the
two agonists and thereby disrupts the dichotomy of trust (Jesus) versus betrayal (Judas), as does the fact that guilt and innocence change
places within the historical trajectory. The contrast between Jesus
and Judas in the Passion depends on a subversive similarity resistant
to erasure, a fearful symmetry eminently suitable to a narrative that
generally imagines the good of salvation arising from the evil of crucifixion. Countless elaborations of the Passion testify to the urgency
of the need to blame someone, anyone, for the crucifixion of Jesus or
for humanity's unredeemed state—mortality, suffering, injustice—to
find a culprit and excoriate him, human or divine. But the one on
the "most wanted" list is the one "wanted most."[22] At every stage
of the historical process that moves Judas from disgrace to dignity,
doubling proves how unfeasible it is to locate an uncontested target
of blame. All of the most challenging re-creations of Jesus and Judas
point in this direction: toward humanity's need to fix responsibility for crucifixion or for mortality, suffering, and injustice, and the
impossibility of doing so. Doubling thus works to break the cycle of
scapegoating.[23]

For permutations of the doubling within the historical trajectory illuminate the contextual ambiguity and interconnectedness of

Jesus and Judas, the mutability of ethical judgments about trust's betrayal. To the extent that the doubling surfaces emphatically, it dramatizes the division human beings feel as they are simultaneously pulled toward trust and toward the betrayal of trust or distrust, the reciprocity or interdependency of the graced and the disgraced, illustrating how each may work for or with the other, and therefore how dependent good is on evil, evil on good. Over the historical route recorded in this volume, attention to the similarities shared by Jesus and Judas, rather than their antipathy, is supplemented by creative artists' focus on the differences within each of them, as both Jesus and Judas increasingly evince ambivalent, conflicted interiorities. Mirroring between Jesus and Judas, like subjective differences within each of them, counteracts or subverts outright vilification of the twelfth apostle. It recurs not only in painting and literature but also ceremonially: the Judas of the Paschal is the seventh or middle candlestick in churches, which rose nearly to the roof and on which was placed at Eastertide the wax paschal candle. Symmetry explains, too, why the slang oath or exclamation of surprise "Judas Priest" is a euphemism for Jesus Christ. Perhaps Judas has gone ignored because scholars have been smitten with a bad case of catoptricophobia, a fear of mirrors (that explains superstitions about broken mirrors and that sometimes has me in its grip).[24]

Curiously, Judas can be fully exonerated only by configurations that blame God or the Son of God for humanity's unredeemed state. Treachery simply attaches to another agent. Prominent in the twentieth century, this narrative has been recently replaced by a version without a single target of blame (the one centering on anomalous characters), a formulation that tends to abide in unresolved perplexities (without a confirmed resurrection). Generally, though, it seems that someone must be accountable: if not Judas, then Jesus; if not Jesus, then God. Yet doubling even in the most blame-targeting of these scenarios (the pariah plot) frustrates simple finger-pointing. Historically, as Judas progresses from disgrace to dignity, Jesus does not follow the opposite track; he does not devolve into disgrace. Instead and steadily, Jesus loses potency. Jesus and the trust he embodies become increasingly frayed, vulnerable—progressively more implicated in alien and alienating forces that hem him in and hamper the salvation he seeks to bring about.

Rather than thinking sequentially about the trajectory of Judas's evolution (as I have just done), the thinkers and artists discussed in these pages brought various logics to bear on the betrayal. A follower who betrays his leader offers a textbook case for exploring the criteria needed to evaluate an action as good or evil. Often the reasoning of novelists, painters, dramatists, poets, and theologians draws on or replicates that of secular specialists in moral philosophy, whose three divergent approaches to ethics clarify why Judas continues to leave us with a conundrum. If we broach the puzzle of Judas through the criteria established by ethicists, conflicting judgments emerge with regard to his conviction or vindication: evaluations will differ, depending (in large part) on whether they are based on consequence, on principle, or on character.[25]

First, consider the claims of those who focus on consequence, defining right action in terms of the good of a beneficial outcome. One could argue that the ancient Gospel of Judas, as well as some modern works in harmony with Gnostic approaches to the Passion, present the idea that Judas helped Jesus achieve his godhood and then take the assumption of consequentialism to its logical conclusion: they leap over the horror of the crucifixion Judas triggered to ascribe to him its ultimate consequence, the good of redemption. Valuing the greatest good for the greatest number of people, those concerned with ultimate consequences would see Judas's actions as virtuous, whether or not he meant them to be. Betrayal was necessary to bring about the salvation of humanity through Jesus' death and resurrection. "The necessary one, without which not," in Howard Nemerov's phrase, enacts a *felix culpa* or "fortunate fall," for without Judas's betrayal there would be no promise of eternal life.

But this biography has focused on conduct, as do many moral philosophers. Unlike those who stress consequences, ethicists who emphasize the maxims and rules regulating right conduct would probably judge Judas's behavior to be impermissible, his decisions unethical. Breaking a promise or trust: with regard to special obligations (having taken on the role of an apostle pledged in loyalty to his teacher), didn't Judas shirk his duties to or breach his contract with Jesus and thereby fail to pay an owed debt of gratitude? The fidelity due a leader or teacher makes Judas's negotiations with Jesus' adversaries traitorous. Lying: didn't Judas violate Jesus' rights and injure him by evading or overtly misspeaking the truth (at the Last Supper)? Duties to oneself: in taking his life, didn't Judas violate his obligations to existence? If everyone were to act in the manner of Judas—Kant's categorical imperative suggests that personal actions should be based on maxims that could become universal laws—where would we be?

When one turns away from principles to matters related to character, such factors as knowledge, intentionality, personality traits, and temperament may mitigate judgments of the moral agent.[26] Within this framework, the strongest vindication of Judas endows him with benevolence, justice seeking, or courage in his dedication to a principle outside himself. Thinking first of others, Judas acted as he did because he was devoted to a cause or an idea. In various reinventions of the biblical narrative, integrity, contrition, love, and bravery have also been attributed to Judas's decision to commit suicide. A modified defense of Judas's moral character is offered by artists who imagine him to have based his actions on false beliefs or miscalculations. Less of a vindication but still an exoneration of sorts, a third approach points to his unruly temperament, disposition, or personality: rash or confused, captivated or depressed, Judas could not have done otherwise, for he was propelled by cosmic or psychological forces over which (he felt) he had no control. *Akrasia*—meaning a lack of command over oneself or weakness of will—might be said to describe a Judas who betrays despite his own best interests.[27]

Various philosophical approaches provide innumerable views of Judas as an admonitory figure who proves how difficult it is to generalize about betrayal. If one factors in Nietzsche's scathing attack on Judeo-Christianity as a religion of ressentiment—the morality and exaltation of the weak projecting their hostility onto the strong—anger at Judas takes on a somewhat different cast. The relish in Judas's punishment and suffering displayed (at least at times) by interpreters of the Passion narrative counterpoints Jesus' message of compassion with barely concealed Christian vengeance against a powerful dissident. Freud's explanations of masochism and sadism would provide yet another analysis of the appeal of suffering (exemplified by Jesus) and of causing suffering (in Judas). These aspects of the death drive propel humanity toward nonexistence, the inorganic past from which all organisms grow, lifelessness, nonbeing, *thanatos*.[28] On the historical map of Judas's progress with Jesus that I have traced in this volume, Nietzschean and Freudean approaches typify two recurrent phenomena: de-vilification and doubling.

Over time, aesthetic responses to Judas's trajectory tend to extenuate or reverse the more severe judgments of antiquity and the premodern period. By means of the doubling between Jesus and Judas, many artists clarify the evolution of Christians' attitudes toward Judaism, at least in the rarefied worlds of the arts and the humanities, from strenuous efforts to disown Christianity's Jewish origins to equally strenuous efforts to acknowledge or champion Judaism as well as Christianity's profound historical, textual, and theological attachments to Judaism. To that extent, Judas's growing dignity attests to the emergent force of interfaith consciousness and coalitions. Curiously, though, something can get lost in Judas's absolution. Notwithstanding the anger of Jewish scholars at anti-Semitic deployments of Judas as well as the discomfort of Christian commentators, the four Gospel accounts—contradictory though they are—create in the twelfth apostle a figure of crucial and, I will finally argue, abiding ethical and psychological consequence.

"SURELY, NOT I?"

Despite all the disagreements surrounding the sundry interpretations of Judas, one constant can help us steer toward what these diverse reconfigurations share. Narrative logic required someone to hand Jesus over to his enemies in the Temple. That someone could have been an undercover Temple official, of course, a figure like Caiaphas. Instead, *the betrayer comes from within,* and so he might have been, say, Peter. But these two candidates, with whom Judas is often aligned and who could have been his stand-ins, have been fixed respectively in the Temple and in the apostle camps, as the story comes down to us. Should Caiaphas and Peter penetrate into each other's realms, they would immediately turn into a figure like Judas, a passer or poser. By virtue of handing Jesus over *from the apostles to the Temple,* the agent of betrayal would necessarily be linked to both Jesus' followers and their opponents, as Judas is. Judas thus functions to an extent as a subordinate agent of the plot, as many commentators have duly noted. Why, then, is this side effect so frequently reinvented in subsequent ages?

One nice analogy for Judas's function is offered by the architectural spandrel.[29] The term *spandrel,* which derives from a diminutive of the span or distance between the outstretched thumb and last finger, refers to structures formed inadvertently because of the need to connect two arches or the curve of an arch and a rectilinear molding. The spandrel arises as a secondary consequence of other (primary) architectural decisions, but of course it can then be ornamented or utilized as an important space in and of itself. Think of the Temple authorities and the apostles as two arches for which Judas provides the linkage. Imagining Judas as a spandrel helps us appreciate the bond he furnishes between Jewish followers of Jesus and Jews faithful to the Temple. Although in and of itself the spandrel has no purpose—it developed only to support the arches—*after* its creation it often boasts ornate sculptural and mosaic designs or offers storage.

The temporal distinction suits Judas's case. We know so little about him in the earliest Gospel of Mark because he is simply a needed narrative device and of secondary consequence in Jesus' Passion. Yet his shady character morphs over time into a multifaceted mosaic of infinite adaptations.

Still, why must there be a betrayer from within who hands Jesus over from the apostles to the Temple? Wouldn't it be easier to target the imperialist Romans by having Jesus arrested during a crackdown by the colonizers? Some functionary in Pilate's imperial hierarchy might have been a logical contender. However, precisely because the foundations of Jesus' being and faith were Jewish, early Christians had to establish their identity by distancing themselves from their Jewish origins.[30] The foreign occupier, already marked as an alien, does not require the same rigorous and explicit rejection as the Temple, and therefore pagan Rome recedes in importance. A Jew was needed to hand Jesus over not to the Romans but to the Temple. And of course only a Jew could provide the resonant doubling with Jesus we have traced throughout these pages, a doubling that stages Christianity's efforts to separate from and yet remain attached to its Jewish roots. For centuries, we have seen, Judas did embody the Jews.

Throughout most of history, Judas functions as the usual suspect for every imaginable wrong, providing a template of the bad character ascribed to Jewish people who are generally assumed or imagined to be male. In place of the convoluted trajectory of doubling mapped earlier in this chapter, another simpler story could be told and often was. In this easier tale, which also must repress many elements in the cruxes of the Gospels, human beings locate the cause of the problem, the reason why life is not as it should be, and exterminate the brute so that all manner of things will be well. Both at the beginning of Judas's postbiblical life and toward the end of it, as well as intermittently in between, writers and painters have followed early church fathers in casting the twelfth apostle in the role of the scapegoat: a symbol to promote enmity. Besides being accused of the nefarious acts of theft and lying and murder, Judas often incarnates the deadly or mortal sins that destroy the soul. To these, he adds despair and hypocrisy as well as schadenfreude: a twisted joy in observing the pain of others.

In the anti-Semitic imagination, Jews are men disposed to be treacherous, mercenary, self-destructive, and contaminating. But like Judas, Jews have also been imagined as consequentially instrumental, well-intentioned but ensnared in false belief systems, perversely weak willed, perversely strong willed, and simply sadistic. Unhappily, to my mind, nefarious characterizations of Judas tend to be accompanied by an emphasis on his Jewishness. Anomaly-, lover-, heroic-, or savior-Judas often surfaces as a Palestinian or Israeli oddity, while pariah-Judas frequently embodies Judaism. Why, in the early years of the church's establishment, did Judas alone of all the apostles become identified as Jewish? The simplest explanation relates to the mechanisms of projection and separation anxiety: Christian Jews or Jewish Christians, inevitably unfaithful to their origins and thus deserters or renegades from the Jewish traditions into which they or their families had been born, alleviated their sense of guilt by projecting betrayal onto a Jewish Judas; Gentile converts could differentiate their adopted Christianity by disavowing its hyphenated intimacy with a now treacherous Judas-Judaism. Judas supplied a crucial figural means by which a faith increasingly dominated by Gentiles managed to disclaim or forget its Jewish origins.

Just as an offspring develops into maturity by individuating from a parent, Christianity differentiated itself by first rejecting and later admitting and then sometimes cherishing its Jewish roots.[31] Patriarchal at its core, Judaism nevertheless often provoked the intensely ambivalent reactions generally accorded a mother, the figure Jamaica Kincaid once called "Mrs. Judas" (130).[32] In early art, a repudiated Judaism or the Temple in Jerusalem was personified by means of the female figure *Synagoga:* blind or losing her crown, wearing a yellow dress, tempted by Satan, with reddish hair, and accompanied by Eve or contrasted with Mary (Pinson 150, 162). Counterbalanced against *Ecclesia* (a church also often figured as womanly), *Synagoga* looks like a female Judas. Insofar as Judas reflects the ways in which

Christians have imagined Jews and the Temple as the counterpart, companion, or alternative to Jesus and the church, the twelfth apostle illuminates the feminization of (male) Jewry.[33]

Whereas Jesus figures the new Adam, Judas, who sometimes eats before he entices others into temptation and is often accompanied by reptilian familiars, functions as a male analogue of Eve.[34] Judas has been stamped with the infamy of Cain, Esau, Judah (the brother of Joseph), Ahithophel (the suicide disloyal to King David), Herod Agrippa (eaten by worms), and Job (inexplicably afflicted by God), but especially Eve, who brought sin, mortality, pain, shame, and incessant labor into the world.[35] The supposed weaknesses of Eve—"her curiosity, vanity, insecurity, gullibility, greed, and lack of moral strength and reasoning skill"—all apply to Judas, as do "her supposed greater powers of imagination, sensuality, and conspiracy" (J. Phillips 62). Especially during premodern times, when Jews along with heretics, female prostitutes, and lepers were identified as contagious pollutants, Judas with his bloody emissions and sinful carnality recalls the physicality of Eve's descendants. Oral gratification characterizes Judas's kissing, informing, and devouring, as it does Eve's eating. Not an enemy but a cherished intimate and trusted confidant, Judas resembles Eve in violating a trust, making the beloved vulnerable and specifically vulnerable to death. Like Eve's, Judas's domination by Satan endows him with a power that cannot easily be withstood. Like Eve, Judas—delivering Jesus or embracing him—has been contrasted with Mary.

Yet Eve suffers alongside and with Adam, whereas Judas does not share in Christ's martyrdom (in most accounts). In addition, many of us may suspect that we might be tempted by a luscious fruit in the garden or by a desire for wisdom, but few of us feel that we would set out to ensnare a devoted friend or revered teacher. Some of us experience the pain of childbearing, but fewer of us (I hope) spontaneously explode or undergo demonic possession. Innumerable creative writers have suggested that Eve has recourse to the excuse that Adam—given his primacy in one account of creation—must take ultimate responsibility for the fall and in any case should not have heeded her advice.[36] And of course Judas, except in Monty Python's zany world, is always a man. So what does this Eve genealogy signify for a male character?

A masculine apostle inflicted with Eve's fallen nature proves, as she does too, that there is no disgust without desire, no desire without disgust.[37] But disgust could be more easily emphasized with respect to Eve because of her femininity: she was, after all, the Other, since the default position for human was male. Eve's female body sufficiently emblematized an otherness that in Judas—not only a man but also a disciple—had to be reinforced through the punitive spiritual and physical maladies he was made to suffer and exemplify. As greater crimes and punishments accrue, disgust is divorced from desire in a figure meant to be repudiated. Likened to a stillbirth or abortion in some depictions, the twelfth apostle has been diagnosed with blindness, bloody emissions, bulimia, a cloven palate, colic, cretinism, dysentery, elephantiasis, erectile dysfunction, leprosy, Lesch-Nyhan syndrome (compulsive self-injury), measles, obesity, putrefying flesh, rabies, restless leg syndrome, schizophrenia, spirit possession, spontaneous intestinal eruptions, and suicidal impulses (to follow the example of Saramago's deity by listing the maladies alphabetically). While such pathologies often accompany Judas's most villainous manifestations, all his incarnations (taken together) reflect a multiple personality disorder related directly to the knots and cruxes of the Gospels (taken together).

A male Eve, Judas—rejecting or accepting, promoting or curtailing Jesus' potency—inhabits a decidedly queer place in the Western imaginary. To the extent that Judas stands for the poser or passer—a person who is not what he seems to be—he reflects anxieties about all sorts of banned or ostracized groups, not just Jews. An apostle in an all-male circle, associated with anality and with the disclosure of secrets, Judas retains his masculinity, but he is not always manly—because of his resemblance to Eve and also because of his removal

from the paternal order. Neither an inheritor nor a biological progenitor (in most retellings), he locates his most important relationship in and with his sparring partner, Jesus. Sometimes the glamour
Judas displays appears to spring from the illicit same-sex desires that
he embodies, or his sinister reputation appears to derive from the
fear that such desires inspire.[38] At other times and in diverse contexts,
though, Judas represents a range of quite various and variously stigmatized populations—criminals, heretics, foreigners, Africans, dis-
sidents, the disabled, the suicidal, the insane, the incurably ill, the
agnostic. Members of these groups, too, have been faulted for posing
or passing as (alien) insiders. Potentially convertible, all such outcasts
might be thought to be using camouflaging techniques to infiltrate,
hide out, assimilate, and thereby turn a treacherous trick; or maybe, it
is assumed, they believe that they have experienced a genuine conversion until a relapse disproves it.

At sundry points in his imagined history, then, Judas reflects
ambivalence about those who cannot be assimilated or integrated
into normative categories. He returns again and again because, as
innumerable practitioners of psychoanalysis have interminably
informed us, the repressed always returns. In pernicious representations of people considered anathema, Judas signifies the duplicity
of a turncoat, the faltering irresolution of a snitch. When viewed up
close and personal, his hedged or divided loyalties relate to conflicted,
blurred, or hybrid identifications: a mixture or *Mischling,* he returns
another repressed—namely, that hyphenated composite called Judeo-
Christianity, a dual heritage for one of the largest and one of the
smallest world populations. In contemporary times, he stands for
groups enthralled by belief systems to which they cannot fully commit, in itself not a minuscule percentage of living people. At moments
in his trajectory he becomes a demon, a debased spiritual force for
evil, but at other moments a daimon, an elevated spiritual force for
good. Each one of these propositions could be modified and applied
to various societies' attitudes toward the outcast constituencies Judas

represents—homosexuals, for instance, or the mentally ill—thought at various times to be duplicitous, divided, hybrid, vacillating, satanic or saintly.

From this discouragingly familiar perspective, Judas induces the suspicious second-person singular: the disavowed "you," not the "me." Here I am advancing a somewhat different point than the one made by George Steiner about the Passion. Confronting the "radiant imperatives" of Jesus' commandments "of total altruism, of universal love and compassion, of readiness for transcendence," Steiner has explained, we encounter our own weakness for an "*imitatio* [that] proves too arduous" and "turn in hatred and self-hatred on those whom we are unable to emulate, whose exigencies leave us naked" (*No Passion Spent* 398). At least historically speaking, most people in Western civilization have turned not against the figure of perfection but instead against the figure of *im*perfection and thus against one who represents all-too-human shortcomings that bar such emulation.

Detested Judas—the disavowed "you"—reflects the perspective of a history overwhelmingly composed by those working at distinguishing themselves from what is held to be abhorrent or shameful. But the greatest artists have understood that such a personage—whether Jewish or homosexual, African or heretical, disabled or insane— cannot be sufficiently addressed through the second-person singular. For the recurrent doubling I have traced intimates that such a "you" could have been or might be or may become or perhaps is "me." More importantly, no matter how often Judas took on stereotypically Semitic or African or insane features, thinkers true to the foundational texts had to number him among the twelve; they had to admit that the betrayal of Jesus to those outside his following came from *someone within*.

Transnational and multilingual, the preeminently imperfect disciple often roots himself in the resistant power of corruption or the persistence of anguish, regardless of the various geographical routes he navigates. That C. K. Stead is a renowned New Zealand author, while Knut Ødegård is Norwegian and Nino Ricci Canadian, underscores the cosmopolitan traveling that Judas has undertaken in these pages. Born in the Middle East, Judas has appeared in Italian and English legends and plays, Australian and German visual art, Greek and Portuguese and French fiction, and Irish as well as North and South American folk art and poetry. He emerges in an aesthetic tradition dominated not exclusively but primarily by male, Christian artists.[39] The most innovative painters, poets, and novelists in this aesthetic history lived in Catholic countries notable for their clerical, religion-drenched cultures. Imaginatively engaged with the Gospels, these artists have enlarged on one or another detail about Judas recounted by Mark, Matthew, Luke, or John, while disregarding various contradictory claims in the Gospels.[40] Because betrayal remains all too relevant an ethical quandary, because Judas resembles a spandrel—standing in the gap between us and them, friend and enemy, insider and outsider—we can imagine Judas as the lost apostle recurrently found in translation: lost, as in lost to salvation; lost, as in debarred from discipleship; lost, as in representing the lapsed and forlorn; but found again in virtually every language community of every historical moment. To the Gnostics, he was the thirteenth apostle and, given his replacement by Matthias in Acts, he functions as the thirteenth disciple after the crucifixion in the New Testament as well: an unlucky number that registers the appeal of a figure perpetually lost and found.

The sumptuous destitution of Judas's configurations underscores the Hebrew etymology of his name. Ironically, in light of widespread assumptions about his nature, the name Judah in Hebrew means "he who is praised."[41] Precisely because of his troublesome role, Judas has to be praised as an indispensable creature. For he has continually—since biblical times—prompted the distressing suspicion: "Surely, not I?" (Mark 14:19) or "Is it I, Lord?" (Matthew 26:22). Not the disavowed "you," but the fearful "I?" or the "I" one desperately wants to deny is what Mark and Matthew record. Whether spoken by the eleven or by the twelfth, whether meant as a protestation or a cover-up, the query expresses anxiety: a burdensome intimation returns its speaker to the humiliation of admitting an abiding propensity for betrayals, errors, lapses, aberrant desires, and instincts not exteriorized in others but located instead within the compromised self.[42]

Struggling to disclaim guilt, Judas Iscariot resembles Judah in Genesis (who sold his brother Joseph into slavery for twenty pieces of silver) but also diverges from this predecessor. For long after the selling of Joseph, when Judah in Genesis had to convince his father to entrust him with another beloved son, he vowed to be "accountable" for Benjamin: "If I do not bring him back to you and set him before you, then let me bear the blame forever" (Genesis 43:9). Judah in Genesis eventually receives a pardon precisely because conscience does not make a coward of him: he offers to make the supreme sacrifice; he accepts full responsibility for putting his brother in jeopardy. Unlike Judah in the Hebrew Bible, Judas Iscariot in the New Testament bears blame precisely because all-too-human frailty causes him to equivocate about his trustworthiness. The prevaricating or self-deluding query "Surely, not I?" or "Is it I, Lord?" expresses apprehension about one's own unreliability and therefore about becoming burdensome or dangerous to oneself, to those entrusted into one's care, and thus meriting rejection. The gravity of Judas's case therefore grounds Jesus' grace. It conveys disquietude about humanity's capacity for faltering and sinning. To the extent that the twelfth apostle embodies all those deprived of honor, he generates a history clarifying not merely the faltering or sinning of others but also feelings about one's own faltering or sinning, which may be experienced internally as a profoundly nauseating sense of defilement and pain.[43]

A symptom of disgust or self-disgust, nausea affixes to Judas and nausea explains why he so often succumbs to the eating disorder called pica, the craving to eat nonnutritive substances. Compulsively consuming the inedible, the twelfth apostle swallows or gags on or vomits coins, insects, and birds, just as he and the people he represents are said to engage in hematophagy (ingestion of blood), urophagia (consumption of urine), and cannibalism. What should not go in must come out—sometimes orally, sometimes anally—through a regurgitation or bursting that replicates his recurrent demotion from discipleship: he who should not have been included must be expelled.

Although biblical accounts of Judas's possession by the devil may appear folkloric (and were translated into alternative terms by later artists), they perfectly capture a psyche that feels foully and internally pervaded by forces that need to be purged. In *The Dark Night* (composed in 1584–85), St. John of the Cross described the afflicted soul, which feels "as though *an enemy is within* it who . . . will awaken and cause trouble" (chap. 7, section 6; emphasis mine). Judas resembles individuals troubled by the frightful feeling "that they truly bear *within themselves* every reason for being rejected and abhorred by God" (chap. 7, sec. 7; emphasis mine). Sickened by what he has ingested and in turn abhorrent to many of his chroniclers, a queasy Judas bears all the mental and physical ills to which flesh is heir because—standing at the slash between us/them, friend/enemy, insider/outsider—he takes in what ought not to be internalized: ideas, feelings, desires, identifications, compulsions deemed pernicious or appalling. Judas exemplifies the condition of wretchedness; our understanding of him clarifies not only feelings about our own faltering or sinning but also the ethical quandary of injustice and the psychological condition of despair.

Judas's representational history plays a key role in the history of ethics because he embodies precisely "the sense of human misery" that Simone Weil considered "a precondition of justice and love" (*Iliad* 34). A Jewish thinker who prayed to Jesus Christ but remained outside the church, Weil used terms applicable to what Judas's trajectory conveys: "He who does not realize to what extent shifting fortune and necessity hold in subjection every human spirit, cannot regard as fellow-creatures nor love as he loves himself those whom chance separated from him by an abyss" (*Iliad* 34–35). More recently, in a study unrelated to biblical matters, Eve Kosofsky Sedgwick illuminated the psychological perplexities pertinent to Judas's sense of himself as a misfit isolated from all others by shifting chance or neces-

sity. According to Sedgwick, the "threshold" of "the depressive position" is the "very difficult understanding that good and bad tend
to be inseparable at every level." One feels "depressive realization,"
then, "in the forms of remorse, shame, the buzzing confusion that
makes thought impossible, depression itself, mourning for the lost
ideal, and—often most relevant—a paralyzing apprehension of the
inexorable laws of unintended consequences" (637). An emissary of
depression, Judas intimates that the inseparability of good and bad
breeds mournful trepidation about the harms our acts and those of
our closest associates can and do cause.

No matter how variously configured, the repressed that returns
through Judas is a sickening acknowledgment of one's own capacity for treachery or of one's own vulnerability to unintended consequences. Nor does such self-knowledge guarantee liberation from
harm doing. With a title that captures a personage often profiled as
two-faced, Anne Sexton's poem "The Legend of the One-Eyed Man"
crystallizes this point in a couplet: "The story of his life / is the story
of mine."[44] The betrayer within is necessary because in this narrative
the betrayer always resides within. With regard to Judas, the long
history of art concurs with Mark and Matthew: the pronouns the
Passion narrative demands are *I* and *me, we* and *us.* We betrayed
Jesus; we betray ourselves. This is the genius of making the betrayer
a disciple. Jesus was hurt by the very people he came to redeem. In
Acts, even the apostle often viewed as an anti-Judas, Peter, asserts of
Judas, "he was numbered among *us* and was allotted his share in this
ministry" (1:17; emphasis mine).

No matter how isolated Judas may be in paintings of the Last Supper, no matter how shamefully hunchbacked or cringing or twisted,
the twelfth apostle nevertheless participates as an invited, if not
cherished, guest in Jesus' company: a stranger but also a neighbor,
an indigenous foreigner. A friend who becomes a foe, Judas stands
between amity and enmity to signify how difficult it is to take to
heart Jesus' injunction to "Love your enemies and pray for those

who persecute you" (Matthew 5:44), to "Love your enemies, do good to those who hate you, bless those who curse you, pray for those who abuse you" (Luke 6:27–28). Is it a coincidence that this native informer is often situated closest to us, the viewers, or do such painters as Crespi and Ratgeb, the Master of the Housebook and the ancient Ottonian artist, Rubens and Holbein intuit Saramago's insight about Judas—that "he will always be one of us, we may not know what to do with him, but he will go on being one of us" (372)? Judas and his role in the Passion have to be praised for his uncanny share in the ministry, reminding Gospels interpreters (whatever their religious affiliation) about our continual inability to fathom the principles governing human nature, our own and that of others. As was true of the doubling, here again we see the passer or poser reminding us normal, genuine, authentic types that, alas, we might just be the very one we guard ourselves against becoming.

In addition, the twelfth apostle does not easily fit the manifold purposes that innumerable thinkers have attributed to God in relation to the creation, and thus he stymies facile speculations about the purposefulness of the world we inhabit. For this reason, the philosopher of religion Donald M. MacKinnon once argued,

> It is sheer nonsense to speak of the Christian religion as offering a solution to the problem of evil. There is no solution offered in the gospels of the riddle of Iscariot through whose agency the Son of man goes his appointed way. The problem is stated; it is left unresolved, and we are presented with the likeness of the one who bore its ultimate burden, and bore it to the end, refusing the trick of bloodless victory to which the scoffers, who invited him to descend from his cross, were surely inviting him. (92–93)

According to MacKinnon, "What the gospels present to us" is not a "solution" but rather "the tale of an endurance": "Christianity takes the history of Jesus and urges the believer to find, in the endurance of the ultimate contradictions of human existence that belongs to its very substance, the assurance that in the worst that can befall his creatures, the creative Word keeps company with those whom he has called his own" (93).

I would add only that Christianity's refusal to offer a solution to the riddle of Judas—"the problem is stated; it is left unresolved"—makes especially resonant an apostle who also bore the "ultimate burden" of evil "and bore it to the end."[45] Judas endured "the worst that can befall" God's creatures and did so generally *without* "the creative Word" keeping him company. In the Passion narrative, one and only one apostle suffered, like Jesus, a death that brings about salvation—in Judas's case, a death with the power of quickening the understanding of those grappling with exclusion or abandonment. "Is not Judas also, in his own place and after his own fashion, *the* outstanding apostle?" Karl Barth asked, thereby providing evidence that his own scrupulous attention to the Gospels could offset the anti-Semitic uses to which he often put them: "Is he not the holy one among them—'holy' in the old meaning of the term, the one who is marked, branded, banned, the one who is burdened with the divine curse and thrust out, the one who is thus brought into remarkably close proximity to Jesus Himself?" (*Doctrine* 479). As always with Judas a paradox surfaces: by failing to solve the problem of evil posed by Judas, Christianity succeeds in addressing it but also in admitting its insoluble potency. An unresolved conundrum will remain current and provocative, will undoubtedly continue to call forth responses. For the believer, paradoxes transcend reason without dislodging faith, since they present "fumbling cognitive ways of pointing toward spiritual truths that can never be adequately pictured" (Madden and Hare 66).[46]

Like the other disciples and like numerous people in ancient Palestine, Judas at the start of his story appears to have dedicated himself to the coming of a messiah who would bring about the end of human history, the beginning of the final glory foreseen by Isaiah:

For out of Zion shall go forth instruction,
    and the word of the Lord from Jerusalem.
He shall judge between the nations,
    and shall arbitrate for many peoples;
they shall beat their swords into plowshares,
    and their spears into pruning hooks;
nation shall not lift up sword against nation,
    neither shall they learn war any more. (2:3–4)

The haughtiness of people shall be humbled,
    and the pride of everyone shall be brought low;
    and the Lord alone will be exalted on that day.
The idols shall utterly pass away.
Enter the caves of the rocks
    and the holes of the ground,
from the terror of the Lord,
    and from the glory of his majesty,
    when he rises to terrify the earth. (2:17–19)

Jesus himself in various prophecies, like Paul later, seemed to believe that the messiah would quickly usher in the messianic age of peace and justice, when all crass values and crude arrogations of power would be shattered.[47] But at one point in his life Judas, who had shared this passionate hope, doubted that such a time was at hand. Whether or not one sustains faith in the possibility of one's own personal redemption, Judas stands for the stubborn fact that the world as we know it remains unredeemed, though not necessarily unredeemable. Writing of Catholics and Protestants in *Sinai and Calvary,* John T. Pawlikowski explains, "We are still awaiting the Messianic Age along with the Jews" (124). Toward the end of the book, he quotes Rabbi Irving Greenberg, asking Protestant, Catholic, and Jewish believers to "wait until the Messiah comes. Then we can ask him if this is his first coming or his second" (228).

Once a Jew for Jesus, Judas became disenchanted, perhaps anxious about the fragility of the colonized Jewish land, perhaps eager or wary about Jesus' ability to inaugurate an earthly or a spiritual kingdom, perhaps enamored or dejected, perhaps inexorably but inexplicably resistant to grace, perhaps enraptured once again by the words of the Hebrew Bible and the authority of the Temple. Or, according to a less influential perspective, Judas promoted Jesus' project at great cost to himself, but in this case, too, he suffered unjustly and therefore registers a profound failure. More than any other figure in the Passion, and because of his fallibility, Judas epitomizes the human difficulty of following Jesus' injunction to "be perfect, as your heavenly Father is perfect" (Matthew 5:48).

The visual and literary artists discussed throughout these pages have produced a kaleidoscope of perspectives by isolating various moments in Judas's life: less frequently his call to discipleship and ministry for and with Jesus; more often his dealings with the Temple authorities, his interactions at the Last Supper, the kiss in the garden, remorse, the return of the silver or buying of a field, and finally death. Taken together, the designs of this series of tableaux encapsulate the course of Western culture in a manner that reflects ourselves stripped of ideals, beholding what everyone fears to be the internal type of all that is hateful, hurtful, or harmful; a self one distressingly might have been or could yet become or fears oneself to be; a soul inhabiting a plot inimical to its well-being. Judas's story addresses injury: he injured and was injured; in an attempt to punish Judas, others have been injured.[48] Not only the damages the twelfth disciple inflicted but also the grievous harms wreaked on innocent people by castigating his evil—these multiplying wrongs intimate that Judas is us. A seeming exception who proves to be the rule, Judas haunts Western culture because he stands for mendacity or vacillation, confusion or qualms not externalized in others but instead dwelling within each and every human psyche. Judas is our mirror.

Judas's bigamous attachments to Jesus and the Temple register a fierce desire to see haughtiness humbled, pride brought low, and the idols pass away, yet also a sorry suspicion that such a day is far hence. The ministry of Judas, like that of the eleven, underscores an enduring longing among many for a time when "neither shall they learn war any more." But his pictorial reincarnations and textual resurrections prompt a woeful mistrust of such a promised end.

NOTES

PREFACE

1. Wilde used the maxim in "The Butterfly's Boswell" (97) and with variations in "The True Function and Value of Criticism" as well as "The Critic as Artist."

2. See Parke's extended discussion of the conflation of biography with autobiography.

INTRODUCTION

1. See Backscheider's discussion of Miles's *God: A Biography* (166–67).

2. After the rise of the prominent stereotype of the Wandering Jew, Cain's murder of Abel was repeatedly used to attribute to Jews their dispersed and fugitive status, while it was deployed in modern times by a number of Holocaust poets to examine the genocidal violence of Nazis against Jews. During the nineteenth century Cain (especially the marked Cain) was at times interpreted as an African or African American by commentators who viewed the mark as a brand of evil, even though it was used by God to protect Cain in the wilderness.

3. In 1935, Barth was "removed from his position at the University of Bonn because of his open opposition to Nazism, and he moved to his native Switzerland. From his position of safety at the University of Basel, he called upon Christians everywhere to oppose Hitler as the epitome of evil" (Ericksen 177). Yet in a 1967 letter, Barth admitted his "allergic reaction" to Jews: "I am decidedly not a philosemite, in that in personal encounters with living Jews (even Jewish Christians) I have always, so long as I can remember, had to suppress a totally irrational aversion, naturally suppressing it at once on the basis of all my presuppositions, and concealing it totally in my statements, yet still having

to suppress and conceal it" (*Letters* 262). Much more nuanced approaches to Judas by Barth will appear in subsequent chapters. For more ample considerations of Barth on Judas, see McGlasson as well as Cane (59–70). On the blindness generally attributed to Jews in medieval Europe, see Kruger (*Spectral Jews* 94) as well as the discussion of Papias in chapter 3.

4. The night into which Jesus sends Judas in John, according to Steiner, "is the instant, the crux . . . in which the Jew-hatred that festers at the absolute heart of Christianity is rooted" (*No Passion Spent* 417).

5. Mellinkoff has studied the anti-Semitic iconography of Judas in art history, as do Celia Lowenstein and Howard Jacobson in their film *Sorry, Judas* (1993).

6. In Bunyan's autobiography, *Grace Abounding to the Chief of Sinners* (1666), the author describes himself being tempted to sell Jesus, as Judas has done, and feels lost and fallen from God's grace before he finally experiences the mercy of God (87, 91, 93). See Ohly (122–24).

7. See chapter 5 for stills from DeMille's movie. DeMille hired Bruce Barton as a consultant, but softened Barton's depiction of Judas in his best-selling *The Man Nobody Knows* (1925): in Barton's popular text, the twelfth apostle is characterized as a "small bore business man" who "'looked out for Number One'" (83).

8. Ray's Judas is torn between Jesus, the Messiah of Peace, and Barabbas, the Messiah of War, as Humphries-Brooks explains (26–28). Similarly, Franco Zeffirelli's Judas in *Jesus of Nazareth* (1977) may be duped, but he is "humanized and fallible," and therefore audiences "can identify with him in a way that we cannot with Jesus" (Humphries-Brooks 75).

9. See Walsh as well as Humphries-Brooks, Reinhartz, and Tatum on Jesus in the movies.

10. I am indebted for this nice insight to Dave McCall's e-mail exchanges.

11. Dinzelbacher goes so far as to assert that "I hardly know any sources in which [Judas's] action is represented as typically Jewish" (80–81). I am indebted to James Rasmussen for the translations.

12. Even theologians attempting to acknowledge how Christian preaching may have facilitated the Nazi genocide ignore Judas. See, for example, Pawlikowski, whose *Christ in the Light of Jewish-Christian Dialogues* discusses representative theologians without any reference to Judas. The Holocaust meditations in *Jesus, Judaism, and Christian Anti-Semitism*, edited by Fredriksen and Reinhartz, contain no mention of him.

13. In a helpful e-mail, David Brakke points out that "*dusangelion* (or *dysangelion*)" is only a theoretical word, and even the verb and adjective forms occur quite infrequently.

14. With a different aim, Barth extensively discusses various handing overs (*Doctrine* 483–89), making the point that "Judas is the first link in the chain" (460) of hands delivering Jesus to the high priests. Cane points out that "both

Augustine and Origen are perceptive enough to notice the linguistic linkage of the 'handing over' of God and of Judas" (120).

CHAPTER 1

1. In addition to Cane's theological work, I will subsequently also draw on Saari's personal book about suicide, which discusses Judas in the synoptic Gospels. I concern myself at the end of this chapter with the flurry of books about Judas that followed and focused on the publication of the Coptic Gospel of Judas.

2. Beyond the books about Judas mentioned here, I will be drawing on a large number of scholarly articles, but I will also use many recent books about Jesus to interpret his antagonist. As a nonspecialist, I follow college teachers and rely throughout on *The HarperCollins Study Bible*, by Meeks and Bassler.

3. The Sayings Gospel Q is a hypothetical text reconstructed by means of material that Matthew and Luke added to Mark, and it is assumed to have "made no reference at all to Judas" (Robinson 5).

4. According to Goldstein, in authentic passages from the tannaitic period (the first two centuries C.E.) "we find that there was a person called Yeshua, Yeshu, Yeshu Hanotzri or Yeshu ben Pandera who practiced magic and who healed people, that this was regarded as sorcery, that for enticing and leading the people astray he was hanged on the eve of Passover," and that he "had five disciples: Mattai, Nakkai, Netzer, Buni, Todah" (96). Schäfer disagrees with those who deny the authenticity of tannaitic Jesus passages; however, he also argues that "The historical Jesus does not appear in our rabbinic sources" (8). See the end of chapter 3 for an account of a medieval Jewish legend about Jesus and Judas.

5. Maccoby claims that "The whole story of the betrayal was invented not less than 30 years after Jesus's death" (25). In *From Jesus to Christ*, Fredriksen agrees that "the task of the Passion narratives" was to position Rome and Christianity "on the same side against the Jews": "the evangelists' image of a Jesus beleaguered by constant Pharisaic opposition draws more on the circumstances of their own day than on the Palestinian ministry of Jesus" (105, 106).

6. Kermode speculates that at "an earlier stage," Judas "had no part in the scene of the Last Supper. He was worked into it later, when he took over the function of Betrayal, so becoming the agent by which the story is moved from its first to its second 'act'" (*Genesis* 84).

7. In *Jesus*, Ehrman discusses these criteria in a succinct and lively manner (87–95).

8. Most scholars now agree that Mark was composed in 68–70 C.E., Matthew in 80–85, Luke in 80–85 (his Acts in 100), and John in 90–95. I am indebted

throughout to the rich background on the Gospels provided by linguists, historians, theologians, and literary interpreters. Like them, I refer to Mark, Matthew, Luke, and John as the authors of the Gospels, although such names are only a convenience. The first three are called the synoptic Gospels, because they tend to present a similar view, and thus are usually distinguished from the last. Of course, the differences between the four Gospels on which my next chapter focuses narrowly concern the figure of Judas.

9. Saari follows Klassen here, although Saari's book is informed by his belief that Judas is a wholly fictitious character invented in Mark's Gospel as part of his critique of the twelve disciples. McGlasson finds this argument about multiply-inflected "handing over" in Barth (143–44). Cane also argues of 1 Corinthians that "it is not clear from the Greek if this [*paradidōmi*] is meant to be a reference to Judas, or whether Pilate, the high priests, or even God is the agent referred to" (21). Since "the New Testament writers chose a verb with the primary meaning of 'hand over' when they could have used one meaning 'betray,'" Cane argues, "they set up linguistic parallelism between the actions of Judas, other agents, and God" (24). He also discusses various translations of "betray" and "hand over" in subsequent biblical publications and commentaries (113–26).

10. Spong looks at precisely the same evidence to argue that it proves one must be suspicious about the historical basis of Judas: "The whole story of Judas has the feeling of being contrived" (203).

11. Klassen (30) lists seven other male characters with the name Judas in the New Testament: the son of the patriarch Jacob (Matthew 2:6); Judah in the genealogy of Jesus (Luke 3:30); Judas, the brother of Jesus (Matthew 13:55; Mark 6:3); Judas the Galilean (Acts 5:37); Judas Barsabbas (Acts 15:22, 27, 32); and Judas of Damascus (Acts 9:11).

12. The *Anchor Bible Dictionary* provides an excellent summary of scholarship on "Iscariot," which scholars have attributed to the Hebrew word for "false one," to the Hebrew root meaning "deliverer," and possibly to the designation of a hometown; however, none of these claims has been legitimated (3: 1091–92). See also Brown, who includes a bibliography to his appendix 4 on Judas (2:1411–18); Meier (210); and Cane (16–18).

13. In Brown's judgment, "attention to all the evidence supports the thesis that one of the Twelve named Judas gave Jesus over to the authorities who arranged his death" (2:1396). See also Nickle (29) and Klassen (74). Crossan writes: "I accept Judas as a historical follower of Jesus who betrays him. I do not think he was a member of the Twelve, because that symbolic grouping of Twelve new Christian patriarchs to replace the Twelve ancient Jewish patriarchs did not take place until after Jesus' death" (75). Pagels and King state that "it is likely that someone in the movement did betray Jesus" and base their supposition on its being "an enormous disgrace" that Jesus was turned in by one of his clos-

est followers (30). Of course, not everyone agrees: "The betrayal theory of the Disciples has not been proved. Any number of things could have happened to Judas between the time he left the Upper Room, and his arrival at Gethsemane" (Wilson 200). The fact that Paul does not name Judas led J. M. Robertson to judge Judas fictitious in *Jesus and Judas* (1927).

14. In *Jesus and Yahweh*, Bloom explains that he is "unhappy when Father Meier argues for the historicity of Judas Iscariot, who appears to me and to others—Jewish and Gentile—a transparently malevolent fiction that has helped to justify the murder of Jews for two thousand years" (24). In his review of Bloom's book, Kermode tellingly notes that "as a good Gnostic [Bloom] prefers to think that Jesus escaped execution and eventually made his way to North India. (Bloom, who entertains that conjecture as fact, dismisses Judas Iscariot as fiction. I think this is right, but in view of Bloom's capricious attitude toward fiction and fact it makes little difference which he was; Bloom can believe what suits him)" ("Arguing" 41).

15. Strauss, who discussed the impossibility of harmonizing Matthew's and Luke's etiology of the Field of Blood, concluded that "we cannot well doubt the existence of a piece of ground so named," but added: "That it really had a relation to the betrayer of Jesus is less certain" (665). Benoit analyzes the contradiction between Matthew and Acts as well as efforts to harmonize the accounts. Moreover, he states: "Tradition has always located Hakeldama in Ayub, at the foot of Siloam, where the three valleys of the Kidron, the Tyropoeon and the Wady Hinnom meet" (200). Called the "Gate of the Potsherds" or the "Gate of the Pottery," it was "a good place for those artisans who found there the water needed to work their clay" (201).

16. Crossan explains that his "*guess* is that Judas may have been captured from among Jesus' companions during the Temple action and eventually told them *who* had done it and not just *where* he was" (81). In *The Lost Gospel of Judas Iscariot*, Ehrman guesses that Judas divulged Jesus' private communications about his future rule as the king in the Kingdom, confidences that could then be used to accuse him of calling himself King of the Jews (165).

17. A fragment attributed to Papias (ca. 130 C.E.) elaborates briefly on Judas (see Marique), as do Irenaeus of Lyons (ca. 130–200) and Epiphanius of Salamis (ca. 310–403), who mention a "Gospel of Judas." Origen (ca. 185–254), Cyril of Syria (ca. 279–303), and Theophylactus (eleventh century) mention Judas. There is also a gospel epic written by Sedulius in the fifth century, and a fifth- or sixth-century Arabic Infancy Gospel. But all these sources, most of which will be discussed in my third and four chapters, postdate the Gospels.

18. Although Galambush does not discuss Judas, she explains the decisive consequences of the disappearance of observant Jewish Christians "from the Christian imagination": "If Christians could no longer imagine a fully Jewish Christianity—a sect that non-Jews joined only through conversion to

Judaism—then they could no longer understand the New Testament's invective against Jewish-Christian opponents. At that point the 'children of the devil' were no longer understood to be Jewish Christians who happened to disagree with John; they were the Jewish people as a whole" (308–9).

19. Armstrong explains that Jesus' "disciples believed that he would soon return to inaugurate the Messianic Kingdom of God, and, since there was nothing heretical about such a belief, their sect was accepted as authentically Jewish by no less a person than Rabbi Gamaliel, the grandson of Hillel" (79). She goes on to state that Jesus' "followers worshipped in the Temple every day as fully observant Jews," until at a later date "the New Israel . . . would become a Gentile faith" (80).

20. Segal similarly writes that "Judaism and Christianity can essentially claim a twin birth. It is a startling fact that the religions we know today as Judaism and Christianity were born at the same time and nurtured in the same environment" (1).

21. In *Border Lines,* Boyarin brilliantly argues that "Judaism is not and has not been, since early in the Christian era, a 'religion' in the sense of an orthodoxy whereby heterodox views, even very strange opinions, would make one an outsider" (13), although Christianity did constitute itself as a series of religions.

22. In an introduction to a book by a German author about Judas, Steiner notes ongoing repression of the fact that Judas was connected with recurrent violence against the Jews: "It is in the name of Judas' alleged betrayal and of the deicide which it provokes, that Jews were hounded to pitiless death from those very times onward in which Judas looms in Christian literature and iconography. It is countless Jewish men, women and children who suffered ostracism and martyrdom in the black lights of Judas' fate as it has been proclaimed and imagined by Christians" (foreword xiii–xiv).

23. On disk 2 of *Shoah,* the crowd before the church describes how the Jews in their community were penned into the church and then loaded onto gas vans to be murdered. A man steps forward to "explain" what the crowd behind him believes: that the rabbi of the community himself told the victims that "around 2000 years ago, the Jews condemned the innocent Christ to death," and therefore "the time has come" for them to acquiesce in the fate ordained in Matthew. Before resorting to the religious justification for the murder of the Jews, some in the crowd mention that the Jews had gold in the suitcases that were collected in the church.

24. See the complete English translation of *The Passion Play,* ed. William Stead, as well as Shapiro's *Oberammergau.*

25. A good example of virulently anti-Semitic rhetoric that lacks any mention of Judas is *Discourses against Judaizing Christians* by Saint John Chrysostom, a fourth-century orator who attacked Jews not just as the killers of Christ but also as drunks, animals, demons, and diseased pollutants: "The man who does

not have enough of loving Christ will never have enough of fighting against those who hate Christ" (177). Clearly these sermons were addressed to those who "profess you are a Christian, but you rush off to their synagogues" (238). The author wishes to prove Christianity diametrically opposed to Judaism in order to secure the fidelity of his community: "Why are you mixing what cannot be mixed? They crucified the Christ whom you adore as God. Do you see how great the difference is? How is it, then, that you keep running to those who slew Christ when you say that you worship him whom they crucified" (78–79). In Ruether's overview chapter on the *adversos Judaeos* tradition from the second to the sixth century (117–82), she never mentions Judas, because the tradition attacks Jews without any need for him to play a central rhetorical role.

26. Jews fared "considerably better" under Muslim rule than in early Christian Europe, according to Laqueur (192). To be sure, as Laqueur explains, one can find "quotations stating that *jihad* (holy war) is the sacred duty of every Muslim believer, that Jews and Christians should be killed, and that this fight should continue until only the Muslim religion is left (Sura 8:39)"; however, "the Koran also says that Muhammad had Jewish friends and there is even a verse that can be interpreted as saying that Allah promised Jerusalem to the Jews. Verses preaching tolerance can be found: there should be no coercion in matters of religion (Sura 2:256); both Moses and Jesus were genuine prophets; Jews and Christians are referred to as *ahl al-kitab* (the People of the Book) and they should be better treated in Muslim societies than pagans" (192). In *Under Crescent and Cross,* Mark Cohen discusses "the myth of the Islamic-Jewish interfaith utopia" (5) with a special emphasis on the medieval period. With specific reference to Judas, the Muslim tradition surfaces in the Gospel of Barnabas, discussed in chapter 4.

27. Dylan's lyrics appear in his 1963 antiwar song "With God on Our Side." They raise the possibility that Judas resembles all warring people who claim God's sanction or that all warring people who claim God's sanction resemble Judas.

28. Contemporary songs with references to Judas include "Amarok—Zorn Des Lammes III" by Nagaroth, "At Least I Know I'm a Sinner" by Atreyu, "The Ballad of Frankie Lee and Judas Priest" by Bob Dylan (this the inspiration for the name of the band Judas Priest), "It Was As If the Dead Man Stood upon the Air" by Norma Jean, "Judas" by Depeche Mode, "Judas Iscariot" by Rick Wakeman, "The Man's Too Strong" by Dire Straits, "Masters of War" by Bob Dylan, "Omerta" by Lamb of God, "Pride (In the Name of Love)" by U2, "Truly, Truly This Is the End" by Zao, "Until the End of the World" by U2, "Brainsaw" by Therapy, "Judas My Heart" by Belly, "Judas" by Helloween, "Kiss of Judas" by Stratovarius, "Judas Be My Guide" by Iron Maiden, "Age of False Innocence" by Blind Guardian, "Behold Judas" by Hate Eternal, and

"Don't You Grieve" by Roy Harper. In addition, the Smashing Pumpkins produced two B-side collection albums: *Pisces Iscariot* and *Judas O*.

29. Reinhartz points out that "the transformation of Jewish children into demons is apparently a figment of Judas' guilty and tortured mind," but then links the sequence to "the age-old trope of Jews as the children of the devil" (194).

30. That the ancient Gnostics preserved a Gospel of Judas—not included among the forty-six apocryphal texts recovered in 1945 near Nag Hammadi, in Upper Egypt—became clear only when the text was being sold. Quoted in articles about the discovery, leading voices in the Catholic Church argued that a rehabilitation of Judas might solve "the problem of an apparent lack of mercy by Jesus toward one of his closest collaborators" (Owen 3). Monsignor Walter Brandmüller, head of the Pontifical Committee for Historical Science, and Vittorio Messori, a prominent Catholic writer close to Pope Benedict XVI and the late John Paul II, are quoted in Owen. Robinson describes in detail Monsignor Brandmüller's repudiation of newspaper reports as well as his statement that "There is no campaign, no movement to rehabilitate the traitor of Judas" (180).

31. For a recent overview of scholarship on the controversial disciple to the apostles Mary Magdalene, see Acocella. Dart's article describes the recovery of the Gospel of Judas, as does Krosney's book.

32. Pyper discusses Henryk Panas's *The Gospel according to Judas* (1973; trans. 1977), Michael Dickinson's *The Lost Testament of Judas Iscariot* (1994), Ernest Sutherland Bates's *The Gospel according to Judas Iscariot* (1929), Daniel Easterman's *The Judas Testament* (1994), Peter van Greenaway's *Judas!* (1972), and Cecil Lewis's *The Gospel according to Judas* (1989), all composed before the discovery of the Coptic Gospel of Judas (as was Pyper's essay).

33. In *The Lost Gospel of Judas Iscariot*, Ehrman argues that "The Christian tradition has consistently and increasingly portrayed Judas in a bad light" (138), a point I debate throughout the remaining chapters.

34. See, for instance, Ehrman's book on the Coptic Gospel (*Lost Gospel*) as well as Pagels and King's. Robinson is an exception here.

35. In an essay, DeConick judges the jubilation over what she believes to be a mistranslated Gnostic Judas-savior in light of a widespread wish to reconcile Christianity to Judaism. In her book, she judges the Gospel of Judas to be a "parody" about a "'demon' Judas written by a particular group of Gnostic Christians known as Sethians" (4).

CHAPTER 2

1. Especially useful on the various sources, authorship, historical background, theological resonance, and interconnections of the Gospels of Mark, Matthew, and Luke is Nickle. On John, see Kysar.

2. On the widening division between Jews and Christians after the Jewish-Roman War, see both books by Fredriksen. The collection she edited with Reinhartz includes excellent essays on anti-Judaism in the New Testament, although they do not focus on Judas.

3. In other words, I do not consider whether the Gospels should be interpreted as "history recalled" or "prophecy historicized." The words in quotes derive from Crossan's *Who Killed Jesus?* (159); the debate between Crossan and Raymond Brown about the status of the Gospels is well elucidated by Jeremy Cohen (23–25).

4. According to McGlasson, Barth agrees with Nickle's analysis: for him, too, "Absolute blindness, absolute misunderstanding, absolute error, absolutely wrong ideas, absolute denial; such is the picture of apostleship" (108).

5. Borg and Crossan explain, "The exclamation is warranted. Josephus reports that the largest stones measured 69 feet long, 9 feet high, and 8 feet wide" (75); however, they also agree that Mark's is a story of "*failed discipleship*" (91), making Judas's betrayal "simply the worst example of how those closest to Jesus failed him dismally in Jerusalem" (107). The logic of their subsequent argument—"By reporting that Jesus sent *two* disciples to make clandestine arrangements for the Passover meal, Mark has Jesus withhold from Judas its precise location, so that Judas cannot tell the authorities where to find Jesus during the meal" (111)—seems more tenuous.

6. Borg and Crossan interpret the woman with the ointment "as the first believer" in Jesus and a "model leader," because she was the first to trust his prophecies and "drew the obvious conclusion" (104–5).

7. On the derivation of "the Son of Man" from Daniel 7:13, see Segal (68–80).

8. In his commentary on Luke, Fitzmyer argues that "even though one is hard put to establish the historicity of Judas' kiss, the substance of the episode of the arrest has to be reckoned as historical" (*Gospel* 2:1449).

9. Briskin associates the kiss with David's general, Joab, who greets the traitorous Amasa as a "brother," takes hold of his beard "as if to kiss him," and then stabs him (2 Samuel 20:9), as well as with Proverbs 27:6: "Wounds by a loved one are long lasting; / The kisses of an enemy are profuse" (Briskin 192). Robinson points out that Matthew's Jesus cautions against being called "rabbi" (23:8) and thus Judas, the only one to use the term, is shown to be an unworthy disciple (18–19).

10. The early church father Tertullian (ca. 155–230) raised precisely this question: "For what need of a traitor was there in the case of one who offered Himself to the people openly, and might quite as easily have been captured by force as taken by treachery?" He answered it by explaining that the betrayal was necessary because Christ was "One who was accomplishing prophecies. For it was written, 'The righteous one did they sell for silver' " (351). The reference to silver, pertinent to Matthew, comes from Amos 2:6.

11. According to Sanders, who is interested in the historical Jesus, the charge of blasphemy "looks like Christian creativity": "Some early Christians wanted to attribute his death to confessing the christology of the church. Christology separated the new movement from its mother, and naturally they wanted their own distinctive views to go back to Jesus. Titles, however, play such a minor part in the synoptic gospels that we must doubt that they were the real issue at the trial" (270–71). Fredriksen, in *Jesus of Nazareth, King of the Jews*, explains why most scholars consider Mark's presentation of the trial less historically useful than John's (221–25). Borg and Crossan state that the Greek can be translated either "I am" or "Am I?" (24, 130).

12. Schweitzer explains, "For a hundred and fifty years the question has been historically discussed why Judas betrayed his master. That the main question for history was what he betrayed was suspected by few . . ." (353). Schweitzer believed that Judas betrayed the messianic secret. Ehrman makes this claim historically: "What, then, did Judas betray to the authorities? This private teaching of Jesus. That's why they could level the charges against Jesus that he called himself the Messiah, the King of the Israel. He meant it, of course, in the apocalyptic sense. They meant it in a this-worldly sense. But he couldn't deny it when accused. For that *was* how he understood himself, and the twelve disciples all knew it" (*Jesus* 218).

13. In *The Lost Gospel of Judas Iscariot,* Ehrman surmises that this line can be understood as Judas asking the authorities to take Jesus away "securely" and speculates that perhaps Judas "didn't want Jesus—or the disciples—to be hurt in the mayhem" (166). Cane agrees about a word that can be translated "securely" or "safely": "Is Judas concerned for Jesus' safety, or simply that in no circumstances should he be allowed to escape? Or perhaps even something of both?" (47).

14. On Jewish anti-Semitism, see Gilman. On Matthew as the most Jewish-identified of the Gospel authors, see, for instance, Ehrman's chapter titled "Jesus, the Jewish Messiah: The Gospel According to Matthew" in *The New Testament* (92–111). Many commentators have noticed that Matthew's Jesus is a new Moses: he comes out of Egypt, he delivers five major speeches (matching the five books of the law), he gives sermons on mountaintops (as did Moses on Sinai), and he seeks not to abolish but to fulfill the law.

15. "One of the most distinctive features of Matthew is the ferocity of anti-

Jewish polemic and this seems to be related to the evangelist's original purposes. Polemical sayings are found already in Mark and in Q, but Matthew has sharpened and extended these traditional considerably. . . . Perhaps the most plausible explanation of Matthew's intensified anti-Jewish polemic is that Matthew's communities have recently parted company with Judaism after a period of prolonged hostility" (Stanton 75).

16. To be sure, some of Matthew's citations demonstrating prophecies fulfilled include lines of scripture that do not appear in the Hebrew Bible, as a number of scholars have pointed out.

17. Where Matthew deviates from Mark, as here, scholars identify his source as Q. In contrast to Peter's role in Mark, Matthew's Peter is, according to Jesus, the "rock" upon which "I will build my church" (16:18).

18. Perhaps the most curious (and unconsciously anti-Semitic) use of the thirty pieces appears in Kierkegaard, according to Hans-Josef Klauck. He mentions that Kierkegaard once was tempted to doubt the historical veracity of the Jew Judas precisely because he was "so unconcerned with money" (26)! The passage in Kierkegaard can be found in *The Moment and Late Writings* (44–45).

19. See Briskin for this and other analogues of Judas in the Hebrew Bible.

20. In parables, Matthew's Jesus also uses the word *hetairos,* or friend (20:13, 22:12).

21. In the next verses (27:9–10), Matthew identifies the returned thirty pieces of silver as a fulfillment of Jeremiah, a connection discussed by Paffenroth (*Judas* 117). The potter's field evokes Jeremiah's spoiled potter's clay that the Lord destroys, as he would destroy an evil nation (Jeremiah 18:7). Maccoby links the potter's field to Jeremiah 19 in order to question the Gospel authors' propensity to reverse the intentions of the Hebrew Bible (47). Ehrman points out that "Scholars have long puzzled over why Matthew indicates that this Scripture passage comes from Jeremiah when it appears to come from Zechariah" and goes on to posit that perhaps various sources were blended (*Lost Gospel* 28). Galambush attributes the allusion to Jeremiah (even though "Jeremiah's prophecies include no passage even vaguely resembling the quotation Matthew attributes to him") to the fact that "Matthew would seemingly rather make up his own prophecy than recount events *not* 'foretold by the prophets' " (76).

22. Gärtner provides an extensive analysis of the shared typology of Judas and Ahithophel (30–39).

23. The first to consider Judas as proving the power of Jesus' teaching and therefore as not a case of complete apostasy is Origen (ca. 185–254) in *Against Celsus* 2.11. The Greek word applied to Judas as he feels remorse is *metamelētheis,* which suggests "a conscious decision, one made over time" (Saari 92). In the translation of some editions, Judas does not repent but is "seized with remorse" or "feeling remorse." Theologians argue about whether the repentance of Judas

was genuine, because the Greek word used might involve merely a change of mind (Cane 48). Saari believes that the introduction of the word "forgiveness" (in the reference of Matthew's Jesus to the wine as his blood) might imply that Judas is forgiven (90). As the next chapter indicates, some premodern interpreters believed that Judas had not truly repented; however, their "condemnation cannot be sustained on the basis of the text. . . . According to Matthew, Judas's act of self-destruction was the measure of his repentance" (Droge and Tabor 114).

24. "Paul refutes this argument by turning it upside down," damning the Jewish law as a curse, "while Christ, by hanging on a tree, took the curse of the Law upon himself," or so Ruether interprets Galatians 3:10–14 (101).

25. "Is he going to kill himself?" is a question "the Jews" ask when Jesus explains, "I am going away" (John 8:21–2). In *Christ,* Miles mentions John Donne's defense of suicide, *Biathanatos* (ca. 1647), "in which Jesus himself is chief among the exemplary suicides of the past" (169), as well as the theological work of Pierre-Emmanuel Dauzat, *Le Suicide du Christ* (1998), which dates the idea back to the Gospel of John.

26. "It was not until the sixth century that voluntary death was decreed illegal, and the only scriptural reference offered to support the ban was an appeal to the Sixth Commandment: 'Thou shalt not murder'" (Saari 72).

27. Mark's "fondness for the historical present" was not shared by his successors: "Whereas Matthew retained twenty-one instances of the one hundred fifty-one times Mark used that tense, in Luke only one survived" (Nickle 142).

28. On Luke's emphasis on the Holy Spirit and the Gentile church, see Fredriksen (*From Jesus to Christ* 27–36).

29. Ananias is possessed by Satan in Acts 5:3.

30. I am indebted here to David Brakke's translation.

31. The first commentator to attempt to harmonize the account of Judas's death offered by Matthew and Luke was Theophylactus, who in the eleventh century describes Judas as so afflicted with dropsy that his immensity caused the tree to bend, and he continued to live until he burst asunder (see J. Harris). J. Rendel Harris, establishing parallels between Luke's account and the death of Nadan in the story of Ahikar, the grand vizier of Sennacherib, considers this account unreliable but also finds Matthew's account historically improbable.

32. Briskin quotes 2 Chronicles 21:15: "As for you [Jehoram] you will be severely stricken with a disorder of the bowels year after year until your bowels drop out" (194). See also Fitzmyer (*Acts* 220). Syriac, Armenian, and Arabic versions of the traitor Nadin's fate include the words "*swelled, burst,* and *scattered,*" according to Crossan (74). Saari quotes Wisdom 4:19, where the dishonorable and anguished death of the godless is described (114).

33. Psalms are repeatedly quoted in relation to Luke's Judas, according to Cane, in order to emphasize the "theme of fulfillment and providence" (54):

Judas's death "cannot be read as tragic," but instead in these contexts as "in accordance with scripture and therefore the purposes of God" (54). The second quotation comes from Psalm 109:8 and is invoked by Luther (who is discussed in chapter 3).

34. Like Stanton (115), many biblical scholars argue that John's "Jews" cannot be considered a religious or ethnic group, but should instead be understood to refer to religious authorities opposed to Christian teaching. They therefore find John anti-Jewish yet not anti-Semitic; however, John often refers not to the chief priests or the Pharisees but simply to "the Jews" and he does so many more times than do Mark, Matthew, or Luke.

35. Because this passage appears after Jesus has explained that his believers must eat his flesh and drink his blood, Pagels and King view it as a possible link to the Gospel of Judas, whose author agrees with John's Jesus that the spirit, not the flesh, gives life (52–53). They then go on to interpret the Gospel of Judas as an attack on "people like 'the twelve' [who] practice eucharist and sacrifice and encourage others to follow their lead" in martyrdoms that proliferate suffering (65).

36. Miles describes the Jews' situation this way: "The choice Rome has offered [the leaders] is the classic oppressor's choice: Either you police yourselves or we police you. In defense of the bargain he has made, Caiaphas offers the classic collaborationist argument: Fewer will die if we do our own killing" (*Christ* 193).

37. Sanders believes that in fact "Jesus was dangerous because he might cause a riot, which Roman troops would put down with great loss of life," and thus he judges John's presentation of Caiaphas as "entirely appropriate" (272) to the historical context; that is, Caiaphas "did not act because of theological disagreement, but because of his principal political and moral responsibility: to preserve the peace and to prevent riots and bloodshed" (273). In *From Jesus to Christ,* Fredriksen finds that John's scenario "offers both a more credible 'offense' on the part of Jesus and a more direct connection between his offense and his execution" (109).

38. Gärtner states that these are the only two places in which the phrase "son of perdition" appears in the New Testament (26).

39. Schäfer attributes the "strongly anti-Jewish bias" in John to "a bitter struggle between the established Jewish and the emerging Christian communities, a struggle moreover that was waged by both sides with the gloves off" (128).

40. Steiner notes the contradiction with 6:70, where Judas is described as the disciple "who is a devil," which he believes "discloses the tension, the unresolved awfulness in what some commentators have had the honesty to call 'a Satanic sacrament'" (*No Passion Spent* 416). Stanton describes the "awkward breaks in sequence, known as aporias," that have led to theories about several

difference sources for John's Gospel (104–5), as well as the "awkward transitions" that may be the result of "later insertions into the gospel" (106).

41. J. Albert Harrill, e-mail to author, June 2006.

42. For a discussion of the significance of this "Judas (not Iscariot)" in John 14:22, see chapter 5.

43. As late as 1946, Halas argued that "Matthew and John were eyewitnesses of the events that transpired at the Last Supper. Mark derived his information from St. Peter, who was certainly present when the Eucharist was instituted. Luke was not an Apostle but a companion of Paul, who had not known Christ according to the flesh (Gal. 1:23). The last two were obliged to secure material for their writings from tradition and by the meticulous questioning of eyewitnesses" (127–28). Today, scholars agree that the authors of the Gospels were not eyewitnesses.

44. To his credit, Cane attempts to provide a "full account of the totality and particularity of the Gospel accounts of the incarnate Christ" (181) with respect to Judas, but he must go beyond the facts supplied in the Gospels to do so. Specifically, he invents a theological fantasy about "the descent of the dead Christ" that offers "hope for Judas, and indeed hope for all people" (185).

45. According to Ruether, "Modern historians usually explain this [shift in blame] as due to the exigencies of the gentile mission. Since the Christians were now preaching to the Gentiles, they wished to play down any hostility of the gentile government" (88).

46. "As we move sequentially from Mark, through Matthew and Luke to John," Borg and Crossan explain, "that original emphasis on Jewish supporting crowd versus Jewish high-priestly authority diminishes significantly" (90).

47. See Barth on Paul's relation to Judas (*Doctrine* 501–3) and Cane on Barth (65–66).

48. In *Christ in the Light of the Christian-Jewish Dialogue,* Pawlikowski proves that there were disputes not only between these groups but within each of them as well (76–107). He emphasizes Jesus' close connections with the Pharisaic movement. See also chapters 7 and 8 of Pawlikowski's *Sinai and Calvary.*

49. Brown argues that "No Gospel account specifically describes Judas receiving the bread/body or the wine/blood" (2:1398); however, the scenes in the synoptic Gospels suggest that all twelve are present. Exactly when Judas leaves the table has been a question of much interest to theologians over the centuries.

50. Derbes and Sandona also rely on Barasch's book. Another nice demon appears with Judas, holding the money bag and departing the last supper, in Peter Pourbus's rendition (1548): Judas rushes toward the clutches of an attending skeleton-devil who looks female (with a maid's cap, leggings) but has muscular limbs ending with clawlike hands and feet.

51. Jeffers's play, *Dear Judas,* is discussed in chapter 5.

CHAPTER 3

1. That there is no single or simply adolescent Judas in premodern times (a ridiculously capacious term I am using to cover a huge temporal swath) will become clear in the next chapter, which explores a mature Judas in this same period. In other words, I am not labeling antiquity or the medieval period as "immature." Although most historians trace an escalation in anti-Jewish attitudes during the twelfth century and frequently use such designations as early Middle Ages, High Middle Ages, and late Middle Ages, the latter usually taken as ending around 1520, the recurrence of Judas's morphing and the need to cover so many centuries of his development have encouraged me to use the umbrella term "premodern."

2. That the line—from an 1855 poem by Robert Browning ("Childe Roland to the Dark Tower Came," l. 84)—comes from a much later date than the period under discussion does not render it less apposite.

3. The exoneration of God by blaming Judas continues even in excellent biblical scholarship today. Consider Borg and Crossan, who ask, "Was the death of Jesus the will of God?" and justify their negative answer by explaining that "Judas might not have betrayed Jesus" (161).

4. Cane quotes Aquinas's similar proposition in *The Summa Theologica* that God delivered Christ out of love, whereas Judas delivered him out of avarice: "It was from love that the Father delivered Christ, and Christ gave himself up to death; it is for that reason both are praised. Judas however delivered him out of avarice, the Jews out of envy, and Pilate because of the worldly fear he felt towards Caesar, which is why they all have such bad names" (123). Cane also discusses the propensity of early theologians to assume that Judas did not participate in the Eucharist or the foot washing at the Last Supper (see his chapter 3). As late as 1946, Halas asked, "Did Judas Iscariot partake of the Eucharist together with the rest of the Apostles" and answers, "Recent opinion of theologians and scripturists favors the absence of Judas" (104).

5. The complex subject of Christian heresies is outside the scope of this book; however, interested readers can find background information in the book by Wakefield and Evans as well as that by Lambert.

6. Irenaeus, the late second-century church father, referred to Papias's telling a story about the abundance Jesus promised to bring to earth: "'And the betrayer Judas,' he said, 'did not believe but asked "How then can the Lord bring forth such produce?"' The Lord then replied, 'Those who come into those times will see'" (quoted in Ehrman, *Lost Gospel* 45). I am arguing not that fragmentary texts about Judas from antiquity by Papias and others directly influenced the visual artists of the Middle Ages and Renaissance, but instead that their recycling helps explain the pictorial conventions governing later depictions of Judas.

7. The diagnosis of elephantiasis is given in 1874 by Farrar (587).

8. Judas therefore epitomizes the fear of pollution analyzed by Mary Douglas in transitional cultures when new social boundaries are being established and thus anxiety about their dissolution escalates, in this case the orthodoxies being established by the Church. See Douglas's *Purity and Danger* as well as R. I. Moore's use of it in his study of the persecution of heretics, Jews, lepers, and homosexuals (100–123).

9. See J. Rendel Harris for different explanations of how Judas could both hang and explode: for example, in the seventh century Theophylactus believed that Judas hanged himself to get to Hades before Jesus and ask his forgiveness, but because the tree bowed down he lived until his dropsy made him burst apart.

10. For a discussion of the Latin word *suspensus* used by Jerome, see Murray II (2:338), whose section on the medieval Judas extensively analyzes shifting attitudes toward suicide.

11. The best book on the guilt associated with suicide and Judas is by Saari.

12. Snyder quotes Aquinas: "'Judas indeed had fear and sorrow because he lamented his sin; but he did not have hope. And such is the penitence of the wicked.'" She adds, "Calvin sees in Judas the type of the reprobate who could be oppressed with horror and remorse but was unable really to hate his sin and humble himself. Judas is a grim reminder that, while mercy is open to all, despair may inhibit the operation of its own cure; salvation is not automatic" (34). Ohly explains the symmetrical opposition of the sinful sinner Judas and the saintly sinner Gregorius: "*Desperatio* and *poenitentia,* penitence and despair, stand side by side" (16). He also describes a passage of Mechthild of Magdeburg's thirteenth-century *The Flowing Light of Divinity,* in which Lucifer and Adam lay the foundation stones of Hell together with Judas, who delivers four blocks of sin: "lying, treason, despair and suicide" (37).

13. The Jesuit exegete Cornelius a Lapide (1567–1637) connected Judas's last name to his cupidity: "Iscariot means in Hebrew the same as mercenary, for *sachar* is merchandise. And this well agrees with Judas who made merchandise of Christ" (quoted in Mormando 181).

14. I am indebted here to a September 15, 2006, e-mail from Dyan Elliott.

15. Braswell discusses Judas in Chaucer's *Pardoner's Tale*. Bernard of Clairvaux conceded that "We have known many fall into the Devil's power in this regard, drowning or hanging themselves" (Murray 1:364). Thus, as Murray argues, "If Judas, though guilty, was wrong to kill *him*self, how much more wrong it is for an innocent person to do so" (2:114).

16. Taylor ("Gallows") also recounts folklore about the oak, the tamarind, and the redbud.

17. Ruether quotes the words of the fourth-century poet Prudentius: "From place to place the homeless Jew wanders in ever-shifting exile, since the time

when he was torn from the abode of his fathers and has been suffering the penalty for murder and having stained his hands with the blood of Christ, whom he denied" (134). According to a number of the church fathers, the Jew descended not from Abraham but from Cain.

18. In Paffenroth's translation, "blood" and not "pus" flows over Judas's body (*Judas* 23). Halas also translates the passage "worms mixed with decaying blood flowing from the entire body" (154).

19. The stench of the blasphemer whose body teems with worms and decomposing flab is recorded by the fourth-century church historian Eusebius in his account of the emperor Galerius's fate and is discussed by Ehrman (*Lost Gospel* 46).

20. "The thirteenth-century monk Caesarius of Heisterbach would feminize the Jews—who in the course of the high Middle Ages would come to be increasingly associated with the diabolical—by alleging that Jewish men were subject to a debilitating flux of blood on Good Friday," according to Dyan Elliott (*Fallen Bodies* 7). Halas connects the swelling of Papias's Judas to the ordeals of a woman accused of adultery (Numbers 5:21, 22, 27), which include "the swelling of her womb" and "the rotting of her thigh" (155–56).

21. This wasteland is related to the landscape T. S. Eliot would later lament in "Burbank with a Baedeker, Bleistein with a Cigar" (1920): "The rats are underneath the piles. / The jew is underneath the lot . . ." (ll. 22–23).

22. Linking Judas to the Antichrist, Sullivan interprets the lack of Jewish features and the lack of any attempt to suggest avarice in this image in terms of the "economic and political conditions that resulted from the intense iconoclasm of radical reformers during the 1520s" (98).

23. According to Dyan Elliott, Inquisitor Stephen of Bourbon, who believed that burning heretics "give forth a disgusting stench," also argued that they die "with their eyes cast down in sorrow" (*Proving Women* 62).

24. Such a view of the devil as the creator of Judas's soul was confessed by Bonigrino of Verona, a heretic (specifically a Cathar), when questioned during the late thirteenth-century Inquisition: "If Judas's soul was evil, then it was made by the devil" (Lansing 89).

25. Besides Sullivan, see Blumenfeld-Kosinski, who discusses the caesarean birth of the Antichrist (138–42).

26. According to Otis, in the Middle Ages "the social group which prostitutes most resembled was that of the Jews" (69). Mellinkoff points out that disreputable prostitutes were made to wear blond wigs or yellow headbands ("Judas's Red Hair" 44). Kruger explains that "Jews were frequently associated with female prostitutes, with both sometimes similarly treated as polluting presences" (*Spectral Jews* 83).

27. Derbes and Sandona review a host of scholars who have filled in the intellectual history of usury as unnatural breeding.

28. Freud's essay "Character and Anal Eroticism" links avarice and revenge-fulness to the anal stage and discusses the long mythological "identification of gold with faeces" (174).

29. The section from Walter of Wimborne's "De Symonia et Avaritia," trans-lated by Bonnie Erwin, begins this way:

The traitor lives again who betrayed Christ,
The seller lives again who sold Jesus,
Everywhere the truth of goodwill is lost.
Alas, wretched Judas, through whom it thus has come to pass!

The traitor lives again who on account of reward
Summons again the old crime of purchasing;
The greedy one resumes that wretchedness
Which, when it rustles, causes the entrails to burst forth.

Having been cut off, the offspring of Judas are removed,
Who pollute the household of the church and the king;
For a long time the law has been announced, and justice has been
     maintained,
But Judas returns, who murders the law.

Mark Cohen discusses the negative sentiments generated against Jews as mer-chants and moneylenders during the medieval period (79–88).

30. Frequently two-faced, often shown in profile by painters, Judas is pre-sented in a stereotypical manner by Andreyev: "The face of Judas, too, was double: one side, with its black, keen, observing eye was living, mobile, ready to gather into a multitude of irregular wrinkles. The other side was free from wrinkles, deathly smooth, flat and rigid; and though in size it was equal to the other, it seemed immense because of the wide-open, sightless eye" (50).

Ohly translates a ninth-century set of verses in which Judas returns to destroy believers: "Behold, Judas rises again, here comes the impious one" (96).

31. This stanza is in Nirenberg's translation (62) of Walter of Wimborne.

32. That Luther gives Judas the name Shariot indicates that he is responding to the Jewish medieval legend discussed at the end of this chapter. In *Sermons on the Passion of Christ,* Luther explains about the twelfth apostle that "Because he thus gave place to sin, his carnal security finally brought him so far that the devil completely possessed him and urged him on to the attainment of his outrageous purpose of betraying his dear Lord and Master for fifteen florins" (47). According to Luther, the Catholic Church, its bishops, and its priests betray Christ: "see the pope, for instance; he has the very bag of Judas hanging

from his neck, and is so fond of money and possessions that he takes them in exchange for the gospel, which he betrays and sells, and with which he deals as the Jews dealt with the Lord Jesus before Caiaphas and Pilate!" (49).

33. These noncanonical gospels probably date from the late first or early second century C.E.

34. Along with the others, Judas asks pious questions, such as "Tell [us, L]ord, what [existed] before [heaven and] earth came into being," so as to be enlightened by instruction; and like them, having received it, "he bowed down and he [worshipped] and he offered praise to the Lord" (Schneemelcher 305, 306). Indeed, in this apocryphal Coptic codex, "Judas raised his eyes and saw a very high place, and he saw the place of the abyss below" (307), illuminating him (along with Matthew and Mary) about Jesus' mission on earth.

35. In the Acts of Andrew and Paul, Satan determines to keep Judas's soul; however, "Jesus ordered Michael to take away Judas' soul also, that Satan's boast might be proved vain" (J. Elliott 302). Because Judas "had destroyed his own hopes by worshipping Satan and killing himself," he is "sent back till the day of judgement" (302).

36. "Some of them say that it was because Christ was wicked that he was betrayed by Judas, because he, Christ, wanted to distort what pertains to the law. They admire Cain and Judas, as I said, and they say: For this reason he betrayed him, because he wanted to destroy sound teachings" (Epiphanius 134). Other speculations by Epiphanius are quoted and discussed in chapter 4. On the Cainites, see Ehrman (*Lost Gospel* 62–65).

37. According to an e-mail from Dyan Elliott, John Nider's fifteenth-century *Formicarium* details different forms of possession. Although some possessed people are innocent, possession can also be a punishment for sin—as exemplified, according to Nider, by Judas.

38. According to Dinzelbacher, "The fish-thief Judas is practically a type of its own" (30).

39. A revolting image of obscenity that was placed on church doorways and the gates of cities, the *Judensau* capitalizes on the animalization, blindness, scatology, and gluttony that Judas emblemizes in antiquity and the medieval period. Jews, forbidden by the laws of kashrut to eat pork, become pig suckers; the carnal Jews guzzling at the sow's teats or asshole are the antitype of Christians who worship the Lamb of God. According to Bynum, in the early modern period the *Judensau* did not merely "announce that Jews were unwelcome," for it functioned "in a talismanic way to ward off their presence or ensure that they would not return from exile" (14).

40. Indeed, writes Luther, if Christians were to tolerate Jewish depravity, "What a great saint the traitor Judas would be in comparison with us!" (*Selected Psalms* 273).

41. "Origen (185–255 A.D.) claims that the sop which Christ gave to Judas was actually the consecrated Eucharist"; "St. Leo the Great (ca. 400–461 A.D.) identifies the morsel of dismissal with the Holy Eucharist" (Halas 109, 113).

42. A fly-, bird-, dog-, worm-, blood-, or feces-infected Judas may have contributed to medieval beliefs that Jews poisoned wells: one panel of Piero Della Francesca's Frescoes of the Legend of the True Cross (ca. 1450s) depicts a hung Judas being pulled out of a well. A color photograph and diagram of the frescoes appears in *History of Italian Renaissance Art,* by Harrt and Wilkins (315–16). An extensive discussion of medieval beliefs in Jewish host desecration can be found in Rubin.

43. Klauck discusses the anti-Semitism of Abraham a Sancta Clara's *Judas the Arch-Rogue* (18). Many of the host desecrations decried by Abraham are performed by Christians unworthily taking the host and suffering as a consequence.

44. Drawing on the scatological iconography associated with Judas, one famous literary example of ritual murder occurs in Chaucer's *Canterbury Tales* (ca. 1400), specifically in the story the Prioress tells about Jewish mercenary and murderous enterprises. Chaucer's nun eulogizes a pious Christian boy killed by Jews who slash the child's throat (because his praise of the Virgin infuriates them). The actions of the Jews, dedicated to "their foul lucre, by usury gained, / —Hateful to Christ, by Christian folk disdained—" (ll. 4–5; p. 160), take on added resonance when the slashed victim is thrown into a latrine:

> This cursed Jew, as the little child passed by,
> Grabbed him and held him in a cruel grip,
> And cut his throat and threw him in a pit.
> It was a cesspit that they threw him in,
> Where these Jews used to go to purge their bowels. (ll. 570–74; p. 162)

Cast into a pit where the Jews defecate, the child's "blood cries out upon [the] fiendish deed" of the "fiendish nation" (ll. 581, 576; p. 163). The tale thereby demonstrates that "The serpent Satan, our first enemy, / . . . has his wasps' nest in the hearts of Jews" (ll. 558–59; p. 162). Chaucer's narrator tells her tale about child murder because of reports alleging the crucifixion of one Hugh of Lincoln. As Kruger has shown, Middle English texts tend to contrast "the Christian body, attacked but preserved, and the Jewish body, foul (purging its 'entraille' [573]), attacking innocence, justly destroyed" ("Bodies of Jews" 306).

45. The 1235 charges, Langmuir shows, accused "Jews in Germany . . . of ritual murder, but not a crucifixion. The accusation was the novel one of ritual cannibalism, and it was made at Christmas, not at Easter or Passover" (268). Langmuir points out that "in every case for which we have fair evidence [about

ritual murder] it is far more likely that Jews did not do it and that someone else did" (296). Kruger argues that the charge confirms depictions of European Jews whose circumcision was linked in the Christian imagination to "a lack of Jewish 'virility' ": " 'the wound of circumcision' entails, on the one hand, a lack in Jewish gender and sexuality and, on the other, a compensatory violence directed against the unwounded bodies of Christians" (*Spectral Jews* 82).

46. For medieval woodcuts and manuscript illustrations of ritual murder as well as host desecration and image desecration, see Zafran.

47. "Only be sure that you do not eat the blood; for the blood is the life, and you shall not eat the life with the meat" (Deuteronomy 12:14).

48. Whereas Jews were accused of drinking blood and eating flesh at Passover, it was at Passover in the synoptic Gospels that Jesus instituted the Eucharist, urging his disciples to eat his body and drink his blood. In a passage from the Gospel of John that might bring to mind cannibalism, Jesus goes into graphic detail:

> "Very truly, I tell you, unless you eat the flesh of the Son of Man and drink his blood, you have no life in you. Those who eat my flesh and drink my blood have eternal life, and I will raise them up on the last day; for my flesh is true food and my blood is true drink. Those who eat my flesh and drink my blood abide in me, and I in them." (6:53–56)

Directly after this pronouncement, the apostles express shock—"This teaching is difficult; who can accept it?" (6:60)—and Jesus himself asks, "Does this offend you?" (6:61). Schäfer discusses anti-Jewish and anti-Christian charges of cannibalism in antiquity (100–102).

49. "If Judas, in some sense, begets Iago, he most assuredly engenders Shylock" (Steiner, *No Passion Spent* 416). See Paffenroth's discussion of other Shakespeare plays with allusions to Judas (*Judas* 79–82).

50. Gilman discusses the slippage between circumcision and castration within the context of Jewish anatomical difference (119, 127). On the pointed hat, see Lipton (15–21).

51. From the first accusation of Jewish ritual murder in 1130 England until the 1650s, when the Amsterdam rabbi Menasseh ben Israel felt the need to refute the charge in order to gain Jews readmission into England, Jews were accused of bloodletting. See Shapiro (*Shakespeare and the Jews* 89–111) as well as Langmuir.

52. In an article titled "The Thirty Pieces of Silver," Hill translates the account of Godfrey of Viterbo, who died in 1191 and whose *Pantheon* describes the coins given by the Magi, left behind by Mary, found by shepherds, restored to Jesus, given to Judas as treasurer, cast down by him, and used to buy the Potter's Field. "Perchance thou thinkest, reader, that my words agree not together,

since I have written that those coins were of gold. . . . But it is even as I have said; for it was the custom of the ancients to use more than one name for gold, and to call different metals by the name of silver" (93). In the medieval *Life of Judas* that Ohly publishes, the thirty pence are the same "thirty pence for which Joseph was sold by his brothers, lord Jacob's sons, in the land of Egypt, and thereafter they had been preserved as a true inheritance for many thousand years among the Jews, who bought our lord for those same pence from Judas, and they are the coins of Ishmael, and every one of them is worth ten ordinary pence" (Ohly 149).

53. On German Passion plays, see Ohly (72–102), who argues, "The lamentations of Judas find echoes in those of Faust. Judas sees that by betraying Christ he has sold himself to the devil, just as Faust sold himself when he betrayed God and made a pact with Satan" (74).

54. I am using Jean Hollander's translation and Robert Hollander's notes (Dante 486–88).

55. Cane points out that "Satan and Judas are bound together in opposition to God's purposes. . . . Lucifer executes God's judgement on Judas, who in his turn silences Lucifer" (168). The grinning face has also been interpreted as a more generalized mythological beast that feeds on men. As a sort of hell mouth, Satan of course might be chomping on any damned soul.

56. Without reference to Judas, more extended analyses of anti-Semitism in Dickens's *Oliver Twist* (1837–39) and Trollope's *The Way We Live Now* (1875) appear in Derek Cohen and Heller.

57. As one scholar notes, "the sexual and vampiric, as well as pathogenic associations of . . . blood-sucking, and the combination of . . . infection, unnatural sexuality, and blood lust" link its protagonist with anxiety about the influx of Jewish immigration into England at the end of the nineteenth century (Malchow 153). See also Zanger.

58. An Oedipus-Judas can be found in Arnoul Gréban's *Mystère de la Passion* (composed between 1450 and 1455) and in Jean Michel's *Mystère de la Passion* (printed ca. 1490), according to Kahn. The medieval idea that a deceptive "God causes evil and sin" and that therefore an individual's culpability should be reduced is discussed by Dyan Elliott in *Proving Woman*, where she points out that a chancellor of the University of Paris entertained the idea that "since the Jews regarded Christ as a destroyer of the law, they would have sinned by not crucifying him" (246–47).

59. See Laeuchli's analysis of Origen's Judas.

60. See Baum ("Medieval Legend") for an exhaustive history of the transmigration of this Oedipal version of Judas's life in medieval legend as well as Edmunds, Archibald (107–10), and Ohly (especially 33). About the *Golden Legend*, Ehrman remarks: "Prior to the Protestant Reformation, this was the

most widely read book in all of Christendom, for many people their principal source of 'knowledge' about the early medieval church" (*Lost Gospel* 48). Paffenroth shows how much the legend of Judas-Oedipus has in common with the lives of Saint Gregory, Saint Andrew, and Saint Albans (*Judas* 73–75). Ohly includes an appendix, "Unpublished *Life of Judas* from the Schaffhausen Lectionary," which is dated 1330. The Oedipal-Judas continues to exert influence: both Denise Levertov's "The Peachtree," within the sequence "During the Eichmann Trial," and Anne Sexton's "The Legend of the One-Eyed Man" elaborate on *The Golden Legend*.

61. Steinberg discusses "the erection motif" on the figure of the dead Christ by speculating on its relationship to paintings of the circumcision of the baby Jesus: "if the truth of the Incarnation was proved in the mortication of the penis, would not the truth of the Anastasis, the resuscitation, be proved by its erection?" (91). For Judas, of course, the symbolism operates quite differently.

62. See the discussion of Saramago's novel in chapter 6. Various versions of *The Golden Legend* find enough that is good or representative in Judas to accord him some reward. In John Mirk's collection of homilies (ca. 1403), for instance, "the fiend [who] could not draw Judas's soul out by the mouth that had kissed the mouth of God's son so soon before" managed to "burst Judas's stomach" and bear his soul to hell; however, Saint Brendon later encounters Judas on the sea, where—placed there "out of God's courtesy" every Sunday "from evensong to evensong, and from midwinter to the twelfth day, and during the Passion-day of our lady, and on Candlemass-day"—he can "refresh the great heat" he suffers (79–80).

63. Theologians such as Aquinas pioneered the concept of the "just price," which made interest and even usury somewhat respectable (see Little).

64. Translation by Bonnie Erwin of a text printed by Axton from a manuscript in Trinity College, Cambridge, B.14.39 (fol. 34). In his discussion of the ballad, Baum compares it to a Wendish folk song in which Judas gambles and loses his money, then sells his master, but is forgiven by God. According to Baum, the ballad's plot draws on one of the oldest apocrypha, the fragmentary Coptic Gospel of the Twelve Apostles, where "it is the wife of Judas who is at the bottom of all his villainy" ("English Ballad" 185). In two Coptic fragments, a henpecked Judas's betrayal is blamed on the nefarious influence of his Eve-like wife (J. Elliott 163).

65. The York Corpus Christi plays were staged as early as 1376 and performed annually until the late 1500s. For a study of the cycle as sacramental theater, see Beckwith.

66. Similarly, in his 1534 *Treatise upon the Passion,* Sir Thomas More used the word "monopoly" to describe the greed of merchants who follow in the footsteps of Judas (78). See Sacks on this passage (265).

67. Arthur explains of *Elene*, "even Satan can see that while he once had a sort of victory through the actions of another Judas, this Judas has now furthered the process of his defeat" (119).

68. Quoted by Axton (181); translation by Bonnie Erwin.

69. I am indebted to Ellen MacKay for this approach to the play, which can be found in a collection of early English drama edited by John Coldewey (Croxton *Play*). According to Arthur, "*The Play of the Sacrament* resulted in anti-Jewish riots" (127).

70. Murray translates Theophylact of Ochrid (a biblical interpreter, ca. 1200): "when Judas saw Jesus arrested and condemned to death he was struck by contrition that events had turned out otherwise than expected, so he hanged himself in order to get to Hell first, and procure his salvation by throwing himself on Jesus' mercy" (2:363).

71. I am indebted to Dyan Elliott's translation of the Latin at the base of this engraving, which concludes with the phrase "And Judas hung the sad burden on the branches."

72. See also Schonfield (42–43). Jeremy Cohen describes a version in which one "Gisa" bows to "Yeshu the Wicked" and the sages grab him to kill him on the eve of Passover (146–47). As Cohen explains, the legend "depicts Jesus and his followers as fomenting a rebellion in the Jewish community and as undermining its religious law, order, and unity. In a word, it justifies his execution" (147). In an analysis of late talmudic evidence of Jesus, Schäfer describes the contempt with which Jesus is treated in counternarratives that maintain Jewish responsibility for Jesus' death but insist that "there is no reason to feel ashamed because we rightfully executed a blasphemer and idolater. Jesus deserved death, and he got what he deserved" (9).

73. Judas "acted foully and polluted Jesus, so that he became unclean and fell to earth, and Judas also with him. [[And for this deed they weep bitterly on their night, yea, for the deed that Judas did to him]]" (Schonfield 45; brackets his). Some scholars interpret this event as Judas ejaculating or urinating on Jesus.

CHAPTER 4

1. See Brown (1:252) as well as Mormando (183).

2. A standard Pauline letter closing, the phrase appears in 1 Corinthians 16:20; 2 Corinthians 13:12; 1 Thessalonians 5:26.

3. Exceptions include paintings of Jupiter embracing or kissing Ganymede as well as representations of Jonathan and David, Damon and Pythias.

4. The first Shakespeare quote comes from *The Tragedy of King Richard the Second* (3.2.129), the second from *The Third Part of King Henry the Sixth* (5.7.34).

5. Frank postulated Judas as the speaker of Dickinson's Fr. 562 (J. 394), although others—including Mossberg (132–33)—offer provocative interpretations of this text.

6. Foucault famously argued that the homosexual was invented in the nineteenth century, but he was referring to the homosexual as an identity category used to discipline and punish a class of people. Many scholars of antiquity and the Middle Ages (on whom I draw) discuss same-sex love in early times. In "Forgetting Foucault," Halperin explains that "the canonical reading of the famous passage in *The History of Sexuality,* volume 1, and the conclusion conventionally based on it—namely, that before the modern era sexual deviance could be predicated only of acts, not of persons or identities—is . . . as inattentive to Foucault's text as it is heedless of European history" (29).

7. Hand ("The Birthday" 3, 5, 7) makes it clear that in folklore the birthday is a day of ill-omen, so I am of course reading against the intended grain.

8. According to Mormando (182), "The influential *Revelations* of the fifteenth-century mystic Saint Bridget of Sweden had publicized the fact—communicated to her by the Virgin Mary herself—that Judas was small in height (and hence Jesus had to lean down to respond to his kiss)."

9. See Thomas on the wide range of meanings that have accrued to different types of kisses.

10. "Till at least the late fifth and sixth centuries of Christendom," Steiner stated (before the recovery of the Coptic codex), "Judas was, in certain religious communities, revered for his self-sacrifice, for the necessary holiness of his deed" (*No Passion Spent* 415).

11. Produced either in the late Middle Ages or the early modern period, composed originally in Spanish and Italian, and first translated into English in 1908, the Gospel of Barnabas is a harmonized version of the New Testament in 222 chapters. Jesus, here not the Son of God, foretells the coming of the messiah, Muhammad. Many Muslim scholars have assumed its authenticity, whereas most Western scholars have not. For background, see Leirvik, who interprets the Gospel of Barnabas "as part of an Islamic literature of resistance 'from below,' directed against Christian empires and missionaries" (20). Before the crucifixion of Judas, the Gospel of Barnabas describes the twelfth apostle as a traitor, an unbeliever, a hypocrite, and a thief; but after Jesus is taken away to heaven, Judas cannot convince anyone that Jesus' magic has transformed him into his teacher's image. Judas is crucified in the place of Jesus, despite his protestations that he is actually Jesus' betrayer.

12. I am indebted to Stephen D. Moore, who describes how the fathers of the church approached the Song of Songs (*God's Beauty Parlor* 21–89). I am arguing not that the artists I discuss were motivated by the Song of Solomon, but rather that their portraits of the same-sex embrace charge the figure of the bonded male couple with erotic and spiritual power.

13. On the top of his rendition of the betrayal, Fra Angelico has painted parts of the verse from Psalm 41:9 (with its reference to the one who "ate my bread" lifting "his heel against me") and at the bottom parts of Matthew 26:49 (with its description of Judas coming up to Christ and hailing him as "Rabbi").

14. In *The Lost Gospel*, Ehrman quotes Ambrose, onetime bishop of Milan: "[Judas] kissed the Lord . . . with lips, this kiss the Jewish people have, and therefore it is said, 'This people honor me with their lips, but their heart is far from me' " (50).

15. Mormando supplies historical information proving that both the kiss of peace and the Judas kiss were imagined as mouth-to-mouth kisses (184–86). Penn quotes Augustine:

> The kiss of peace is a great sacrament. Just as you kiss, so too love. Do not be Judas. The traitor Judas kissed Christ with his mouth, he plotted with his heart. But perhaps someone has enmity against you, and you are not able to convince or persuade him [to forgive]. Compel yourself to tolerate. Do not return him evil for evil in your heart. He hates. You love and, untroubled, kiss [him]. (116)

Penn also quotes Origen:

> [Paul] first teaches that kisses, which are given in church, are chaste. At that time there are no rivalries as there was from Judas, who gave a kiss with his lips and considered treachery in his heart. A kiss, in truth, is first faithful, in order that we might say that it is chaste. (117)

16. Raced representations thereby gloss the second Response of the third nocturn for Good Friday in the Breviary—"Iesum tradidit impius summis principibus sacerdotum et sorioribus populi" (The wicked man betrayed Jesus to the chief priests and elders of the people)—as well as the second Response of the second nocturn for Good Friday: "Tenebrae factae sunt, dum crucifixissent Iesum Judaei" (It became dark when the Jews crucified Jesus). Oesterreicher (29) contrasts the first line to the more anti-Semitic second line as well as the second Response of the second nocturn of Maundy Thursday: "Denariorum numero Christum Iudaeis tradidit" (For a handful of coins he delivered Christ to the Jews).

17. I am indebted to Bonnie Erwin for this translation from the Latin of Sedulius.

18. "O innocent lamb of God, why you and that wolf?" asks the German abbot Ekbert of Schönau, the author of *Stimulus amoris* (Prick of Love), when meditating on the "bloodthirsty beast approaching for a kiss of [Jesus'] mouth" (quoted in J. Cohen 126).

19. Dyer, among others, makes this point (17). Another image of a darkened Judas embracing a whitened Jesus appears in *The Kiss of Judas* (end of fifteenth century) by Jean Bourdichon, which can be viewed on the Web at the Bridgeman Art Library, <http://www.bridgeman.co.uk> (MMT 181594).

20. Paffenroth explains that Othello's likening himself to "the base Indian" appears as "Iudean" in folio 1, and connects not only the Moor's murderous kiss but his subsequent suicide to Judas (*Judas* 80). But perhaps the reference is to the place Judea, rather than to the person of Judas.

21. Iago recounts a dream kiss he received while sleeping with Cassio: according to Iago's scheming story, the dreaming Cassio—thinking his bedfellow was Desdemona—would "kiss me hard / As if he plucked up kisses by the roots / That grew upon my lips, lay his leg o'er my thigh, / And sigh, and kiss, and then cry 'Cursed fate / That gave thee to the Moor!' " (Shakespeare, *Othello* 3.3.424–28).

22. Brooks has discussed the enclosed garden—the scene of (often mute) virtue recognized and acknowledged, the stark contrast between salvation and damnation—in later secular and melodramatic literature.

23. William Blake used a marked disparity in age to contrast a youthful and energetic Jesus with an aged and rigid-looking Judas in *Judas Betrays Him* (ca. 1803–05), a pen and ink on paper owned by the Tate Museum.

24. Consider Jorg Breu the Elder's *Betrayal and Arrest of Christ* on the Melk Altar (1502) and *Betrayal and Arrest of Christ* by the Nuremberg Artist (1400–1410), or that of the Artist of Rueland Frueauf the Elder's Circle in Regensburg (1440–1507).

25. On anti-Semitism and Dürer's various depictions of the Passion, see Price (169–93).

26. In *Sermons on the Passion of Christ*, Luther describes the shameful fall of Peter and then asks, "why is it that Peter does not hang himself like Judas?" The answer is that "Peter, no doubt, remembered the Word of the Lord Jesus; this saved him" (108). See Ohly on medieval writers (32) as well as his quotation of François Mauriac: " 'Very little would have been needed for the tears of Judas to be allied in the memory of mankind with those of Peter' " (32). John Calvin argued "that the one [Peter] was received into favour again with God, and the other [Judas] cast away, but because the one did, by a lively faith in him who he had denied, take hold upon the mercy of God; and the other wanted faith, whereby he did despair of the goodness and mercy of God . . ." (quoted in Cane 141). Up to the present day, Judas appears in relation to Peter. Ray Anderson's *Gospel according to Judas*, for instance, is composed because "Jesus found Peter before he could drown himself in his own remorse and sorrow": "In this spirit, let's suppose that a conversation occurred between Judas and the risen Christ" (4).

27. The black Judas and blond and fair Jesus in a color rendition of the 1508

Dürer can be seen on the Web at Art Resource, <http://www.artres.com> (ART157499).

28. "As to the Apostles' exact place, we know that St. John occupied the couch next to Jesus, for he reclined on His bosom (Jn. 13:23)," Halas explains (96). Moore quotes Bernard of Clairvaux's *Sermons on the Song of Songs*: "For [John's] soul was pleasing to the Lord, entirely worthy both of the name and the dowry of a bride, worthy of the Bridegroom's embraces, worthy that is of leaning back on Jesus' breast. John imbibed from the heart of the only-begotten Son what he in turn had imbibed from the Father" ("Song of Songs" 342). A contemporary historian of homosexuality in the biblical world, Martti Nissinen, points out that "public expressions of homosexuality were regarded as anomalous, idolatrous, and indecent" in Jesus' time, explaining that "the relationship between Jesus and the beloved disciple has been recently considered as a training relationship akin to the ideal in Plato's Athens"; however, he determines that "the homoerotic or pederastic dimension of their relationship could be argued only in a strained way from very limited material" (118, 121–22).

By the end of the nineteenth century, oddly, one C. S. Griffin advanced the idea encapsulated in his book's title: *Judas Iscariot, the Author of the Fourth Gospel* (1892). A twentieth-century poem about John falling asleep "on the breast of the Master" includes a meditation on John seeing himself "with the face of Judas" and feeling "the heft of / the moneybag in his hand" (see Rózewicz). Michael Dickinson's curious *The Lost Testament of Judas Iscariot* (1994) posits a Judas closest to Peter and jealous of John: "I couldn't understand why the Master should single him out for favour over the rest of us. Why he had the place at his right hand at meal times and was fed with sops by his own hand" (41–42). The Reverend Michael Jude Fay, a Catholic priest who pilfered $1.3 million from St. John's Church in Darien, Connecticut, spoke about the link between Judas and John during his trial: Leonardo da Vinci, he recounted, found a handsome model of John for his "Last Supper," but not until many years later did he find a grotesque enough model for Judas, only to be shocked to learn that this disheveled man had been the model for John (Cowan).

29. Barth suggests that Judas's restitution constitutes a truer repentance than Peter's (*Doctrine* 466) and quotes one C. Starke: "Peter, thou art also a brother of Judas" (475). Brodie reads the scene in John's Gospel as linking Peter's swordplay to a "darkness of mind" related to "the Satanic darkness of Judas" (527).

30. The painting in plate 5 is considered a later copy (by a follower of Carracci), now at Princeton, of the original (currently privately owned in Genoa). For purposes of simplicity and because the provenance of the Princeton canvas remains unknown, I refer to it as Carracci's.

31. Since Judas stands leaning forward but behind Jesus, that kiss might recall

the act of sodomy painted by a number of Carracci's relatives and contemporaries. "Revealing like no other oral activity the powerful connection, in fantasy and physiology, between mouths and genitals, kissing is indeed a 'softened hint' at the sexual act" (A. Phillips 97). "Canon lawyers of the thirteenth century, in their more systematic definition of the laws of sexual conduct, often equated kissing with the major misdemeanour of fornication (sexual intercourse between an unmarried man and a woman) and the even more serious crime of adultery" (Camille 152). Bersani and Dutoit explain that "a heterosexual artist such as Annibale Carracci would have no trouble painting a frankly homosexual scene (there are, for example, two small homosexual scenes on the Farnese ceiling)" (*Caravaggio's Secrets* 10–11). For historical background on sodomy, see Jordan.

32. Bersanit and Dutoit state that Roberto Longhi's 1960 identification of the witness as one of Caravaggio's self-portraits "has generally been accepted" ("Beauty's Light" 20). See this article as well as their book on Caravaggio, *Caravaggio's Secrets*. The fascinating story of how this long-lost painting was found and restored is told by Harr.

33. Some commentators read the horrified man at Christ's back as John the Evangelist.

34. Guercino's *Betrayal of Christ* (ca. 1621) picks up on the idea of distinguishing the soldiers from Judas by means of an armored Roman who—as he flings a rope around Jesus' neck—literally separates Judas from Jesus.

35. On "consuming trauma," see Yaeger.

36. In relation not to painting but to the Passion narrative, Maccoby advances this idea and views Judaism as superior to Christianity because Judaism did abolish human sacrifice, "not even retaining it in the form of myth, as did Christianity" (95).

37. Walsh, who views Pasolini's movie as a Marxist interpretation of Matthew, points out that the film increases Judas's "perfidy," but adds that "In Pasolini's light, then, we cannot look at Matthew's cross without thinking of Judas hung" (114). Reinhartz argues that "Given Pasolini's own homosexuality, his allusion to the homoerotic potential in this intense relationship [between Jesus and Judas] is not surprising" (168). Judas is played by Otello Sestili and Jesus by Enrique Irazoqui.

CHAPTER 5

1. The fact that Judas, like the Jesus to whom he is dedicated, becomes a patriot at this stage of his career does not, of course, stop the Jewish priests and Caiaphas from playing the role of villainous Christ-killers.

2. See Paffenroth (*Judas*) on such figures as the American lecturer Telemachus Thomas Timayenis (1853–1918)—who proposed resettling Jews in New Mexico—and the Scottish novelist Eric Linklater (1899–1974).

3. Jeremy Cohen includes an illustration from *La libre parole* (November 10, 1894), titled "A propos de Judas Dreyfus" (139); Maccoby discusses two pamphlets excoriating Dreyfus, *In the Time of Judas* and "The Spectacle of Judas" (120). Both suggest that Dreyfus as Judas was assumed to be crucifying "the master (in Dreyfus's case, France) whom he claimed to serve" (J. Cohen 138).

4. Strauss "will not maintain" that covetousness was Judas's motive (610), and concludes about contradictory Gospel accounts of Judas's death that "we scarcely know with certainty concerning Judas even so much as that he came to a violent and untimely death" (668). Dismissing avarice as a motive, Renan argues that "the curses with which [Judas] is loaded are somewhat unjust. There was, perhaps, in his deed more awkwardness than perversity" (194).

5. The term *counterhistory* begs the question of history in the Gospel narrations. Throughout I use this term to describe reinventions of the Passion narrative that contradict or supplement (with new material) the accounts of Mark, Mathew, Luke, and John—without in any way claiming that the Gospels should be understood as historically factual. The complex works in this transnational trajectory exhibit sundry formal characteristics that I have had to relegate to the background so as to foreground the contours of Judas's development.

6. Besides "Judas," see "On the Irish Bishops," where Swift exclaims, "How should we rejoice, if, like Judas the first, / Those splitters of parsons in sunder should burst?" (ll. 39–40).

7. Lamb's animosity may have been inspired by Mackintosh's reversal of his earlier support of the French Revolution, by rumors of his appointment to a government position in India, or by a feud between Mackintosh and Coleridge.

8. See also Hollander and Schwartz for background on the composition of this painting.

9. These lines from the fourteenth-century *Cursor Mundi,* translated by Bonnie Erwin, are quoted in Patterson (415).

10. Cane also discusses Buchanan's *The Wandering Jew* (1893) in terms of a Judas who explains that he died because "I knew the Man whom I had slain was not Messiah" (151), a supposition discussed in my final chapter. In an eighteenth-century text about Judas, John Bonar sets out to prove that "this apostate *Judas,* instead of disproving Christianity in any point, prov[es] it in every one" (4). To Bonar, Judas is "a man of sense and ability" who ultimately "was firmly persuaded, that Jesus was an innocent person, and the true Messiah" (36–37).

11. Longing to teach the Gospels and to become like his teacher, T. Sturge

Moore's Judas hears "wonderful words, nay, even new parables / Worthy of Jesus, beat[ing] about his brain" (20). Judas does agree to show the way to Jesus in Gethsemane, but only because he mistakenly hopes "to save" Jesus by "leading [the captors] astray" (49). In the garden, he does not kiss but is instead kissed (50). Paffenroth points out that Judas's and Jesus' "goodness and enlightenment are contrasted with the supposed primitive barbarism of Judaism" in Moore's poem (*Judas* 54).

12. See Paffenroth (*Judas* 101–10) as well as Ernest Temple Thurston's *Judas Iscariot* (1923), James Lewis Milligan's *Judas Iscariot* (1929), and Sybil Morley's *Judas: A Poem* (1932). Thurston's Judas, who leaves his lover to follow Jesus, responds to her death with an (unsuccessful) effort to resurrect her, for "To raise up the dead even and cast out devils, He gave us power" (99). The temptress Shikona causes Judas to betray Jesus in Milligan's play, where she mourns over his dead body, "Who was this Man that He should take my place, / Turn you from love, and bid you make an end?" (31). In Taylor Caldwell and Jess Stearn's *I, Judas* (1977), Judah decides to leave his seductive betrothed, Rachel, to follow Jesus, at which point his mother for the first time uses the Greek version of his name, Judas (101). At the end of the novel, she informs him that Rachel killed herself because of the shame of carrying Judas's illegitimate child. An irate Magdalene also calls Judah Judas after he refers to her as a prostitute (248). And Jesus in this novel understands "how hard it is for you, Judah, to remain celibate" (246).

13. For a more complete musical analysis, see Paffenroth ("Character of Judas").

14. Matthew Arnold's "Saint Brandan" (1860) recounts the once-a-year "respite" from hell Judas receives to "staunch with ice [his] burning breast" because of an act of charity early in his life (ll. 28, 69). Rudyard Kipling's "The Lance Chantey" (1892) imagines God on Judgment Day about to "gather up the sea," but determining against such an act when the souls of mariners, of slaves, of the Apostle Paul, and also of Judas plead with him: "Lord, hast Thou forgotten Thy covenant with me? / How once a year I go / To cool me on the floe? / And Ye take my day of mercy if Ye take away the sea" (ll. 12–15).

15. See, for example, Ehrman's *Jesus*. Ehrman views Albert Schwietzer (in 1906) as the first to establish the tradition of seeing Jesus in the Jewish tradition of apocalyptic prophets (*Lost Gospel* 149).

16. In Caldwell and Stearn's *I, Judas,* the patriotic twelfth apostle believes that Jesus will be "tried and acquitted" and that Jesus "can conquer death itself" (271, 272), so he therefore goes forward with the plot: "I wanted to see Jesus challenged, so he could confront the Romans and triumph over them, and yet I had no wish to play the betrayer, even innocently" (278–29). But in Pilate's court, he is overcome by lust for a virgin and rapes her, thereby clearly demonstrating that he is destined for a bad end.

17. For a twentieth-century novelistic version of this tradition, see G. A. Page's *The Diary of Judas Iscariot or the Gospel according to Judas* (1912). In Robert Graves's *King Jesus* (1946), Jesus instructs Judas "to buy a sword with which to kill his master." A loyal Judas worries, "How could he take the life of the man he loved best?" and assumes he was chosen because he was "the only one who had realized" the doctrine Jesus was preaching (309). Although he does do Jesus' bidding, Judas attempts to hatch a plot to save him, but it fails.

18. In Story's dramatic monologue, the perspective of the Roman narrator could be interpreted as a sly authorial comment on pagan opacity. In any case, we are left in the dark—by Story but also by De Quincey, Horne, and Ward—about what Jesus' perspective might have been on the evolving Passion narrative.

19. Jeffers's Judas feels haunted by a bird's pain, as by "Flogged slaves and tortured criminals, and bitter deaths of the innocent. Who created it? Who can endure it? Does no one, / Not even our Lord, feel it all but I alone?" (17). Vaughn discusses the influence of Noh plays on the complex temporal framework of Jeffers's play.

20. Jeffers also hints that Jesus knows exactly what he is doing when he preaches what will necessarily get him not only arrested but also crucified as a firebrand, a rabble-rouser. In particular, he stresses Jesus' foreknowledge and acquiescence to his fate. Throughout the verse play, all the characters refer to "the net" (of fishermen or of God's will) to emphasize how they are all caught and tangled in a script not of their own devising.

21. According to one of Sayers's interpreters, Judas—who explains that he trusts nobody, believes in nothing but what he can see and handle—represents the type of "reformer" still "with us": "a self-described humanitarian who will unhesitatingly walk over any number of human beings in the service of what he considers a noble cause," he stands for "the modern temper" (Kenney 238).

22. Even the more conflicted avatars of Judas tend, like Ernest Sutherland Bates's protagonist at the close of *The Gospel according to Judas* (1929), to justify their actions in moral terms: "I loved my Master whom I slew, nor would I have betrayed him but that I loved even more the truth" (226). Bates's novel, which depicts a Gnostic Judas himself betrayed by the Temple priests, is discussed by Pyper (113).

23. See Herman (16), who points out that activists protested against not only DeMille (a self-identified half-Jew), for undertaking the direction of a film that could inflame anti-Semitism, but also "Rudolph (Caiaphas) and Joseph (Judas) Schildkraut—both full-fledged Jews—[who] had no excuses for taking part in the film, and their participation drew much vitriol" (18). Humphries-Brooks argues that because DeMille's Judas is wealthy and uses Jesus for personal rewards, he along with Caiaphas is associated with Jewishness and with money and betrayal (14, 16, 17).

24. The incident is mentioned by Verneuil (261) and seems especially resonant given the anti-Semitic stereotypes often associated with Bernhardt's image, which are discussed in Ockman and Silver (36–43).

25. Simone Weil explained her determination to remain outside the church because of "the use of the two little words *anathema sit*": "I remain beside all those things that cannot enter the Church, the universal repository, on account of those two little words" (*Waiting for God* 33). She associates these two words with the church's establishment of a "sort of totalitarianism in Europe in the thirteenth century" (37). Cameron writes about Weil's feeling of having been "incorrectly assimilated" (130).

26. A dactylic foot contains a stressed and two unstressed beats; the name Judas Iscariot is a double dactyl, as is the name Jesus of Nazareth. In the double dactylic poem, "all the lines except the rhyming ones, which are truncated, are composed to two dactylic feet" (as Hecht and Hollander explain this rigorous form in their introduction to *Jiggery-Pokery* [27]). My use of the rubric Judas the Obscure differs from that of Paffenroth (*Judas*), who uses it (as a chapter title) to emphasize the obscurity of early approaches to Judas.

27. Prayers to Saint Jude are obviously motivated by the hope of saving some-one from a desperate situation that seems hopeless. Paradoxically, devotion to Saint Jude itself became a lost cause when his name was besmirched by its resemblance to Judas's. Orsi explains that Judas's bad reputation histori-cally occluded the apostle Jude, whose followers therefore work to emphasize their contrasting natures: "Judas was treacherous and underhanded, Jude is loyal, dependable, and straightforward" (99–100); however, the two figures "are inseparable; the Patron Saint of Hopeless Causes is Judas inverted" (100). In *The Secret Supper,* a recent novel about Leonardo da Vinci's *Last Supper,* Javier Sierra postulates a Gnostic artist who painted himself "as Saint Jude, the 'good' Judas," with his back turned toward Jesus (201), while it is Peter (not Judas) on the canvas who holds a knife.

28. Little Jude's suicide note—"*Done because we are too menny*" (Hardy 405)—has frequently been interpreted in light of Malthusian population theory and with a focus on its aesthetic outrageousness, as Matz explains (529–32).

29. Most readers view Hardy's novel as an attack on institutions of higher education that exclude the poor and on the bankruptcy of marriage.

30. The suicidal image of Willem van Swanenburg may have influenced Rem-brandt's painting of the penitential Judas. Schwartz claims that the "closest known antecedent to the rare subject is one of the prints in the series of peni-tents by Willem van Swanenburg after Abraham Bloemaert. . . . The pose of Judas is a variant on that of St. Peter in the same series" (75).

31. As O'Malley puts it, "Time is the murderer and the avenger but time destroys itself in the process" (663).

32. The suicides of Islamic prisoners were dubbed "asymmetrical warfare"

by the officer in charge of the U.S. base at Guantánamo in 2006 (Risen and Golden). Father Time recalls Herman Melville's "Bartleby, the Scrivener" (1853), for both of their lives and deaths express a preference not to follow directions, not to exist, if living involves accepting a role in a suspect story not of their own devising. On Melville's relation to Poe, see Fleissner.

33. See Žižek on Job (*Puppet* 125) as well as Miles (*God*).

34. For an analysis of how Yeats's *Calvary* operates along the lines of the mystical vision he was evolving with his wife, see Haswell.

35. An excellent discussion of "The Imp of the Perverse" appears in Elmer (130–37).

36. In the Middle Ages, as chapter 3 argued, suicide was as damning a sign as a demon. The money bag appears in a number of the paintings reprinted in chapter 3; it can also be seen in Lucas Cranach the Younger's *Epitaph for Joachim of Anhalt* (1565), where Judas conceals not only the money bag but also a knife.

37. I am indebted to Andrew H. Miller's interpretation of Kierkegaard's *Sickness unto Death*.

38. Calvin goes on to argue that his view of a Judas handed over "to Satan for torment without hope of relief" proves Catholicism to be erroneous: "If the papists were right in what they teach about penitence in their schools, one could find nothing lacking in Judas, as all their definition of it would apply to him. We can pick out the contrition of heart, the confession by the mouth, the satisfaction in deed, which they speak of. Whence we gather that they only grasp the outer shell, and omit the chief part which is the conversion of man to God, when broken with shame and fear, the sinner renounces himself, in order to give himself over to follow righteousness" (175).

39. The words in quotation marks come from an 1827 sermon of Nathanael Emmons, a Calvinist who is quoted by Cane (158).

40. A very different and much earlier poem also juxtaposes woeful Judas's fate against Jesus' loving promises of infinite compassion. In a 1912 ballad by Cale Young Rice, titled "The Wife of Judas Iscariot," Judas's widow expresses horror that the savior of mankind could have used and abused her husband's confidence in him. The shocked widow of this counterhistory weeps over her dead husband's body, crying out "'Judas! Judas! What has He done, / The Christ you followed so!'" She then asks, "'Was He the Christ and let it be?'" The secret of her husband's mission or identity remains hidden from a world that misunderstands it and him: "'None in the world shall ever know / Your doubts of Him but I!'" (373–74). Not only will his wife alone realize that Judas's act was motivated by his suspicions; she alone will understand that Judas's fate might be thought to justify those misgivings.

41. An introduction to Kant's rule is furnished by Marcia Baron (10–13).

CHAPTER 6

1. Piero Ricci, who interprets the Borges tale, states that "in Hebrew script a single letter—*dàleth*—differentiates the name of Judas from the magic letters, the *Tetragrammaton,* which may not be either written or spoken" (18). He then argues that "The name of Judas thus constitutes the *incipit* of a new system of writing" (24).

2. Klauck discusses Klopstock's Judas and in particular his "attempts to force Jesus to accept the messianic ruling role, which he resists" (24).

3. Hitler exploited both Catholic and Protestant church leaders, but some of his speeches suggest that he believed that "religions are all alike. . . . They have no future." In the speech in which this sentence appears, Hitler rejected efforts to see Christ as Aryan: "Whether it is the Old Testament or the New, or simply the sayings of Jesus according to Houston Stewart Chamberlain—It's all the same old Jewish swindle. It will not make us free" (quoted in Head 68). A recent analysis by Herf is a good example of scholarship that examines propagandistic newspapers, books, posters, speeches, and legislation in light of a Nazi myth about an international Jewish conspiracy, one that did not rely on Christian iconography. Quite a few Nazi leaders resembled Martin Bormann in considering Nationalist Socialism superior to Christianity, which had been tainted by its Jewish roots.

4. Klein discusses this theological theme in Germany before, during, and after the Holocaust (92–126).

5. One elliptical allusion to Judas appears after the war in Jerzy Kosinski's novel *The Painted Bird* (1965), which describes the agony of a boy abandoned during the Holocaust and then repeatedly abused by a sadistic farmer and his menacing dog, Judas. The ten-year-old boy, a paradigmatic victim, is strung up on two hooks driven into the beams of the farmhouse ceiling, and fears falling prey to the murderous attacks of Judas: "I wondered why he went on hanging me up. Did he really expect the dog to kill me when it had failed to do so all these times?" (134).

6. Dieckmann discusses the *Voelkische Beobachter* newspaper caricature (16).

7. Dieckmann's quotation of the poem makes it clear that it conflates Judas's appearance and victory in Germany with burning and martyrdom and murder (17), terrifying threats to the citizenry that must be countered.

8. Most accounts of the film stress that it was shown to the SS before they undertook various genocidal campaigns and to local occupied populations before Nazi "actions" against the Jews. See the discussions of Schulte-Sasse (47–91) as well as Friedman (120) and Klotz (97). Weinstein discusses *Jew Süss* as an assimilation narrative illustrating the concept of allo-Semitism.

9. Hitler follows his warning—"With satanic joy in his face, the black-haired

Jewish youth lurks in wait for the unsuspecting girl whom he defiles with his blood"—by associating Jewish sexual predators with black rapists: "It was and it is Jews who bring the Negroes into the Rhineland, always with the same secret thought and clear aim of ruining the hated white race by the necessarily resulting bastardization, throwing it down from its cultural and political height, and himself rising to be its master" (325).

10. Friedman sees Levy as "the non-assimilated counterpart in his natural stage," setting up "the "caftan Jew/camouflaged Jew" as "the two stages of social integration" (123).

11. King notes, "Unlike an editing device such as the cut, the dissolve does not signify a 'clean' break," but instead "embodies what [Julia] Kristeva calls 'the in-between, the ambiguous' " (24).

12. Klotz discusses the Jew as vampiric (100), as does King (27).

13. As in anti-Semitic propaganda—for example, the notorious fake known as the *Protocols of the Elders of Zion* (published in 1903 and 1905 and reissued as "one of the sacred texts of National Socialism")—Jew Süss operates on the assumption that for Jews in general it is indispensable "*to undermine all faith, to tear out of the minds of the GOYIM the very principle of Godhead and the spirit, and to put in its place arithmetical calculations and material needs*" (Bernstein x, 307–8).

14. King analyzes in detail how *The Eternal Jew* uses the dissolve (32–34), as does Clinefelter (138).

15. Throughout *The Eternal Jew,* Jews are compared to Africans and African Americans: jazz musicians and African influences on art create "niggerized and bastardized" productions, which demonstrate that the "rootless Jew has no feeling for the purity and neatness" of German culture. There is also a stress on "degenerative" Jewish pornography and transvestism, with footage of performers in drag.

16. By interpolating a clip from *The Rothschilds* (1934), a fanciful account of the well-known family, the editor could use the American film to illustrate how wealthy Jewish people pretend to be poor so as to evade the tax collector. As presented in this movie-within-the-documentary, each of the Rothschild sons assimilates into a different European society, one becoming a Frenchman and another Italian, one an Englishman and another Austrian; a map thus can display their metastasizing spiderweb of global economic networks. Buttressing the repeated accusation that Jews do not labor like honest workers but instead play and steal, the sequences emphasize lucrative Jewish cheating and double-dealing. Said to hold "one thing of value—money," the Jews of Poland are shown starting up businesses with trash and a tray, then moving up to stands and small shops, until "the most unscrupulous have warehouses and banks."

17. Along these same lines, a long interpolated clip from Peter Lorre's portrayal of a child murderer in Fritz Lang's *M* (1933) is said to justify the murderer.

18. This gruesome sequence closes with Hitler's promise that should the Jews instigate another world war, he would effect "the destruction of the Jewish race in Europe"; then, as band music plays, crowds enraptured by their "Sieg Heils!" and soldiers dedicated to keeping the race pure are pictured under the waving swastika-emblazoned flags.

19. In relying on Jeremiah (19:6) to conflate Judas's Field of Blood with the "valley of Slaughter" deserved by those who have shed innocent blood, Seth Libby argues, Matthew used "Jeremiah's proclamation against Jerusalem and its people" to heighten "the guilt and culpability of the Jews" and of Judas (34).

20. Trained partly in the States, where he learned to prize African American forms of spirituality, Bonhoeffer was well positioned to critique the racism of Nazi propaganda, and in 1939 he joined a conspiracy against Hitler. Bonhoeffer believed that the church "looks full of hope upon those who have returned home from the people of Israel, upon those who have come to believe in the one true God in Christ" ("Kirche" 50). Yet he lagged in his efforts to combat anti-Semitism. I am by no means attempting to disparage the ultimate sacrifice he made. His biographer Bethge explains how "tormented" Bonhoeffer felt after he decided not to conduct a funeral service for a Jew (275), and Bethge also believes that Bonhoeffer realized his response to the times was "a very tardy one" (830). Kenneth Barnes negotiates a middle course between contemporary scholars who present Bonhoeffer as a courageous moralist and those who view him as "'the best of a bad lot'" (110–11). Baranowski argues that "Bonhoeffer's example holds for the church the vision of absolute, principled opposition in the Third Reich against a picture of Protestant behavior now widely acknowledged to have been wanting" (127).

21. I am grateful to James Rasmussen for this and other translations of the German. Writing about this same passage, Littell contrasts Bonhoeffer the courageous dissident with Bonhoeffer the thinker: "The man whose humanity and decency led him to run risks for Jews and to oppose practical Antisemitism was better than the bad theology which laid the foundations for Christian Antisemitism" (51).

22. Fackenheim recounts testimony by Irving Greenberg about a Slovak rabbi who asked Archbishop Kametko to save Slovak Jews from deportation. Kametko replied, "It is not just a matter of deportation. You will not die there of hunger and disease. They will slaughter all of you, old and young alike, women and children, at once—it is punishment that you deserve for the death of our Lord and Redeemer, Jesus Christ. You have only one solution. Come over to our religion, and I will work to annul this decree" (11). In 1933, according to Kenneth Barnes, "the Aryan Paragraph became official policy in the Prussian church," suspending non-Aryans from the clergy (113). During the late thirties, many members of the Confessing Church took loyalty oaths to Hitler, much to Bonhoeffer's distress (K. Barnes 122).

23. *Die Grundlagen des neunzehnten Jahrhunderts* (*The Foundations of the Nineteenth Century;* 1899) by Chamberlain, who was born in England but married Wagner's daughter and was naturalized as a German citizen, "sold 60,000 copies in eight editions over ten years" (Head 64). "According to the prophets of Germanic Christianity," Mosse explains, "the Jew lacked a soul, all virtues, and the capacity for ethical behavior for the reason that Judaism was a fossilized legalism" (129).

24. Littell quotes the *Deutsche Christen,* explaining that "A special edition of the four gospels was published free of Jewish influence" (53). Heschel concludes, "The example of the Aryan Jesus is an important phenomenon in the history of theology because of the enormous influence exerted by German Protestant biblical scholarship to this day" ("Quest" 84). After Hitler's rise to power, even a Protestant theologian like Gerhard Kittel, whose early work defended Judaism and the centrality of the "Old" Testament in the New, disassociated biblical Jews from what was presumed to be a degenerate modern Jewry (Ericksen 61, 68).

25. Bonhoeffer does go on in this passage to repeat the apostles' "is it I?" in order to engage their perplexed anxiety that they might have to identify themselves as sinners. Niemöller also meditates on Judas: "The cold hatred of the Jewish authorities fills us with horror, the groundless and unfathomable treachery of Judas makes us shudder" (141); then he goes on to argue that "Pilate nevertheless becomes the hangman of the man whose life he has tried to save" (143).

26. Barth repeatedly reviles Judas and the Jews. "Both [Matthew's and Luke's] accounts of what happened to the reward of Judas confirm the fact that both Judas and Judah—Judas as the embodiment of Judah, and Judah as embodied in Judas—have, in fact, no future as such and in and for themselves"; "This Judah and Jerusalem can only perish and disappear, to make way for another" (*Doctrine* 469, 470). Such a view could be held by Jewish thinkers as well. Robert Coles quotes Simone Weil—"'Jahveh made to Israel the same promises as the devil did to Christ'"—and then explains that "Her historically knowing and able mind refused for even a moment to examine the relationship of the Jews to Jesus—the splits among the Jews, the complexities of a particularly confused historical moment. Simone Weil pays no attention to those Jews who followed Jesus, the disciples and authors of the Gospels" (60–61).

27. "Alas, poor Judas, what hast thou done" comes from a fourteenth-century Passiontide hymn "Laus tibi, Christe, qui pateris" (Praise be to thee, Christ, who dost suffer), often sung in German: "Oh Du armer Judas, vas hastu gethon." The verses "reproach Judas rather than sympathizing with him. Alas for poor Judas: he is lost" (Ohly 78). One year later (after Kristallnacht), Bonhoeffer cautioned his seminarians, "When today the synagogues are set afire, tomorrow the churches will burn" (quoted in K. Barnes 123).

28. Both sentences are discussed by Fackenheim (13). The first scholar was Eberhard Bethge, who is quoting from Bonhoeffer's *Ethics*, which he edited and which is also discussed by Kenneth Barnes (126); the second was William J. Peck.

29. On how "the Jewishness of Jesus served as a central trope" for Jews as well as Christians in Germany (11), see Heschel's book *Abraham Geiger and the Jewish Jesus*. Chagall severely revises Gauguin's impressionistic vision in *Yellow Christ* (1889), where pastoral fields surround a Jesus visited by three serene women in peasant hats and aprons.

30. The idea of a sacred death—wherein a single and sanctified individual lays down his life in a voluntary affirmation of faith—is annulled during the Holocaust by the millions sentenced to wholesale destruction by the Nazis. By considering Chagall's Jesus in relation to Bonhoeffer's 1944 view that "The church stands, not at the boundaries where human powers give out, but in the middle of the village," one can measure how far Bonhoeffer has moved away from supersessionism: "That is how it is in the Old Testament, and in this sense we still read the New Testament far too little in the light of the Old" (*Letters* 282). Or again when Bonhoeffer claims that the Christian "must drink the earthly cup to the dregs, and only in his doing so is the crucified and risen Lord with him, and he crucified and risen with Christ": "This world must not be prematurely written off; in this the Old and New Testaments are at one" (337).

31. According to Bonhoeffer, a church fighting only for its own self-preservation cannot bring redemption: "Christian thinking, speaking, and organizing must be born anew" out of "prayer and righteous action among men" (*Letters* 300). To that extent, he calls to mind the thinking of liberation theologists.

32. Littell's claim is related to but somewhat different from Steiner's view: "the Cross stands beside the gas ovens," he believes, "because of the ideological-historical continuity which connects Christian anti-Semitism, old as the Gospels and the Church Fathers, to its terminal eruption in the heart of a Christian Europe" (*No Passion Spent* 395).

33. Two other works by Anderle, his *Judas* (1995) and his *Variation on Giotto's Judas Kissing Christ* (1993), can be seen in color plates reprinted in Anderle (266, 267).

34. The drawing resembles much of Anderle's other work, where "brutality wins out over understanding, aggression over humility, stupidity over knowledge" (Machalický 14).

35. The Jesuit Joseph Bonsirven is quoted by Amishai-Maisels (102).

36. This insight into Job derives from Žižek's interpretation in *The Puppet and the Dwarf* (126). A statement by Miles about a different moment in God's evolving identity illuminates Chagall's Christ: "it is not the Jews who have failed him but he who has failed the Jews" (*Christ* 180). The difference between Miles's murdered God and Chagall's is that the former does offer his followers eternal life.

37. See Oesterreicher (1–136), who explains that "From the time of Christian antiquity up to that of Vatican II, there had been hardly any development of the Church's teaching on the mystery of Jewish existence" (39), though of course there were many debates about such other subjects as the Eucharist, the triune God, etc. Jeremy Cohen discusses the Second Vatican Council in terms of its conversations about the relationship between the Catholic Church and Jews (171–82).

38. Intriguingly, in the work of this African American poet, the monstrous weight of the silver in Judas's palm is described as "thirty *white* coins" (295; emphasis mine). Is Cullen imagining Judas as Jesus' slave, one who *must,* under severely constrained circumstances, do his master's bidding?

39. "Judas projects Jesus' own daemonic nature. This is implicit in all the dreams in the novel; it becomes explicit at one point when Jesus, hearing Judas' voice, recognizes it as the deepest voice of his own deepest self" (Bien 71).

40. At Kazantzakis's seder, Jesus fills Judas's glass with salt water "overflowing" (423) and his own "brimful" (*Last Temptation* 423). Though the others only sip a few drops, Jesus and Judas drain their glasses. When Jesus feels himself losing heart, Judas and Jesus join glances—"the one stern and merciless, the other beseeching and afflicted. A split second only—and straightway Jesus shook his head, smiled bitterly at Judas" (426). While the other apostles at table despair at the necessity of the crucifixion, Jesus nods to Judas, who grasps his crooked staff and rushes out. In the garden, Jesus greets soldiers and Levites—"Welcome to the envoys of my God" (433)—with no mention of Judas's presence, and no kiss.

41. The Greek Orthodox Church excommunicated Kazantzakis, the Roman Catholic Church banned the book, and bishops denounced the movie because it dishonored Jesus (presumably by presenting him as weak-willed); Jeremy Cohen discusses how this attack damaged Jewish movie producers (243).

42. Brelich's Dupin also postulates an imperialistic God who similarly thinks of Israel, "What mattered the little nation's immense disillusion compared to the enormous advantage that would accrue to Him? Why go looking for trouble with the Jews when, with a skillfully conducted policy, He could win over and conquer the *damned* by the millions" (105). In addition, Dupin argues that in the Passion, Jesus was "sent more to save the Father than to save humanity" (107).

43. Disturbing as such an idea of a ruthless God might be, it can be traced back to the ancient Gnostics, who believed that the biblical God was not the ultimate divinity but instead an ignorant, bloody power to whom should be attributed all misfortunes. As markedly as Kazantzakis's depiction of the Passion differs from Saramago's, the Greek author also exploits Gnostic ideas about divinity, which are discussed in Meyer's essay "Judas and the Gnostic Connection."

44. Saramago's judgment against this bloodthirsty God resembles the Gospel of Judas's attack on the eleven apostles' false religion, a response not to Jesus' teachings (which only Judas understands) but instead to a God who demands human sacrifice. Pagels and King read the Gospel of Judas as a savage attack against Christians who promulgated an ethics of martyrdom and self-sacrifice.

45. Kazantzakis also particularly calls into question the veracity of Matthew throughout his novel, by having Jesus read Matthew's reports of his acts and words only to reject them as "Lies! Lies! Lies!" (*Last Temptation* 391).

46. It seems probable that *The Last Temptation of Christ*'s exoneration of Judas reflects a widespread intuition about the relationship between the pariah Judas and the "final solution" as well as the succession of genocides, religious wars, and ethnic conflicts that followed in its wake, though Lew Wasserman, the Jewish chairman of MCA (the parent company of Universal Pictures, which made the film), was excoriated for "fomenting anti-Jewish hatred by allowing the distribution of [Scorsese's] film" of the novel (Tatum 181).

47. Felstiner discusses the phenomenon of quarreling with God in the verse of Paul Celan, and I analyze it in the verse of contemporary poets writing in English (Gubar 227–40).

48. In *The Work of Betrayal,* Brelich's Dupin rejects such a hypothesis of a manipulative Jesus precisely because it tarnishes Jesus' name: "to transform, to deform a human being for one's own purposes, bringing down upon him eternal damnation and the contempt of posterity" would "definitely compromise" Jesus' morality (129). These bleak allegations remain merely implicit in *The Last Temptation of Christ,* because Kazantzakis offset them by bracketing Judas's eventual fate and by emphasizing his proactive role in a voluntary partnership approached somewhat timorously by Jesus.

49. As Mossinsohn's Judas explains well into the book, "Jesus refused to be told upon whom had fallen the miserable lot of pointing him out. He pleaded with Barabbas not to tell the real truth to the informer. Had I known that it was Jesus' wish to be crucified, to serve as a cause for inciting a storm of rebellion, the beginning of the revolt, and that his tortured body was to serve as fuel for the fire, I would have refused to carry out the order" (189). In this convoluted counterhistory, a surviving Judas keeps telling his intimates that he is the betrayer; however, most of them remain convinced that "Cain is Judas Iscariot" (201). When Judas finally meets up with Paul and asks, "Call me Judas!" Paul labels him mad because Judas "has already taken his own life in Jerusalem" (285). Jackson discusses the sensation of violation that accompanies betrayal.

50. Schonfield's approach on the surface is more respectful about Jesus' intentions. Yet in his account, at the anointing Jesus' "stratagem was . . . designed to pile on the pressure at the crucial moment and induce the traitor to act" (135).

This episode convinced Judas, who had heard Jesus repeatedly talking about his imminent betrayal and death, that "Jesus expected to be betrayed" (135).

51. The twelfth apostle—upset that he has admitted his part in the scheme to the narrator of *A Time for Judas*—kills himself because he was tempted to confide the true story, which was supposed "to be silence and mystery" (Callaghan 185). Ironically, then, Callaghan's Judas hangs himself "for telling the truth" that Jesus wanted covered up (196).

52. In Michael Dickinson's novel, Jesus informs the narrator, Judas, that "he wanted me to go to the Temple priests and offer to hand him over to them" (92). Jesus' plan is to get arrested but then released by the people's "popular choice" in the Passover amnesty (93); however, in this curious fantasy another follower is crucified instead, and then Judas encourages Jesus to "perform the ultimate miracle of his career" by staging his own resurrection (142). Dickinson's Judas recounts the scene: "Summoning up all my strength, I smashed the hammer down on the nail and felt it pass through his hand into the wood beneath. The Master screamed and blood spattered out, wetting my face and shirt. I became hysterical and, sobbing and jabbering, begged him to forgive me for hurting him, but fiercely he demanded that I pull it out swiftly and do the other hand, and I obeyed him, wild with grief at the spilling of his precious blood and his shriek of pain" (144).

53. Cane interprets Borges's story as "unique" in that "it is not even that equal gratitude is due to Judas and Jesus, as Judas is alone truly deserving of praise," for "in his destruction Judas can look, from a certain perspective, to be the one 'lost for the sins of the world'" (162).

54. A reviewer of Kennelly's book glimpses the hells of Dante and Hieronymus Bosch inside its pages and recognized in its author "a modern sensibility struggling with medieval demons," in particular the demonic Judas (Augustine Martin's review in the *Irish Independent* is quoted on the back of *The Little Book of Judas*).

55. Althusser's now classic list of "ideological State apparatuses" (or ISAs), produced in 1969, probably did not influence Kennelly. Nevertheless, the poet ambitiously tracks the Judas-effect on each of these formations, which Althusser lists as follows:

— the religious ISA (the system of the different Churches),
— the educational ISA (the system of the different public and private "Schools"),
— the family ISA,
— the legal ISA,
— the political ISA (the political system, including the different Parties),
— the trade-union ISA,

— the communications ISA (press, radio and television, etc.),
— the cultural ISA (Literature, the Arts, sports, etc.). (143)

For another critical approach to *The Book of Judas*, see Roche's fine essay.
56. Given the importance of female actors in the Passion as well as the centrality of women in the history of Christianity, male domination in the Catholic
Church is the most obvious social injustice explored by Kennelly, who wrote
one poem with a title that sounds like a group of backup singers: "The Twelve
Apostlettes" (137).

CHAPTER 7

1. Pyper likewise takes notice of "novelists who speak for Judas," the apostle
made to represent "the truth of death" (119). Similarly, Barth balances the
"'for' of Jesus," with his power of grace, and the "'against' of Judas," with his
weakness of human wickedness (*Doctrine* 477).
2. Encapsulating the link between Judas and the Jews, Jews (in the context of
this list) are prominently depicted in the New Testament as not converted to a
religion they were explicitly offered.
3. The political as well as life-affirming spirit of Judas Day is discussed by
Lamadrid and Thomas, who include wonderful pictures of some of these
Mexican Judas figures. Diego Rivera painted a mural in Mexico City, *Burning
Judases* (1924–26).
4. Significantly, Judas celebrations occurred after sacred cathedral and church
bells were silenced during Holy Week, replaced by rattles. Beezley recounts
the use of pig bladders (120), but he also describes bakers stuffing rolls in
the Judas effigy, soap makers soap, and butchers chunks of meat, supplying
rewards strewn to crowds of revelers. Following the logic of such thinkers as
Bakhtin and Natalie Zemon Davis, Beezley views these Judas Days as festivals
of misrule (108).
5. The biblical scholars Borg and Crossan explain that "while we were growing up, the only thing worse than being a 'doubting Thomas' was to be a
'Judas.' But there is no condemnation of Thomas in the story [told by John]"
(203). That doubt has historically been externalized in the Jews is apparent in
the charge of host desecration (discussed in chapter 3). In a fictional biography
of Judas by Ken Smith, Judas "felt the entire sorrow that he had not seen Jesus
in his risen state as had all the others, though he admitted that he had no right
to see him" (433). Smith's Judas conspires with James and Simon to place Jesus
before the Sanhedrin, in the (mistaken) belief that by so doing Jesus "will have
the opportunity to tell to the world of theology what we know of him" (382).

Ray Anderson's *Gospel according to Judas* also includes a Judas who records that "The eleven other disciples, my former companions, each met Jesus after his resurrection" (143).

6. Barth uses an extended comparison of Judas and Paul to argue that "Judas says No, Paul says Yes" precisely because the former did not witness Jesus' death: "it is by the death of Jesus that the Judas in Paul dies, and Paul is cleansed and liberated from his own past, so that he is no longer capable of what Judas inflicted upon Jesus" (*Doctrine* 501).

7. According to Cane, Robert Buchanan's *The Wandering Jew* imagines Judas believing that the man he killed "was not Messiah" (151).

8. Because Judas "was an exceptional man," Klausner argues, Jesus accepted him; "not till the very last did Jesus recognize in him that base character which made him a traitor" (285).

9. Mailer's Yeshua realizes regarding Judas, "If he would betray me, his suffering would be greater than mine" (200). And the kiss in the garden proves to Yeshua that Judas "knew he loved me too, and more than he could ever have believed" (209). At news of the suicide, Yeshua cannot speak but "would have wept. From one side of my heart or the other" (218).

10. Judas in Nino Ricci's novel *Testament* feels trapped between loyalty to anti-Roman insurrectionists and devotion to Jesus. Better educated than the other apostles and convinced of "how little of value there was in the world, how men were deceitful and base and would espouse to you the loftiest ideals in one breath and contradict them in the next" (121), Judas nevertheless finds in Jesus a new vision appealing enough to betray all his oaths and risk his own life by warning Jesus of the danger he would encounter in Jerusalem. When Jesus is accused by the governor, his crime of treason is sealed by guilt through association—namely, his past association with Judas, "a suspected rebel" (432).

11. In Archer and Moloney's *The Gospel according to Judas by Benjamin Iscariot,* the Scribe tricks a loving Judas into believing that Jesus will be rescued and then hands Jesus over to Caiaphas. Peter refuses to help Judas bear witness on Jesus' behalf.

12. This tradition of imagining a Judas who lived longer continues in biblical scholarship today. Borg and Crossan speculate, "had Judas not killed himself or died suddenly, we may imagine that even the betrayer would have been restored to relationship and community" (126).

13. The rationale for keeping Judas at the center and sidelining Jesus has been the plethora of books about various incarnations of Jesus—as devoted shepherd, king of kings, prince of peace, liberator—compared to the paucity of approaches to Judas, his major agonist. See, for instance, Pelikan.

14. In a similar vein, Guirgis's Jesus tells Judas, "You were my heart!" (103). Guirgis includes a speech by Mary Magdalene in which she declares, "I think

he was Jesus's favorite too . . . Judas was almost an alter ego to Jesus—he was the shadow to Jesus's light" (60; ellipsis his). In Panas's *The Gospel according to Judas* (originally published in Polish in 1973), Jesus says to Judas, "You have been like a mirror, like a judge, weighing my every word, my every action" (188–89). This skeptical Judas serves Jesus by leaving him before the events that result in his death. In *The Flight of the Feathered Serpent,* Cosani's Judas follows his statement about being the "no" to Jesus' "yes" with a promise, "I will be your reflection" (188). In the first and fifth chapters of her book, Bartsch traces back to Seneca the ancient idea of the pedagogic mirror—the gaze is turned back on itself, so that the observing self can be illuminated or taught by the objective self it sees.

15. The notion of "therapeutic trust" is attributed to H. J. N. Horsburgh in the helpful overview on trust provided by McLeod.

16. The author of Acts also asserts, "It is through many persecutions that we must enter the kingdom of God" (14:22).

17. I am indebted to conversations with Sandra Macpherson, whose ideas about strict liability illuminate the link between tragedy (in which characters recognize their responsibility without being directly at fault) and the rise of the novel.

18. According to Baier, "Trust comes in webs, not in single strands, and disrupting one strand often rips apart whole webs" (134). The trajectory of the relationship between Jesus and Judas suggests that when a single thread of trust tangles, the web may break or a different strand may bear the load.

19. An interpretation of the Passion, Melville's novella *Billy Budd, Sailor* hinges on this exchange of good and evil, as Barbara Johnson shows in an essay that has deepened my understanding not only of Melville's evil Claggart but also of Judas.

20. Jesus may also sound cynically idealistic to a skeptical Judas. Linda Charnes examines "cynical idealism," which is evident when people doubt their own actions but mask that doubt with "the brittle bravado of idealist enthusiasm" (2), a concept discussed by the philosopher Peter Sloterdijk in *A Critique of Cynical Reason.*

21. Discordant as the multiple perspectives on the Passion are, evil generally does not appear to be situational: the decision or desire to inflict harm, regardless of which approach prevails or which cruxes in the New Testament it draws on, rarely arises out of dehumanizing or authoritarian social systems such as those described by Stanley Milgrim in his infamous obedience studies or more recently by Zimbardo in *The Lucifer Effect.* Despite the Roman occupation of Jerusalem, the Passion story seldom lends itself to the judgment that abusive deeds ought to be deemed the by-product of miserable or coercive environments (such as military bureaucracies or prisons). In some interpretations, it seems dispositional (the consequence of psychology), in some cosmic

(the consequence of the forces ruling the world), in some societal (the result of competing values). Not merely a construct or by-product, evil (or the infliction of injury) generally abides with agency, whether human or divine.

22. In the poem "Zone," Kennelly's Judas knows that "I'm the one who's wanted most," though his enemies seek to set up a border zone, "Dividing me from my redeemer; but the bond / Between that man and me will go on and on / Despite church, state, stories of betrayal and murder" (109).

23. Girard famously viewed the resurrection of the innocent Christ as a break in the cycle of violence he locates in scapegoating.

24. Doubling explains why Judas's history contains so many vampires, doll-like effigies, and animal familiars. Rogers discusses catoptricophobia and "the primitive soul-doubles" of "ghosts, revenants, vampires, werewolves," etc. (8–9). As in the ancient world, "the mirror provides a tool for the splitting of the viewer into viewing subject and viewed object, judging 'I' and judged-to-be-lacking 'me'" (Bartsch 23). Mirroring of the self, according to Bartsch, occurs "in the weakest of senses, since none of these sources suggests that the momentary dislocation of self-identity leads to any permanent sense of self-spectatorship or self-judgment" (23).

25. Throughout this section, I am indebted to Kieran Setiya. The contrasts pursued in the next three paragraphs refer loosely to the recent classification of moral theories as consequentialist, deontological, or virtue-ethical (all discussed by Kagan).

26. Just as for the particularist philosopher no two cases are exactly alike, so numerous successors of Mark, Matthew, Luke, and John present sometimes strikingly, sometimes minutely different circumstances in their literary recounting or visual portrayals of the betrayal story. Kagan notes that particularism is "philosophically *uninteresting*" (185). Yet what might seem philosophically uninteresting—the rejection of generalizations about doing right and doing wrong—becomes aesthetically powerful and fascinating.

27. A more nuanced statement of virtue ethics appears in Setiya (38, 67, 70).

28. See Faulkner for a recent response to Freud's theories in "Beyond the Pleasure Principle."

29. Gould explains why he and Richard Lewontin used the spandrel to describe nonadaptive secondary consequences of brain evolution.

30. Rosenberg describes how early Christians distanced themselves from their Jewish origins in part 1 of his book. Kruger argues of Jewish-Christian relations in medieval Europe that "the Christian incarnational reorganization of history, in working to make fully *past* that which precedes the rupture of the incarnation, operates efficiently to put Judaism to rest, to kill it off (at least, but not only, phantasmatically) and thus to make way for the new Christian dispensation" (3). Yet "Despite all the pressure to disavow, indeed destroy, Judaism, Christianity also expressed a certain need to preserve Jews" (5).

31. The emergence of pro-Zionist evangelical mega-churches in the United States at the start of the twenty-first century illustrates the malleability of Christians' response to Judaism and Israel. According to one Christian thinker, "The Jewish people can define itself in history without Christianity: Christians cannot establish a self-identity except in relationship to the Jewish people—past and present, and whenever the Christians have attempted to do so, they have fallen into grievous heresy and sin" (Littell 66).

32. I am therefore taking issue with the formulation of Boyarin quoted in the introduction, that "Judaism is not the 'mother' of Christianity" (5). Schäfer seems to use the maternal analogue unconsciously: "The Jewish sect triggered by Jesus in Palestine would eventually evolve into a religion of its own, a religion to boot that would claim to have superseded its mother religion . . ." (2).

33. Heschel points out that the Jewish thinker Leo Baeck tended to imagine Christianity as effeminate in contrast to a morally responsible and thus masculine Judaism (*Abraham Geiger* 236).

34. Brunner can stand for the long Christian tradition of thought that compares Adam and Christ: "As in Jesus Christ all have been redeemed, so in Adam all have sinned" (97); "in 'Adam' all are sinners; in Christ, all are redeemed" (99).

35. Judas in his resemblance to Eve bears on Jack Miles's point in his book *Christ*: "The New Testament is like a skin on every square inch of which the Old Testament is tattooed" (65).

36. For an excellent account of feminist approaches to the two creation stories about Eve, see Bellis.

37. Yanay (54) bases her analysis of "the paradox of hatred" on the work of the psychoanalyst William Stekel.

38. The nexus between Judas and homosexuality relates to Boswell's point that "the fate of Jews and gay people has been almost identical throughout European history, from early Christian hostility to extermination in concéntration camps" (14). Passing or posing can, of course, mask gender identity, but the camouflaging of sexuality or sexual orientation, less anatomically apparent than gender, pertains more obviously to Judas. When Judas stands for the linkage of Jews and homosexuals, a connection routed through the first female makes Jewish and homosexual men appear effeminate, unfaithful, devious, and ultimately self-destructive in their influence. Especially in the Nazi period, Judas resembles Iago, a villain also often presumed to be a repressed homosexual. See Adelman, who rehearses this reading of Iago and qualifies it (134).

39. Norman Mailer is quite unusual in this last regard, and the weakness of *The Gospel according to the Son* may be related to his negligible personal investment in the New Testament.

40. In my approach, I have not tried to evaluate the historical bases for representational decisions or to solve theological disputes about configurations of

Judas and their impact on belief systems. The dearth of historical knowledge and the plethora of theological debates would have frustrated efforts to understand Judas's representation over twenty centuries. In appendix 2 of *Christ,* Miles gives a summary of the evolution of literary approaches to the Bible that take a middle course between historical and theological interpretations (265–89).

41. Halas explains that the name Judas "is a verbal noun derived from the Hiphil passive; i.e. the imperfect Hophal of the same root (*yādāh*), so that it means *praised, celebrated, lauded*" (1). Bonhoeffer's curious assertion, quoted in chapter 6, that the twelfth apostle's "name means 'Thanks' in German" may refer to the Hebrew etymology.

42. In a German-language study of Judas, Klauck comes to a similar conclusion. After explaining that "Hatred for Judas must be dismantled precisely so that it cannot continue to nourish subliminally a hatred for Judaism," he then argues: "Through a well-known scapegoat mechanism we have transferred onto Judas whatever aggressions, murderous appetites, avarice and doubtings of the faith hide in us ourselves" (144, 146).

43. The terms used here derive from Simone Weil, who goes on to explain that "This is the presence of evil in us. It is the ugliness in us. The more we feel it, the more it fills us with horror. The soul rejects it in the same way as we vomit" (*Waiting for God* 123).

44. The Filipino poet Emmanuel Lacaba expresses a similar conviction: "Named Judas, born Jesus, named Jesus, born Judas, / I am not what I am, I am what I am not" (372). Ricaredo Demetrillo's "The Scare-Crow Christ" addresses the reader in a comparable vein: "Are you not Judas to this scare-crow Christ?" (410). The editors of the anthology in which his poem appears preface it by commenting, "Simultaneous identification with Jesus and Judas, as in 'The Scare-Crow Christ,' is a recurrent theme in modern Filipino poetry on Christ" (410).

45. Balthasar appears to agree about the riddle of human treachery when he argues that "The inter-play between the God who hands over and the sinners who, in handing over, betray, has an extremely paradoxical character" (110) and when he further asserts that "The handing over of Jesus in the Passion remains a mystery" (110) or that "the very contradiction between human treason and the love of God in giving his Son must be bonded together with the 'contradiction of the Cross' and there find its resolution" (112).

46. Madden and Hare attribute this perspective on paradox to Paul Tillich: "For a believer, Tillich says, the existence of prima facie gratuitous evil does not constitute a reason for giving up his belief in God but simply constitutes one of the ultimate mysteries of religion" (66).

47. Cane discusses Barth's conflation of Judas and Paul, whereby Paul as a persecutor had resembled Judas but also took over Judas's work by "fulfilling what Judas tried to reverse—the faithful handing over of Jesus to the Gentiles"

(64). In Jewish thinking, Paul (who famously converted) can become a figure of treachery somewhat like Judas: "In the process of becoming the Apostle to the Gentiles, Paul also became the 'arch-apostate' of the Jews" (Rosenberg 45).

48. To the extent that Judas is less evil than those who excoriated him, he fits into a larger pattern discussed by Frankfurter: "the real atrocities of history seem to take place *not* in the perverse ceremonies of some evil culture but rather in the course of *purging* such cults from the world. Real evil happens when people speak of evil" (12).

WORKS CITED

Abraham a Sancta Clara. *Sämmtliche Werke* [Collected Works]. Band 4. Passau: Friedrich Winkler, 1835.

Acocella, Joan. "The Saintly Sinner: The Two-Thousand-Year Obsession with Mary Magdalene." *New Yorker* 13 and 20 Feb. 2006: 140–49.

Althusser, Louis. "Ideology and Ideological State Apparatuses (Notes towards an Investigation)." *Lenin and Philosophy, and Other Essays.* Trans. Ben Brewster. New York: Monthly Review Press, 1972. 127–86.

Amishai-Maisels, Ziva. "The Jewish Jesus." *Journal of Jewish Art* 9 (1982): 84–104.

Anderle, Jiří. *Jiří Anderle: Drawings, Prints, Paintings, Objects 1954–95.* Pref. Jiří Machalický. Ed. Jana Steinerová. Trans. Anna Bryson. Prague: Slovart, 1996.

Anderson, Ray S. *The Gospel according to Judas.* Colorado Springs, CO: Helmers & Howard, 1991.

Andreyev, Leonid. "Judas Iscariot." *When the King Loses His Head and Other Stories.* Trans. Archibald J. Wolfe. New York: International Book Publishing, 1920. 45–130.

"The Arabic Gospel of the Infancy of the Saviour." *Apocryphal Gospels, Acts, and Revelations.* Trans. Alexander Walker. Ante-Nicene Christian Library vol. 16. Edinburgh: T. & T. Clark, 1870. 100–124.

Archer, Jeffrey, and Francis J. Moloney. *The Gospel according to Judas by Benjamin Iscariot.* New York: St. Martin's, 2007.

Archibald, Elizabeth. *Incest and the Medieval Imagination.* Oxford: Clarendon, 2001.

Arendt, Hannah. *The Origins of Totalitarianism.* New York: Harcourt, Brace, 1951.

Armstrong, Karen. *A History of God: The 4,000-Year Quest of Judaism, Christianity and Islam.* New York: Ballantine, 1993.

Arnold, Matthew. "Saint Brandan." *The Poems of Matthew Arnold*. Ed. Kenneth Allott. London: Longmans, 1965. 463–66.

Arthur, Ross G. "Literary Jews and the Breakdown of the Medieval Testamental Pattern." *Jewish Presences in English Literature*. Ed. Derek Cohen and Deborah Heller. Montreal: McGill-Queen's University Press, 1990. 113–27.

Atwan, Robert, George Dardess, and Peggy Rosenthal, eds. *Divine Inspiration: The Life of Jesus in World Poetry*. New York: Oxford University Press, 1998.

Augustine. *The City of God, Books I–VII*. Trans. Demetrius B. Zema and Gerald G. Walsh. Intro. Étienne Gilson. Vol. 6 of *The Writings of Saint Augustine*. New York: Fathers of the Church, 1950.

———. *Tractates on the Gospel of John, 112–24; Tractates on the First Epistle of John*. Trans. John W. Rettig. The Fathers of the Church, a new translation; vol. 92. Washington, DC: Catholic University of America Press, 1988.

Axton, Richard. "Interpretations of Judas in Middle English Literature." *Religion in the Poetry and Drama of the Late Middle Ages*. Ed. Piero Boitani and Anna Torti. Cambridge: Brewer, 1990. 179–97.

Bach, Johann Sebastian. *St. Matthew Passion*. Gabrieli Consort and Players. Cond. Paul McCreesh. Deutsche Grammaphon, 2003.

Backscheider, Paula R. *Reflections on Biography*. New York: Oxford University Press, 1999.

Baier, Annette C. *Trust*. The Tanner Lectures on Human Values. Princeton University, 6–8 March 1991. 11 Feb. 2008 <http://www.tannerlectures.utah.edu/lectures/baier92.pdf>.

Bakhtin, Mikhail. *Rabelais and His World*. Trans. Hélène Iswolsky. Bloomington: Indiana University Press, 1984.

Baldwin, Aaron Dwight. *The Gospel of Judas Iscariot*. Chicago: Jamieson-Higgins, 1902.

Balthasar, Hans Urs von. *Mysterium Paschale: The Mystery of Easter*. Trans. Aidan Nichols. Edinburgh: T&T Clark, 1990.

Baranowski, Shelley. *The Confessing Church, Conservative Elites, and the Nazi State*. Texts and Studies in Religion 28. Lewiston, NY: Mellen, 1986.

Barasch, Moshe. "Despair in the Medieval Imagination." *Social Research* 66 (1999): 565–76.

———. *Giotto and the Language of Gesture*. Cambridge: Cambridge University Press, 1987.

Barnes, Djuna. *Nightwood*. London: Faber & Faber, 1949.

Barnes, Kenneth C. "Dietrich Bonhoeffer and Hitler's Persecution of the Jews." *Betrayal: German Churches and the Holocaust*. Ed. Robert P. Ericksen and Susannah Heschel. Minneapolis: Fortress, 1999. 110–28.

Baron, Marcia. "Kantian Ethics." *Three Methods of Ethics: A Debate*. By Marcia W. Baron, Philip Pettit, and Michael Slote. Oxford: Blackwell, 1997. 3–92.

Barth, Karl. *The Doctrine of God*. Vol. 2, part 2 of *Church Dogmatics*. Trans. G. W. Bromiley et al. Edinburgh: T. & T. Clark, 1957.

———. *Letters, 1961–1968*. Ed. Jürgen Fangmeier and Hinrich Stoevesandt. Trans. and ed. Geoffrey W. Bromiley. Grand Rapids, MI: Eerdmans, 1981.

Barton, Bruce. *The Man Nobody Knows*. 1925. Chicago: Dee, 2000.

Bartsch, Shadi. *The Mirror of the Self: Sexuality, Self-Knowledge, and the Gaze in the Early Roman Empire*. Chicago: University of Chicago Press, 2006.

Bataille, Georges. *Erotism: Death and Sensuality*. Trans. Mary Dalwood. San Francisco: City Lights Books, 1986.

Bates, Ernest Sutherland. *The Gospel according to Judas Iscariot*. London: Heinemann, 1929.

Baum, Paul Franklin. "The English Ballad of Judas Iscariot." *PMLA* 31 (1916): 181–89.

———. "The Medieval Legend of Judas Iscariot." *PMLA* 31 (1916): 481–632.

Beckwith, Sarah. *Signifying God: Social Relation and Symbolic Act in the York Corpus Christi Plays*. Chicago: The University of Chicago Press, 2001.

Beerbohm, Max. *Zuleika Dobson; or, An Oxford Love Story*. London: Heinemann, 1911.

Beezley, William H. *Judas at the Jockey Club and Other Episodes of Porfirian Mexico*. Lincoln: University of Nebraska Press, 1987.

Bellis, Alice Ogden. "The Story of Eve." *Helpmates, Harlots, and Heroes: Women's Stories in the Hebrew Bible*. Louisville, KY: Westminster/John Knox, 1994. 45–66.

Benedetti, Sergio. "Caravaggio's 'Taking of Christ,' a Masterpiece Rediscovered." *Burlington Magazine* November 1993: 731–46.

Benoit, Pierre. "The Death of Judas." *Jesus and the Gospel*. Vol. 1. Trans. Benet Weatherhead. London: Darton, Longman, & Todd, 1973. 189–207.

Bernstein, Herman. *The Truth about "The Protocols of Zion: A Complete Exposure."* New York: KTAV, 1971.

Bersani, Leo, and Ulysse Dutoit. "Beauty's Light." *October* 82 (Fall 1997): 17–29.

———. *Caravaggio's Secrets*. Cambridge, MA: MIT Press, 1998.

Bethge, Eberhard. *Dietrich Bonhoeffer: A Biography*. Rev. and ed. Victoria J. Barnett. Minneapolis: Fortress, 2000.

Bidart, Frank. *In the Western Night: Collected Poems, 1965–90*. New York: Farrar Straus Giroux, 1990.

Bien, Peter. *Nikos Kazantzakis: Novelist*. Bristol: Bristol Classical Press, 1989.

Bloom, Harold. *Jesus and Yahweh: The Names Divine*. New York: Riverhead, 2005.

————. "The One with the Beard Is God, the Other Is the Devil." *Portuguese Literary and Cultural Studies* 6 (Spring 2001): 155–66.

Blue, Adrianne. *On Kissing: From the Metaphysical to the Erotic*. London: Gollancz, 1996.

Blumenfeld-Kosinski, Renate. *Not of Woman Born: Representations of Caesarean Birth in Medieval and Renaissance Culture*. Ithaca: Cornell University Press, 1990.

Bonar, John. *Observations on the Conduct and Character of Judas Iscariot, in a letter to the Rev. Mr. J. P. [i.e., James Primrose]*. Edinburgh: W. Sands, A. Murray, and J. Cochran, 1750.

Bonaventure. *The Soul's Journey into God, The Tree of Life, The Life of St. Francis*. Trans. Ewert Cousins. Mahwah, NJ: Paulist Press, 1978.

Bonhoeffer, Dietrich. "Die Kirche vor der Judenfrage" [The Church Before the Jewish Question]. *Gesammelte Schriften*. Vol. 2. Ed. Eberhard Bethge. Munich: Chr. Kaiser, 1965. 44–53.

————. *Letters and Papers from Prison*. Ed. Eberhard Bethge. New York: Macmillan, 1972.

————. "Predigt am Sonntag Judika über Judas" [Sermon on Judas. March 14, 1937]. *Gesammelte Schriften*. Vol. 4. Ed. Eberhard Bethge. Munich: Chr. Kaiser, 1965. 406–13.

Borg, Marcus J., and John Dominic Crossan. *The Last Week: The Day-by-Day Account of Jesus's Final Week in Jerusalem*. [San Francisco]: HarperSanFrancisco, 2006.

Borger, Julian, and Stephen Bates. "Judas: This Is What Really Happened." *Guardian* 7 April 2006. 11 Feb. 2008 <http://www.guardian.co.uk/science/2006/apr/07/comment.frontpagenews>.

Borges, Jorge Luis. "The Sect of the Thirty." *Collected Fictions*. Trans. Andrew Hurley. London: Penguin, 1999. 443–45.

————. "Three Versions of Judas." *Collected Fictions*. Trans. Andrew Hurley. London: Penguin, 1999. 163–67.

Boswell, John. *Christianity, Social Tolerance, and Homosexuality: Gay People in Western Europe from the Beginning of the Christian Era to the Fourteenth Century*. Chicago: University of Chicago Press, 1980.

Boyarin, Daniel. *Border Lines: The Partition of Judaeo-Christianity*. Philadelphia: University of Pennsylvania Press, 2004.

Braswell, Mary Flowers. "Chaucer's Palimpsest: Judas Iscariot and *The Pardoner's Tale*." *Chaucer Review* 29 (1995): 303–10.

Brelich, Mario. *The Work of Betrayal*. Trans. Raymond Rosenthal. Marlboro, VT: Marlboro, 1988.

Briskin, Lawrence. "Tanakh Sources of Judas Iscariot." *Jewish Bible Quarterly* 32 (2004): 189–97.

Brodie, Thomas L. *The Gospel according to John: A Literary and Theological Commentary*. New York: Oxford University Press, 1993.

Brooks, Peter. *The Melodramatic Imagination: Balzac, Henry James, Melodrama, and the Mode of Excess*. New York: Columbia University Press, 1985.

Brown, Raymond E. *The Death of the Messiah: From Gethsemane to the Grave*. 2 vols. New York: Doubleday, 1994.

Browne, Thomas. *Pseudodoxia Epidemica: or, Enquiries into Very Many Received Tenents, and Commonly Presumed Truths*. London: Tho. Harper, 1646.

Browning, Robert. "Childe Roland to the Dark Tower Came." *Robert Browning's Poetry: Authoritative Texts, Criticism*. Norton Critical Edition. Ed. James F. Loucks. New York: Norton, 2007. 134.

Brunner, Emil. *Dogmatics*. Vol. 2, *The Christian Doctrine of Creation and Redemption*. Trans. Olive Wyon. 1952. Philadelphia: Westminster, 1974.

Buchanan, Robert. *The Poetical Works*. Vol. 1. Boston: James R. Osgood, 1874.

Bunyan, John. *Grace Abounding to the Chief of Sinners*. 1666. New Kensington, PA: Whitaker House, 2002.

Burrin, Philippe. "Political Religion: The Relevance of the Concept." *History & Memory: Passing into History: Nazism and the Holocaust beyond Memory*. Ed. Gulie Ne'eman Arad. 9 1/2 (Fall 1997): 321–52.

Bynum, Caroline Walker. "The Presence of Objects: Medieval Anti-Judaism in Modern Germany." *Common Knowledge* 10 (2004): 1–32.

Caldwell, Taylor, and Jess Stearn. *I, Judas*. New York: Atheneum, 1977.

Callaghan, Morley. *A Time for Judas*. New York: St. Martin's, 1984.

Calvin, John. *Calvin: Commentaries*. Trans. and ed. Joseph Haroutunian and Louise Pettibone Smith. Philadelphia: Westminster, 1958.

Cameron, Sharon. "The Practice of Attention: Simone Weil's Performance of Impersonality." *Impersonality: Seven Essays*. Chicago: University of Chicago Press, 2007. 108–43.

Camille, Michael. "Gothic Signs and the Surplus: The Kiss on the Cathedral." *Contexts: Style and Values in Medieval Art and Literature*. Ed. Daniel Poirion and Nancy Freeman Regalado. Special issue of *Yale French Studies*. New Haven: Yale University Press, 1991. 151–70.

Cane, Anthony. *The Place of Judas Iscariot in Christology*. Hampshire, Eng.: Ashgate, 2005.

Carson, D. A. *Divine Sovereignty and Human Responsibility: Biblical Perspectives in Tension*. Atlanta: John Knox, 1981.

Cartlidge, David R., and David Dungan, eds. *Documents for the Study of the Gospels*. Minneapolis: Fortress, 1994.

Charnes, Linda. *Hamlet's Heirs: Shakespeare and the Politics of a New Millennium*. New York: Routledge, 2006.

Chaucer, Geoffrey. "The Prioress' Tale." *The Canterbury Tales*. Trans. David Wright. Oxford: Oxford University Press, 1998. 160–66.

Chudoba, Petr. "Czech Easter—The Chasing and Burning of Judas." *my CzechRepublic*. 1998–2008. 14 Feb. 2008 <http://www.myczechrepublic .com/czech_culture/czech holidays/easter/judas.html>.

Clinefelter, Joan. "A Cinematic Construction of Nazi Anti-Semitism: The Documentary *Der ewige Jude*." *Cultural History through a National Socialist Lens: Essays on the Cinema of the Third Reich*. Ed. Robert C. Reimer. Rochester, NY: Camden House, 2000. 133–54.

Cobbe, William Rosser. *Doctor Judas: A Portrayal of the Opium Habit*. Chicago: Griggs, 1895.

Cohen, Derek, and Deborah Heller. *Jewish Presences in English Literature*. Montreal: McGill-Queen's University Press, 1990.

Cohen, Jeremy. *Christ Killers: The Jews and the Passion from the Bible to the Big Screen*. New York: Oxford University Press, 2007.

Cohen, Mark R. *Under Crescent and Cross: The Jews in the Middle Ages*. Princeton: Princeton University Press, 1994.

Coleridge, Samuel Taylor. "The Rime of the Ancient Mariner." *Lyrical Ballads and Related Writings*. By William Wordsworth and Samuel Taylor Coleridge. Ed. William Richey and Daniel Robinson. Boston: Houghton Mifflin, 2002. 423–41.

Coles, Robert. *Simone Weil: A Modern Pilgrimage*. Woodstock, VT: Skylight Paths, 2001.

Cosani, Armando. *The Flight of the Feathered Serpent*. Trans. Patricia Atkinson and Edith Pritchard. Fremont, CA: Absolute, 2003.

Cowan, Alison Leigh. "37-Month Sentence for Connecticut Priest Who Defrauded Parish." *New York Times* 5 Dec. 2007: C16.

Crossan, John Dominic. *Who Killed Jesus? Exposing the Roots of Anti-Semitism in the Gospel Story of the Death of Jesus*. San Francisco: HarperCollins, 1995.

"The Croxton *Play of the Sacrament*." *Early English Drama*. Ed. John C. Coldewey. New York: Garland, 1993. 277–305.

Culbert, Davis. "The Impact of Anti-Semitic Film Propaganda on German Audiences: *Jew Süss* and *The Wandering Jew* (1940)." *Art, Culture, and Media under the Third Reich*. Ed. Richard A. Etlin. Chicago: University of Chicago Press, 2002. 139–57.

Cullen, Countee. "Judas Iscariot." *Negro Poets and Their Poems*. Ed. Robert Kerlin. Washington, DC: Associated Publishers, 1935. 293–96.

Daily Missal of the Mystical Body. Ed. the Maryknoll Fathers with collaboration of Charles U. Callan. New York: P. J. Kennedy & Sons, 1961.

Dante Alighieri. *Inferno*. Trans. Jean Hollander. Introduction and notes Robert Hollander. New York: Doubleday, 2000.

Dart, John. "Long-lost Gospel of Judas to be Published." *Christian Century* 27 Dec. 2005: 12–13.

Daube, D. "Judas." *Rechtshistorisches Journal* 13 (1994): 307–30.

Davis, Natalie Zemon. "The Reasons of Misrule." *Society and Culture in Early Modern France: Eight Essays*. Stanford: Stanford University Press, 1975. 97–123.

DeConick, April D. "Gospel Truth." Op-ed. *New York Times* 1 Dec. 2007: A15.

———. *The Thirteenth Apostle: What the Gospel of Judas Really Says*. New York: Continuum, 2007.

de Kay, John. *Judas*. With the version in French by J. Coudurier de Chassaigne. [New York: Rullman], 1910.

De Quincey, Thomas. "Judas Iscariot." *The Collected Writings of Thomas De Quincey*. Ed. David Masson. [London]: A. & C. Black, 1897. 8: 177–206.

Derbes, Anne, and Mark Sandona. "Barren Metal and the Fruitful Womb: The Program of Giotto's Arena Chapel in Padua." *Art Bulletin* 80.2 (June 1998): 274–91.

Dickinson, Emily. "'Twas Love – not me –" (Fr. 562). *The Poems of Emily Dickinson*. Ed. R. W. Franklin. Cambridge, MA: Belknap Press of Harvard University Press, 1998. 2:561.

Dickinson, Michael. *The Lost Testament of Judas Iscariot*. Dingle, Ire.: Brandon, 1994.

Dieckmann, Bernhard. *Judas als Sündenbock: ein verhängnisvolle Geschichte von Angst und Vergeltung* [Judas as Scapegoat: A Fatal History of Fear and Retribution]. Munich: Kösel, 1991.

Dillon, Philip Robert. *Judas of Kerioth: A Romance of Old Judea*. New York: Exposition, 1953.

Dinzelbacher, Peter. *Judastraditionen* [Judas Traditions]. Vienna: Selbstverlag des Österreichischen Museums für Volkskunde, 1977.

Donne, John. "Batter my heart, three-personed God." *The Norton Anthology of English Literature*. 7th ed. M. H. Abrams, general ed.; Stephen Greenblatt, associate general ed. New York: Norton, 2000. 1:1271.

———. *The Sermons of John Donne*. Ed. George R. Potter and Evelyn M. Simpson. Vol. 5. Berkeley: University of California Press, 1959.

Douglas, Mary. *Purity and Danger: An Analysis of the Concepts of Pollution and Taboo*. 1966. New York: Routledge, 2002.

Droge, Arthur J., and James D. Tabor. *A Noble Death: Suicide and Martyrdom among Christians and Jews in Antiquity*. New York: HarperCollins, 1991.

Dryden, John. *All for Love: or, The World Well Lost. Plays: All for Love, Oedipus, Troilus and Cressida*. Ed. Maximillian E. Novak, Alan Roper, George

R. Guffey, and Vinton A. Dearing. Vol. 13 of *The Works of John Dryden*. Berkeley: University of California Press, 1984. 3–111.

———. "The Hind and the Panther." *Poems, 1685–1692*. Ed. Earl Miner and Vinton A. Dearing. Vol. 3 of *The Works of John Dryden*. Berkeley: University of California Press, 1969. 119–20.

Durham, John. *The Biblical Rembrandt*. Macon, GA: Mercer University Press, 2004.

Dyer, Joyce. "Frank Bidart's 'The Sacrifice.'" *Notes on Contemporary Literature* 11.3 (May 1981): 8–10.

Dyer, Richard. *White*. New York: Routledge, 1997.

Edmunds, Lowell. "Oedipus in the Middle Ages." *Antike und Abundland* 22 (1976): 140–55.

Ehrman, Bart D. *The Apostolic Fathers*. Vol. 2. Cambridge, MA: Harvard University Press, 2003.

———. *Jesus: Apocalyptic Prophet of the New Millennium*. New York: Oxford University Press, 1999.

———. *The Lost Gospel of Judas Iscariot: A New Look at Betrayer and Betrayed*. New York: Oxford University Press, 2006.

———. *The New Testament: A Historical Introduction to the Early Christian Writings*, 3rd ed. New York: Oxford University Press, 2004.

Elene. *Anglo-Saxon Poetry: An Anthology of Old English Poems in Prose Translation*. Ed. S. A. J. Bradley. London: Dent, 1982. 164–97.

Eliade, Mircea. *The Quest: History and Meaning in Religion*. Chicago: University of Chicago Press, 1969.

Eliot, T. S. "Burbank with a Baedeker, Bleistein with a Cigar." *Collected Poems, 1909–1962*. 1963. Orlando, FL: Harcourt, 1991. 33.

Elliott, Dyan. *Fallen Bodies: Pollution, Sexuality, and Demonology in the Middle Ages*. Philadelphia: University of Pennsylvania Press, 1999.

———. *Proving Woman: Female Spirituality and Inquisitional Culture in the Later Middle Ages*. Princeton: Princeton University Press, 2004.

Elliott, J. K. *The Apocryphal New Testament*. Oxford: Clarendon, 1993.

Elmer, Jonathan. *Reading at the Social Limit: Affect, Mass Culture, and Edgar Allan Poe*. Stanford: Stanford University Press, 1995.

Epiphanius. *The Panarion of St. Epiphanius, Bishop of Salamis: Selected Passages*. Trans. Philip R. Amidon. New York: Oxford University Press, 1990.

Ericksen, Robert P. *Theologians under Hitler: Gerhard Kittel, Paul Althuas and Emanuel Hirsch*. New Haven: Yale University Press, 1985.

Fackenheim, Emil L. "Abraham's Covenant under Assault: The Need for a Post-Holocaust Theology, Jewish, Christian and Muslim." *Good and Evil after Auschwitz: Ethical Implications for Today*. Ed. Jack Bemporad, John T. Pawlikowski, and Joseph Sievers. Hoboken, NJ: KTAV, 2000. 3–20.

Farrar, Frederic W. *The Life of Christ*. 1874. London: Cassell, 1963.

Faulkner, Joanne. "Freud's Concept of the Death Drive and Its Relation to the Superego." *Minerva—An Internet Journal of Philosophy* 9 (2005): 153–76.

Feigenbaum, Gail. "The *Kiss of Judas* by Lodovico Carracci." *Record of the Art Museum* 48 (1989): 2–18.

Felstiner, John. "Speaking Back to Scripture: The Biblical Strain in Holocaust Poetry." *Humanity at the Limit: The Impact of the Holocaust Experience on Jews and Christians*. Ed. Michael A. Singer. Bloomington: Indiana University Press, 2001. 391–99.

Fiore, Kristina Herrmann. "Caravaggio's 'Taking of Christ' and Dürer's Woodcut of 1509." *Burlington Magazine* Jan. 1995: 24–27.

Fitzmyer, Joseph. *The Acts of the Apostles, a New Translation with Introduction and Commentary*. New York: Doubleday, 1998.

———. *The Gospel according to Luke*. 2 vols. New York: Doubleday, 1981.

Fleissner, Jennifer L. "Poe's Imp, Melville's Formula." *Fictions* 4 (2005): 13–27.

Forsyth, Hazel, with Geoff Egan. *Toys, Trifles & Trinkets: Base-Metal Miniatures from London 1200 to 1800*. London: Unicorn, 2005.

Frank, Bernhard. "Dickinson's ''Twas Love—Not Me—.' " *Explicator* 63.1 (2004): 25–26.

Frankfurter, David. *Evil Incarnate: Rumors of Demonic Conspiracy and Ritual Abuse in History*. Princeton: Princeton University Press, 2006.

Fredriksen, Paula. *From Jesus to Christ: The Origins of the New Testament Images of Jesus*. New Haven: Yale University Press, 1988.

———. *Jesus of Nazareth, King of the Jews: A Jewish Life and the Emergence of Christianity*. New York: Knopf, 1999.

Fredriksen, Paula, and Adele Reinhart eds. *Jesus, Judaism, and Christian Anti-Judaism: Reading the New Testament after the Holocaust*. Louisville, KY: Westminster John Knox, 2002.

Freedman, David Noel. *The Anchor Bible Dictionary*. 6 vols. New York: Doubleday, 1992.

Freud, Sigmund. "Character and Anal Eroticism." *The Standard Edition of the Complete Psychological Works of Sigmund Freud*. Vol. 9, *1906-1908: Jensen's 'Gradiva' and Other Works*. Trans. under the general editorship of James Strachey, in collaboration with Anna Freud, assisted by Alix Strachey and Alan Tyson. London: Hogarth, 1959. 168–75.

Friedman, Régine Mihal. "Male Gaze and Female Reaction: Veit Harlan's *Jew Süss*." *Gender and German Cinema: Feminist Interventions*. Ed. Sandra Frieden, Richard W. McCormick, Vibeke R. Petersen, and Laurie Melissa Vogelsang. Vol. 2, *German Film History/German History on Film*. Providence: Berg, 1993. 117–33.

Frye, Northrop. *The Great Code: The Bible and Literature*. New York: Harcourt, 1982.

Galambush, Julie. *The Reluctant Parting: How the New Testament's Jewish Writers Created a Christian Book*. New York: HarperSanFrancisco, 2005.

Gambetta, Diego. "Can We Trust Trust?" *Trust: Making and Breaking Cooperative Relations*. Ed. Diego Gambetta. Oxford: Blackwell, 1988. 213–38.

Gärtner, Bertil. *Iscariot*. Trans. Victor I. Gruh. Philadelphia: Fortress, 1971.

Gillet, Joseph E. "Traces of the Judas-Legend in Spain." *Revue Hispanique* 65 (1925): 316–41.

Gilman, Sander. *The Jew's Body*. New York: Routledge, 1991.

Girard, René. *Violence and the Sacred*. Trans. Patrick Gregory. Baltimore: Johns Hopkins University Press, 1977.

Glock, Charles Y., and Rodney Stark. *Christian Beliefs and Anti-Semitism*. New York: Harper & Row, 1966.

Goldstein, Morris. *Jesus in the Jewish Tradition*. New York: Macmillan, 1950.

Gopnik, Adam. "Jesus Laughed." *New Yorker* 17 Apr. 2006: 80–81.

The Gospel of Barnabas. Ed. and trans. from the Italian MS in the Imperial Library at Vienna, by Lonsdale and Laura Ragg. Oxford: Clarendon, 1907.

The Gospel of Judas. Ed. Rodolphe Kasser, Marvin Meyer, and Gregor Wurst, with additional commentary by Bart D. Ehrman. Washington, DC: National Geographic, 2006.

Gould, Stephen Jay. "The Exaptive Excellence of Spandrels as a Term and Prototype." *Proceedings of the National Academy of Sciences in the United States of America* 94 (1997): 10750–55.

Graves, Robert. *King Jesus; and, My Head! My Head!* Ed. Robert A. Davis. Manchester: Carcanet, 2006.

Greenblatt, Stephen. "The Wound in the Wall." *Practicing New Historicism*. Ed. Catherine Gallagher and Stephen Greenblatt. Chicago: University of Chicago Press, 2000. 75–109.

Gubar, Susan. *Poetry After Auschwitz: Remembering What One Never Knew*. Bloomington: Indiana University Press, 2003.

Guirgis, Stephen Adly. *The Last Days of Judas Iscariot*. New York: Faber & Faber, 2006.

Halas, Roman B. *Judas Iscariot: A Scriptural and Theological Study of His Person, His Deeds and His Eternal Lot*. Washington, DC: Catholic University of America Press, 1946.

Halperin, David M. *How to Do the History of Homosexuality*. Chicago: University of Chicago Press, 2002.

Hand, Wayland D. "The Birthday of Judas Iscariot." *Modern Language Forum* 25 (March 1940): 1–8.

———. *A Dictionary of Words and Idioms Associated with Judas Iscariot: A Compilation Based Mainly on Material Found in the Germanic Languages*.

University of California Publications in Modern Philology 24, no. 3. Berkeley: University of California Press, 1942.

Hardy, Thomas. *Jude the Obscure*. 1895. London: Macmillan, 1960.

Hare, David. *The Judas Kiss*. London: Faber & Faber, 1998.

Harper, Phillip Brian. *Private Affairs: Critical Ventures in the Culture of Social Relations*. New York: New York University Press, 1999.

Harr, Jonathan. *The Lost Painting*. New York: Random House, 2005.

Harris, J. Rendel. "Did Judas Really Commit Suicide?" *American Journal of Theology* 4 (1900): 490–513.

Harris, Thomas. *Hannibal*. New York: Delacorte, 1999.

Harrt, Frederick, and David G. Wilkins. *History of Italian Renaissance Art: Painting, Sculpture, Architecture*. 5th ed. New York: Abrams, 2003.

Haswell, Janis. "Resurrecting *Calvary*: A Reconstructive Interpretation of W. B. Yeats's Play and Its Making." *Yeats's Collaborations: Yeats Annual 15*. London: Macmillan, 2005. 159–89.

Hawker, Robert Stephen. "The Kiss of Judas." *The Poetical Works*. Ed. Alfred Wallis. London: John Lane, 1899. 96.

Head, Peter M. "The Nazi Quest for an Aryan Jesus." *Journal for the Study of the Historical Jesus* 2.1 (2004): 55–89.

Hecht, Anthony. "Handicap." *Jiggery-Pokery: A Compendium of Double Dactyls*. Ed. Anthony Hecht and John Hollander. New York: Atheneum, 1983. 43.

Hecht, Anthony, and John Hollander. Introduction. *Jiggery-Pokery: A Compendium of Double Dactyls*. Ed. Anthony Hecht and John Hollander. New York: Atheneum, 1983. 3–31.

Held, Robert. *Inquisition/Inquisición: A Bilingual Guide to the Exhibition of Torture Instruments from the Middle Ages to the Industrial Era*. Florence: Qu d'Arno, 1985.

Herbert, George. *George Herbert*. Ed. Louis L. Martz. Oxford: Oxford University Press, 1994.

Herf, Jeffrey. *The Jewish Enemy: Nazi Propaganda during World War II and the Holocaust*. Cambridge, MA: Harvard University Press, 2006.

Herman, Felicia. "'The Most Dangerous Anti-Semitic Photoplay in Filmdom': American Jews and *The King of Kings* (De Mille, 1927)." *Velvet Light Trap* 46 (Fall 2000): 12–25.

Heschel, Susannah. *Abraham Geiger and the Jewish Jesus*. Chicago: University of Chicago Press, 1998.

———. "Quest for the Aryan Jesus: The Archaeology of Nazi Orientalist Theology." *Jews, Antiquity, and the Nineteenth-Century Imagination*. Ed. Hayim Lapin and Dale B. Martin. Potomac: University Press of Maryland, 2003. 65–84.

Hill, G. F. *The Medallic Portraits of Christ, The False Shekels, The Thirty Pieces of Silver*. Oxford: Clarendon, 1920.

Hitler, Adolf. *Mein Kampf*. Trans. Ralph Manheim. 1943. Boston: Houghton Mifflin, 1999.

Hollander, Martha. "Losses of Face: Rembrandt, Masaccio, and the Drama of Shame." *Social Research* 70 (2003): 1334–39.

Horne, Richard H. *Judas Iscariot. Bible Tragedies*. London: Newman, 1848. 115–91.

Hughes, Kirk T. "Framing Judas." *Semeia* 54.1 (1991): 223–38.

Humphries-Brooks, Stephenson. *Cinematic Savior: Hollywood's Making of the American Christ*. Westport, CT: Praeger, 2006.

Irenaeus of Lyons. *St. Irenaeus of Lyons Against the Heresies*. Trans. and annotated by Dominic J. Unger, with further revisions by John J. Dillon. Vol. 1. New York: Paulist Press, 1992.

Jabès, Edmons. "My Itinerary." Trans. Rosmarie Waldrop. *Studies in Twentieth Century Literature* 12 (1987): 3–12.

Jackson, Rodger L. "The *Sense and Sensibility* of Betrayal: Discovering the Meaning of Treachery through Jane Austen." *Humanitas* 13.2 (2000): 72–89.

James, M. R. *The Gospel of Nicodemus, or Acts of Pilate. The Apocryphal New Testament, being the Apocryphal Gospels, Acts, Epistles, and Apocalypses*. Oxford: Clarendon, 1953. 94–146.

Jeffers, Robinson. *Dear Judas and Other Poems*. New York: Liveright, 1977.

Jemmat, Catherine. "Epigram [on Judas]." *Miscellanies in Prose and Verse*. London: Printed for the Author, 1766. 140.

Jerome, Saint. *The Homilies of Saint Jerome*. Trans. Sister Marie Liuori Ewald. Vol. 1. The Fathers of the Church, a new translation; vol. 48. Washington, DC: Catholic University of America Press, 1964.

"The Jesus the Jews Never Knew." [Description of *Sepher Toldoth Yeshu and the Quest of the Historical Jesus in Jewish Sources*, by Frank R. Zindler.] *American Atheists Secure Online Shopping*. 14 Feb. 2008 <https://lightning.he.net/~atheists/catalogue/shop/prod7>.

John Chrysostom. *Discourses against Judaizing Christians*. Trans. Paul W. Harkins. The Fathers of the Church, new translation; vol. 68. Washington, DC: Catholic University of America Press, 1977.

———. *Homilies on the Gospel of Saint Matthew*. Vol. 10 of *A Select Library of the Nicene and Post-Nicene Fathers of the Christian Church*. 1886–90. Ed. Philip Schaff. Grand Rapids, MI: Eerdmans; Edinburgh: T&T Clark, 1991.

John of the Cross, Saint. *The Dark Night. The Collected Works of St. John of the Cross*. Trans. Kieran Kavanaugh and Otilio Rodriguez. Rev. ed. Washington, DC: ICS Publications, 1991. 358–457.

———. *The Spiritual Canticle. The Collected Works of St. John of the Cross*.

Trans. Kieran Kavanaugh and Otilio Rodriguez. Rev. ed. Washington, DC: ICS Publications, 1991. 461–630.

Johnson, Barbara. "Melville's Fist: The Execution in *Billy Budd.*" *The Critical Difference: Essays in the Contemporary Rhetoric of Reading*. Baltimore: Johns Hopkins University Press, 1980. 79–109.

Jordan, Mark D. *The Invention of Sodomy in Christian Theology*. Chicago: University of Chicago Press, 1997.

Kagan, Shelly. *Normative Ethics*. Boulder, CO: Westview, 1998.

Kahn, Jeffrey. "Judas Iscariot: A Vehicle of Medieval Didacticism." Diss. University of Utah, 1976.

Kazantzakis, Nikos. *Christ Recrucified*. Trans. Jonathan Griffin. Oxford: Bruno Cassirer, 1954.

———. *The Last Temptation of Christ*. Trans. P. A. Bien. 1960. New York: Simon & Schuster, 1998.

Kelly, Henry Ansgar. *Satan: A Biography*. Cambridge: Cambridge University Press, 2006.

Kempe, Harry. *Judas*. New York: Mitchell Kennerley, 1913.

———. "Our Thirty Pieces." *The Sea and the Dunes*. New York: Brentano's, 1926. 24.

Kennelly, Brendan. *The Book of Judas*. Newcastle upon Tyne: Bloodaxe, 1991.

———. *The Little Book of Judas*. Northumberland: Bloodaxe, 2002.

Kenney, Catherine. *The Remarkable Case of D.L.S.* Kent, OH: Kent State University Press, 1990.

Kermode, Frank. "Arguing with God." *New York Review of Books* 1 Dec. 2005: 40–42.

———. *The Genesis of Secrecy: On the Interpretation of Narrative*. Cambridge, MA: Harvard University Press, 1979.

Kierkegaard, Søren. *Journals and Papers*. Vol. 2, *F–K*. Ed. Howard V. Hong and Edna H. Hong. Bloomington: Indiana University Press, 1970.

———. *The Moment and Late Writings*. Ed. and trans. Howard V. Hong and Edna H. Hong. Princeton: Princeton University Press, 1998.

———. *The Sickness Unto Death*. Trans. Alastair Hannay. London: Penguin, 1989.

Kincaid, Jamaica. *Lucy*. New York: Farrar Straus Giroux, 1990.

King, Claire Sisco. "Imaging the Abject: The Ideological Use of the Dissolve." *Horror Film: Creating and Marketing Fear*. Ed. Steffen Hantke. Jackson: University of Mississippi Press, 2004. 21–34.

Kipling, Rudyard. "The Last Chantey." *Complete Verse*. New York: Anchor, 1989. 159–61.

Klassen, William. *Judas: Betrayer or Friend of Jesus?* Minneapolis: Fortress, 1996.

Klauck, Hans-Josef. *Judas, ein Jünger des Herrn* [Judas, a Disciple of the Lord]. Freiburg im Breisgau: Herder, 1987.

Klausner, Joseph. *Jesus of Nazareth: His Life, Times, and Teaching.* Trans. Herbert Danby. London: Allen & Unwin, 1925.

Klein, Charlotte. *Anti-Judaism in Christian Theology.* Trans. Edward Quinn. Philadelphia: Fortress, 1978.

Klotz, Marcia. "Epistemological Ambiguity and the Fascist Text: *Jew Suss, Carl Peters,* and *Ohm Krüger.*" *New German Critique* 74 (Spring–Summer 1998): 91–124.

Kosinski, Jerzy. *The Painted Bird.* 1965. New York: Grove, 1976.

Koslofsky, Craig. "The Kiss of Peace in the German Reformation." *The Kiss in History.* Ed. Karen Harvey. Manchester: Manchester University Press, 2005. 18–30.

Krosney, Herbert. *The Lost Gospel: The Quest for the Gospel of Judas Iscariot.* Washington, DC: National Geographic, 2006.

Kruger, Steven F. "The Bodies of Jews in the Late Middle Ages." *The Idea of Medieval Literature.* Ed. James M. Dean and Christian Zacher. Newark: University of Delaware Press, 1992. 301–23.

———. *The Spectral Jews: Conversation and Embodiment in Medieval Europe.* Minneapolis: University of Minnesota Press, 2006.

Kysar, Robert. *John the Maverick Gospel.* Atlanta: John Knox, 1976.

Lacaba, Emmanuel. "When a Cloud Shades the Sun." *Divine Inspiration: The Life of Jesus in World Poetry.* Ed. Robert Atwan, George Dardess, and Peggy Rosenthal. New York: Oxford University Press, 1997. 372.

Laeuchli, Samuel. "Origen's Interpretation of Judas Iscariot." *Church History* 22 (1953): 253–68.

Lamadrid, Enrique R., and Michael A. Thomas. "The Masks of Judas: Folk and Elite Holy Week Tricksters in Michoacán," *Studies in Latin American Popular Culture* 9 (1990): 191. 17 Feb. 2008 <http://www.bsu.edu/classes/magrath/305s02/masks/lamadrid.html>.

Lamb, Charles. "To Sir Mackintosh." *Poems, Plays, and Rosamund Gray.* Ed. William Macdonald. London: Dent, 1903. 195.

Lambert, Malcolm. *Medieval Heresy: Popular Movements from the Gregorian Reform to the Reformation.* 2nd ed. Oxford: Blackwell, 1992.

Langmuir, Gavin I. *Toward a Definition of Anti-Semitism.* Berkeley: University of California Press, 1990.

Lansing, Carol. *Power and Purity: Cathar Heresy in Medieval Italy.* New York: Oxford University Press, 1998.

Laqueur, Walter. *The Changing Face of Anti-Semitism: From Ancient Times to the Present Day.* New York: Oxford University Press, 2006.

Lawrence, D. H. *The Man Who Died.* New York: Knopf, 1928.

Leirvik, Oddbjørn. "History as a Literary Weapon: The Gospel of Barnabas in Muslim-Christian Polemics." *Studia Theologica* 54 (2001): 4–26.

Leo the Great. *Sermons*. Trans. Jane Patricia Freeland and Agnes Josephine Conway. Washington, DC: Catholic University of America Press, 1996.

Levertov, Denise. "ii The Peachtree." From "During the Eichmann Trial." *The Jacob's Ladder*. New York: New Directions, 1961. 64–65.

Levinas, Emmanuel. "Ethics and Spirit." *The Holocaust: Theoretical Readings*. Ed. Neil Levi and Michael Rothberg. Edinburgh: Edinburgh University Press, 2003. 241–45.

Lévitt, Albert. *Judas Iscariot: An Imaginative Autobiography*. [Hancock, NH: Flagstone, 1961].

Libby, Seth. "Judas in History and Myth: A Study in the Trajectories of the Judas Character in Early Christian Literature." Senior Honors Essay in Religious Studies. Indiana University, Bloomington, December 2007.

Lipton, Sara. *Images of Intolerance: The Presentation of Jews and Judaism in the* Bible moralisée. Berkeley: University of California Press, 1999.

Littell, Franklin H. *The Crucifixion of the Jews*. New York: Harper & Row, 1975.

Little, Lester K. *Religious Poverty and the Profit Economy in Medieval Europe*. Ithaca: Cornell University Press, 1978.

Luther, Martin. "On Jews and Their Lies." Trans. Martin H. Bertram. *The Christian in Society IV*. Ed. Franklin Sherman. Vol. 47 of *Luther's Works*. Ed. Helmut T. Lehmann and Jaroslav Pelikan. Philadelphia: Fortress, 1971. 137–306.

———. *Selected Psalms III*. Ed. Jaroslav Pelikan and Daniel E. Poellot. Vol. 14 of *Luther's Works*. Ed. Helmut T. Lehmann and Jaroslav Pelikan. Saint Louis: Concordia, 1958.

———. *Sermons on the Passion of Christ*. Trans. E. Smid and J. T. Isensee. Rock Island, IL: Augustana, 1956.

———. *Vom Schem Hamphoras und vom Geschlecht Christi* [Of the Unknowable Name and the Generations of Christ]. *The Jew in Christian Theology: Martin Luther's Anti-Jewish* Vom Schem Hamphoras, *Previously Unpublished in English, and Other Milestones in Church Doctrine Concerning Judaism*. By Gerhard Falk. Jefferson, NC: McFarland, 1992. 153–224.

Maccoby, Hyam. *Judas Iscariot and the Myth of Jewish Evil*. New York: Free Press, 1992.

Machalický, Jiří. Preface. Anderle 9–15.

MacKinnon, Donald M. *Borderlands of Theology and Other Essays*. Ed. and intro. George W. Roberts and Donovan E. Smucker. London: Lutterworth, 1968.

Madden, Edward H., and Peter H. Hare. "On the Difficulty of Evading the

Problem of Evil." *Philosophy and Phenomenological Research* 28 (1967): 58–69.

Mailer, Norman. *The Gospel according to the Son.* New York: Random House, 1997.

Malchow, H. L. *Gothic Images of Race in Nineteenth-Century Britain.* Stanford: Stanford University Press, 1996.

Malcolm, Janet. "Strangers in Paradise: How Gertrude Stein and Alice B. Toklas Got to Heaven." *New Yorker* 13 Nov. 2006: 54–61.

Marique, Joseph M. F. "The Fragments of Papias." *The Apostolic Fathers.* Trans. Francis X. Glimm, Joseph M. F. Marique, and Gerald G. Walsh. The Fathers of the Church, vol. 1. Rev. ed. Washington, DC: Catholic University of America Press, 1962. 373–89.

Matz, Aaron. "Terminal Satire and *Jude the Obscure.*" *ELH* 73 (2006): 519–47.

McClellan, George Marion. "The Feet of Judas." *Negro Poets and Their Poems.* By Robert Kerlin. 2nd ed. Washington, DC: Associated Publishers, 1935. 177–78.

McGlasson, Paul. *Jesus and Judas: Biblical Exegesis in Barth.* Atlanta: Scholars, 1991.

McLeod, Carolyn. "Trust." 20 Feb. 2006. *Stanford Encyclopedia of Philosophy.* 17 Feb. 2008. <http://plato.stanford.edu/entries/trust/>.

McNally, Terrence. *Corpus Christi.* New York: Grove, 1998.

Meditations on the Life of Christ: An Illustrated Manuscript of the Fourteenth Century. Trans. Isa Ragusa. Ed. Isa Ragusa and Rosalie B. Green. Princeton: Princeton University Press, 1961.

Meeks, Wayne A. "A Nazi Testament Professor Reads His Bible: The Strange Case of Gerhard Kittel." *The Idea of Biblical Interpretation: Essays in Honor of James L. Kugel.* Ed. Hindy Najman and Judith H. Newman. Leiden: Brill, 2004. 513–44.

Meeks, Wayne A., and Jouette M. Bassler. *The HarperCollins Study Bible New Revised Standard Version, with the Apocryphal/Deuterocanonical Books.* New York: HarperCollins, 1993.

Meier, John P. *A Marginal Jew: Rethinking the Historical Jesus.* Vol. 3. New York: Doubleday, 1991.

Mellinkoff, Ruth. "Judas's Red Hair and the Jews." *Journal of Jewish Art* 9 (1982): 31–46.

———. *Outcasts: Signs of Otherness in Northern European Art of the Late Middle Ages.* Vol. 1. Berkeley: University of California Press, 1993.

Meyer, Marvin. "Judas and the Gnostic Connection." *The Gospel of Judas.* 137–69.

Miles, Jack. *Christ: A Crisis in the Life of God.* New York: Knopf, 2001.

———. *God: A Biography.* New York: Vintage, 1996.

Miller, Andrew H. *The Burdens of Perfection: On Ethics and Reading in Nine-teenth-Century British Literature*. Ithaca: Cornell University Press, 2008.

Milligan, J. Lewis. *Judas Iscariot: A Poetical Play*. Toronto: Ryerson, 1929.

Mirk, John. *Mirk's Festival: A Collection of Homilies*. Ed. Theodor Erbe. EETS Extra Ser. 96. London: Kegan Paul, Trench, Trübner, 1905.

Moore, R. I. *The Formation of a Persecuting Society: Power and Deviance in Western Europe, 950–1250*. Oxford: Blackwell, 1987.

Moore, Stephen D. *God's Beauty Parlor: And Other Queer Spaces In and Around the Bible*. Stanford: Stanford University Press, 2001.

———. "The Song of Songs in the History of Sexuality." *Church History* 69 (2000): 328–49.

Moore, T. Sturge. *Judas*. London: J. Richards, 1923.

More, Sir Thomas. *A Treatise upon the Passion. Treatise on the Passion; Treatise on the Blessed Body; Instructions and Prayers*. Vol. 13 of *The Complete Works of St. Thomas More*. Ed. Garry E. Haupt. New Haven: Yale University Press, 1976. 1–177.

Morley, Sybil. *Judas: A Poem in 1932 lines, One for Each Year of Our Lord*. Oxford: Blackwell, 1932.

Mormando, Franco. "'Just as Your Lips Approach the Lips of Your Brothers': Judas Iscariot and the Kiss of Betrayal." *Caravaggio and the Baroque Image*. Ed. Franco Mormando. Boston: McMullen Museum of Art, Boston College; distributed by the University of Chicago Press, 1999. 179–90.

Morrison, Toni. *Love*. New York: Vintage, 2005.

Mossberg, Barbara Antonina Clarke. *Emily Dickinson: When a Writer Is a Daughter*. Bloomington: Indiana University Press, 1982.

Mosse, George L. *The Crisis of German Ideology: Intellectual Origins of the Third Reich*. New York: Grosset & Dunlap, 1964.

Mossinsohn, Igal. *Judas*. Trans. Jules Harlow. New York: St. Martin's, 1963.

Murray, Alexander. *Suicide in the Middle Ages*. Vol. 1, *The Violent against Themselves*. New York: Oxford University Press, 1998.

———. *Suicide in the Middle Ages*. Vol. 2, *The Curse on Self-Murder*. New York: Oxford University Press, 1998.

"The Narrative of Joseph." *Apocryphal Gospels, Acts, and Revelations*. Trans. Alexander Walker. Ante-Nicene Christian Library, vol. 16. Edinburgh: T. & T. Clark, 1870. 237–44.

Nemerov, Howard. "The Historical Judas." *Norton Anthology of Modern Poetry*. Ed. Margaret Ferguson, Mary Jo Salter, and Jon Stallworthy. 4th ed. New York: Norton, 1996. 1520.

Nickle, Keith F. *The Synoptic Gospels: An Introduction*. Rev. and expanded. Louisville, KY: Westminster John Knox, 2001.

Niemöller, Martin. *The Gestapo Defied, Being the Last Twenty-Eight Sermons*. Trans. Jane Lymburn. London: William Hodge, 1941.

Nirenberg, David. *Communities of Violence: Persecution of Minorities in the Middle Ages.* Princeton: Princeton University Press, 1996.

Nissinen, Martti. *Homoeroticism in the Biblical World: A Historical Perspective.* Trans. Kirsi Stjerna. Minneapolis: Fortress, 1998.

"Nostra Aetate." *Vatican Council II: The Conciliar and Post-Conciliar Documents.* Ed. Austin Flannery. Northport, NY: Costello, 1975. 738–49.

Ockman, Carol, and Kenneth E. Silver. *Sarah Bernhardt: The Art of High Drama.* New York: Jewish Museum, New York under the auspices of the Jewish Theological Seminary; New Haven: Yale University Press, 2005.

Ødegård, Knut. *Judas Iscariot & Other Poems.* Trans. Brian McNeil. Dublin: Waxwing Poems, 2005.

Oesterreicher, John M. "Declaration on the Relationship of the Church to Non-Christian Religions." *Commentary on the Documents of Vatican II.* [General ed. Herbert Vorgrimler.] Vol. 3. New York: Herder & Herder, 1969. 1–154.

Ohly, Friedrich. *The Damned and the Elect: Guilt in Western Culture.* Trans. Linda Archibald. Foreword by George Steiner. Cambridge: Cambridge University Press, 1992.

O'Malley, Patrick R. "Oxford's Ghosts: *Jude the Obscure* and the End of the Gothic." *Modern Fiction Studies* 46 (2000): 646–71.

Oppermann, Jürgen. "Das Drama 'Der Wanderer' von Joseph Goebbels: Frühformen nationalsozialistische Literatur" [The Drama "The Wanderer" by Joseph Goebbels: Early Forms of National Socialist Literature]. Diss. Universität Karlsruhe, Fak. F. Geistes- und Sozialwissenscaften, 2005.

Origen, *Contra Celsum.* Trans. Henry Chadwick. Cambridge: Cambridge University Press, 1953.

Orsi, Robert A. *Thank You, St. Jude: Women's Devotion to the Patron Saint of Hopeless Causes.* New Haven: Yale University Press, 1996.

Otis, Leah Lydia. *Prostitution in Medieval Society: The History of an Urban Institution in Languedoc.* Chicago: University of Chicago Press, 1985.

Owen, Richard. "Judas the Misunderstood: Vatican Moves to Clear Reviled Disciple's Name," *Times* (London) 12 Jan. 2006: 3, 19.

Paffenroth, Kim. "The Character of Judas in Bach's *St. Matthew Passion.*" *Midwest Quarterly* 36.2 (Winter 1995): 125–35.

———. *Judas: Images of the Lost Disciple.* Louisville, KY: Westminster John Knox, 2001.

Page, Gregory A. *The Diary of Judas Iscariot or the Gospel According to Judas.* London: Charles H. Kelly, 1912.

Pagels, Elaine, and Karen L. King. *Reading Judas: The Gospel of Judas and the Shaping of Christianity.* New York: Viking, 2007.

Panas, Henryk. *The Gospel according to Judas.* Trans. Marc E. Heine. London: Hutchinson, 1977.

Panofsky, Erwin. *The Life and Art of Albrecht Dürer*. 4th ed. Princeton: Princeton University Press, 1955.

Pappano, Margaret Aziza. "Judas in York: Masters and Servants in the Late Medieval Cycle Drama." *Exemplaria* 14 (2002): 317–50.

Parke, Catherine. *Biography: Writing Lives*. New York: Routledge, 2002.

Patterson, Lee. *Chaucer and the Subject of History*. Madison: University of Wisconsin Press, 1991.

Pawlikowski, John T. *Christ in the Light of the Christian-Jewish Dialogue*. New York: Paulist Press, 1982.

———. *Sinai and Calvary: A Meeting of Two Peoples*. Beverly Hills, CA: Benziger, 1976.

Pelikan, Jaroslav Jan. *The Illustrated Jesus through the Centuries*. New Haven: Yale University Press, 1997.

Penn, Michael Philip. *Kissing Christians: Ritual and Community in the Late Ancient Church*. Philadelphia: University of Pennsylvania Press, 2005.

Perella, N. J. *The Kiss Sacred and Profane*. Berkeley: University of California Press, 1969.

Phillips, Adam. *On Kissing, Tickling, and Being Bored*. Cambridge, MA: Harvard University Press, 1993.

Phillips, John. *Eve: The History of an Idea*. New York: Harper & Row, 1984.

Pieper, Jim. *Guatemala's Folk Saints: Maximon/San Simon, Rey Pascual, Judas, Lucifer, and Others*. Albuquerque: University of New Mexico Press, 2002.

Pinson, Yona. "The Iconography of the Temple in Northern Renaissance Art." 25 Feb. 2004 Tel Aviv University, Faculty of the Arts. 17 Feb. 2008 <http://www.tau.ac.il/arts/projects/PUB/assaph-art/assaph2/articles_assaph2/09Pinson.pdf>.

Poe, Edgar Allan. "The Imp of the Perverse." *Collected Works of Edgar Allan Poe*. Vol. 3, *Tales and Sketches, 1843–1849*. Ed. Thomas Ollive Mabbott. Cambridge, MA: Belknap Press of Harvard University Press, 1978. 1217–27.

Prévert, Jacques. "The Last Supper." Trans. Lawrence Ferlinghetti. *Divine Inspiration: The Life of Jesus in World Poetry*. Ed. Robert Atwan, George Dardess, and Peggy Rosenthal. New York: Oxford University Press, 1997. 375.

Price, David Hotchkiss. *Albrecht Dürer's Renaissance: Humanism, Reformation, and the Art of Faith*. Ann Arbor: University of Michigan Press, 2003.

Prose, Francine. *Caravaggio: Painter of Miracles*. New York: HarperCollins, 2005.

Pyper, Hugh S. "Modern Gospels of Judas: Canon and Betrayal." *Literature & Theology* 15.2 (June 2001): 111–22.

Rayner, William. *The Knifeman*. New York: Morrow, 1969.

Reinhartz, Adele. *Jesus of Hollywood*. New York: Oxford University Press, 2007.

Renan, Ernest. *The Life of Jesus*. Buffalo, NY: Prometheus, 1991.

Ricci, Nino. *Testament*. New York: Houghton Mifflin, 2003.

Ricci, Piero. "The Fourth Version of Judas." *Variaciones Borges* 1 (1996): 10–26.

Rice, Cale Young. "The Wife of Judas Iscariot." 1912. *Selected Plays and Poems*. London: Hodder & Stoughton, 1972. 372–74.

Risen, James, and Tim Golden. "Three Prisoners Commit Suicide at Guantánamo." *New York Times* 11 June 2006: A1.

Robertson, J. M. *Jesus and Judas, a Textual and Historical Investigation*. London: Watts, 1927.

Robinson, James M. *The Secrets of Judas: The Story of the Misunderstood Disciple and His Lost Gospel*. San Francisco: HarperCollins, 2006.

Roche, Anthony. "*The Book of Judas*: Parody, Double Cross and Betrayal." *Dark Fathers into Light: Brendan Kennelly*. Ed. Richard Pine. Newcastle upon Tyne: Bloodaxe, 1994. 91–113.

Rogers, Robert. *The Double in Literature*. Detroit: Wayne State University, 1970.

Rollins, James. *The Judas Strain*. New York: HarperCollins, 2007.

Rosenbaum, Ron. *Explaining Hitler*. New York: HarperPerennial, 1999.

Rosenberg, Stuart E. *The Christian Problem: A Jewish View*. New York: Hippocrene, 1986.

Rózewicz, Tadeusz. "The Dream of John." Trans. Victor Contoski. *Divine Inspiration: The Life of Jesus in World Poetry*. Ed. Robert Atwan, George Dardess, and Peggy Rosenthal. New York: Oxford University Press, 1997. 388.

Rubin, Miri. *Gentile Tales: The Narrative Assault on Late Medieval Jews*. Philadelphia: University of Philadelphia Press, 2004.

Ruether, Rosemarie. *Faith and Fratricide: The Theological Roots of Anti-Semitism*. New York: Seabury, 1974.

Saari, A. M. H. *The Many Deaths of Judas Iscariot: A Meditation*. New York: Routledge, 2006.

Sacks, David Harris. "The Greed of Judas: Avarice, Monopoly, and the Moral Economy in England, ca. 1350–ca. 1600." *Journal of Medieval and Early Modern Studies* 28 (1998): 263–307.

Sanders, E. P. *The Historical Figure of Jesus*. London: Penguin, 1993.

Saramago, José. *The Gospel according to Jesus Christ*. Trans. Giovanni Pontiero. New York: Harcourt, 1991.

Sayers, Dorothy L. *The Man Born to Be King: A Play-Cycle on the Life of Our Lord and Saviour*. Grand Rapids, MI: Eerdmans, 1943.

Schäfer, Peter. *Jesus in the Talmud*. Princeton: Princeton University Press, 2007.

Schiller, Gertrud. *Iconography of Christian Art*. Trans. Janet Seligman. 2 vols. Greenwich, CT: New York Graphic Society, [1971–72].

Schneemelcher, Wilhelm, ed. *New Testament Apocrypha*. Vol. 1, *Gospels and Related Writings*. English translation [by A. J. B. Higgins et al.] ed. R. McL. Wilson. Rev. ed. Cambridge: Clarke; Louisville, KY: Westminster/John Knox, 1991.

Schonfield, Hugh J. *The Passover Plot: New Light on the History of Jesus*. London: Hutchinson, 1965.

Schulte-Sasse, Linda. *Entertaining the Third Reich: Illusions of Wholeness in Nazi Cinema*. Durham: Duke University Press, 1996.

Schwartz, Gary. *Rembrandt: His Life, His Paintings*. New York: Viking, 1985.

Schweitzer, Albert. *The Quest of the Historical Jesus*. Trans. W. Montgomery, J. R. Coates, Susan Cupitt, and John Bowden. Ed. John Bowden. Minneapolis: Fortress, 2001.

Sedgwick, Eve Kosofsky. "Melanie Klein and the Difference Affect Makes." *South Atlantic Quarterly* 106 (2007): 625–42.

Sedulius. *Sedulii Opera Omnia*. Ed. Johann Huemer. Corpus Scriptorum Ecclesiasticorum Latinorum 10. Vienna: C. Geroldi, 1885.

Segal, Alan F. *Rebecca's Children: Judaism and Christianity in the Roman World*. Cambridge, MA: Harvard University Press, 1986.

Setiya, Kieran. *Reasons without Rationalism*. Princeton: Princeton University Press, 2007.

Sexton, Anne. "The Legend of the One-Eyed Man." *Live or Die*. Boston: Houghton Mifflin, 1966. 22.

Shachar, Isaiah. *The Judensau: A Medieval Anti-Jewish Motif and Its History*. London: Warburg Institute, 1974.

Shakespeare, William. *The Complete Works of Shakespeare*. 4th ed. Ed. David Bevington. New York: HarperCollins, 1992.

———. *Love's Labors Lost*. Shakespeare, *Complete Works* 34–74.

———. *The Merchant of Venice*. Shakespeare, *Complete Works* 178–215.

———. *Othello*. Ed. E. A. J. Honigmann. The Arden Shakespeare. Walton-on-Thames: Thomas Nelson and Sons, 1997.

———. *The Third Part of King Henry the Sixth*. Shakespeare, *Complete Works* 586–627.

———. *The Tragedy of King Richard the Second*. Shakespeare, *Complete Works* 725–62.

———. *The Winter's Tale*. Ed. J. H. P. Pafford. London: Methuen, 1963.

Shapiro, James. *Oberammergau: The Troubling Story of the World's Most Famous Passion Play*. New York: Vintage, 2000.

———. *Shakespeare and the Jews*. New York: Columbia University Press, 1996.

Shelley, Percy Bysshe. "Epipsychidion." *Shelley's Poetry and Prose: Authorita-tive Texts, Criticism*. Ed. Donald H. Reiman and Sharon B. Powers. Norton Critical Edition. New York: Norton, 1977. 373–88.

Shklar, Judith N. *Ordinary Vices*. Cambridge, MA: Belknap Press of Harvard University Press, 1984.

Sierra, Javier. *The Secret Supper*. Trans. Alberto Manguel. New York: Atria, 2004.

Sloterdijk, Peter. *Critique of Cynical Reason*. Trans. Michael Eldred. Foreword Andreas Huyssen. Minneapolis: University of Minnesota Press, 1987.

Smith, D. Moody. *John among the Gospels*. 2nd ed. Columbia: University of South Carolina Press, 2001.

Smith, Ken. *Judas: A Biographical Novel of the Life of Judas Iscariot*. San Jose: Writer's Showcase, 2001.

Smith, W. B. "Judas Iscariot." *Hibbert Journal* 9 (1911): 529–44.

Snyder, Susan. "The Left Hand of God: Despair in Medieval and Renaissance Tradition." *Studies in the Renaissance* 12 (1965): 18–59.

Spong, John Shelby. *The Sins of Scripture: Exposing the Bible's Texts of Hate to Reveal the God of Love*. San Francisco: HarperCollins, 2005.

Springer, Carl P. E. *The Gospel as Epic in Late Antiquity: The Paschale Carmen of Sedulius*. New York: Brill, 1988.

Stanton, Graham. *The Gospels and Jesus*. 2nd ed. New York: Oxford University Press, 2002.

Stead, C. K. *My Name Was Judas*. London: Vintage, 2006.

Stead, William T., ed. *The Passion Play at Oberammergau, 1930*. London: Ernest Been, 1938.

Steinberg, Leo. *The Sexuality of Christ in Renaissance Art and in Modern Oblivion*. New York: Pantheon, 1983.

Steiner, George. Foreword. Friedrich Ohly. *The Damned and the Elect: Guilt in Western Culture*. Cambridge: Cambridge University Press, 1992. xi–xiv.

———. *No Passion Spent: Essays, 1978–1996*. New Haven: Yale University Press, 1996.

Sterne, Laurence. *The Life and Opinions of Tristram Shandy*. 1760–67. Ed. Melvyn and Joan New. New York: Penguin, 2003.

Stoker, Bram. *Dracula*. 1897. Ed. John Paul Riquelme. New York: Bedford/St. Martin's, 2002.

Story, W. W. *A Roman Lawyer in Jerusalem: First Century*. Boston: Loring, 1870.

Strack, Hermann L. *The Jew and Human Sacrifice*. Trans. Henry Blanchamp. London: Cope & Fenwick, 1909.

Strauss, David Friedrich. *The Life of Jesus Critically Examined*. Trans. George Eliot. 1846. Ed. Peter C. Hodgson. Ramsey, NJ: Sigler, 1994.

Sullivan, Lee R. "The Hanging of Judas: Medieval Iconography and the German Peasants' War." *Essays in Medieval Studies* 15 (1999): 93–101.

Swift, Jonathan. "Judas." *The Complete Poems.* Ed. Pat Rogers. New Haven: Yale University Press, 1983. 498–99.

———. "On the Irish Bishops." *The Complete Poems.* Ed. Pat Rogers. New Haven: Yale University Press, 1983. 499–500.

Swinburne, Algernon Charles. "Dirae: 4. Papal Allocution." *The Complete Works of Algernon Charles Swinburne.* Vol. 2, *Poetical Works.* Ed. Sir Edmund Gosse and Thomas James Wise. London: William Heinemann; New York: Gabriel Wells, 1925. 350.

Synan, Edward A. *The Popes and the Jews in the Middle Ages.* New York: Macmillan, 1965.

Tatum, W. Barnes. *Jesus at the Movies: A Guide to the First Hundred Years.* Rev. ed. Santa Rosa, CA: Polebridge, 2004.

Taylor, Archer. "The Burning of Judas." *Washington University Studies* 11.1 (1923): 159–86.

———. "The Gallows of Judas Iscariot." *Washington University Studies* 9.2 (1922): 135–56.

Tertullian. *The Five Books of Quintus Sept. Flor. Tertullianus against Marcion.* Trans. Peter Holmes. Edinburgh: T. & T. Clark, 1868.

Thomas, Keith. Afterword. *The Kiss in History.* Ed. Karen Harvey. Manchester: Manchester University Press, 2005. 187–203.

Thurston, E. Temple. *Judas Iscariot: A Play in Four Acts.* London: G. P. Putnam's Sons, 1923.

Tillich, Paul. *Systematic Theology.* Vol. 2, *Existence and the Christ.* Chicago: University of Chicago Press, 1957.

Trachtenberg, Joshua. *The Devil and the Jews: The Medieval Conception of the Jew and Its Relation to Modern Anti-Semitism.* 1943. Cleveland: Meridian, 1961.

Varriano, John. "Caravaggio and Religion." *Caravaggio and the Baroque Image.* Ed. Franco Mormando. Boston: McMullen Museum of Art, Boston College; [Chicago]: distributed by the University of Chicago Press, 1999. 191–207.

Vaughn, Eric. "*Dear Judas*: Time and the Dramatic Structure of the Dream." *Robinson Jeffers Newsletter* 51 (July 1978): 7–22.

Verneuil, Louis. *The Fabulous Life of Sarah Bernhardt.* Trans. Ernest Boyd. New York: Harper & Brothers, 1942.

Volkov, Shulamit. "Antisemitism as a Cultural Code: Reflections on the History and Historiography of Antisemitism in Imperial Germany." *Leo Baeck Institute Year Book* 23 (1979): 25–45.

Voltaire, François Marie Arouet de. *Philosophical Dictionary.* Trans. Peter Gay. New York: Basic Books, 1962.

Voragine, Jacobus de. *The Golden Legend: Readings on the Saints.* Trans. William Granger Ryan. Vol. 1. Princeton: Princeton University Press, 1993.

The Voyage of Saint Brendan: Journey to the Promised Land. Trans. John J. O'Meara. Atlantic Highlands, NJ: Humanities, 1976.

Wakefield, Walter L., and Austin P. Evans. *Heresies of the High Middle Ages.* New York: Columbia University Press, 1991.

The Wakefield Mystery Plays: The Complete Cycle of Thirty-Two Plays. Ed. Martial Rose. New York: Norton, 1969.

Walsh, Richard. *Reading the Gospels in the Dark: Portrayals of Jesus in Film.* New York: Trinity Press International, 2003.

Walter of Wimborne. "De Symonia et Avaritia." *The Poems of Walter of Wimborne.* Ed. A. C. Rigg. Toronto: Pontifical Institute of Mediaeval Studies, 1978. 113–43.

Ward, Frederick William Orde. "Judas Iscariot." *Matin Bells and Scarlet and Gold.* London: Roxburghe, 1897. 213–20.

Warner, Marina. *Alone of All Her Sex: The Myth and the Cult of the Virgin Mary.* London: Weidenfeld and Nicolson, 1976.

Weber, Annette. "The Hanged Judas of Freiburg Cathedral: Sources and Interpretations." *Imagining the Self, Imagining the Other: Visual Representation and Jewish-Christian Dynamics in the Middle Ages and Early Modern Period.* Ed. Eva Frojmovic. Boston: Brill, 2002. 165–88.

Weil, Simone. *The Iliad, or The Poem of Force. War and the Iliad.* By Simone Weil and Rachel Bespaloff. Trans. Mary McCarthy. New York: New York Review of Books, 2005. 3–38.

———. *Waiting for God.* Trans. Emma Craufurd. 1941. New York: Perennial Classics, HarperCollins, 2001.

Weinstein, Valerie. "Dissolving Boundaries: Assimilation and Allosemitism in E. A. Dupont's *Das alte Gesetz* (1923) and Veit Harlan's *Jud Süss.*" *German Quarterly* 78 (2005): 496–516.

Wesley, John. "God's Sovereign, Everlasting Love." *The Poetical Works.* London: Wesleyan Conference Office, 1868.

Wiesel, Elie. *Night.* Trans. Stella Rodway. New York: Bantam, 1960.

Wilde, Oscar. "The Butterfly's Boswell." *Art Journal* April 1887: 97–103.

Williams, Linda. "Of Kisses and Ellipses: The Long Adolescence of American Movies." *Critical Inquiry* 32 (2006): 288–340.

Wilson, A. N. *Jesus.* New York: Norton, 1992.

Wistrich, Robert S. *Hitler and the Holocaust.* New York: Modern Library, 2001.

Woolf, Virginia. *Orlando.* 1928. New York: Harvest-Harcourt, 1956.

Wright, James. "Saint Judas" *Saint Judas.* Middletown, CT: Wesleyan University Press, 1959. 56.

Yaeger, Patricia. "Consuming Trauma; or, The Pleasures of Merely Circulating." *Journal X* 1 (1997): 225–51.

Yanay, Niza. "Understanding Collective Hatred." *Analyses of Social Issues and Public Policy* 2.1 (2002): 53–60.

Yeats, W. B. *Calvary. The Collected Poems of W.B. Yeats*. New York: Macmillan, 1934. 288–94.

Yerby, Frank. *Judas, My Brother: The Story of the Thirteenth Disciple*. New York: Dial, 1968.

York Cycle of Mystery Plays: A Complete Version. Ed. J. S. Purvis. New York: Macmillan, 1957.

Zafran, Eric M. "The Iconography of Antisemitism: A Study of the Representation of the Jews in the Visual Arts of Europe, 1400–1600." Diss. New York University, 1973.

Zanger, Jules. "A Sympathetic Vibration: Dracula and the Jews." *English Literature in Transition, 1880–1920* 34.1 (1991): 33–44.

Zimbardo, Philip. *The Lucifer Effect: Understanding How Good People Turn Evil*. New York: Random House, 2007.

Žižek, Slavoj. *The Puppet and the Dwarf*. Cambridge, MA: MIT Press, 2003.

———. *Tarrying with the Negative: Kant, Hegel, and the Critique of Ideology*. Durham: Duke University Press, 1993.

PERMISSIONS ACKNOWLEDGMENTS

INDEX

Page numbers in *italics* refer to illustrations. Page numbers beginning with 355 refer to notes.